DATE DUE			

CONSTITUTIONAL
HISTORY OF THE
AMERICAN REVOLUTION

CONSTITUTIONAL HISTORY OF THE AMERICAN REVOLUTION

THE AUTHORITY OF RIGHTS

John Phillip Reid

THE UNIVERSITY OF WISCONSIN PRESS

Published 1986

The University of Wisconsin Press
114 North Murray Street
Madison, Wisconsin 53715

The University of Wisconsin Press, Ltd.
1 Gower Street
London WC1E 6HA, England

First printing

Printed in the United States of America

For LC CIP information see p. 374

ISBN 0-299-10870-8

For
G. O. W. Mueller and Freda Adler
of Rutgers University

CONTENTS

vii

CONSTITUTIONAL
HISTORY OF THE
AMERICAN REVOLUTION

INTRODUCTION

Rights were taken seriously in the eighteenth-century British Empire: the rights of the individual, the rights of Englishmen, the rights of mankind. People cherished them, championed them, and defended them. "I speak, Sir, as a friend of England and America," John Wilkes boasted to the Speaker of the House of Commons, "but still more to universal liberty, and the rights of all mankind." "The rights of *America* have often been declared to the public," John Mackenzie reminded South Carolinians. "Related strokes on the anvil, tempers the metal: They cannot be too often mentioned." Because Americans took rights seriously, they were intent on claiming them during the controversy leading to the Declaration of Independence. That is why they betrayed such anxiety about losing their rights when they perceived those rights threatened by British government policy in the decade and a half before 1776. "The bare Mention of the Word *Rights* always strikes an Englishman in a peculiar Manner," Chief Justice Thomas Hutchinson told the 1769 session of the Suffolk County (Massachusetts) grand jury. "But, in Order to support and defend the Rights, of which we are so fond, we ought to have a just Apprehension of what they are, and whereon they stand." The task Hutchinson set for the grand jury is the task of this study: to identify the rights that Americans feared were in jeopardy, and to learn on what theory of law they claimed those rights.[1]

This study seeks to dispel several notions about the American Revolution. One, which follows from the assertions that rights were taken seriously and that they were constitutional, is the notion that the Revolution was unconcerned with constitutional and legal ideology. Another is the claim that colonial Americans "failed to define their liberty, [or] to catalog their rights." The task undertaken in the first chapters is to show that the colonists not only cataloged their rights, they also were in general agreement about their definitions and purpose. Eighteenth-century constitutional rights, however, were not twentieth-century constitutional rights. For example, a right given much emphasis then — one of the most cherished and utilized that the British people possessed — was the right of petition. It is so unimportant now that it is seldom mentioned in treatises on American constitutional law. By contrast, rights that today monopolize our attention, such as freedom of occupation, the right to abortion, freedom of association, the rights of women, and the right to privacy, were unknown during the revolutionary era. The closest that eighteenth-century political theorists came to discussing privacy was when British pamphleteers protested the cider excise of 1763. "Is not subjecting the *dwelling houses of private persons*, to be *entered* and *searched* at every hour of the day by any petty excise officer . . . very great grievances?" it was asked. "Nay, is it not striking at, and undermining the very foundations of our constitution?" The language seems to presage the twentieth-century American constitutional right of privacy, but only in the most attenuated sense. The "very great grievances" referred to by the writer were not invasions of privacy, but arbitrary entrances and general search warrants.

Other rights now extant existed in quite different guises during the eighteenth century. One example is the right to trial by jury. No civil privilege was more highly cherished in the European or American dominions of George III than jury trial. It is one we think we still possess — but do we? In the eighteenth century the privilege of jury trial did not include the right to professional counsel in felony prosecutions, or the right of defendants accused of crime to testify on their own behalf. A second example is freedom of printing and publication. "The LIBERTY of the PRESS is one of the most valuable privileges of Englishmen," a barrister contended in 1768, and the political literature was filled with defenses of the right, claiming that it "is undoubtedly a very great benefit in our constitution," and asserting that should the right be abrogated "we shall *then* be truly without a constitution." It was not the same freedom of the press that we know today, however, for there was no right to publish criticism of public officials or to report certain happenings such as parliamentary debates.[2]

Another notion this study seeks to correct is the thesis that American whigs, unable to answer British constitutional arguments, were forced to abandon claims to English rights "and resort instead to the natural rights of man rather than those peculiar to Englishmen. This was finally and fully accomplished by the Declaration of Independence in 1776, a document that essentially repudiated concepts that had been developed and elaborated upon for three-quarters of a century." But, aside from rhetoric in the preamble, the Declaration of Independence does not contain claims of natural rights. All rights asserted in the Declaration were English rights, recognized and protected by British constitutional doctrine. Moreover, it is not true that the American argument shifted during the revolutionary debate. Colonial whigs asserted their rights as "Englishmen" and only as Englishmen. They did not claim American rights or British rights, except to the extent that American rights and British rights were concurrent with or derived from English rights. The colonists began the controversy with the mother country because they feared losing English rights, and they declared independence only after being convinced that English rights would be lost or drastically curtailed should they remain within the British Empire.[3]

The bulk of this study—the chapters following those identifying the rights that Americans claimed to possess and believed London was encroaching upon—will consider the theoretical bases upon which those rights were said to be constitutional. The question of the source of rights, or why people said they were entitled to rights, has received much less attention than have the rights themselves, their identification, and their definition. The difficult question is not what rights were, but how and why they existed, and how they were secured. The easy answer—one we must realize is very superficial—is that rights originated in and were protected by the British constitution. Certainly that was the basic theory, stated often enough in the eighteenth century: that the constitution and rights were one.[4]

Not only was the constitution the chief protector of civil rights, but there were also quite a number of English-speaking people in the eighteenth century who judged the legitimacy of a constitution by how well it secured those rights. "[A] Constitution in its Proper Idea," the freeholders of Concord, Massachusetts, voted three months after the Declaration of Independence, "intends a System of Principles Established to Secure the Subject[s] in the Possession and enjoyment of their Rights and Priviliges [sic], against any Encroachments of the Governing part." "A good constitution," the Reverend Ebenezer Bridge had told Massachusetts lawmakers nine years earlier, is one "that secures the mutual dependence of the sovereign or ruling powers, and the people on each other,

and which secures the rights of each, and the good of the whole society."
There was no other concept that so well exemplified the eighteenth-
century idea of a civil right than the concept of security. In fact, some
legal theorists defined the word "constitution" to mean security of rights.
"The British constitution is made to secure liberty and property," *Demophoon* told the *Political Register*, "whatever takes away these, takes away
the constitution itself, and cannot be constitutional." That statement by
Demophoon reveals yet another eighteenth-century definition of "constitution" or "constitutionalism." An act of power that jeopardized established norms for securing rights was not "constitutional." David Hartley,
who was negotiator for Great Britain at the Treaty of Paris ending the
American Revolution, applied that definition when he observed that a
"limited excise" (that is, one affecting only traders) "may be called a constitutional excise," but a "general excise" (one permitting revenue agents
to enter private houses) "is unconstitutional." The first was "consistent
with the liberty of the subject," the second was "totally repugnant to the
freedom of our constitution." It was that meaning of "constitution" that
the freeholders of Middlesex had in mind when telling the king that his
"servants have attacked our liberties in the most vital part," that is, freedom of elections, and "they have torn away the very heart-strings of the
constitution." There were students of the constitution who would have
made the relationship between constitutionalism and people's rights a
restraint on the government itself. "A *constitution* is the *organization of
the contributed rights* in society," John Dickinson theorized. "GOVERNMENT
is the EXERCISE of them. It is intended for the benefit of *the governed*;
of course [it] can have no just powers but what conduce to *that end*."
Indeed, there were even writers who used the word "constitution" as if
its meaning was limited to rights, most often saying either that the constitution was nothing less than a collection of individual rights, or that
its chief function was to protect rights.[5] The constitution, William Jones
explained, "is the great system of public, in contradistinction to private,
and criminal, law, and comprizes all those articles, which Blackstone ar-
ranges, in his first volume, under the rights of persons." The "British civil
constitution," Robert Robinson contended, "is a phrase, strictly speaking, expressive first of a natural constitution of rights native and inherent
in all the inhabitants of this kingdom and in all mankind — next a body
of laws, peculiar to this kingdom, declaratory of these natural rights —
and lastly, of a form of making and executing these laws by king, lords,
and commons, the safety and excellence of which consists in each constituent part retaining its own nature, and place." Robinson, by deriving
personal rights of citizens from nature and depicting constitutional rights
as a codification of natural rights, was not unique, but he was among

the minority of eighteenth-century legal theorists. As the following chapters will show, it was much more representative of eighteenth-century legal thought to locate the authority for rights not in nature but in some other theoretical basis, such as ownership or purchase.[6]

A final prefatory point, one that cannot be elaborated now but that will become obvious further on in this study, is that the word "constitution" did not mean in the eighteenth century what it means now — at least, not what it means in the twentieth-century United States. It is well to remind Americans, as the fact is often forgotten, that when colonial whigs said that Great Britain threatened their rights or was denying them rights, they were not claiming that Great Britain acted illegally, only that she acted unconstitutionally. The word "constitutional" was not synonymous with "legal." "The post of a minister . . . in Great Britain, is not constitutional; but it is necessary," an anonymous pamphlet author noted in 1761. He meant that George III's first minister occupied an unconstitutional office, not an illegal one. The point was made often about Britain's regular army. "I presume," John Trenchard wrote, "no Man will be audacious enough to propose, that we should make a Standing Army Part of our Constitution." There was a standing army in the country then, and it was legal. The same was true in 1729 when William Shippen told the House of Commons that "we have just heard it laid down for Doctrine, *that tho' our Government is not military, tho' an Army is not Part of our Constitution, yet it will be necessary to continue our present Army . . . for many Years longer.*" Of course there were actions both unconstitutional and illegal, as when an army officer, on his own authority, without a request from a magistrate, employed troops to suppress a civilian riot and committed an assault on a citizen. The police action was unconstitutional, and the battery was a crime. If no trespass occurred, however, if the soldiers dispersed the crowd without harming or touching anyone, then the officer's conduct would have been only unconstitutional, not illegal.[7]

The distinction between "constitutional" and "legal" should be kept in mind, not only so that words may be understood in their eighteenth-century context, but also to appreciate the scope of this study. It is called a "constitutional history" because that is what it is — *constitutional*. Limited to the *constitutional* reasons for the American Revolution, it is not concerned with its *social* causes, *political* aspects, *economic* origins, or *nationalistic* motivations. It is also not a *legal* history, for this study does not discuss the role played by nonconstitutional law in the coming of the American Revolution. As an example, consider one of the best known of all British constitutional rights, freedom of the press. Highly cherished as it may have been in constitutional theory and contemporary political literature, this right was not a factor in the revolutionary controversy between Great Britain and the colonies. It was, by contrast, a serious grievance in Ireland, where the British government jailed newspaper editors for sedition and confiscated their printing presses. In the colonies the British government would have suppressed publications had the conditions of law allowed. American printers, however, were never tried for libel or sentenced to prison, even though they frequently published material that would have precipitated severe prosecutions had they been in Ireland. The reason is that colonial whigs controlled both the grand and traverse juries, and the British government could neither indict nor convict its critics. Using a vocabulary that distinguishes between "constitution" and "law," or "constitutional law" and "nonconstitutional law," it would be said that a history discussing why American whigs could not be indicted, and what this fact purported, is a "legal" not a "constitutional" history. It would tell the story of how "the conditions of law" affected the coming of the American Revolution, a *legal* history that has been partly told in another book. It should be considered a nonconstitutional topic, for it was "constitutional" only because whig control of colonial juries eliminated from the constitutional debate preceding the American Revolution a potential constitutional grievance — a major constitutional grievance in Ireland but one not known in the North American colonies.

A final caution must be mentioned: this book is limited to constitutional rights. It does not deal with other aspects of the constitutional history of the American Revolution such as the authority to tax, the concept of representation, the authority to legislate, the concept of liberty, the doctrine of sovereignty, or the principle of constitutional rule. These general topics, which are not discussed in this volume, include most of the constitutional issues that American whigs debated with imperialists during the revolutionary epoch. Among these are the tension between two constitutional theories, the distinction between right and power limiting sovereign command, the legislative nature of ministerial instructions to colonial governors, the concept of arbitrariness, the doctrine of consent, the corporation theory, the commercial contract, the imperial contract, the taxation-legislation dichotomy, and several other issues.

CHAPTER ONE

THE ENGLISHNESS OF RIGHTS

When the ailing James Otis retired to the country on the advice of his physician, the people of Boston, assembled in their town meeting, voted him thanks "for his undaunted Exertions in the Common Cause of the Colonies, from the Beginning of the present glorious Struggle for the Rights of the British Constitution." The description, "Rights of the British Constitution," was unusual, but not ambiguous. The Stamp Act Congress, in its petition to the king, a document Otis helped draft, had spoken of "securing the inherent Rights and Liberties of your Subjects here, upon the Principles of the *English* Constitution." Although one might object that there was, in 1765, no such thing as an English constitution, the claim could not be misunderstood. What was being sought was both English and British — English rights under the British constitution. Quite often colonial whigs professed to be defending American rights, as when the Stamp Act Congress asserted "the most Essential Rights and Liberties of the Colonists," and the people of Lebanon, Connecticut, wrote of "the rights of America." Although the language was less precise than we would like, the meaning was clear enough. Colonial whigs might speak of American rights but they were thinking of English rights guaranteed to Americans by the British constitution. Those were the rights Virginia's House of Burgesses meant when asking for "our just Liberties

9

& Privileges as free born British Subjects," or, as New Hampshire's House of Representatives told the burgesses, "those Liberties and priviledges which are the Impregnable Bulwarks of the British Government."[1]

The argument must not be misunderstood. It is not just that American whigs were defending English rights. More to the point, they were not defending or seeking other types of rights. American rights were not generally questioned by the London government during the revolutionary controversy, and therefore were not at issue. And Americans, both whigs and loyalists, were not interested in British rights that were not English rights. They never sought Scottish rights and the last thing they wanted were Irish rights. It was for English rights that they disputed. The fact is not certain, but it is possible that only once did a suggested claim for a non-English right appear in the revolutionary literature. Significantly, it was not asserted in any official remonstrance, declaration, petition, or letter voted by a unit of colonial government or by a whig committee. Rather, it is to be found in a pamphlet written by Arthur Lee and published anonymously in London. Lee thought that the provision against standing armies in the "Declarations of Rights for Scotland" was more suitable for the colonies' protection than was the related provision in the English "Declaration of Rights." England's Declaration provided "That the raising or keeping a standing army within the Kingdom, in time of peace, unless it be with consent of Parliament, is against Law." The Scottish Declarations said "That the sending of an army, in a hostile manner, upon any part of the Kingdom, in a peaceable time, is contrary to Law." "With how much more propriety," Lee asked, "may the Colonies declare, 'That the sending an army among them in a hostile manner, to collect taxes not authorised by the consent of their Representatives, and to enforce laws made without their consent, is dangerous, arbitrary, and illegal'?" Lee was not asking for a Scots right. He was redrafting a Scots right to help solve the American constitutional crisis. It is possible that this was not the only occasion during the revolutionary controversy that a non-English constitutional right was suggested as a model for Americans. If, in fact, other rights were suggested they most likely were natural rights, and their very paucity proves the rule that it was English rights that were at issue.[2]

Rights such as the one Lee cited, promulgated in constitutional instruments like the Bill of Rights or the Petition of Right, were reasonably precise. Most rights asserted in eighteenth-century Great Britain or British North America were more vague. This fact was due in large part to the nature of British constitutional doctrine, arising from unwritten tradition, which had no supreme tribunal for settling controversies and clarifying specifics, and also in small part to a belief held by some legal theorists that it was best to keep rights somewhat imprecise. "It perhaps would be dangerous," a reviewer for *The Scots Magazine* explained, "to inquire too curiously into the strict and punctual legality of all the powers exercised by government, and all the privileges claimed by the subject. . . . There are mysteries in politics, as well as in religion, which a good politician, and a good Christian, should endeavour to believe, without attempting even to understand. May the right of resistance in the people be for ever supposed! may it never be defined or explained!"[3]

Vagueness, whether deliberate or unintentional, was not a consideration when claiming eighteenth-century constitutional rights. They were asserted as fiercely as if they were clearly defined and as if there were a tribunal to which one could appeal for both their definition and their enforcement. It was a matter of the highest constitutional priority with eighteenth-century British subjects that their rights, no matter how general or abstract, be absolutely secured, and they insisted on their security with language that may strike us in the twentieth century as too general and abstract to be constitutionally useful. The New York Assembly was enunciating the basic constitutional principle on which colonial whigs would make their stand when, at the beginning of the controversy, it resolved that Americans "owe Obedience to all Acts of Parliament not inconsistent with the essential Rights and Liberties of *Englishmen*, and are intitled to the same Rights and Liberties which his Majesty's *English* Subjects both within and without the Realm have ever enjoyed."[4] The rights New York asserted may seem imprecise today. They were sufficiently specified for eighteenth-century constitutional advocacy.

BESTNESS OF RIGHTS

One fact that is not a puzzle today is why Americans of the revolutionary period clung so tenaciously to their English rights. It is doubtful if there was any literate person in the eighteenth-century British Empire who was not aware of why rights had to be maintained. To hear or read about civil rights was part of the intellectual and political environment of educated English-speaking people. Indeed, it was probably impossible to avoid the topic since there was nothing of which political writers boasted more than of British rights. And why not? As was said in a 1766 London pamphlet entitled *British Liberties*, the rights of Englishmen were the world's best. "As at present we live under a government, the most perfect in *Europe* . . . it is the indispensible interest and duty of every true *Briton* to maintain those privileges . . . upon which all our temporal (and in a great measure our eternal) happiness, safety, and well being depends."

One fact making the government so perfect was that Britain, in the words of Sir William Blackstone, was "[a] land, perhaps the only one in the universe, in which political or civil liberty is the very end and scope of the constitution." "The idea and practice of this political or civil liberty," Blackstone explained, "flourish in their highest vigour in these kingdoms, where it falls little short of perfection . . . the legislature, and of course the laws of England, being peculiarly adapted to the preservation of this inestimable blessing even in the meanest subject." Blackstone believed that these rights—"the rights of Englishmen"—"were formerly, either by inheritance or purchase, the rights of all mankind; but, in most other countries of the world being now more or less debased and destroyed, they at present may be said to remain, in a peculiar and emphatical manner, the rights of the people of England."[5]

That was the boast: Great Britain and her colonies were unique because the rights that the British people enjoyed were unique. British rights were unique both for their security and their quality. They were secured because the British government was the government "best calculated to preserve and secure" rights.[6] That security was thought by some observers to be, as Blackstone said, just about perfect. "Never was a People possessed of greater Privileges than we are," the pastor of Windham's first church told Connecticut's legislators in 1763. "We enjoy our Rights without fear of loosing them, by the hands of violence, or the Oppression of the Mighty."[7]

The second consideration making British liberties the world's finest was their quality. "All these birthrights and privileges of Britons," Arthur Young pointed out, "form a system of liberty, so happily tempered between slavery and licentiousness, that the like is not to be met with in any other country on the globe." New Englanders agreed. "[W]e are a people, an empire so highly exalted in civil and religious privileges above far the greatest part of the World," Stephen Johnson told Rhode Islanders. They lived, it was boasted in Connecticut, under "the happiest constitution and form of government in the whole world."[8]

What the happiest constitution meant was, of course, the happiest people in the universe. It is astonishing the degree to which everyone was believed to share that happiness. Great Britain, a member of the Middle Temple marveled, "is that *Community*, in which every *Member* enjoys as much Freedom, as is consistent with the *Good of* the *whole*." What that meant for an individual Briton, George III told Parliament, was "to be the freest member of any civil society in the known world." It is hard today to believe some of the claims for British civil rights. Not only were rights nearly perfect, they were also applied perfectly, applied, that is, to every individual with perfect equality, to every person no matter how insignificant or whether a Roman Catholic or non-Anglican Protestant.[9]

It was a rare eighteenth-century legal theorist who found blemishes within the perfect system of British rights. And when any were discovered, they often were dismissed as mere irritations, not flaws needing reform. Indeed, if the British had a complaint about civil rights, it was that they were too extensive and too favorable to individual liberty. Preaching to the University of Cambridge in 1771, the Reverend John Gordon complained that English laws "pulled" too "much towards the side of Freedom," in part because "our juries, those great bulwarks of English Liberty, have been carefully instructed to attend rather to the consequences of their verdict upon the liberty of the subject, than its relation to either equity or justice." That Gordon criticized the jury was unusual. Hardly anyone else did. The eighteenth-century British thought the right to jury trial one of their most precious rights, along with the right to property and the right to security. The remarkable, almost smug, satisfaction everyone expressed regarding jury trial even extended to Ireland, where the population was overwhelmingly Catholic and only Protestants were allowed to serve on juries or practice as defense attorneys. "The Innocent are defended, and the Criminal has no reason to complain," the Anglican bishop of Ossory boasted of the Irish when preaching the 1766 assize sermon for the Leinster circuit. We must be cautious about labeling the bishop a hypocrite, even though at that time Ireland was one of the most harshly governed and oppressed states in Western Europe. For most people rejoicing in the perfection of British civil and political rights, it quite likely seemed immaterial that most Irish and all Roman Catholics did not share the personal privileges possessed by English, Scots, and Americans. Indeed, the fact that they did not may even have helped to highlight just how perfect were British rights by providing such a contrast. What is unmistakable is that the perspective, emphasizing that the British alone had the English system of jury trial, blinded people to other considerations, and led them to suppose that if their institutions were unique, it followed that the rights those institutions protected must be the best.[10]

Another reason why Americans believed that British rights were the best in the world was that the British were the world's best people. Today it is difficult to recapture the extent to which the eighteenth-century English, Scots, and Welsh admired themselves. Almost as perfect as the system of rights that they possessed, they were the finest, most generous, kindest, most compassionate people on earth, inhabiting the best land, drinking the best water, living the best lives, and eating the best roast beef. "[T]he better sort of people in this country," Humphry Sydenham reminded the House of Commons in 1745, "have always, till of late years, been remarkable for their bravery, generosity, and hospitality, and those of inferior rank, for their honesty, frugality, and industry." The British of that day, an anonymous writer claimed that same decade, were "as generous and beneficent a People, as are to be found on the Earth; they love Liberty, and they enjoy it; and, to their immortal Honour be it spoken, they are such true Friends of Liberty, that they would willingly sacrifice a great Part of the Blessings that they derive from it, to procure a like Degree of Freedom to their Neighbours. As they are brave and bountiful, so they are naturally penetrating and judicious." He meant that the British were so unselfish they wished that everyone possessed English civil liberties. In fact, it was sometimes said they even wished the French had them, a particularly generous hope as everyone knew that the French were not capable of appreciating rights, certainly not of enjoying them as they were enjoyed in Great Britain. It was even possible that no other people could do so. Arbitrary government was so widespread in the eighteenth century that it was hard to imagine anyone else cherishing rights as did the British, especially the English.[11]

There was just one other people besides the English capable of understanding and cherishing rights—the North American colonists, who were also British. "*My Lords*," the New York Assembly petitioned Britain's House of Lords, "we are *Englishmen*, and as such, presume ourselves intitled to the Rights and Liberties, which have rendered the Subjects of *England* the Envy of all Nations." They wanted those rights partly for the following reasons: because they were entitled to them, they owned them, had always enjoyed them, and would be treated unequally with other Britons if denied them. There is also another reason, so obvious it easily could be overlooked. Americans were not different from other British subjects. They had been taught since birth and they believed that English rights were the finest in the world; they also suspected that they enjoyed those rights even more extensively than did their fellow subjects living in Great Britain itself, the acknowledged home of civil rights. Massachusetts farmers, one anonymous writer boasted in 1754, "live as they list, their Estates are their own, absolutely their own in Fee. No Lords over them, nor Quit Rents to pay, all are free Men and their Estates free, and they like *Gideon's* Brethren, *each one resembles the Children of a King*."[12]

There was irony or inconsistency to Americans possessing such perfect rights under the best of constitutions and yet claiming those rights as shields against the edicts of the best of all constitutional governments. When the colonists resisted that government to secure their rights, critics said that they were not securing rights; rather, they were jeopardizing them. "No *country* under *heaven* enjoys more *religious* and *civil privileges* than we do," an incredulous Massachusetts tory wrote in 1774.

"[M]any thousands in the world, who are groaning under the weight of despotic power, would think themselves extremely happy, if they could enjoy the same rights and privileges we are favored with."[13]

For American whigs there was no inconsistency. Perceiving the British government as threatening their rights, they opposed London — not to be free of British rule, but to preserve English rights. How, they asked, could free people act otherwise? "These are the rights, without which a people cannot be free and happy," the Continental Congress explained in an address to the French in Quebec. "These are the rights, a profligate Ministry are now striving, by force of arms, to ravish from us, and which we are, with one mind, resolved never to resign but with our lives."[14]

CHAPTER TWO

RIGHTS IN GENERAL

The American colonists were interested in "two great points," Thomas Pownall, former governor of Massachusetts, asserted in 1764. Those two points were "the establishment of their rights and privileges as *Englishmen*, and the keeping in their own hands the revenue, and the pay of the officers of government, as a security for their conduct."[1] Events would prove Pownall prophetic. Had Parliament during the next decade left the Americans undisturbed in these "two great points," the Revolution might not have occurred.

To catalog what the colonists meant by "their rights as Englishmen" is an easy task, as those rights were clearly and frequently stated. To assess the relative importance attached to particular rights is more difficult. The right to consent to taxation, the right to representation, the right to resist unconstitutional government, and the right to liberty, were so vital due to the dynamics of the prerevolutionary debates, they took on an existence separate from the general claim to English rights. That is, they became so central to the constitutional dispute, they assumed the character of discrete issues and can be treated by historians as separate topics deserving individual studies. These rights, although mentioned in this study, are not discussed to the extent that they would be in books devoted to the constitutional authority to tax, the constitutional principle of government by representation, the constitutional right of resistance, or the constitutional concept of liberty. At the other extreme were rights that contributed little to the coming of the American Revolution. An example was the right of the British to be free of a standing army. That right had been one of the most persistent staples of English and British constitutional rhetoric, yet for most of the revolutionary period the right had slight impact on the crisis leading to revolution. Even so, it should be noted that American whigs thought the right in sufficient peril for the Maryland Convention to describe "any standing army" as "dangerous to liberty," and for the Continental Congress to mention standing armies as a grievance in the Declaration of Independence.[2]

There were other rights besides the right of the people to be free of standing armies that were not in constitutional controversy, yet were occasionally asserted. One, claimed by the Provincial Congress of Georgia, was the "right to examine with freedom and to pass censure or applause upon every act of government." It is quite likely the British, had they been able, would have curtailed this right, but it was beyond their governmental capabilities to restrict American speech, and the colonists could not make it a grievance. Another, stated by both Georgia's Commons House of Assembly and the Continental Congress, claimed "the benefit of such of the *English* Statutes as existed at the time of . . . Colonization." Denial of such laws to Americans might have constituted a constitutional grievance had it been fact, which it was not. What was true was that Parliament denied to the colonists the benefit of several significant statutes, such as the Habeas Corpus Act, the Act of Settlement, and the Bill of Rights. These were, however, postcolonization laws, not the precolonization laws Congress complained of. It would have been difficult to make them an issue, as colonial assemblies could have enacted them into law without parliamentary approval. Only had that legislation been vetoed by London would Americans have had a grievance — a grievance about arbitary government quite different from claiming the right to enjoy British legislation.[3]

CONTINENTAL RIGHTS

Some rights claimed by American whigs need not be considered in this study because they were never at issue. An example, provided by Georgia's Commons House, was the right of the colonies not only "peaceably to assemble and consider of their Grievances, and petition the King," but also "that all Prosecutions, Prohibitory Proclamations, and Commitments for the same are illegal." Rights such as these must be distinguished from rights substantively in controversy. The rights of legislators to assemble when not called into session by the Crown, or to meet in provincial conventions or Continental Congresses, and to petition, were in contention. The right to be free of prosecution for assembling or petitioning was not. No one was prosecuted or committed for exercising those rights.

A second category of rights claimed by colonial whigs that does not merit extensive consideration is that asserted by individuals or by informal gatherings of small groups. We must seek what Edmund S. Morgan has called "the official colonial position." It is to be discovered in the resolutions, memorials, petitions, remonstrances of the elected colonial assemblies and of the delegates sent to the Continental Congresses by those assemblies. Also of significance, although of proportionally less weight, are resolves of New England town meetings and, for colonies south of New England, grand jury presentments, county conventions, and mass gatherings in the larger communities called with sufficient notice by recognized whig leaders. In this scale of "official" value, the Declaration of Rights by the first Continental Congress ranks highest as the most authentic statement of rights by American whigs. Of comparatively less significance, by contrast, is the Virginia Declaration of Rights of 12 June 1776, or the bills of rights in the early state constitutions, as these were concerned with future principles of governance, not with the prerevolutionary controversy.

There is yet another qualification. The Continental Congress may have been the most "official" voice of American whigs, but not every right it stated became significant because of its imprimatur. Consider the "right" it claimed "of holding lands by the tenure of easy rents, and not by rigorous and oppressive services, frequently forcing the possessors from their families and their business, to perform what ought to be done, in all well regulated states, by men hired for the purpose." This right to socage or freehold tenure is mentioned in the Congress's address to the inhabitants of Quebec. It is peculiar to French Canada. Residents in the older British colonies did not hold their lands by service, and the right to unencumbered tenure was not a factor in their revolutionary controversy with Great Britain.

This book will be concerned only with *official* claims to rights in actual controversy. The place to start, therefore, is with the first official list of claimed rights, a list drafted during the earliest moments of the revolutionary controversy: Patrick Henry's famous resolves, adopted by Virginia's House of Burgesses in May 1765. Passed in response to the Stamp Act, they were limited to threats posed to rights by that act, yet they presaged all the claims that later would be made by American whigs.

Henry asserted three rights. The first was the English right of equality, in this case equality between the American and European subjects of George III. The colonists, the Virginia resolves maintained, were entitled to "all the Liberties, Privileges, Franchises, and Immunities, that have at any Time been held, enjoyed, and possessed, by the people of *Great Britain*"; that is "all Liberties, Privileges, and Immunities of Denizens and natural Subjects, to all Intents and Purposes, as if they had been abiding and born within the Realm of *England*." The second English right asserted was the one most directly imperiled by the Stamp Act, the right to be taxed only by representation. The third, closely related to the second, was government by consent: "the inestimable Right of being governed by such Laws, respecting their internal Polity and Taxation, as are derived from their own Consent."[4]

Compare these Virginia resolves to the Declaration of Rights promulgated by the Continental Congress nine years later, when all American grievances had been identified and colonial whigs were becoming apprehensive that parliamentary disregard for the rights asserted might lead to civil war. The Declaration was the most comprehensive statement of colonial privileges made during the revolutionary period. In contrast to Henry's resolves, which were concerned with the single issue of internal taxation, it listed all the rights Americans had been claiming with only a few omissions such as the right to have judges serving at good behavior rather than the Crown's pleasure. Nine significant rights were asserted.

The first, a major legacy of English constitutional history, traceable to the earliest origins of the common law, was the right to life, liberty and property. The colonists, it was said, "are entitled to life, liberty, and property: and they have never ceded to any sovereign power whatever, a right to dispose of either without their consent."

The second right was equality, stated in terms of the emigration contract. The first settlers, on emigrating to North America, had carried all English privileges with them, and they and their descendants continued to possess them to the extent that "their local and other circumstances enable them to exercise and enjoy." This was a claim both to a right — the right to equality — and the assertion of a source of rights: equality with the British people. Another example of a source of rights stated by Congress as a right was a resolution claiming that "these, his Majesty's, colonies, are likewise entitled to all the immunities and privileges granted and confirmed to them by royal charters, or secured by their several codes of provincial laws."

Third was the right of representation. It was, as usual, coupled with a denial that Americans were represented in the British Parliament. Rather, as the Delaware Convention had explained two months earlier, "the only lawful Representatives of the freemen in the several Colonies are persons they elect to serve as Members of the General Assembly thereof." From that principle of British constitutionalism, it followed that it was "the just right and privilege of the said freemen to be governed by laws made by their General Assembly in the article of taxation and internal police."

The fourth, fifth, and sixth rights claimed were "the common law of England," which meant the law of England, not Great Britain, the "inestimable privilege" of trial by jury, the main institutional bulwark of English common law, and "such of the English statutes, as existed at the time" of colonization. Many Americans thought of jury trial not merely as a right to defense against a criminal charge, but as the guarantee that rights would be preserved. As the Connecticut House of Representatives expressed it, the people had a right "not to be disseized of their liberties or free customs, sentenced or condemned, but by lawful judgment of their peers."

The seventh claim was to the right of petition and the eighth was to be free of standing armies "without the consent of the legislature of that colony in which such army is kept." Two auxiliary rights, attached to the last, were mentioned in the Declaration of Independence when George III was indicted for affecting "to render the military independent of and superior to the civil power" and for conspiring with Parliament to quarter "large bodies of armed troops among us."

Congress's last asserted right was concerned with free government, not with personal liberty. Free government, according to current British constitutional theory, was balanced government, under which the branches of the legislature were mutually independent. The Continental Congress claimed this ideal when resolving that "the exercise of legislative power in several colonies, by a council appointed, during pleasure, by the crown, is unconstitutional, dangerous, and destructive to the freedom of American legislation."[5]

Not all rights claimed by the Continental Congress were mentioned in the Declaration of Rights. Some, omitted from the Declaration, were included in Congress's letters to the British people and to the inhabitants of Quebec. Among these was the most cherished of eighteenth-century rights, the ancient English right to be free of "an arbitrary form of government." Another, inherited from the late seventeenth century when a few high-church clergymen preached the duty of passive obedience and the doctrine of nonresistance, was the right to defend liberty even against constitutional government should government act unconstitutionally. "[W]e never will," the Congress exclaimed, "submit to be the hewers of wood or drawers of water for any ministry or nation in the world." Less lofty in concept, yet also English in origin, were two other rights, one that Americans did not yet possess, but claimed on the basis of equality, and a second that, by contrast, they possessed much more fully than did any other British subjects, even those living under the common law in England and Wales. The one they did not yet enjoy was the right to habeas corpus. The other was freedom of the press, a right that the colonists had learned from recent experience promoted "union among them" and provided an effective means "whereby oppressive officers are shamed or intimidated into more honourable and just modes of conducting affairs."[6]

RIGHT TO PETITION

During the eighteenth century rights were generally stated as "rights to" or "rights from," rights to do an act or enjoy a benefit, or rights to be free from some action, most likely governmental. Grievances were the other side of rights and often a grievance complained of was a right denied. An example is the seventh right claimed by the Continental Congress in 1774, the right to petition. In the Declaration of Rights petitioning was stated as a privilege denied. In its memorial to the American people, Congress mentioned it not as a right but as a grievance. "Humble and reasonable petitions from the Representatives of the people," Congress complained, "have been frequently treated with contempt." The phraseology could easily have been as positive as negative and stated as a right. "[N]o people," an eighteenth-century pamphlet boasted, "have a more ample claim to the *Right of Petitioning*, than the people of Great Britain." Indeed, the right was as old as constitutionalism in England, endorsed both by Charles I and his opponents, who made it an article in the earl of Strafford's impeachment, charging that he issued a proclamation "to inhibit the King's subjects to come to the fountain, their Sovereign, to deliver their Complaints of Wrongs and Oppressions." The House of Commons reaffirmed the right of petition during the reign of Charles II, and its denial was one of the grievances against James II. In 1701, in response to a memorial claiming that it was "the undoubted Right of the People of England" to petition the House of Commons, the Commons resolved "That it is the UNDOUBTED RIGHT of the People of England to petition or address to the King for the Calling, Sitting, or DISSOLVING Parliaments; and for the REDRESSING OF GRIEVANCES." When Americans claimed it as a right, they were claiming it as an English right.[7]

During the 1770s the right of petition stirred more controversy in the mother country than in the colonies. There it was thought to be one of the most basic of British civil rights. Baron Rokeby, for one, maintained

that it was as absolute as any right could be. The right included petitioning either house of the legislature, and even the king directly. It was, in
fact, said to be a British "birth right and inheritance . . . to petition the
throne," to ensure that "the crown *can* and *does* learn the *real* and the
universal sense of the people, and may be more certainly informed of
it than it can by any vote or resolution of parliament."[8]

The right of petition was controversial in Great Britain during the 1770s
because George III became annoyed at the number of petitions he received
from the City of London, demanding that he take actions that he either
did not wish to take or that he thought to be unconstitutional. In 1775
it was announced that the king would no longer receive London's petitions while sitting on the throne unless they came from the lord mayor
and aldermen "in their corporate capacity." Petitions could still be handed
to palace officials, but the king would not accept them personally or listen
to them being read. When the mayor, aldermen, and livery of London
next attempted to present a petition — one that dealt with American
rights — George III refused to accept it from the throne. "Resolved," London's Common Hall voted, "[t]hat the King is bound to hear the petitions of his people, it being the undoubted right of the subject to be heard,
and not a matter of grace and favour."[9]

Coming out of the same constitutional tradition and claiming the same
constitutional right, American whigs echoed London's grievance except
that their complaint was not against the Crown but rather against Parliament. It was the House of Commons that refused to receive colonial
petitions.[10] One reason was that many protested Parliament's attempts
to tax the colonies and the House of Commons had a rule not to accept
petitions on money bills. There was some dispute as to whether the rule
was evenly applied. The Commons refused to receive petitions on the
Stamp Act, for example, yet just two years earlier had permitted the reading of petitions against the British Cider Excise Bill, some of which raised
issues remarkably similar to American grievances about the stamp tax.[11]
The rule was, however, at least as old as a sessional order adopted in 1706
and a standing order of 1713. It had been invoked to bar American petitions against the Sugar Act of 1733, even though that same year petitions
had been accepted from British cities protesting the wine and tobacco
excise imposed in Great Britain.[12] There were various rationales for this
rule — "petitions were not admitted as against the taxes themselves, but
only as against the mode of collecting them" — but, as they were generally
discriminatory in their application, they did not quiet American apprehensions that their perceived right to petition Parliament was in jeopardy and even, in certain circumstances, nonexistent.[13]

A second parliamentary excuse for refusing to accept some American petitions was more perilous to colonial constitutional rights. It was, as Lord North explained, that "the honour of Parliament required, that no paper should be presented . . . which tended to call in question the unlimited rights of Parliament." Thomas Hutchinson complained that the colonists raised such issues in their petitions "with design to prevent their being received," but if American whigs were sincere about their constitutional claims they had to assert a constitutional defense and deny the authority of Parliament. By the dynamics of eighteenth-century constitutional politics, not to question an asserted power was to concede the government's right to exercise it. Parliament's rule that its "unlimited rights" could not be questioned was tantamount to telling Americans they had to surrender the constitutional defense before they could exercise their constitutional right to petition.[14]

Even though both the British and the Americans thought petitioning one of the great rights of the eighteenth century, its denial was not a significant grievance in the coming of the American Revolution. After all, colonists asserted the right for one purpose—to explain, defend, and secure other rights. As those other rights came to be more and more threatened, the right of petition tended to be seen as less significant, so that by 1775 the Continental Congress no longer mentioned it either as a right or a grievance. "That our petitions have been treated with disdain," Congress explained to Jamaica's Assembly, "is now become the smallest part of our complaint."[15]

Rule of Law

The right of petition was both specific—to voice a particular complaint or solicit a particular favor—and general: the right's chief function was to protect all other rights. A second general right, guarding other rights, was the right to common law, a right claimed by all the colonies. In its more narrow aspect, the right was a claim to the doctrines and forms of common law, both public and private. At its broadest, it embraced more than rule by British constitutional law and blended into the notion of rule by law, for the right claimed the protection of law binding not only on the judiciary but also on the sovereign, and was superior in form, content, and substance to legislative promulgations. In eighteenth-century legal theory, there could be no absolute rights of persons if Parliament was constitutionally empowered to promulgate absolute law. It was that issue—whether parliamentary supremacy meant parliamentary sovereignty—that made the right to common law a central part of the American whig constitutional case.[16]

The ultimate right sought was neither the right to specific English common-law doctrines nor British constitutional-law principles, but rather, the right to be governed by the rule of law. "[T]he indisputable right of every Englishman to the common laws of the land" meant "that no freeman shall be deprived of his life, liberty, or property, but by the law of the land, that is, the due process of law." The basic premise, Ambrose Serle reminded eighteenth-century British readers, was that "liberty rests upon a government by law" and government ruling by the rule of law was "government proceeding upon common, determinate, and well-known principles."[17]

The most important principle of the British concept of rule by law was that no person was above the law or, expressed more aptly, no person was the law. The ideal of constitutional government, Richard Price wrote, was "men over *themselves*," not "men over other men." The most usual way of stating the proposition was to describe the British constitution as "a government of *laws*, not of *persons*." Another way was to boast that "the Glory of this constitution" was "comprised in three words, *government by law*." Jonathan Mayhew of Massachusetts was referring to the rule of law when he reminded the colony's lawmakers that "in all free constitutions of government, law, and not will, is the measure of the executive Magistrate's power." In the mother country twenty-three years later the archbishop of York was thinking of the same concept when observing that, although "[t]he passions of men are restless and enterprizing . . . the supremacy of law is a steady and uniform rule to which those, who mean well, may in all circumstances safely adhere."[18]

TIMELESSNESS OF RIGHTS

Some rights asserted by American whigs can be identified by time. Consider two resolutions, one voted by "towns" of Massachusetts's Middlesex county, the other by the Continental Congress. "*Resolved*," the towns proclaimed, "That every people have an absolute right to meeting together to consult upon common grievances, and to petition, remonstrate, and use every legal method for their removal." "It is," the Congress declared, "indispensibly necessary to good government, and rendered essential to the English constitution, that the constituent branches of the legislature be independent of each other; that, therefore, the exercise of legislative power in several colonies, by a council appointed, during pleasure, by the crown, is unconstitutional, dangerous, and destructive to the freedom of American legislation." These two resolves can be dated at 1774 or later, because before 1774 there would have been no reason to have asserted the rights they mention. Both lay claim to rights threatened by the Massachusetts Government Act of 1774 and it is only because of that act that they were made issues by colonial whigs.[19]

The evidence has sometimes been misinterpreted. Because colonial whigs claimed rights not previously mentioned or added new grievances to familiar complaints does not mean that they changed their argument about rights, that they demanded new rights as time went on, or that they were uncertain about their rights. From the beginning to the end of the revolutionary controversy, American whigs relied on the same rights: their rights as Englishmen. It was parliamentary assertions of governmental power, not shifting colonial constitutional theory or aspirations, that caused different rights to be stressed in different years. In a sense, the Americans were reacting very much as the British had reacted during the early 1760s when they "discovered" the right against general search warrants and made that right a major issue in contemporary politics. They did not, of course, discover the right. What they discovered was that it could be abused in ways previously not suspected or not understood. The seizure of John Wilkes's papers from Wilkes's home under the authority of a general warrant caused the alarm, but reaction to the seizure did not lead to the invention of a new right. In legal theory and in the minds of common lawyers, the right had always existed. It just had not entered constitutional consciousness until threatened by the Wilkes precedent. The same was true for rights that Americans would claim. An example is the right to trial at the venue. That right was not an issue during the Stamp Act crisis and there was no reason to assert it. The Stamp Act had jeopardized the right to trial by jury but not the right to jury trial in the vicinage. Trial at the venue did not become an issue until late in the controversy when an act of Parliament authorized trial in England for treasons committed in the colonies. Before that authority was asserted by London, American whigs had no reason to claim that they had a right to trial in the vicinage. That they made it a grievance — charging George III in the Declaration of Independence with "transporting us beyond seas to be tried for pretended offenses" — does not mean, as is sometimes said, that the Americans shifted or added to their constitutional demands. The right to trial at the venue had always existed and the colonists had always enjoyed the execution of it in security. The right became part of the constitutional case against parliamentary rule because for the first time in history Parliament was asserting the authority to conduct American treason trials in England rather than in the colonies.

Writing in 1769 on the topic of John Wilkes's expulsion from the House of Commons, Nathaniel Forster made a commonplace statement about

British rights. "Every one knows the general rights, which all ENGLISH men claim and enjoy in common with each other," he wrote. Forster was understood by educated people to mean not just eighteenth-century Englishmen, but Englishmen of every epoch. Rights were conceived as being timeless, as having always existed, at least as long as there had been an English nation. The compounding of the constitutional present with the constitutional past was characteristic of common-law thought. An instance is the assumption by eighteenth-century lawyers that the rights codified in Magna Carta had been as viable in Anglo-Saxon times and were still as viable during their own day as they had been when the great charter was first promulgated — and that they were the exact same rights. William Prynne was thinking and writing in this manner when he listed what he said were the fundamental, unalterable, immutable rights of the English people. Any colonial whig who came across Prynne's list of ten rights would have recognized their immutability for, even though published in 1654, they included at least six that were very much at issue in the 1770s and at the heart of the dispute with the mother country. They were: (1) taxation by representation; (2) trial by law and jury; (3) no standing mercenary army; (4) no property taken but by due process of law; (5) laws enacted only by consent in Parliament; and (6) frequent legislative sessions. Moreover, claiming these rights was not a new constitutional development in the colonies. They had always been claimed as part of America's common-law birthright, and like their fellow British subjects, colonial whigs during the prerevolutionary decade assumed that they had always existed and had always been enjoyed.[20]

The quality of timelessness that eighteenth-century rights possessed dictates the historical tale to be told. The pattern of change that provides the thrust of most twentieth-century histories would distort eighteenth-century legal thought. The context in which rights were diminished or defended might change, and hence the arguments of both the government, championing change, and the opposition, defending rights, were altered to meet the changed circumstances. But the eighteenth-century perception of rights did not change, not even over a much longer stretch of time than that which encompassed the constitutional debates leading to the American Revolution. It would be unhistorical to seek the usual history. The history of rights in the American Revolution is not the story of the evolution of changing rights but of the role of legal doctrine, of the impact of what were perceived as timeless rights on a dynamic constitutional controversy. We must not ask how rights were altered by events but, rather, how events were altered by rights.

CHAPTER THREE

THE RIGHT TO PROPERTY

In the eighteenth-century pantheon of British liberty there was no right more changeless and timeless than the right to property. There is probably also no other right that today is more closely associated with eighteenth-century American whigs. Students of the Revolution have occasionally depicted the right to property as the American constitutional epitome, a broad concept that possibly colonial whigs concocted and on which they conferred an air of constitutional legitimacy by grounding it in natural-law principle. The right to property was stated so frequently and with such repetitive expression that anyone familiar with the revolutionary literature will readily recognize when colonial whigs were claiming the right. Consider three quotations from books published during the era of the American Revolution:

> 1. The security of private property, and of private rights of every kind, is the root of commerce, of population, of riches, and of strength in every state; and the statesman, who takes any step by which those private Rights are rendered precarious, discovers himself to be but ill qualified for the place he fills.

> 2. I have no Notion of *Slavery*, but being bound by a Law, to which I do not consent.— If one Law may be imposed without Consent,

any other Law whatever may be imposed on us without our Consent. This will naturally introduce *Taxing* us without our Consent. And this as necessarily destroys our *Property*. I have no other Notion of Property, but a Power of disposing of my Goods, *as* I *please*, and not as another shall command. Whatever another may *rightfully* take from me, I have certainly no Property in.

3. One of the principal effects of the right of property is, that the king can take from his subjects no part of what they possess; he must wait till they themselves grant it to him: and this right, which . . . is, by its consequences, the bulwark that protects all the others, has moreover the immediate effect of preventing one of the chief causes of oppression.

Familiar as these three statements of property rights may seem to students of the American Revolution, none was concerned with colonial rights. The first was asserted in a 1772 London pamphlet protesting Parliament's plans to take the property of the East India Company. The second is by William Molyneux, defending Irish, not American, rights. And the third is by the Swiss theorist, J. L. De Lolme, describing contemporary British constitutional rights.[1]

The fact is that like all other rights claimed by colonial whigs, the American constitutional epitome was not an original American constitutional idea. It was not *sui generis* and it certainly was not a notion lifted from natural law. It was *the* basic concept of English law, the chief contribution made by the ancient common law of England to eighteenth-century British constitutional law. Sir Dudley Digges outlined the conceptual framework in 1628, the year of the petition of right, when he told the House of Lords that the English "have a true Property in their Goods, Lands, and Possessions," without which "there can be neither Law [n]or Justice in a Kingdom; for this is the proper object of both." Also addressing the lords, but in 1675, the duke of Buckingham said, "There is a thing called Property, (whatever some men may think) that the People of England are fondest of. It is that they shall never part with, and it is that His Majesty . . . has promised to take particular care of." After the Glorious Revolution and the ascendancy of the whig political philosophy, property became enshrined as a constitutional principle central to the preservation of freedom. "*Liberty, Property,* and *Life*," William Robertson asserted in 1713, "are the *Trinity,* which the *Whigs* do most adore! . . . They are the *Trinity* which our Laws seem to worship here on Earth." Robertson not only approved the worship, he maintained that whigs had the right to resist arbitrary authority in defense of their trinity.[2]

It would be a serious mistake to think of the right to property as a legal abstraction or as a clever bit of constitutional sloganeering camouflaging the reality of governmental confiscation. The right to property was a viable constitutional concept, often enforced in English constitutional law.[3] Moreover, the right had always been an active part of the constitution of British North America. During the 1740s, for example, a Massachusetts justice of the peace won praise for ordering the return of a servant whom a recruiting officer had enlisted in the military service. "In this," an anonymous writer insisted, "he is justified by the Original, Fundamental and Irrepealable Law of Government, the Security of Property." A few years later the same issue arose in Pennsylvania where the governor condemned the enlistment of servants as "an unconstitutional and arbitrary Invasion of our Rights and Properties." A point very evident in the twentieth century, although probably not noticed in the eighteenth, is that in these two situations the right to property was considered more important and was accorded priority over the right to personal liberty.[4]

THE CENTRALITY OF PROPERTY

Long before the era of the revolutionary controversy, the centrality of property to the definition of liberty, to the rule of law, and to constitutionalism had become established British legal dogma. John Brown, in one of the most widely read books of the day, detailed the decline of morals in Great Britain, yet found three British attributes to praise. They were the spirit of liberty, the spirit of humanity, and "the pure Administration of Justice, as it regards private Property." Most observers of that day probably would have described these as a single virtue, for the dominant theory was that liberty and good laws depended on the sanctity of private property. Francis Stoughton Sullivan, Royal Professor of the Common Law in Trinity College, Dublin, even suggested that the way to discover the origin of the English constitution was to trace it back to the time when real property ceased being granted annually and temporarily, and was given for life or became inheritable. William Blackstone, Viner Professor in Oxford University, insisted that "there is nothing which so generally strickes the imagination, and engages the affections of mankind, as the right of property; or that sole and despotic dominion which one man claims and exercises over the external things of the world, in total exclusion of the right of any other individual in the universe."[5]

To measure the eighteenth century's respect for property we need not be persuaded by what law teachers said. Of course they praised private ownership; it was part of their definition of law, freedom, and civilization. Better to seek the thoughts of nonlawyers and when doing so it is impossible not to be impressed with attitudes manifested toward private property by eighteenth-century British public opinion. A striking instance is provided by arguments justifying sinecures supported by tax revenues. "To hold an office, whether a useful one or not, was regarded by the holder as equivalent to holding a piece of property." A legal perspective from which we can view the concept of "public office as private property" may help clarify the concept. Consider, as an example, the twentieth-century academic position of a tenured professorship. Today we think of the grant of academic tenure as the creation of a contractual right. In the eighteenth century it would have been thought a form of freehold of which the grantee was seised and even people who disliked the office or wanted it abolished felt the occupant, as the owner of property, should be compensated for loss before the office was eliminated.[6] A similar theory was endorsed by *Junius* when opposing John Wilkes's plan to "disfranchise" rotten boroughs — once-thriving towns that despite being depopulated continued to send members to Parliament, generally the appointees of a single "owner." Rotten boroughs, *Junius* admitted, might be an abuse of the constitution but they were owned by individuals and to reform them would be confiscation perhaps "fatal to the liberty and property we are contending for." Or to return again to Blackstone, consider his surprising explanation why the Crown was barred from pardoning a criminal convicted on the information of an informer. "*[T]he informer hath acquired a private property in his part of the penalty.*" With the conviction the right of property had vested and should not be taken away.[7]

Later generations, to suit their own predilections, would interpret Blackstone as saying that rights of property were immutable. To an extent he did say that, but the immutability came from immutable law, not from abstract speculation. Law — or perhaps we should say the rule of law — protected property, made property a legal right, and gave property its meaning by defining it. "[A]ll our peace, plentie, civilitie, and moral honestie, dependeth upon the Law," John Davies, attorney general of Ireland, wrote during the early 1600s. "That we enjoy our lives, our wives, our children, our lands, our goods, our good names, or whatsoever is sweet and dear unto us, we are beholden unto the Law for it." It was "the law which protects our property," Matthew Gwinne remarked in his inaugural lecture as professor of physic at Gresham College, and Sir Edward Coke said that he printed his *Reports* for "the common good . . . in quieting and establishing the possessions of many." During the famous army debates at Putney in 1647, Henry Ireton, moderate spokesman on constitutional matters for the parliamentary army (and Oliver Cromwell's son-in-law), asserted that "[t]he Law of God doth not give me property, nor the Law of Nature, but property is of human constitution. I have a property and this I shall enjoy. Constitution founds property."[8] Ireton's theory that law was the basis of all property rights presaged that of eighteenth-century American whigs. They too defined law as the consent of the governed expressed either through representation or the original contract, and premised rights neither on power nor nature but on positive law.[9]

For seventeenth-century English Puritans and eighteenth-century American whigs to base private rights to property on positive law did not mean those rights were subject to the arbitrary domination of the state. That might have been the implication in the nineteenth century after law was acknowledged to be not custom nor contract but the command of the sovereign. It is sometimes assumed by legal scholars that law was command during the era of the American Revolution, but that is an error. To a remarkable extent law even in the eighteenth century was still thought of as it had been in medieval times, as *the sovereign* and not as the command emanating from the sovereign. To say that property was the product of positive and not natural or divine law, therefore, was to say that property was subject to the absolute dominion of neither the private owner nor the public legislature.[10]

The paradox is deeper than it appears. The right of property was exclusive, but only to the extent that law protected it.[11] But even though the right was not immutable, the law protecting it was, and that law was itself something in which individuals owned property rights.

LIBERTY AND PROPERTY

The law, John Lind told American whigs, was a fence that guarded property, warning them that by opposing British law they weakened the fence and endangered their property. Some decades earlier, Bishop Gilbert Burnet had applied the same metaphor to the House of Commons. When the Commons acted against the prerogative pretensions of James II, he said, it was as "the great Fence" defending "two sacred Things, *Liberty* and *Property*." The association between liberty and property was at least as old as Parliament's struggle against the House of Stuart. The antiroyalist lawyer Henry Parker described Charles I's constitutional and political ambitions in terms every parliamentary proponent could endorse. "[H]e ever intended his people should enjoy property of goods, and liberty of persons, holding no King so great, as he that was King of a rich and free people: and if they had not property of goods, and liberty of persons, they could bee neither rich nor free."[12]

The seventeenth-century English constitutional maxim making liberty depend on security in private rights to property may be the most familiar legal doctrine identified by historians of that period. At the Putney debates one Leveler army officer thought that Ireton was arguing that it was impossible to have liberty without taking away all private rights of property. But few in the seventeenth century could have had such a thought. What Ireton did was draw a distinction between constitutional liberty which "may be had and property not be destroyed," and natural liberty which "cannot be provided for in a general sense, if property be preserved." He meant that natural liberty, at least in theory, implied a lack of restraints that not only endangered property, but could also destroy constitutional liberty. And when liberty and property were associated, it was constitutional liberty, not natural liberty, that was meant. Another way to put it was "rule of law." Among Sir Roger Twysden's definitions of liberty are "la franchise de la terre," "le droit du royalme," and "the law of the land." Liberty was associated with "law" partly because "law" was associated with property. People of the seventeenth and eighteenth centuries would have found it difficult to imagine "law" not protecting property. That was, after all, law's function. One way of stating the constitutional case against prerogative taxation or ship money was to point out that prerogative taxation was "destructive to the fundamentall laws of this realm, and to the subjects right of property and liberty."[13] "To be an Englishman," William Penn argued, "is to be a free man . . . to hold his liberty and possessions by laws of his own consenting unto." When Massachusetts leaders in the 1690s were deliberating whether to accept the new charter offered by William and Mary or to hold out for restoration of the old one, a group of Nonconformist clergymen in England urged them to accept. "*Your present* Charter," they wrote, "*secures Liberty and Property, the fairest Flowers of the Civil State.*"[14]

Americans did not have to be told that liberty and property were inseparable. The Delaware House of Assembly knew what it was about when describing the right of trial by jury as "the great Preservative of public Liberty and private Property." What better way to emphasize the jury's constitutional significance? Earlier, William Livingston of New York and Richard Bland of Virginia explained why both public liberty and private property had to be preserved, Livingston stressing their importance, Bland their frailty. "[W]e are," Livingston wrote, "blessed with civil Liberty, and the inestimable Privilege of unprecarious Property. Without these, all our natural Advantages, would be no more than a beautiful unanimated Picture." Bland thought them both so fragile they were, in fact, precarious. "LIBERTY & PROPERTY," he wrote, "are like those precious Vessels whose soundness is destroyed by the least flaw and whose use is lost by the smallest hole. Impositions destroy their Beauty nor are they to be soldered by patch-work which will always discover and frequently widen the original Flaw."[15]

There may have been no eighteenth-century educated American who did not associate defense of liberty with defense of property. Like their British contemporaries, Americans believed that just as private rights in property could not exist without constitutional procedures, liberty could be lost if private rights in property were not protected. "The right of property," Arthur Lee reminded people on both sides of the Atlantic, "is the guardian of every other right, and to deprive a people of this, is in fact to deprive them of their liberty." It might be argued that Pennsylvania's John Dickinson said the opposite to Lee when, instead of asserting that property guarded liberty, he claimed that "Liberty is the great and only Security of Property." It would be wrong to push the inconsistency too far. What have in the twentieth century become separated may have been so united in the eighteenth century that one could not be conceived of existing independently of the other. "*Liberty* and Property," a correspondent reminded readers of the *Boston Gazette*, "are not only join'd in common discourse, but are in their own natures so nearly ally'd, that we cannot be said to possess the one without the enjoyment of the other."[16]

From the perspective of today, the close association between constitutional liberty and private ownership of property rights provided unexpected twists to prerevolutionary American arguments. For example, when Parliament ordered the port of Boston closed to commerce in retaliation for the Tea Party, members of Virginia's House of Burgesses condemned the statute as a deprivation of property endangering liberty. The act, they argued, "most violently and arbitrarily deprives them [Bostonians] of their property, in wharfs erected by private persons, at their own great and proper expence, which act is, in our opinion, a most dangerous attempt to destroy the constitutional liberty and rights of North America." Perhaps we should not find the burgesses's emphasis on property rights surprising. They were only repeating what John Davies, attorney general of Ireland, had maintained early in the previous century. "The first and principal cause of making kings," he wrote in a law treatise, "was to maintain property and contracts, and traffic and commerce among men."[17]

CHAPTER FOUR

THE RIGHT TO SECURITY

The words of John Davies should be marked. When American whigs said the same, and they often did, their thoughts have sometimes been traced back to John Locke and they have been called Lockean. Locke did express the same principle and many eighteenth-century writers on both sides of the Atlantic quoted his words. "The great and *chief end*," Locke said "of Mens uniting into Commonwealths, and putting themselves under Government, *is the Preservation of their Property*." But when we find the principle expressed many years earlier by an Irish attorney general and other common lawyers, we may wonder if the designation Lockean is not an oversimplification.[1]

The word most often used to state the legal concept was "end"—the end of government. "[T]he great end of Government, [is] the Preservation of Property," the minister at Norwich, Connecticut, assured that colony's Assembly in 1752. "[T]he true end and intention of all government," an anonymous Pennsylvanian wrote twenty-three years later, "[is] the security of property." It should be noted that the Pennsylvanian was writing about the revolutionary controversy and stated the principle as a ground for reconciling the colonies with the mother country. Also significant is the fact that John Pym had used the same word in the 1641 Parliament, as did Earl Camden who served a brief term as lord chancellor during the 1760s. "The great end for which men entered into society," Camden declared, "was to secure their property."[2]

There was another way to state the principle, a broader way that redefined it as a separate British right securing other things besides property. It was the right to security.

"[T]he right of personal security," an opponent of the British Cider Act explained, "consists in the legal enjoyment of life, limb, body, health, and reputation." It could be phrased either as an end of government—"the Design of Civil Government is the Security and Peace of all its Subjects," London's William Stephens wrote in 1709—or as the end of law—"The End of Law is to Secure our Persons and Estates," New York's Samuel Mulford declared five years later. Quite often the right was defined without mentioning either property or estates. Government existed, Noah Hobart told Connecticut's governors, "to render every Member of the Community secure and safe in the Possession of Life and Liberty, Reputation and Ease."[3]

We no longer think of security as a "right." In fact, legal values have changed so drastically over the last two centuries that there is a danger we cannot reconstruct eighteenth-century constitutional thought and that we miss some of the subtleties of the revolutionary debate. It may be that the right to security is even more elusive than the disparaged, misunderstood right to property. Can we today appreciate what Thomas Burnet meant in his *Essay upon Government* when he defined government in the eighteenth century as security? The "Definition of Government" (which "cannot be well disputed"), Burnet wrote, was "[t]he due Administration, Application, or Execution of these Laws, which the Society has devised for the security of their several Rights and Properties." The *London Journal*, Robert Walpole's newspaper, said that it was the "sole Duty" of the civil magistrate, "by the impartial Execution of equal Laws, to secure to every one of his Subjects the *Possession* of Things belonging to *this Life*." We may find incomprehensible, perhaps even troublesome, the belief that the "sole Duty" of government was to secure material possessions. If so, it is one more indication of how much closer the legal mind of the eighteenth century was to medieval constitutionalism than to twentieth-century British or American constitutional law. Until the nineteenth century the right to security, and especially that most important subsection of the right—security of property—was the essence of English constitutionalism. At Putney during the 1640s, Henry Ireton called it "the most fundamental part of your constitution." A hundred years later, two decades before the Stamp Act, a Massachusetts pamphleteer wrote of "the Original, Fundamental and Irrepealable Law of Government, the Security of Property."[4]

GOVERNMENT AND PROPERTY

American whigs not only accepted the English definition of liberty as security in property, they made it an article of constitutional faith. James Otis, one of the few to speak of "private property" rather than just "property," even termed it an absolute right. "The absolute rights of Englishmen," he wrote on behalf of the Massachusetts House of Representatives, "are the rights of *personal security, personal liberty*, and of *private property*." John Dickinson, more a legal traditionalist than Otis, stressed security in terms of property itself. "Men," he contended, "cannot be happy, without Freedom; nor free, without Security of Property; nor so secure, unless the sole Power to dispose of it be lodged in themselves."[5]

These statements of Otis and Dickinson, and many others written and uttered by revolutionary whigs, have been interpreted as evidence of an emerging colonial political theory. Better to recognize that here were Americans clinging to a common-law definition of liberty, a definition popularized in Stuart times when the Parliamentary party, guided by common lawyers, seized on the notion of security of property as the best guarantee of life and liberty. The seventeenth-century constitutional formulation, still current in eighteenth-century British North America, provided the citizen with protection from arbitrary government by identifying the individual in terms of property, and property in terms of legality and rights. The American emphasis on property was not, therefore, as the British historian L. B. Namier has contended, something that "stood in the centre of their thinking," with liberty "merely a function and safeguard of 'property'." It was, rather, the essential element without which people had no liberty. "[A]s Liberty is at the Bottom of all our Enjoyments," New York's Assembly explained to the king, "your Majesty's Subjects can neither be happy nor rich, but in the independent Fruition of their Property." Liberty, not property, was the center of constitutional thinking, but property was also near the center because without security of property an individual could not be independent. The connection between English legal theory and American constitutional reality comes to the fore in relation to property and freedom by comparing the theory as stated in *Cato's Letters* in 1721 with the colonial reality described forty-eight years later by a British traveler in Massachusetts. "[A]ll Men," Thomas Gordon contended,

> are animated by the Passion of acquiring and defending Property, because Property is the best Support of that Independency, so passionately desired by all Men. Even Men the most dependent have it constantly in their Heads and their Wishes, to become indepen-

dent one Time or other; and the Property which they are acquir-
ing, or mean to acquire by that Dependency, is intended to bring
them out of it, and to procure them an agreeable Independency.

Alexander Cluny, traveling in North America in the 1760s, found independent people of Gordon's or *Cato*'s type in Massachusetts, and stressed that
it was property and the law of property that made them independent.
Massachusetts citizens, he wrote, "pride themselves more than any other
People upon Earth in that Spirit of Freedom, which first made their Ancestors leave their native Country and settle there."

The People of *New England* owe that Independency of Individuals,
in which the very Essence of true Liberty exists, and which is the
best Protection of it, to a particular Law of Inheritance, by which
the Possessions of the Father are divided equally among all his Children; so that they are kept in that happy Mediocrity, which by oblig-
ing them to turn their Thoughts to Industry, in order to avoid Want,
exempts them from Temptation to, as well as denies them the Means
of gratifying Luxury; and at the same Time, by supplying them with
a Foundation for that Industry to work upon, exempts them also from
the Necessity of submitting to any Encroachment on their Liberty.

One of the New Englanders of whom Cluny wrote, the Suffolk County
lawyer Josiah Quincy, Jr., thought that security in property provided even
more than the independence that made people free. It provided the foundation for civilization itself. Without "private property, and personal security," Quincy maintained, "men will descend into barbarism, or at best
become adepts in humiliation and servility; but they will never make a
progress in literature or the useful arts."[6]

It was liberty or personal independence that made civilization possible and property indispensable. For the citizen to be secure in individual
rights, property also had to be secure. That reason was why the Massachusetts House of Representatives joined security of right to security in
property when condemning parliamentary taxation of the colonies. "The
security of right and property," it told the earl of Shelburne, "is the great
end of government. Surely, then, such measures as tend to render right
and property precarious, tend to destroy both property and government,
for these must stand or fall together. . . . The House intreat your Lordship to consider, whether a colonist can be conceived to have any property which he may call his own, if it may be granted away by any other
body, without his consent." The representatives were saying more than
that parliamentary taxation was unconstitutional. They were saying that
the imperial government, "the great end" of which was to secure prop-

erty, was not protecting property but making it insecure. In the seventeenth century, Samuel Nowell had told another generation of New Englanders that the Lord would punish rulers who illegally seized their constituents' estates. To render property rights precarious was a sin in government giving sanction to rebellion. It was a concept on which Bostonians had acted in 1689, when they rebelled against Governor Edmund Andros and placed him under arrest, in large part because he had made property rights insecure by introducing arbitrary procedures illegal by the maxims of common law. Resistance on behalf of property security was not merely a right, it may have been a duty owed to what a Connecticut clergyman called "the God of Civil liberty and property." "[I]f I am not mistaken," Abel Stiles wrote his nephew, also a clergyman, during the Stamp Act crisis, "the present existence of our English happifying Constitution, is next to providence owing to sundry Spirited, united efforts formerly made against unconstitutional measures." The Stamp Act was one of those measures. "Shall Revelation say stand fast and contend earnestly for the Faith — and doth not the God of Nature, the God of Civil Liberty and property say stand fast. . . . Pray what forbids us to resist even unto blood, where that freedom is in question, the death of which is the death of property, as the pregnant mother's death is fatal to the infant unborn."[7]

CHAPTER FIVE

THE RIGHT TO GOVERNMENT

In seeking to reconstruct the foundations of American government as they were laid by the Founding Fathers, the greatest risk we run is that we no longer understand the purpose and scope of eighteenth-century rights as they were understood in the eighteenth century. Do we today understand the eighteenth-century right to property? Current twentieth-century law and social theory lead to the hypothesis that the type of "property" intended to be secured was tangible goods, especially the material assets of substantial estates. The concept of property and the principle of the right to property — a "doctrine, so convenient to all property owners, and so perfectly adapted to the existing social and political situation"— was put forth not to secure privileges for all people, but to guarantee the material holdings of the most propertied, and to liberate the very wealthy from political, legal, and moral control. The point is best made for Great Britain in the age of the American Revolution by considering the striking extent to which the death penalty punished offenses against material property.[1]

There is evidence supporting these suppositions, especially if we give weight to the influence of John Locke, for he and his followers were concerned with the security of material gain. Moreover, during the eighteenth century the traditional, customary property rights of the peasantry — in open fields, pannage, pasture, and the forest — were eroded by judgments at common law and by parliamentary statutes promoting the emerging capitalist aspirations of the dominant landed class. Even the champions of democratic reform in the late eighteenth century sought mainly to broaden the electoral base of representation, and not to tamper with the existing economic order.[2]

Yet we must be careful that an anachronistic appraisal of the economic and social order, realistic perhaps by twentieth-century standards, does not intrude on the theoretical premises of received constitutional doctrine. There is no evidence that political and legal theorists of the eighteenth century understood economic matters as we understand them today, or that the hundreds of writers who praised the "best" of all possible constitutions did not believe that it shed its blessings on all economic classes, poor as well as rich, and that they did not think the rights of property benefited the masses as much as the few. The doctrine of security of property was not concocted to justify the contemporary economic arrangement. It existed during all of recorded English history, going back to the prefeudal Saxon era of the "good old law" when the "rights in property" possessed by individuals constituted "an absolutely sacred part of the whole absolutely sacred legal order."[3]

The right to property and the right to security can be understood only in their eighteenth-century context, not from the latter-day insight of Marxist revelation. The concept of property and security of property were civil rights that encompassed a view of the world that defined for eighteenth-century English-speaking people the meaning of law, liberty, and constitutional government. It defined, in fact, yet another right, the right to government of a certain type, to a limited government of constitutionalism such as was believed to exist only in Great Britain. In the last chapter it was noted that Thomas Burnet defined government as the execution of laws securing rights and properties. A good government, a fit government, "a mild and propitious Government," was one that "pursues for its end the Security, Ease, and Welfare of its People." For the individual citizen of Great Britain that meant a constitution securing private property, a security that "will continue his birthright as long as that constitution shall remain inviolate and in its full vigor." It meant, in other words, the right to limited, or what today is called, constitutional government.[4]

Not only was the security of property the purpose of government, it was the very definition of government by law, for a government that failed to protect property ceased to be a government. It was, in fact, a definition encompassing the entire American constitutional case against parliamentary taxation. "If," a writer observed in a 1774 issue of the *Lon-*

don Gazetteer, "any man, or body of men, claim a right to take away at pleasure from other men their property, and to dispose of it as they please such claim tends to a dissolution of society." This constitutional theory was based on a combination of the ancient concept of the original contract with its attendant right of rebellion (discussed in chapter 16) and the English legal principle that government existed for the security of property. Applying this definition of government to the American colonies in 1771, Allan Ramsay argued:

> Nothing will contribute so much to the peace, harmony, and order of our distant provinces, as a thorough conviction, in their own minds, that they are perfectly secure in the enjoyment of all their constitutional rights; and that no partial laws may affect their property, by which they can be charged more, for the expence of government, than what in justice, and equity, they ought to pay.[5]

REPRESENTATION AND PROPERTY

Just as the concept of property was part of the definition of constitutional government, so law was part of the definition of property. One could not have property without security, and security came from law capable of restraining government, that is, from government by the rule of law. *Cato* had that definition of property in mind when he wrote that in "the Eastern Monarchies" and Turkey "there is neither Liberty, Property, true Religion, Art, Sciences, Learning, or Knowledge." Virginia's Richard Bland stated the legal principle in as concise language as did anyone writing before the Stamp Act. "The Rights of the Subjects," he explained, "are so secured by Law that they cannot be deprived of the least part of their property without their own consent. Upon this Principle of Law, the Liberty and Property of every Person who has the felicity to live under a British government is founded." After passage of the Stamp Act Americans realized that Bland's principle might not apply to them if Parliament was allowed to define the legal meaning of the word "consent." John Dickinson, therefore, restated the principle, although still in terms of "liberty" and "property," when he wrote that "as we can have no Property in that which another may of Right take and dispose of as he pleases, without our Consent; and as the late Acts of Parliament assert this Right to be in them, we cannot enjoy freedom until this Claim is given up, and until Acts made in Consequence of it be repealed."[6]

The constitutional principle of "consent" was a legal entity separate from property and must be treated in its turn. For the purpose of this discussion it is enough to note that the concept of "consent" entered into what can be labeled the negative definition of property because anything that could be taken from its possessor without the possessor's consent was not property. In 1775 Lord North proposed ending the dispute about taxation by applying for requisitions. Parliament would inform the colonial assemblies what revenues were required and leave to each colony to raise the money. Only if a colony failed to comply would Parliament tax directly. The Continental Congress rejected the plan. "This," it resolved, "leaves us without any thing we can call property."

It is sometimes suggested that the definition that "property" was not "property" if possessions could be taken without the possessor's consent was *sui generis* to the American whigs, concocted by them in desperation because they were unable to formulate principled legal arguments to support their case against parliamentary supremacy. Nothing can contribute more to our misunderstanding of the constitutional origins of the American Revolution than such assumptions. The legal definition associating "property" with "consent" was not only a constitutional maxim inherited from seventeenth-century England, it also had been current in the colonies long before the Stamp Act. In 1708, for example, the New York Assembly asserted "that it is and always has been the unquestionable right of every freeman in this colony that he hath a perfect and entire property in his goods and estate. . . . That the imposing and levying of any monies, upon his Majesty's subjects of this colony, under any pretence or color whatsoever, without consent in general assembly, is a grievance and a violation of the people's property." The 1689 New England revolution was explained by a contemporary partly on the grounds that the magistrates who were overthrown had "Invaded *Liberty* and *Property* after such a manner, as that no Man could say anything was *his own*."[7]

The principle may seem extreme, that property was not property if, without the possessor's consent, government could disturb its legal possession. Yet the principle followed from the basic premises of eighteenth-century constitutional theory, entailing not only the definition of property, but the meaning of "good" government and the right to security. "The *end* of all government being *common security*," *Mutius Scaevola* explained in the *Boston Gazette*, "Imposition of laws or taxes on any community without their consent, being inconsistent with the faintest idea of public or private *security*, is utterly subversive of all good *government*." The principle deserves close attention by students of the American Revolution, for when property is defined as a legal possession that cannot be taken from the possessor but with the possessor's consent, some revolutionary statements assume clearer meaning. With it in mind, we can better understand what people in Middlesex County, Virginia, meant when they termed taxation without representation "a Subversion of Property," and what the British political writer James Burgh meant when he argued that parliamentary taxation of the colonies "is subversive of liberty, [and] annihilates property." "[I]f any thing is to be taken from the colonies, without the consent of their own representatives," an anonymous pamphlet printed in London asserted, then it followed that whatever was not taken was held by the Americans "by mere grace and favour: for it cannot be said that they have any property in that, which another whom they have never seen, can grant away at pleasure."[8]

It was also this definition that explains why so many American arguments about the right to property were framed in absolute terms giving the appearance that the protection of material acquisitions was the main consideration of the law.[9] Property rights were exclusive not due to natural-law theory but because their constitutional protection was so broad and the margin for their constitutional deprivation so narrow: there was no constitutional justification for taking property except consent.

It would be stretching legal theory to say that government existed in eighteenth-century Great Britain to guarantee property, the right to property, and the security of property. Yet the stretch is less farfetched if we keep in mind the doctrine of consent and the British constitutional manifestation of legislative consent: parliamentary representation. The lesson is not only that possessions government can confiscate without consent of the possessor or the possessor's representative were not "property." Just as telling is that it was property that was represented in the legislature, the institution where consent was expressed, and the property represented was landed property, not just any kind of material wealth. "The Owners of the Land," a progovernment pamphlet pointed out during Walpole's administration, "are properly the *Body* of the Nation. These, in this Island, are strictly the *People* of *Great Britain*."[10] This doctrine was one of the few concerning which American constitutional theory separated from British constitutional theory. In the colonies the general understanding was that localities or people should be represented, and when, following the Revolution, property was made a basis for representation, that property was not land but taxable wealth in general. This study, however, is not the place to discuss representation. The topic is mentioned only for the light it sheds on the right to property and the right to restrained government.

Some aspects to the representation of land help illustrate the eighteenth-century concept of rights in property. The first is that the representation of land justified taxing persons who could not vote. These people, known as nonelectors, were, in legal theory, represented because their property was represented. The nonelectors were protected from arbitrary taxation,

William Knox pointed out, because of "the fixed landed property which
every member of Parliament must have within the kingdom of Great Britain, for as all taxes do ultimately affect the land-owner, the non-electors
from this circumstance derive a security that the members of Parliament
will be careful not to tax them immoderately or unnecessarily, as they
would thereby burden themselves also." The argument was valid only
as far as Knox was correct about all taxes eventually falling on landed
property. There were observers who denied that fact, yet even those calling for reform of parliamentary representation often wanted the representation of property, not the representation of people, reformed.[11] The
idea that property and not people was represented, after all, was but a
mechanism for enforcing the right to security and therefore for putting
into operation the constitutional ideal that the right to property limited
government. The same was true for the second aspect of property representation that illustrates the eighteenth-century notion of property rights.
Again, the argument becomes circular. As Thomas Gordon pointed out,
one of the purposes for having representative government was to place
sound officials in a position "to defend publick and private Property from
the unclean and ravenous Hands of Harpyes," in other words, for the
security of property. It was the ownership of land, not just wealth, that
made such men dependable because it assured their independence and
enhanced the likelihood of their civic virtue.[12] As the author of *Civil Liberty Asserted* explained in 1776, "the Laws of every Civil State in the world
chiefly relate to property, and therefore men of property are those whose
especial duty, as well as interest it is to take care of the equity, impartial-
ity, and justice of the Laws; that every one be equally protected in the
quiet possession and enjoyment of all which of right belongs unto him."[13]

THE DEFINITION OF PROPERTY

Not only was property defined in similar terms on both sides of the
Atlantic during the revolutionary era; American whigs also insisted on
the constitutional right to property using the same definition of property
used by English lawyers as early as the Petition of Right Commons in
1628.[14] The definition could be stated positively or negatively. The governor of Rhode Island was positive when explaining that the meaning
of the British constitutional principle that citizens could not be forced
to part with property except by laws to which they had consented "is
really to be possessed of property and to have something that may be called
one's own." A few years later, people in the same colony made the point
negatively. "[T]here can," the voters of Providence resolved, "be no prop-

erty in that, which another can, of right, take from us without our consent."[15] Either positively or negatively, it was the same definition.

> *The New York General Assembly:* [A]ll real Property is lost, whensoever it becomes subordinate to Laws, in the making of which, the Proprietor does not participate.

> *Arthur Lee:* The right of giving property, by the consent of the possessor, is inherent in the very idea of property. It is original, prior, and paramount to all positive laws.

> *London's Lord Mayor John Wilkes:* The very idea of property excludes the right of another's taking any thing from me without my consent, otherwise I cannot call it my own. What property have I in what another person can seize at his pleasure? If we can tax the Americans without their consent, they have no property, nothing which they can call their own.[16]

It may seem peculiar that the constitutional meaning of "property" was defined in terms of the very controversy itself, or, as Georgia's Provincial Congress expressed the idea, taxation without the consent of those taxed was "diametrically opposite to every idea of property." By this definition, therefore, in 1776 "property" meant a right secure from parliamentary interference, at least as long as Americans were not represented in Parliament. The conclusion becomes less inexplicable when we recall that the colonial whig case against parliamentary taxation was the same case that Parliament once made against the prerogative taxation of Charles I. For Sir Edward Coke and his fellow members of the Commons of 1628, property and security were both defined in terms of what the *king* constitutionally could not do. For the Americans of a century and a half later, property and liberty were defined in terms of what *Parliament* constitutionally could not do. The New York Assembly wrapped up all three concepts — liberty, security, and property — in the same argument. "Without such a Right vested in themselves, exclusive of all others, there can be no Liberty, no Happiness, no Security; it is inseparable from the very Idea of Property, for who can call that his own, which may be taken away at the Pleasure of another?"[17]

When they are read today, many constitutional allegations voiced by American whigs convey a fanatical touch. An example is the repeated claim that if, in just the smallest amount, they were taxed without their consent they would have "no property" to call their own. But worries that appear inordinate when judged by our constitutional experience become more moderate when restored to the context of their British background and to a legal world in which constitutionalism and limited

government depended on the constitutional right to property and security. We must not forget that what really mattered to the eighteenth-
century legal mind was the right itself. When eighteenth-century political theorists wrote that property unprotected from governmental whim
and fancy was not property, they were saying that the right, not the property, must not be diluted. The right was, after all, the foundation not
just of property, but of liberty and government itself. The salient fact
is not that the doctrine was extreme but that its defense had to be stead-
fast, for, as a New Englander wrote of the Boston Port Act, Parliament's
statute closing Boston's harbor in punishment for the Boston Tea Party,
"[w]e do not pretend to hold our property on the fickle tenure of indul-
gencies of Parliament, but on the firm foundation of right."[18]

CHAPTER SIX

THE JURY RIGHT

The right to trial by jury, unlike the rights of property, security, and eighteenth-century government, is a right we think we know. We do, but only in an attenuated form. We no longer know the right as it existed in the age of the American Revolution. Certainly we cannot recapture the extreme euphoria of British and colonist alike when they thought of jury trial. The extravagant eulogiums they heaped on the jury right have a ring of propagandist gasconades for the twentieth-century ear.[1]

For English-speaking people of the eighteenth century, trial by jury was not only "one of the most fundamental principals of our present happy constitution," it was also the most happy fundamental of the world's happiest constitution. Sir William Blackstone thought it as fundamental as anything else in British constitutional law: it could not "be altered but by a parliament." John Cartwright wanted it more fundamental than that. As an old man writing in the nineteenth century he would have made the right to trial by jury fundamental in the old English and future American sense of the word: unalterable even by Parliament. The Constitution, he wrote in 1823, expressing a legal concept that, as theory, had contained some validity in Britain in 1776 but none by 1823, "is paramount to, and a *Law* to the *Legislature* — that is, a *limit* it cannot pass. . . . [N]either *Law*, nor any act of the *Legislature*, can by possibility take away the inherent right of a JURY to exercise its juridical functions while acting in strict fidelity and allegiance to the CONSTITUTION."[2]

We may dismiss Cartwright's constitutional theory but not the constitutional tradition from which he wrote. Almost any legal positivist of the eighteenth century who asserted that Parliament was both supreme and sovereign would have hesitated before answering the question of whether Parliament could abolish trial by jury. It is possible that as late as 1776 a majority of common lawyers would have been too confused or too annoyed to have given an unequivocal answer. The point is not that the law was uncertain or that the legal certitude of the nineteenth century was legal ambivalence in the eighteenth. The point, rather, is the sacrosanct centrality of jury trial in British constitutional thought during the age of the American Revolution.

The most significant definition of trial by jury during the revolutionary period was formulated by the Continental Congress. Bowing to the leadership of Lord North's administration, Parliament had refused to grant jury trial to recently conquered Quebec and Congress hoped to persuade Canadians they had been discriminated against in a very significant way. It can be assumed that much thought was given to this explanation of a right unknown to the people addressed but whom American whigs wanted to convince was a right worth rebelling for.

> This provides, that neither life, liberty nor property can be taken from the possessor, until twelve of his unexceptionable countrymen and peers, of his vicinage, who from that neighbourhood may reasonably be supposed to be acquainted with his character, and the characters of the witnesses, upon a fair trial, and full enquiry face to face, in open Court, before as many of the people as chuse to attend, shall pass their sentence upon oath against him; a sentence that cannot injure him, without injuring their own reputation, and probably their interest also; as the question may turn on points, that, in some degree, concern the general welfare; and if it does not, thei[r] verdict may form a precedent, that, on a similar trial of their own, may militate against themselves.[3]

THE VALUE OF JURY

It would be well to heed what the Congress thought important. It tells us why eighteenth-century people living in common-law jurisdictions valued juries. For them the right to trial by jury was an essential element in their definition of restrained government. Juries checked official power by ensuring that government was less arbitrary. Trial without jury, Maryland legislators explained during the Stamp Act crisis, "renders the Subject insecure in his Liberty and Property." The earl of Chatham told the House of Lords that the jury was the bulwark of an Englishman's "personal security and property"; the New York Assembly added that the jury was "essential to the Safety" of the "Lives, Liberty, and Property" of British subjects; and Virginia's burgesses agreed that it was "the surest Support of Property."[4]

Juries secured the right to property by providing determiners of facts who (1) were disinterested and not associated with the Crown, and (2) shared with the litigant a community interest in the security of his property. Their presence alone precluded secret trials and furnished the citizenry with a shield against venal jurists, purchased testimony, dependent officials, and partial judgments.[5]

The most significant British right that juries guarded, even more priceless than the right to property, was liberty and its enjoyment. Eighteenth-century literature boasting British liberty was filled with pages explaining how citizens and dissenting groups could utilize the right to jury trial to preserve their right to liberty.[6] One needs only read the political platitudes bandied about during the age of the American Revolution to discover the close association between the right to jury trial and the existence of liberty in the minds of people living in the various common-law jurisdictions. To London's Common Council, jury trial was "that sacred Bulwark of *English* Liberty," and to the New York grand jury it was "the very foundation of *British* liberty." It was "the grand Bulwark of LIBERTY" to the Maryland House of Representatives, and "that inestimable privilege and characteristic of English liberty" to the Massachusetts General Court.[7] On both sides of the Atlantic any deprivation of trial by jury was decried as diminishing liberty. In New England the voters of Salem bemoaned Parliament's extension of trial at admiralty without jury as "destructive of Liberty." In the mother country an article entitled "On the Perversion of Law from its constitutional Course" raised the same warning against "encroachment of judges" on the autonomy of juries. The right to trial by a jury uncontrolled by the court, it was said, "is so essential a part of our constitution, that the liberty of the subject is violated, whenever the least attempt is made to break through this sacred rule, which will admit of no exception."[8]

During the seventeenth century the jury performed several roles as the guardian of liberty, primarily as the preserver of fundamental law even against parliamentary enactment.[9] By the 1760s, with parliamentary supremacy superceding the rule of customary law, the emphasis shifted to the role of the jury as a shield against government oppression, or, in the words of Charles Carroll of Carrollton, as "the best security against the encroachments of power, and consequently the firmest support of liberty." Ideally, the right to trial by jury stood as "an insuperable bar against the power of Sovereign over subject." "Juries are not only a most reasonable and most equitable means of determination in matters of meum and tuum between man and man," Baron Rokeby believed, "but they are likewise a very excellent safeguard of the general rights of the community against the attacks and the attempts of princes, of ministers or of any other powerful persons." The reason was that jurors "represent in their province the public, not by election, but as a fair, equal, indifferent part and pattern of the whole."[10]

The institutional function must not be misunderstood. Power was feared in the eighteenth century, whether it was government power, royal power, aristocratic power, or "mobocracy." The very existence of power, rather than its abuse, raised concern. All authority was dangerous, but not all power was illegitimate. Only authority checked by procedural rules was "lawful." The purport of the rules did not matter; it was the existence of rules and their procedure that counted. Rules and procedure meant that power was exercised in prescribed ways, making it less dangerous than unrestrained authority. Power was relatively less fearful in proportion to the procedures or restraints surrounding it. In the vocabulary of the eighteenth century the most feared power was "arbitrary" power. The concept of arbitrariness may have been the most prominent element in the definition of liberty during the second half of the eighteenth century. To be free of arbitrary power was to possess liberty. The measure of liberty was not the freedom people enjoyed from government restraint, but the procedural restraints surrounding government. The importance of trial by jury to the preservation of liberty lay in the mere facts that it existed and all citizens were entitled to its "benefits" before they could be put in jeopardy of life and limb, not whether it provided a "fair" trial, allowed the defendant to tell his story (no party could testify), or if the jurors were impartial, were representative of minorities, of all social classes, or were communicants of any but the official religion.[11]

It may be that colonial constitutional thought envisioned an additional purpose to trial by jury along with protection of property and the preservation of liberty. It is a major theme of this study that American constitutional ideals were British constitutional ideals, and that there were few differences in legal thought between the two parts of the empire. There were, however, some differences, or perhaps changes in perception and emphasis, separating American constitutionalism from that of the mother country. The major ones were the diverging theories of representation and consent to government. A minor one, discernible primarily in the thoughts of John Adams, was an emerging colonial stress on the

jury as a democratic institution. In the mother country praise was heaped
on trial by jury for providing commoners with judgment by their equals.[12]
What was meant, however, was that the day laborer might be judged
by the younger son of a duke or the dissenting cottager by a member of
the established church who owned vast estates. They were equals in that
all were "commoners." John Adams, by contrast, lived in a land where
jurors were in fact as well as theory generally the social and political if
not the economic equals of criminal defendants and civil parties. He considered the jury more an instrument of commonality or lower-class protection than did his contemporaries in Great Britain. The perceived value,
however, was less the nineteenth-century value of democratic expression
than the traditional, medieval value of restraint upon government. "As
the Constitution requires, that, the popular Branch of the Legislature,
should have an absolute Check so as to put a peremptory Negative upon
every Act of the Government," Adams argued, "it requires that the common People should have as compleat a Controul, as decisive a Negative,
in every Judgment of a Court of Judicature."[13]

Localism was another American change of emphasis. It was, of course,
not new to English legal theory as trial at *nisi prius* had long been a
common-law ideal. Colonial isolation and the parliamentary innovation
of internal legislation, however, gave localism a new association with jury
trial during the American revolutionary era. The "excellence" of trial by
jury, North Carolina's James Iredell boasted, "consists in being judged
by Men who are equally interested with the Prisoner in preserving the
law from violation"; jurors who "may be placed in a situation to be affected
by *their own precedents*," yet "at the same time that the principles of
self-defence will urge them to condemn *the guilty*, the care of their own
preservation (if no higher principle actuates them) will prompt them to
acquit *the innocent*." There was even a theory, advanced by Connecticut's Benjamin Trumbull, that a vicinage jury gave a criminal defendant
more than a sympathetic hearing; it provided a more knowledgeable
judgment.[14]

A special American attachment for juries arose from the colonial worry
about English common lawyers appointed by London to preside over colonial courts who, it was feared, had a greater attachment to imperial rule
than to impartial justice. It was a matter of intraempire balance, of preserving the autonomy of the peripheral from the strength of the center,
not unrelated in constitutional practice to the check that seventeenth-
century common-law juries had placed on prerogative courts. The judge
might be sent out from the mother country to promote the interests of
the Empire, but if the judge was unable to function without a jury of
the neighborhood, imperial legislative and judicial mandates might have

to be tempered to conform to a local constitutional consensus. For that reason, New England, where most judges had always been native sons, not placemen, felt a particular menace when violations of the Stamp Act were to be prosecuted in vice admiralty; that is, not at common law, but before a Crown-appointed judge sitting without a jury. Taking away the ancient right of being judged only by peers, the voters of Boston complained, "deprives us of the most essential Rights of *Britons*, and greatly weakens the best Security of our Lives, Liberties and Estates; which may hereafter be at the Disposal of Judges who may be Strangers to us, and perhaps malicious, mercenary, corrupt and oppressive."[15]

THE THREAT TO JURY

From the beginning of English and British attempts to enforce imperial law in the colonies, local, common-law juries were barriers defending what colonists perceived as local rights against parliamentary encroachments.[16] Juries, in other words, were constitutional instruments of regional autonomy, a role that Parliament sought to nullify when it created vice-admiralty courts: civil-law tribunals that did not refer the decision of fact to juries. For about three-quarters of a century these imperial courts, although unpopular with some sections of the colonial population, were not constitutional issues, for Parliament had promulgated them by virtue of its constitutional authority to regulate imperial trade. It was not until Parliament adopted the policy that led to the Revolution, introducing legislation depriving Americans of jury trials at the venue in matters not connected with imperial or international trade, that American whigs realized that vice admiralty might be a constitutional grievance. Even then the jurisdiction was not challenged as an instrument of enforcement within its traditional sphere of trade regulation, but for the potential of what it might become: a new breed of prerogative court, serving not the Crown but Parliament.[17]

The Stamp Act was the start — Parliament's first attempt in a matter not concerned with trade regulation to curtail the right to jury trial in the colonies. Prosecutions for violation of the Act — refusal to pay the stamp tax or to use stamped paper as specified by the statute — were not cognizable at common law as constitutional custom dictated, but prosecuted in vice admiralty with both law and fact determined by an imperially appointed judge applying civil, not common, law. The statute was repealed before it could be enforced, a fact immaterial to the constitutional controversy. As with every other parliamentary tax imposed on the colonies during the era of the American Revolution, the grievance was not economic but constitutional, and in eighteenth-century constitutional polemics the threat or potential of enforcement could be as grievous as actual enforcement. There were two rights in jeopardy — the right to be taxed only by consent and the right to trial by jury — and the Stamp Act, repealed or not, was proof that Parliament, a legislature in which Americans were not represented, would not hesitate to deprive Americans of those fundamental rights.[18]

In resolution after resolution and instruction after instruction, legislative bodies and town meetings educated colonial citizens about their endangered right to jury trial; it was an astonishing outpouring of constitutional arguments. Educated Americans, with only the most cursory and superficial glance at the current political literature, had to have been aware that their elected representatives were fearful that the treasured right to trial by jury was perilously threatened.[19]

We will never be certain, but it can be plausibly argued, that the Stamp Act did more than any other piece of parliamentary legislation to erode the colonists' faith in British constitutional rule, and in restrospect the rulers of Parliament appear recklessly foolish to have risked so much antagonism for so little. Yet a strong case can be made for the need to suspend the right of trial by a jury of the vicinage if imperial law was to run in North America. The fact that colonial whigs controlled local juries and in some colonies used them to defeat imperial policy and nullify parliamentary statutes is one of the most dramatic and least understood of the legal conditions leading to the American Revolution. To defy what they considered unconstitutional parliamentary commands by applying what can be called "whig law" or seventeenth-century English constitutional ideals, colonial juries not only protected local citizens from imperial prosecutions, they also punished royal officials "guilty" of enforcing "unconstitutional" imperial law.[20] The central administration in London had compelling reasons to curtail colonial jury trials. The difficulty was that no matter what remedy it applied, it had to tread on one of the most sensitive and fundamental of British constitutional rights.

Other imperial attempts similar to the Stamp Act, to curtail colonial juries by depriving common-law courts of jurisdiction and assigning it to vice admiralty, will be mentioned in the chapter that discusses the jury and admiralty grievances. At this point our concern is with the tactics that Parliament employed threatening jury trial in the colonies. There was one other besides utilizing vice admiralty. It did not deny Americans the right to a trial by jury when accused of a criminal offense. Rather, the method was to deny the right to a jury of the vicinage by shifting trial from the venue where the alleged crime had been committed to some jurisdiction less hostile to imperial constitutional aspirations.

American whigs labeled trial away from the vicinage unconstitutional,[21] but they were on somewhat insecure grounds as there was constitutional precedent for it in the law of the mother country. For example, a British statute authorized transfer of treason trials to any county the administration thought would enhance conviction. The best-known instance of shifting the venue was the prosecution in English counties before English jurors of Scots following the Rebellion of 1745 when, in many Scottish localities, "all the inhabitants [had] participated in the same crime." Another example was the notorious Black Act of 1723, which provided that members of the lower classes accused of proaching and other proscribed actions could be tried in any English county.[22]

These precedents were important to the question of the legality of ordering trial away from the vicinage, but apparently not on the question of constitutionality. Despite statutory law, there was a general perception on both sides of the Atlantic that persons accused of common-law crimes had a constitutional right to trial at the venue. Even in cases of high treason, Baron Auckland had stated in the 1771 edition of *Principles of Penal Law*, "[t]he jurors must, by the common law, be of the same county wherein the offence was committed."[23]

The matter of trial at the vicinage became an issue in the revolutionary controversy because Parliament committed a stupid blunder. The two Houses voted an address to George III advising him that a statute of Henry VIII providing for trial in England of persons accused of treasons and misprisions of treason committed outside the realm was applicable to the American colonies and urged that the statute be enforced. Parliament later reinforced the law of Henry with a new statute—"an act for the better securing his Majesty's dock-yards"—authorizing that certain crimes committed outside the realm could be indicted and prosecuted in any county within the realm.[24] The "dockyards" bill was primarily intended to frighten whig leaders in Massachusetts. Instead, it strengthened the American whig constitutional case against parliamentary rule and colonial resistance to imperial law.

Some weak efforts were made toward enforcing the Dockyards Act for alleged treasonable conduct in Massachusetts and Rhode Island, and the law officers ruled the Act applicable to the Boston Tea Party. But it is doubtful if any attention was given either to how the Act would be implemented or even to whether it could be. In truth, Great Britain lacked both the practical capability and the constitutional apparatus for ordering an American tried in England for alleged crimes committed in the colonies. Any imperial official attempting to enforce either the act of Henry VIII or the Dockyards Act ran the risk of indictment by the local colonial grand jury for attempted kidnapping.[25]

The law of Henry VIII and the dockyards statute, together with the Administration of Justice Act (one of the Massachusetts "intolerable acts" passed in 1774) which permitted trial of an imperial official accused of homicide to be removed anywhere in the Empire, served no purpose but to inflame whigs. Some of the strongest constitutional rhetoric of the revolutionary era was written in condemnation of these laws. The resolutions, protests, and denunciations voted by colonial assemblies and whig bodies were not just constitutional arguments, they were also statements of constitutional defiance.[26] "*Resolved*," the first Congress voted, "[t]hat the seizing or attempting to seize any person in America, in order to transport such person beyond the sea for trial of offences, committed within the body of a county in America, being against law, will justify, and ought to be met with resistance and reprisal."[27]

Imperialists might fault the extreme rhetoric of American radicals but the British administration was really to blame. The legislation should never have been enacted. It is no justification that it appeared to be necessary. We may admit that imperial statutes such as the Stamp Act and the White Pine Act would not be enforced by colonial juries. But extending vice admiralty or changing the venue were not practical solutions. The administration should have realized it could not enforce such statutes, but apparently gave the matter little thought. Instead, by promulgating laws certain to irritate American constitutional sensibilities and of dubious constitutionality, London permitted colonial whigs to associate their constitutional defense of rights with the legendary struggles of Lord Coke and the seventeenth-century common lawyers who quashed Star Chamber and other prerogative courts. In truth, all that Parliament accomplished in threatening the right of colonists to trial at the vicinage was to tarnish its own image as an instrument of constitutional rule, and needlessly to raise doubt in American minds whether they could ever again be secure under the British constitution.[28]

THE BRITISH ANALOGY

The American constitutional defense was but a British constitutional echo. British constitutional language to the west was not appreciably more extreme than British constitutional language to the east. In London, the mayor, aldermen, and livery condemned the Dockyards Act, saying that it converted a person accused of crime into "a victim to Ministerial vengeance," and charging that by the Massachusetts Administration of Justice Act "Soldiers and others, in *America*, have been instigated to shed the blood of the people, by establishing a mode of trial which holds out impunity for such murder." Edmund Burke, in one of the most celebrated political publications of the revolutionary controversy, his letter to the Bristol sheriffs, asserted that if the statute of Henry VIII were applied as Parliament interpreted it, "almost all that is substantial and beneficial in a trial by jury is taken away from the subject in the colonies." He meant that to have a criminal trial shifted from an American venue to an English county was, for a colonist, substantially the same as being deprived of the right to trial by jury itself. "A person is brought hither in the dungeon of a ship's hold: thence he is vomited into a dungeon on land; loaded with irons, unfurnished with money, unsupported by friends, three thousand miles from all means of calling upon, or confronting evidence, where no one local circumstance that tends to detect perjury, can possibly be judged of; — such a person may be executed according to form, but he can never be tried according to justice." Burke wrote these words in 1777, two years after the fighting had begun.[29]

The salient feature of Burke's letter is not that he said rebels had a right to juries, but that he made the point with arguments American whigs also used. This fact deserves attention if we are to understand the constitutional aspects of the American Revolution. The American echo of British constitutional slogans does not prove the colonists constitutional mimics. It demonstrates the extent to which the colonial whig legal case was a product of the accepted, established, taught tradition of English and British constitutionalism. The polemics were the same because the constitution was the same. London's *Public Ledger* condemned the rise of prerogative courts in the seventeenth century and Henry VII's creation of Star Chamber in 1487 for the same reasons colonial whigs warned Americans about seventeenth-century prerogative courts and quoted the words of Lord Coke: to defend with a constitutional argument the right to trial by jury.

When British whigs encountered a statute depriving them of trial by jury in exactly the same manner that the Stamp Act had attempted to deprive Americans of trial by jury, their protests were worded precisely as were American protests. One British statute, the cider excise, provided for prosecutions before a judge sitting without a jury, a departure from constitutional practice, the *North Briton* charged, repealing "the most favourite law of our constitution, which has ever been considered as the birth-right of an *Englishman,* and the sacred *palladium* of liberty; I mean the trial by JURY." Addressing their representatives in the Commons, people of Devon, speaking much like Massachusetts voters and Virginia burgesses, wanted the excise repealed for "precluding the right of trial by Juries, that pledge of Liberty, that inestimable inheritance, that free-born privilege of *Englishmen.*"[30]

The jury issue was similar to just about every other constitutional issue during the age of the American Revolution. When alarmed by matters also alarming to Americans, British whigs made the same arguments as colonial whigs. An example is the Quebec bill. There were writers in the mother country who condemned Parliament's refusal to grant jury trial to Canadians just as vehemently as did Americans and on the same constitutional grounds. Sign the bill into law, the Corporation of London warned the king, and "both the persons and properties of very many of your Majesty's subjects are rendered insecure and precarious."[31]

Even where the jury issue in the mother country differed from the jury issue in the colonies there were similarities. Several controversies surrounding trial by jury in England did not exist in the colonies. They bear mentioning, however, for they were extensively debated and discussed in British pamphlets and newspapers, contributing in some degree to colonial consciousness of the threat to jury trials existing under current standards of British constitutionalism.

During the age of the American Revolution, British subjects living in England and Wales were concerned with three threats to their right of trial by jury that were not the concern of British subjects in North America: (1) trial by information and attachment; (2) trial by the House of Commons; and (3) trial at common law with jurors restricted to questions of fact — that is, judges narrowly defining the jury's area of competency.

The first, trial by information and by attachment, is the least important as it received little publicity in the colonies and was primarily an attack on the grand rather than the traverse jury. Critics of these innovations, which attempted to streamline the judicial process by bypassing juries, were often legal theorists who thought and argued much like American whigs. Interpreting constitutionalism as custom rather than command, they could not brook departures from the traditional safeguards of jury trial, especially departures mandated by parliamentary will rather than constitutional evolution.[32]

The second challenge to trial by jury in the mother country came from parliamentary privilege. The Commons, jealous of what it perceived as its rights and dignity, sometimes ordered people imprisoned for contempt without any trial except an appearance at the Bar of the House. In one instance the lord mayor and two aldermen of London arrested agents of the Commons sent to seize printers suspected of publishing parliamentary proceedings. Although in their defense, the three officials pleaded the ancient privileges of the City, they were ordered committed to the Tower of London without being able to present that defense to a jury.

In the 1760s and 1770s, the people in Britain most critical of commitment for contempt of Parliament were John Wilkes and his followers, a political movement closely watched and emotionally supported by American whigs. In a proceeding that was arbitrarily *sui generis* yet bore some resemblance to conviction by attainder, the Commons had barred Wilkes from taking his seat as a member despite his election by Middlesex County. It did so by summary vote without trial. His supporters among the Middlesex electors made a fetish of instructing their representatives "[t]o endeavour to continue to use, and to conform our old constitutional and only rightful trial — by jury." One of the reasons why the City of London knowingly accepted the risk of irritating George III by asking him to adjourn Parliament and call elections was preservation of jury trial. If only there was a new House of Commons freely elected, the king was told in 1770, it would surely "secure to us that sacred bulwark of English liberty, *the trial by jury*, against the dangerous designs of those who have dared openly to attempt to militate its powers, and destroy its efficacy."[33]

The third perceived threat to jury in the mother country came from common-law judges. It was an argument closely followed in the colonies, and one that would be repeated in America following independence when lawyers of the Jeffersonian persuasion, in the name of the people, sought to keep questions of law as well as fact within the purview of the jury, and lawyers of the Hamiltonian persuasion, believing that the rule of law required certainty and predictability, succeeded in separating questions of law from questions of fact, making law exclusively the business of the court and limiting jurors to decisions of fact. In Great Britain, or more properly, in England, during the two decades of the American Revolution, the issue was the more traditional one of authority, expressed by the judge, versus liberty through customary constitutional law, entrusted to the jury. "Britannicus," writing for the *Political Register*, summed up in popular terms the case for liberty.

> It has lately been by some confidently asserted, that juries are not judges of law, but of fact only: What can be more false? What more injurious to the subject? Or, what can tend more to overturn all our laws and liberties? For if this pernicious doctrine should be allowed, juries would be so far from being a security to the subject, that they would be then a snare; and that which our ancestors intended as a bulwark to defend our lives and properties, would become a strong engine to batter them down; because any person might then be prosecuted for the most innocent action; nay, indeed, for acting according to any law of the land, which arbitrary power did not like, and found guilty, and punished at the pleasure of the court; for they need only to charge such action in the information to be seditious, traitorous, &c. and then to prove the fact, and the jury must of course bring him in guilty, if they are not judges of law, but of fact only.[34]

The ideal norm, expressed in a 1766 pamphlet entitled *British Liberties*, was that "judges are no more than the mouth tha[t] pronounces the words of the law, mere *passive* beings, incapable of moderating either its force or rigour." Or, as stated several times in a slogan drawn from the old constitution of restraint on government rather than the new constitution of sovereignty, "In England the judge checks the jury, the jury controuls the judge, and the law rules both."[35]

The idea behind that slogan was not quite the nonsense it may seem today, but it was based on a decaying constitutionalism that was being undermined by the resurgent toryism of common-law judges. Lord Mansfield, chief justice of King's Bench, led the assault, ruling in the trial of Henry Sampson Woodfall, the publisher of *Junius*'s letters, that in prosecutions for seditious libel the jury was to determine only if the defendant had printed and sold the objectionable literature; whether the words were libelous was a question of law for the court. For the next few years, the half decade before the Declaration of Independence, the British press was filled with polemics attacking Mansfield and what were perceived as new definitions of law, government power, and personal security. "It must be granted," a pro-American, antiadministration pamphleteer wrote, summing up a popular argument, "that the two great supporting pillars of the constitution — are — our trials by *Jury* — and the liberty of the press. By rendering Juries, Cyphers — both these pillars would be blown up *at one blast*."[36]

CHAPTER SEVEN

EQUALITY OF RIGHTS

"The excise has been lately extended in this country," Richard Hussey, barrister and bencher of the Middle Temple, was quoted as telling his colleagues in the House of Commons, but he believed "no Minister would dare to propose to take away the trial by jury in all cases relating to the revenue. We should be shocked at this proposal here; why should the honest Americans be more submissive?" For us today Hussey seems to be talking politics, but American colonists listening to his speech would have thought he was talking constitutional law. He stated a constitutional right, the right to equality, a right of special interest as it is only the second so far encountered in which colonial constitutional theory diverged from that of the mother country. The divergence was not in definition, but in emphasis. The concept of equality was expanding in American jurisprudence, largely in reaction to the imperial relationship, and was emerging as a right utilized to protect other rights. Consider, for example, its use by "about 1200 Freemen and Freeholders of New York City" who argued that to be deprived of trial by jury meant that they were not treated equally with other British citizens. "Without these Bulwarks our Fellow Subjects in England would not think themselves either safe or free; nor can we see any Reason why American Subjects should not set an equal Value upon these Privileges, which are equally essential to both."[1]

The same complaint was directed against the vice-admiralty jurisdiction. Voters of Boston were disturbed to find in the same statute reforming vice admiralty in the colonies — indeed, on the "same Page"—

> "that all Penalties and Forfeitures which shall be incurred in Great Britain, shall be prosecuted Sued for and recovered, in any of his Majestys Courts of Record in Westminster, or in the Court of Exchequer in Scotland respectively." Here is a Contrast that stares us in the Face! A partial distinction that is made between the Subjects in *Great Britain* and the Subjects in America! the Parliament in one Section guarding the People of the Realm and securing to them the benefit of a tryal by Jury and the Law of the Land, and by the next Session [*sic*] depriving Americans of those important Rights.[2]

The grievance was twofold: Americans were denied a British constitutional right and were not treated equally. "[W]e are unhappily distinguished from our fellow subjects in Britain," the government of Rhode Island complained.[3] "Why are not His Majesty's good Subjects of *Great Britain* thus treated?" the voters of Cambridge, Massachusetts, asked. "[W]hy must we in *America* . . . be thus discriminated?"[4]

Inequality was a matter proven by facts and American apprehensions of inequality were disputed on the facts. It was pointed out that in Great Britain stamp duties and most excises were recoverable without a jury, indeed that most revenue matters tried in the mother country were without juries.[5] Unlike so many other disputes of facts, such as the imperial contract, this contention of fact drew little argument from American whig writers. They thought it largely irrelevant. Both the right to jury trial and the right to equality were still violated. The right to trial by jury was not less a constitutional right because it was denied to someone else. And although in Great Britain the government prosecuted some tax questions without juries, generally they were tried before justices of the peace or other common-law judges by common-law procedures, and not in civil law. The denial of common law made Americans unequal with their fellow subjects and was *per se* a denial of their right to equality.

There were two ways that the concept of equality was stated during the eighteenth century. One was to speak of equality not as a constitutional right, but as a source of rights. Because all British people were equal they shared an equality in rights and the rights of one were the rights of all. If the English, Scots, or Irish claimed a particular privilege, the principle of equality gave an equal claim to Carolinians, New Yorkers, or Jamaicans. The other way of stating equality was as a constitutional right. Most often the right of equality was asserted to secure a right al-

ready possessed by the British on the grounds that Americans had a right
to equality, or, to state the principle most narrowly, a right to an equality
of rights. The first use of the equality concept will be discussed in chapter 10. The second is the subject of this chapter.

The Equality Dilemma

The right of equality was stated most frequently by American whigs
when denying Parliament's authority to tax them. The primary right asserted was the right to be taxed only by consent. A secondary right was
the right to equality: to be taxed as were the British living at home, or
Protestants in Ireland, by constitutional consent.[6]

Taxation, of course, is only one example. The claim to equality covered the entire range of American assertions to rights. After all, the colonists only had to show that a right they were claiming was a British right
and they could add the count of equality.[7] In fact, it is somewhat ironic
that the equality principle was so easily formulated during the revolutionary controversy, for it was not easily applied. For one thing, American whigs had to be careful how they argued it. An instance of a wrong
application was tucked away in the decade's most influential study of the
imperial constitution, Governor Thomas Pownall's book on colonial administration. Pownall granted that the colonists had an equal claim with
the British to British rights, but not on the American ground of constitutional equality. He put it instead on what whigs thought the worst of
all constitutional grounds, parliamentary supremacy.

> By the very act of extending the power of parliament over the Colo-
> nies, the rights and liberties of the realm must also be extended to
> them, for, from the nature of the British constitution, from the con-
> stitution of parliament itself, they, as parts, can be subject by no other
> mode, than by that in which parliament can exercise its sovereignty;
> for, the nature of the power, and the nature of the subjection must
> be reciprocal.

Pownall's constitutional theorem was more annoying than dangerous
for American whigs. As they denied his first premise — parliamentary
supremacy — they did not have to answer his conclusion that the right
to equality rested on the constitutional principle that parliamentary power
had to be applied equally. Far more troublesome was an argument for
parliamentary supremacy deduced from American whig demands for
equality with their fellow subjects in Great Britain. Equality of rights,

the colonists were told, implied equality of obligations, making Americans equally bound with the British to obey lawful enactments of Parliament. The controversy had begun with the very first American whig assertion to equality in rights, Virginia's Stamp Act resolutions. *"Resolved,"* the House of Burgesses had proclaimed, "That . . . the Colonists aforesaid are declared entitled to all Liberties, Privileges, and Immunities of Denizens and natural Subjects, to all Intents and Purposes, as if they had been abiding and born within the Realm of *England."* "Quere," William Knox asked, "[i]f they had been *abiding and born within the realm of England,* would they not have been bound by acts of parliament?"[8]

The fact is that American whigs had difficulty with the equality principle simply because its formulation was so easy. What was easy for them, after all, was equally easy for the other side. The imperialists also pleaded the equality principle, even using it to make the colonial claim to equality appear to be constitutionally contradictory. A striking example was the American whig assertion that the doctrine of equal rights gave the colonists the right to legislate for themselves on the same constitutional basis that Parliament legislated for the British. Imperialists countered that that argument led not to American equality but to British inequality. "I have the best authority for saying," Knox told the public in 1789, that George III "very early declared it to be his determination rather to cast off the revolted Colonies entirely, than consent to give up the authority of the Supreme Legislature over them; or allow them to possess superior advantages to those enjoyed by his European subjects." The American constitutional pretension — to be entitled to equal rights and yet be independent of Parliament — was said to be an "absurdity" and "ridiculous." "[I]t seems parliament has a right to *benefit* the colonies, but not to *bind* them," Knox wrote. "Its power over the colonies is somewhat like that allowed by the deists to the Almighty over his creatures, he may reward them with eternal happiness if he pleases; but he must not punish them on any account."[9] The rival perspectives, British imperial and American whig, were far apart. The British imperial perspective was described by a critic of John Dickinson: "The constitution does not mean to draw a line betwixt the rights of the subjects in Great Britain, and the rights of the colonists, THEREFORE the just conclusion is, *both have the same rights,* both are under the controul of parliament." The colonial whig perspective was best described by Dickinson's fellow Pennsylvanian, James Wilson: "Can the Americans, who are descended from British ancestors, and inherit all their rights, be blamed — can they be blamed *by their brethren in Britain* — for claiming still to enjoy those rights? But can they enjoy them, if they are bound by the acts of a British parliament?" These contrary perspectives created a constitutional dilemma leading to a constitutional dead end. "They insist upon a right to the privileges of British subjects," a writer for a London political journal said of the colonists, "and we insist upon their being subject to the British constitution. But how they can be subject to the British constitution without being entitled to the privileges of British subjects, will need some ingenuity to make out."[10]

CHAPTER EIGHT

AUTHORITY OF RIGHTS

In the preface to the Virginia edition of John Dickinson's *Farmer's Letters*, Richard Henry Lee praised Dickinson for "contending for our just and legal possession of property and freedom. A possession that has its foundation on the clearest principle of the law of nature, the most evident declarations of the *English* constitution, the plainest contract made between [the] Crown and our forefathers, and all these sealed and sanctified by the usage of near two hundred years." It would be well to pay close attention to what Lee wrote. He was not saying what some twentieth-century readers may think he said. He was not claiming rights. Rather, Lee was stating some of the authority for rights — that is, he was delineating part of the constitutional explanation why Americans said they had a right to rights. Most of what colonial whigs said about rights had to do with the basis for the authority for rights, rather than their definition. The rights were British rights and well known. Why Americans were entitled to them was more controversial and more complicated. Lee identified four sources — natural law, the British constitution, colonial charters, and immemorial custom — but whigs relied on many more authorities for their claim to rights than those four.[1]

When American whigs asserted rights, they did not do so to advance theoretical hypotheses, but to oppose British manifestations of authority.

Essentially, London had three legal justifications for its constitutional pretensions: (1) parliamentary authority to tax the colonies; (2) parliamentary authority to bind the colonies by legislation in all cases whatsoever; and, to a lesser degree, (3) ministerial authority to govern by executive instructions. Colonial whigs interposed the doctrine of rights in opposition to these powers. They claimed immunity from imperial taxation and the privilege of legislating for and governing themselves by virtue of constitutional rights derived from certain sources and supported by certain constitutional authorities: (1) their rights as Englishmen; (2) natural law; (3) the emigration contract; (4) the original contract; (5) the original American contract; (6) the emigration purchase; (7) colonial charters; (8) equality with other British subjects, especially with Protestants in Great Britain and Ireland; (9) principles of the British constitution; and (10) principles of the customary American constitution.

As with the rights themselves, the claim to constitutional authority for these rights was stated in the alternative. Some arguments were advanced to support specific contentions; others such as natural law could be asserted in almost every situation. It was a matter of rhetoric as well as legal theory. In a set of resolutions denigrating vice admiralty and the taking of property by parliamentary statutes to which Americans never consented, the House of Burgesses complained that Virginians were being deprived "of those great and fundamental Rights, which, until lately, they have constantly enjoyed, and which they and their Forefathers have ever claimed as their unalienable Rights as Men, their Constitutional Rights as Subjects of the British Empire, and their Right by Charters granted to the first Settlers of this Distant Country by his Majesty's Royal Ancestors, *Kings of England*." Six days later the burgesses petitioned George III "to secure to us the free and uninterrupted Enjoyment of all those Rights and Privileges, which from the Laws of Nature, of Community in general, and in a most especial Manner, from the Principles of the *British* Constitution, particularly recognized and confirm'd to this Colony by repeated and express Stipulations, we presume not to claim, but in common with all the rest of your Majesty's Subjects, under the same or like Circumstances." In the first, the resolution, the burgesses claimed rights on the authority of fundamental law, custom, inheritance, natural law, constitutional law, charter, and contract. In the petition to the king, the authorities named were natural law, the British constitution, contract, and equality with other British subjects.[2]

Another preliminary point deserving mention is that American whigs employed rather peculiar expressions when identifying the authority for rights claimed. They spoke, for example, of privileges that were "the Purchase of the People" obtained with "valuable Considerations," "the Purchase of their Ancestors, as a gracious and royal Reward of the Merit and Services of their Forefathers, and as one of the best Inheritances they left to their Children," and of "those rights and immunities which were purchased for us, by the lives and blood of our worthy ancestors, and secured to us by solemn stipulation (or contract) with our late majesties King William and Queen Mary." Such expressions may strike the uninformed reader as American bombast, the language of politics rather than of law, used to claim bogus rights for which there was no constitutional authority, and which could be supported at best by passionate pleas. The language, however, was the same vocabulary Britons used to delineate legal rights and to explain the constitutional authority for rights. A favorite word on both sides of the Atlantic was "blood." An authority for rights was that "our ancestors redeemed" those rights "with their blood," "sealed with their blood," "purchased for us with their blood," or "purchased with seas of blood, to entail upon their posterity."[3]

This sort of language was not confined to British political pamphlets. It was familiar fare in official resolutions and in petitions to Parliament. London's Common Council, for example, warned the king of "the desperate Attempts which have been, and are too successfully made . . . to subvert those sacred Laws which our Ancestors have sealed with their Blood." And in words reminiscent of many American petitions, the East India Company protested that legislation intruding upon corporate management was "subversive of those rights which they held under their charter; the original privileges of which, and the continuation thereof, have been purchased by their predecessors from the public for a valuable consideration, and repeatedly confirmed by several acts of parliament." The legal principle was that rights had been acquired by "purchase," and rested on the authority of implied contract and prescriptive custom. That was the meaning the earl of Chatham intended to convey to the House of Lords when he spoke of America's "dear-bought privileges," and what London's Council was thinking of when it told the Commons that the East India Bill would, if enacted, destroy "the most sacred rights of the subject, purchased for a valuable consideration, and sanctified by the most *solemn charters* and *acts of parliament*."[4]

THE IMMEMORIALITY OF RIGHTS

"[T]he British subjects in America have equal rights with those in Britain," Rhode Island's governor, Stephen Hopkins, wrote when claiming that an American right was the right to British rights. "[T]hey do not hold those rights as a privilege granted them, nor enjoy them as a grace and favor bestowed, but possess them as an inherent, indefeasible right, as they and their ancestors were freeborn subjects, justly and naturally entitled to all the rights and advantages of the British constitution." Hopkins postulated a constitutional theory with which all whigs agreed. It is also possible that most tories or conservatives agreed, perhaps even most lawyers including William Blackstone. Writing about the American controversy, John Erskine, the Scottish theologian, defined the concept of a civil right entirely in terms of the theory Hopkins stated. "[A] civil right," Erskine explained, "is that which law and constitution confer, not that which may be derived from the arbitrary bounty of those in authority." The proposition was stated just as frequently by contemporary students of British politics who had no interest in the revolutionary controversy. "The privileges of Englishmen are not a matter of grace and favour, but of right," Joseph Towers argued when commenting on the expulsion of John Wilkes from the House of Commons. Urging his countrymen to take advantage of the Volunteer movement, and restore the "original" constitution, an Irishman endorsed the same doctrine. "[T]he *privileges* we claim are not the *grants* of *Princes*, they are ORIGINAL rights, conditions of the original CONTRACTS, co-equal with *prerogative*, and coeval with our *government*."[5]

Although the doctrine was substantially the same on both sides of the Atlantic — that rights were independent of government and not concessions granted by rulers to the ruled — it is possible that colonial thought was already moving apart from British theory and anticipating the future American constitutional concept that rights were powers not delegated to government but reserved to the people. Such language can be found among nonlawyers as, for example, two preachers of the annual Massachusetts election sermon. "In all governments there is a reserve of certain rights in favour of the people," Charles Chauncy told the legislators in 1747. Rights and privileges "are retained by the people," Charles Turner repeated to the same audience in 1773.[6]

Although language can be found from the eighteenth century saying that rights were grants from the sovereign,[7] we have no way of knowing whether these statements represented serious constitutional theory or were spoken without thinking through their implications. Even if serious, they were the minority view. The dominant, taught legal doctrine went back at least to Sir Edward Coke and the early Stuarts. James I tried to establish the contrary principle when he told the Commons that its rights "grow from precedents which shews rather a toleration than inheritance." His son, Charles I, had to retreat, however, acknowledging that Parliament's liberties "are not of grace, but of right."[8] The repetition over the decades of that theme shaped what would evolve as whig constitutional theory,[9] a theory summed up by the perception from which Magna Carta was universally viewed. Every authority denied that Magna Carta had been a grant of newly recognized rights. Rather, it had been a statement of ancient common-law privileges, "recognitions," as Lord Chancellor Somers explained, "of what we have reserved unto ourselves in the original institution of our government, and of what had always appertained unto us by common law and immemorial customs."[10]

It has occasionally been suggested that these theories of the origin of civil rights had something to do with history, that they were based on historical fact. Dr. Robert Brady in the 1680s invested much historical scholarship to proving "[t]hat all the *Liberties and Priviledges* the People can pretend to, were Derived from the Crown." His research was unquestionably correct as history but irrelevant as law. When the earl of Chatham, defending the right of Middlesex to elect John Wilkes to the Commons, told the House of Lords that rights were "as old as the constitution itself; the liberties of the people in the original distribution of government, being the first provided for," he was stating a theory of constitutional law, not a lesson from history. It was law based not on the proven facts of historical scholarship, but on speculation from an assumed past. It might be more descriptive, although not quite accurate, to say that we are talking about a legal fiction. Rights were immemorial, those that exist today have existed from a time before there were kings to grant them, and the only evidence necessary to prove immemoriality was that they exist today. Yet immemoriality was not an insignificant allegation: it was the best, the strongest, proof of constitutionality. "Whatever are the Rights of Men *in this Age*, were their Rights *in every Age*; for, Rights are independent of *Power*," one of Robert Walpole's newspapers had explained on behalf of an administration that is often said to have traced the authority for rights only as far back as the Glorious Revolution. "The People have *originally all Right in themselves*: They *receive* none from *Governors*; but Governors *receive* all from them." It did not matter that the thesis could not be proven historically. What counted was that it be legally controlling. Ironically, the very act by kings in seeming to grant rights, as in Magna Carta, the Petition of Right, and the Bill of Rights, strengthened the theory, for in law, when a right that previously existed in less definite precision is defined, it is added to, and one thing added in theory was a reinforced presumption of immemoriality. "[T]he object of the Bill of Rights was to reassert those parts of the Laws and Constitution which had been violated in act, or of which doubts were entertained," John Brand wrote at the relatively late date of 1796. "Those liberties, when they were fully and completely regained, were then as securely ours as law, in the turbulent state of society which then obtained, could render them; and the explicit acknowledgement of some pre-existing laws and their principles cannot be considered as even a change of them; it cannot amount to new-modelling a Constitution." This theory of law was law and not history; it was as easily supported by historical hypothesis as by pseudohistory. "Had King WILLIAM," Richard Price conjectured about the prince of Orange, "instead of coming over by invitation to deliver us, invaded us; and, at the head of an army, offered us the BILL OF RIGHTS; we should, perhaps, have spurned at it; and considered LIBERTY itself as no better than SLAVERY, when enjoyed as a boon from an insolent conqueror."[11]

The legal imperative of the theory lay in the reality that granted rights are precarious rights, for what is given can be revoked. It was a constitutional truism to which Americans paid close heed. Throughout their history Americans had fought attempts to leave them dependent on rights conferred rather than inherited. That was why they cited their charters as evidence of rights enjoyed or of the emigration contract, but not as the origin or authority for rights.[12]

There was a second imperative, one that by 1765 only a minority of legal theorists in Great Britain shared, but that still dominated constitutional thought in the colonies. It was the supposition that people created their rulers, that as kings governed by authority of law, the law preceded kings. Law and power were all one, not because law was the command of power, but because power was legitimized by law. Quoting John Selden—"My penny is as much my own as the King's ten pence is his: if the King may defend his ten pence, why not Selden his penny?" —Samuel Johnson, the English clergyman and constitutional theorist, asked, "What signifies the King's having more Rights than I, if they be all upon the same Bottom? for if he Invades my Two-pence, at the same time he destroys his own Ten-pence, because he breaks down that Hedge of the Law which secures all Mens Rights."

Another source of authority for civil rights, much less often mentioned in Great Britain than in the colonies, was the people—that is, neither the legislature nor the law was sovereign, but the people. "[A]bsolute Power is lodg'd" in the people, "and from whence all *delegated* Power flows," a Boston editor wrote in 1756, protesting his arrest by the Massachusetts House of Representatives.[13]

One doctrinal derivative of this way of thinking, especially pertinent to the revolutionary debates, was the concept of inalienable rights. The inalienability of rights followed from the premise that they were inherent, not granted. Inalienable rights, in the words of Josiah Tucker, are those rights that "cannot be delegated, or transferred, even with the Consent of the Parties, supposing it possible that such Consent could be obtained." There were various ways to think about the origin of such rights. One was the American way of thinking of them as reserved from government. Another was the British way, saying that they had never been granted by the Crown, that they existed independently of government. For the British that meant separating rights from any notion of royal creativity. For Americans, however, the originating institution against which they had to be on guard was not the Crown but the two Houses of Parliament. If whig theory could not abide even a hint that former kings granted the British their rights, surely any suggestion that Parliament granted American rights could not be tolerated. Remember, John Wesley, a foe of colonial rights, was told, British legislators "can have no right to *grant* privileges to a people, who *have* as much as themselves, an *inherent indefeasible* right to those privileges."[14]

STATUTORY RIGHTS

American whigs had to reject talk that parliamentary grants were authority for civil rights, but that did not mean they rejected parliamentary statutes as evidence of rights. The distinction was drawn by Massachusetts legislators when they resolved that the right of taxation by representation, "together with all other, essential Rights, Liberties, Privileges and Immunities of the People of *Great Britain*, have been fully confirmed to them by *Magna Charta*, and by former and later Acts of Parliament." The legal proposition was that parliamentary recognition reinforced proof of rights, not that rights came from parliamentary promulgation.[15]

There was grave constitutional risk to acknowledging any form of parliamentary power. If Americans claimed statutory rights they could be said to concede statutory authority. "[D]oes not our pleading British Acts of Parliament that were in force before the Colonies were settled, or have been made since," a Bostonian asked, "necessarily imply that our fathers, when they came into this land bro't with them the laws of the realm, and are still obligated to obey the supreme authority of the nation, the acts of which they plead for protection or other advantages?"[16] Despite the risk, there was one important parliamentary statute which the colonies — or at least two, South Carolina and Massachusetts — cited as a source of rights. It was the act of 13 George II that naturalized foreign-born Protestants domiciled seven years in the colonies, and provided that those naturalized "be deemed, adjudged, and taken to be His Majesty's natural-born subjects of the Kingdom of Great Britain to all intents, constructions, and purposes, as if they, and every one of them, had been or were born within the same." The assemblies of the two colonies said that the statute "confirmed" to all Americans the right to an equality in British rights. "No reasonable man," Governor Hopkins argued, "will here suppose the Parliament intended by these acts to put foreigners who had been in the colonies only seven years in a better condition than those who had been born in them or had removed from Britain thither, but only to put these foreigners on an equality with them; and to do this, they are obliged to give them all the rights of natural-born subjects of Great Britain."

The constitutional risk was demonstrated when the argument was turned around and applied against the colonial whigs. The statute was enforced in the colonies, William Knox pointed out, and its enforcement proved — or at least implied — parliamentary supremacy. Foreigners had not only been accepted as citizens, they had also been elected to public office. To say that the statute was also a source of colonial rights, he concluded, reinforced American acknowledgment of Parliament's authority to legislate internally for the colonies.[17]

Rights by Custom

American identification of the authority for their claim to rights was almost always stated in the alternative and the alternatives, like those mentioned in the Connecticut resolutions of June 1774, were all constitutional. The colonists, Connecticut's Assembly resolved, claimed "the rights, liberties and immunities of free-born Englishmen, to which they are justly intitled by the law of nature, by the royal grant and charter of his late Majesty King Charles the Second, and by long and uninterrupted possession." It is indicative of how our legal assumptions have changed since the eighteenth century that we would dismiss the last-mentioned source of rights as the least important. Yet of those cited — natural law, royal grant, charter, and possession — the last was the strongest claim in the eighteenth century, at least if "uninterrupted possession" meant not just prescription but also ownership and even custom. Certainly, in the eighteenth century, as Arthur Lee demonstrated, possession was stronger than charter.[18]

The legal fact could be stated in various ways: "uninterrupted possession," "uninterrupted Practice and Usage," "venerable by long Usage," "constant usage."[19] Both the evidence of proving the right and the authority for the right were found in usage and custom. It was not a political boast but a statement of constitutional law to say that rights had been "sanctified by long usage, a uniformity of principle and practice for ages past." The theory was not only that *"long Possession gives a Title in Law,* or at least enforces it . . . so the *publick Rights of Mankind* acquire Strength by *long Prescription*," but also, as was explained by the barrister who in 1777 was appointed Oxford's Vinerian Professor of Law, immemorial usage was "evidence of common acquiescence and consent."[20]

To say that rights were known by usage was to say they were established by the conventions of civil society — conventions comprising both the practice of the rulers and the understanding of the ruled. For Americans, these conventions were proven by evidence from the English, British, and colonial constitutional past. To learn both the law ways of the rulers and the expectations of the ruled, one had only to appreciate the century and a half of colonial home rule. The appeal was to law — not history. Custom was changeless time, a view of the past in which the civil rights of the present existed in a timeless infinity, a frozen history without origin, without transmission, and without change, an unmeasurable duration during which there were no manifestations of sovereign will except for the implied consent of habitual acquiescence.[21]

It was from custom — from receiving its authority from custom — that the eighteenth-century concept of civil rights obtained much of the theoretical base making it so different from today's idea of personal rights. The old, customary theory of rights was confining when compared to the theory that would emerge in both British and American constitutional law during the nineteenth century. Rights in the eighteenth century were thought of as restraining arbitrary government rather than as liberating the individual. The offspring of a static legality that encased government in a timeless, changeless constitution, the eighteenth-century concept of rights was torn between the ideal of freeing human subjectivity and the reality of confining human subjectivity within the mores of a customary society.

CHAPTER NINE

CONSTITUTIONAL
AUTHORITY

The customary, static constitution of eighteenth-century legal and political theory was on the mind of an anonymous London pamphleteer in 1774. He was searching for ways to resolve the imperial controversy that seemed headed toward civil war, and asked what "ground" held the "medium between the absolute obedience in the colonies to be taxed by parliament, and their total independence." He found the answer in constitutional rights. "This ground is the *English constitution*," he decided, "out of this did the colonies spring, and those that would wish to form a true judgment of the nature of their rights, will not be satisfied in a matter of so much importance, to take their leading principles upon trust and by hearsay, but will for themselves examine the evidence on which they depend."[1]

The theory, that the constitution was a source of rights, not merely an apparatus for protecting rights, was a familiar eighteenth-century truism. It was a concept that would not survive the early nineteenth century when parliamentary supremacy came to be equated with sovereignty over law. Then it would be understood, as A. V. Dicey explained, that "the right to individual liberty is part of the constitution, because it is secured by the decisions of the Courts." That is, he went on, "with us the law of the constitution . . . [is] not the source but the consequence of the rights of individuals, as defined and enforced by the Courts." During the era of the American Revolution perceptions were somewhat different. Rights were not seen so much as deriving from the Constitution as being, as Arthur Lee put it, "coequal with the Constitution." Governor Thomas Pownall thought that "the liberty of the subject" meant the same as "the liberty of the constitution," and Jonathan Mayhew said that "constitutional principles . . . are those of liberty." Quite frequently, rights were said to possess an independent existence, a condition implied by John Reeves when he argued that "nothing is intitled to be called a Constitution, but a system springing out of an act declaratory of abstract principles, as of the Rights of Man."[2]

RIGHTS AT LAW

When claiming the constitution as a source for rights, American assemblies were apt to express the concept in terms of privileges guaranteed by Magna Carta, the Petition of Right, and other great landmarks of English constitutional history.[3] That was not the general eighteenth-century practice, however. Political commentators then were so accustomed to thinking of rights as immemorial, encased in timeless custom existing independently of any creative agency, that they usually did not refer to documents for their authority, and quite often did not even mention the constitution. Rather, they referred to law in general, or the "law of the land." When, for example, the Pennsylvania legislature asserted that the colonists were entitled to "the *noble principles* of English liberty," William Knox ridiculed so lofty a source. "[W]here to find these *noble principles* of English liberty, except it be in the laws of the land, I confess I am ignorant."[4]

Knox thought he was attacking a nonsensical appeal to natural law, and expected his readers to know what he meant by "laws of the land." Perhaps they did, but we must not assume that we do. English-speaking people in the eighteenth century had an intuition for legalism we no longer share. When they said a right was vested by law they might mean a mutable right such as a freeholder's right to vote, conferred by custom, not statute, yet subject to legislative alteration. Usually, however, they meant a higher source, either common law when that concept was equated with constitutional law, constitutional law which the sovereign should not but legally could change, or fundamental law beyond the reach of legislative will.[5]

It is important to keep distinct concepts separate. During the eighteenth century when British lawyers and American whigs used the term "constitutional law" they had in mind a definition similar to that in Canada during the twentieth century. To say that a statute or a governmental action was unconstitutional was to say that it was contrary to the constitution; it was not to say that it was illegal. When eighteenth-century people wished to describe an immutable constitutional law, as the term is now understood in the United States, they did not speak of constitutional law, but of fundamental law. The term "fundamental law" had several usages two centuries ago. One made it synonymous with "constitution." Another had it protective of old and valued customs but not capable of controlling the sovereign. A third limited it to rules governing the functions of the legislative sovereign, such as the requirement that all three branches — king, Lords, and Commons — consent for a bill to become law. In that last sense fundamental law was alterable, although not by the legislature.[6] Yet the most significant use for us, because it was the meaning accepted and acted on by American whigs, was that fundamental law was immutable law beyond the reach of any institution of government. Fundamental law was "unalienable" law and fundamental rights were "unalienable" rights "which mark out and fix the chief lines and boundaries between the authority of rulers, and the liberties and privileges of the people."[7]

Looking back today we have the certitude of knowing that fundamental law, in the sense of unalterable, immutable doctrine, did not exist in Great Britain during the second half of the eighteenth century. If it had ever been part of English jurisprudence, it had been diluted by the Glorious Revolution and destroyed as a viable concept by the Septennial Act of 1716. With that statute, Parliament repealed the Triennial Act, one of the most fundamental parts of the constitutionally sacred revolutionary settlement, and prolonged its own existence from three to seven years. The British legislature, as *Junius* observed, "did what, apparently and palpably, they had no power to do." Allan Ramsay, writing in 1771, thought that the most fundamental of fundamentals had been arbitrarily quashed. "Thus the primary law of our constitution," he bemoaned, "the first principle upon which it was founded, which had stood the test of twelve-hundred years, and been the admiration of many ages, was now reduced to the common level of a nuisance, to be corrected by acts of parliament." The meaning of constitutionality was drastically transformed. Parliament, John Gray pointed out, had "no right to alter fundamental laws without the acquiescence of the people," but the very fact the House of Commons votes a law "supposes the acquiescence of the majority of the people." One consequence we can recognize in twentieth-century America is that there were no longer immutable rights in British constitutional theory. Civil rights existed at the pleasure and caprice of the legislature.[8]

What is obvious to us was not obvious in the eighteenth century. Most students of the constitution refused to admit that Parliament had become omnipotent. No study has been made of what percentage of the population continued to cling to the notion of fundamental law beyond the competence of legislative change, but it was substantial, articulate, and included many men trained in the Inns of Court. Consider that in 1771 *Junius* was writing for a British audience and was supposedly expounding British constitutional theory when he protested a proposed reform of juries. "I would have their right, to return a general verdict in all cases whatsoever, considered as part of the constitution, fundamental, sacred, and no more questionable by the legislature, than whether the government of the country shall be by King, Lords, and Commons. Upon this point, an enacting bill would be pernicious; a declaratory bill, to say the best of it, useless."[9]

Junius's words were neither extreme nor unusual. The only reason they are important to us is that they expressed legal theory commonplace in London at that time. What that fact means is that American whigs should be viewed as less constitutionally eccentric than they otherwise might be. When colonial whigs claimed some rights were immutable, they were expounding valid though anachronistic English constitutional theory.[10]

Perhaps the British realized more clearly than they admitted that they had lost their once-cherished freedom from arbitrary government. It may be they were not unaware, only reluctant to face reality. It was an ambiguity affecting the revolutionary debate, and persuading some members of Parliament to give greater credit to American whig constitutional arguments than have many twentieth-century scholars of the Revolution. George Johnstone, for example, was just one of many members of Parliament with a foot in two constitutional worlds. "Some men who are for simplifying Government," he told the Commons during the debate over the Boston Port Act, "will not allow they conceive that the supreme legislative authority shall not be paramount in all things, and taxation being fully comprehended in legislation, they argue, that the power of the one must necessarily follow that of the other; and yet we find mankind possessed of privileges which are not to be violated in the most arbitrary countries." By 1911, perhaps even by 1850, a House of Commons would not have understood the enigma Johnstone raised. A different constitutional environment existed in the 1770s, and those who listened to Johnstone knew what he meant for they still thought of rights as privileges shielded from the whim of arbitrary power. They also appreciated how the constitutional absolute applied to the American controversy. "We have certain constitutional *Magna Charta* privileges so inviolable and sacred, that every endeavour of the sovereign to diminish them would be void and null," a pamphlet explained in 1766. "Britons are taught to believe so on this side the Atlantic; they would be miserable if this truth should be called in question. Why should *British Americans* have different sensations and judgement?"[11]

The End of Government

"Those laws which prescribe the rights of prerogative, and the rights of the people," the pastor of the Third Church of Hingham noted in the 1768 Massachusetts election sermon, "should be founded on such principles as tend to promote the great end of civil institutions." Some students of the American Revolution have misrepresented statements such as this one, saying that appeals making "the good of society . . . the end of civil government" are evidence that among colonial whigs "[p]opular writers came to scorn appeals to the English constitution, charters, acts of Parliament and the like as the foundation of American rights." Nothing could be further from the truth. "What is the end of government?" was the question most frequently posed by eighteenth-century constitutional theorists. They asked it seeking answers to the nature of government and the meaning of constitutionalism. Another New England clergyman, writing in 1744, explained why. "[T]he Way to know what Branches of natural Liberty are *given up*, and what *remain* to us after our Admission into civil Society," Elisha Williams, who was also a superior-court judge and a member of the Connecticut Assembly, wrote, "is to consider *the Ends* for which Men enter into a State of Government.— For so much Liberty and no more is departed from, as is necessary to secure those Ends; the rest is certainly our own still."[12]

So much was asked during the eighteenth century about the "end of government" that a separate volume could be written on the topic. The best that can be done here is to outline the answers as they relate to the authority for civil rights. What should be kept in mind is that questions about the end of government represent a manner of constitutional reasoning about the nature and limits of state power. When political theorists sought the end of government they sometimes were inquiring about the purpose, policy, and future programs of a government, but much more frequently—in fact, almost invariably during the American Revolution —they were probing the constitutional restraints placed on governors and, therefore, by implication if not explicitly, the rights of the people against their governors. "There is a general rule which includes all the duties of a sovereign, and by which he may easily judge how to proceed under every circumstance," the Swiss Jean Jacques Burlamaqui contended in his 1751 classic, reprinted in London the next year. "*Let the safety of the people be the supreme law*. This maxim ought to be the principle and end of all his actions."[13] It also should set limits to those actions and define the rights of those acted upon.

Almost every conceivable social good was said by some eighteenth-century writer to be the end of government. The rule was to identify just one or two, sometimes three ends, usually broad generalities such as "Peace and Order." It was unusual to list a string of positive or negative ends as a 1710 writer did when claiming that "[t]he very end of Government is to prevent Disorder, Confusion, Injustice, Violence, and perpetual Rapine and Bloodshed."[14] The concept of civil rights was seldom mentioned as an end. The security and preservation of rights were understood to be implied ends, but not the creation of rights. In fact, they were not often referred to as an entity.[15] Even colonial whigs seldom specified rights as ends. One of the few exceptions came from the Massachusetts House of Representatives telling Governor Thomas Hutchinson that "the Rights and Liberties of the People . . . are the great Ends of Government."[16]

Turning from civil goals not considered ends of government to goals that were, four ends of government were frequently mentioned during the eighteenth century. The first was liberty. Liberty was the "direct End" of the British constitution and government existed "for the preservation of civil liberty" or "the enjoyment of liberty."[17] The second was security, not just what we might expect, "the preservation of property," or the security of "rights, liberties and privileges," but, in the words of the Massachusetts Provincial Congress, "the Protection and Security of the People."[18] The third end of government was "good," stated many different ways as "the good of the community,"[19] "the good of society,"[20] "the good of the whole Body,"[21] "the good of the *subject*," "the good of the people," "the Good and *Welfare*" of the people, and "the common good and safety of society."[22] Some dissentient Irish lords employed the most common way of expressing the thought when they said the "only constitutional End" of governmental power was "the Publick Good."[23] The fourth, perhaps referred to more than all the others combined, was some sort of collective or individual "happiness"—"the happiness of the people,"[24] "the Happiness of the Subject,"[25] "the happiness of society,"[26] as well as "Human happiness"[27] and "Public Happiness."[28] Sometimes the end was stated as just plain "happiness," not this kind or that kind,[29] and at other times it was joined with an additional end, such as "the Security and Happiness of Society,"[30] the "Good and Happiness,"[31] and "the liberty and happiness of mankind."[32]

The people of the eighteenth century are entitled to their own institutions, methods of argumentation, and ways of arriving at constitutional conclusions. We may today scoff at talk of "good" and "happiness" and say that here is proof that colonial whigs, knowing they had lost the constitutional case, gave up their claim to positive rights and turned to natural law. But that conclusion just cannot be sustained once the historical record is researched. To ask what was the end of government was a familiar, taught way of arguing constitutional law in the seventeenth and eighteenth centuries. More particularly, it provided a standard by which the constitutionality of governmental actions could be tested, a standard used by lawyers as well as laymen. One of England's greatest judges, Lord Chancellor John Somers, stated what he understood to be the "principal ends of all civil government" in 1681 and then went on to make those ends the measure of constitutionality. Thomas Rutherforth, delivering lectures on the jurisprudence of Grotius at Cambridge in the 1740s, drew from "the end of civil society," which he thought was "the common benefit of the whole," a specific right of the people — the right "in the collective body" to rebel when their governors "make their continuance in power planely and notoriously inconsistent with such common benefit."[33]

American whigs were not departing from British constitutional tradition when they sought the authority for rights in the ends and purpose of government. The Continental Congress was speaking English common law when it declared that "Government was instituted to promote the Welfare of Mankind, and ought to be administered for the Attainment of that End." It was an inexact, polemical, yet quite practical test of the constitutionality of imperial actions. "The primary end of government seems to be, the security of life and property," Richard Henry Lee observed when arguing against London's power to deprive Americans of the right to trial in the venue, "but this ministerial law, would, if acquiesced in, totally defeat every idea of social security and happiness." The same constitutional criterion could be applied to most of the other statutes in controversy, the Massachusetts Government Act, for example, which the king was told was subversive "of the two grand objects of civil society, and constitutional protection, to wit, *Liberties* and *Life*."[34]

There is no need to quote many instances of the technique. One written by John Dickinson should serve as a final illustration for Dickinson would have made the "end of government" the measure for assaying the constitutional controversy between Great Britain and the American colonies. "The happiness of the people is the end . . . of the Constitution," Dickinson noted in Pennsylvania's official instructions to its representatives in the Continental Congress.

> If, therefore, the Constitution "declares by evident consequence;" that a tendency to diminish the happiness of the people, is a proof, that power exceeds a "boundary," beyond which it ought not to "go;" the

matter is brought to this single point, whether taking our money from us without our consent, depriving us of trial by jury, changing Constitutions of Government, and abolishing the privilege of the writ of *habeas corpus*, by seizing and carrying us to *England*, have not a greater tendency to diminish our happiness, than any enormities a King can commit under pretence of prerogative, can have to diminish the happiness of the subjects in *England*.

Or, there are the questions that Benjamin Trumbull asked the citizens of New Haven, Connecticut, in 1773, questions delineating the theme that in the ends for which government was created were to be found authority for the rights of the people. "Is it not," Trumbull asked, "[t]hat the original great design of civil Government is the good of the community? The maintaining and securing the rights, liberties, privileges and immunities of mankind? The impartial and faithful administration of justice? Must not whatsoever therefore, tendeth to deprive mankind of these important rights, and to prevent the impartial administration of justice, be contrary to the great design of government, and subversive of it's noble institution?"[35]

CHAPTER TEN

THE RIGHT
TO ISONOMY

John Dickinson was consistent throughout the revolutionary controversy. The concept of "happiness" that he employed when instructing
Pennsylvania's delegates to the Continental Congress, he had also used
nine years earlier in his *Address on the Stamp Act*. "If," he then wrote,
"the Colonies are equally intitled to Happiness with the Inhabitants of
Great-Britain, and Freedom is essential to Happiness, they are equally
intitled to Freedom." It was a chief thesis of Dickinson's constitutional
jurisprudence that "the inhabitants of these colonies are entitled to the
same rights and liberties WITHIN these colonies, that the subjects born
in *England* are entitled to WITHIN that realm."[1]

We must dwell on these two statements by Dickinson. In them he men-
tioned two different aspects of the equality principle. In the second quotation he said Americans were entitled to the same rights as the British.
That was the right to equality, the right discussed in chapter 7, the right
Lord Shelburne had in mind when saying that during his tenure as secretary of state in charge of colonial affairs, his practice toward the
Americans had been "to hold them as countrymen, fellow-subjects, and
Englishmen."[2] In the first statement Dickinson had also been concerned
with equality, but his emphasis had concentrated on another aspect. The
right he claimed was freedom — happiness through freedom — and equal-

ity was the source of that right. It was because the colonists were equal with fellow subjects that they could claim freedom. The distinction between the right to equality and equality as an authority for rights is blurry and was not made explicitly by American whigs, but it was made implicitly frequently enough to merit separate attention in a study on revolutionary civil rights.[3]

EQUALITY IN RIGHTS

The constitutional principle was repeated over and over during the decade and a half preceding the Battle of Lexington. The right to equality was more than a civil right, it was also a source of rights. Americans were equal to the British and therefore, the Pennsylvania Convention resolved, "are entitled to the same rights and liberties within these colonies that the subjects born in England are entitled to within that realm."[4] The constitutional justification was explained by the Massachusetts House of Representatives. "[A]ll the free subjects of any kingdom," the House told the earl of Shelburne, "are entitled equally to all the rights of the constitution; for it appears unnatural and unreasonable to affirm, that local, or other circumstances, can justly deprive any part of the subjects of the same prince, of the full enjoyment of the rights of that constitution, upon which the government itself is formed."[5]

The constitutional criterion for making equality an authority for rights was much the same as the criterion for the right to equality itself. "The benefits of the constitution, and of the laws," Samuel Cooke explained in 1770, "must extend to every branch, and each individual in society, of whatever degree; that every man may enjoy his property, and pursue his honest course of life with security." Cooke was a bit unusual to speak of individuals. Generally, the emphasis was not on persons but on imperial subdivisions. "Since the constitution of the State, as it ought to be, is fixed," the Massachusetts House told the colonial secretary, "it is humbly presumed that the subjects, in every part of the Empire, however remote, have an equitable claim to all the advantages of it." This argument deserves close attention for it holds the answer to what the eighteenth century meant by the concept of equality. We must be careful not to define the values of the American past by the American present, something easily done when we encounter the word "equality." We find colonial whigs using the word and it looks, sounds, and seems to be defined much like today's word "equality." But when eighteenth-century people spoke of equality, were they speaking of equality of individuals or equality of rights? Of course there were references to personal equality — not to social leveling or to property redistribution, but to people being legally equal. However, we must ask how they were equal, and when we examine the definitions behind the rhetoric one conclusion becomes inescapable. The eighteenth-century meaning of equality of individuals was isonomic. Persons were entitled, as Rhode Island's governor, Stephen Hopkins, said, to "the advantage of just and equal laws," or, as Edmund Burke phrased it, "to equal rights, but to equal rights to unequal things."[6]

It is best to approach equality as an authority for rights in the eighteenth century from the imperial perspective. That perspective may well hold the meaning of eighteenth-century constitutional equality, not so much equality of people as equality of peoples. As a collective people, a separate distinct division of the British Empire, colonial whigs insisted on equality with the peoples of Britain and, to some extent, the Protestants of Ireland. The town meeting of Providence stated the American conditions. "[W]e are willing, and even desirous, of a Continuance of Connexion between the Colonies and Britain, if it may be had upon Terms in any Measure equal."[7]

Colonial whigs seldom said that all individuals, as individuals, were equal. What they generally said was that the American people were equal to the British people. To make a claim to the right to representation on the grounds of equality, for example, the probative fact was that the British people enjoyed that right. It was immaterial that in some colonial assemblies certain people were not represented or that representation was unequal in others. This is an aspect of the whig constitutional argument that sometimes has been misunderstood. It was not a probative fact in the imperial controversy that there were groups within the colonies demanding equality as a *local American right* — the Baptists who wanted an equality of taxation with the Congregationalists and the Anglicans who pleaded their right to a North American bishopric on the grounds that the Moravians and the Catholics of Quebec had bishops. For the whigs to demand equality with the British yet ignore requests for equality in the colonies was not constitutional hypocrisy. The equality issue debated during the revolutionary controversy did not concern local American rights. It concerned American equality to rights that the British possessed as a people. "[T]he question," Governor Hopkins explained, "is not whether all colonies, as compared one with another, enjoy equal liberty, but whether all enjoy as much freedom as the inhabitants of the mother state." Although not indisputable, this meaning of equality lends support to the controversial supposition that the equality boast in the Declaration of Independence — "all men are created equal" — meant not that individuals were equal, but that the American people were entitled to an equality of rights with the British.[8]

David Griffith, the rector of Shelburne Parish, Virginia, came as close as anyone during the prerevolutionary debates to stating as a separate constitutional entity the right to equality between peoples in different parts of the Empire. He also had an explanation why separate peoples within the Empire were entitled to equality with one another: separate peoples were entitled to equality because their individual members were entitled to equality.

> The colonists . . . contend that their fellow subjects in Britain are but their equals: That the power ordained of God; that share of power which exists in the people, is, equally, the privilege of every individual subject: They insist that a Briton cannot boast a single blessing from the constitution, but what an American is, equally, entitled to: They say the claim of the commons of Britain is an innovation; that is unnatural, unjust and oppressive; and destructive of that equal justice and liberty which, by the constitution, was meant to be secured to all.

Americans, Griffith concluded, were "contending with their equals, only; [that is,] with those who are ordained to have no greater share of power than themselves."[9]

The Imperial Inequality

There were two chief arguments used by persons questioning whether the American people could be constitutionally and politically equal with the British people. One was distance and the other was the imperial relationship. Governor Thomas Hutchinson of Massachusetts made the first notorious when he raised it in a private letter obtained and printed by the whigs. "There must be an abridgment of what are called English liberties," he wrote. "I doubt whether it is possible to project a system of government in which a colony 3000 miles distant from the parent state shall enjoy all the liberty of the parent state. I am certain I have never seen the projection. I wish the good of the colony when I wish to see some further restraint of liberty rather than the connexion with the parent state should be broken." George III said much the same, and would have broken the colonial connection before tolerating the chaos of equality. "Distant possession standing upon an equality with the superior state is more ruinous than being deprived of such connexions."[10]

The constitutional potentials of the Hutchinson thesis threatened American rights less seriously than is sometimes thought. The governor had not been referring to what we call civil liberties. The colonists, especially

New Englanders, were the least governed, and most unregulated, people in the Empire. Hutchinson accepted that fact and knew better than any other imperial official that Parliament could do little to alter the realities of legal coercion. The rights he thought had to be abridged were those Americans were claiming in theory—the right of enjoying the same privileges as the British, the privileges they would have enjoyed had they remained at "home."[11]

The second consideration for denying colonial claims that the American people were constitutionally equal to the British people was the imperial relationship. "[C]an anything be more absurd than to draw comparisons between the rights and privileges of countries standing in such degrees to relationship to each other, as the mother-country and her colonies?" a London writer asked in 1766. "[T]he absolute impracticability of vesting the American assemblies with an authority, in all respects equal to that of the mother country, without actually dismembering the British empire must naturally occur to every one," a second London writer argued three years later.[12]

American whigs and their British supporters did not answer these arguments directly. The eighteenth-century principle of equality did not permit modification. Equality either existed whole or did not exist at all. That was why the colonists felt themselves never truer friends to British liberty than when claiming that British rights were theirs by equality. Losing British rights in the colonies, they said, would be a certain first step toward the British people losing British rights at home. Perhaps they were correct at least to the extent that we apply the eighteenth-century conception of rights as restraint on arbitrary government. For it was just after the age of the American Revolution that government in Great Britain finally was acknowledged to be arbitrary, and British rights were seen to exist at the pleasure of the two Houses of Parliament. There may, therefore, have been more merit than has generally been acknowledged to the constitutional theory of a New York pamphleteer who, during the Stamp Act crisis, contended that Americans had no choice but to stand rigidly uncompromising and "claim an *unalienable Right* to all the Privileges of Englishmen.—As Freemen, Subjects of the same Prince, They consider Themselves upon an *equal Footing* with the Freemen of Great-Britain. To suppose any Subordination would be destroying the very Spirit of the English Government."[13]

CHAPTER ELEVEN

THE AUTHORITY
OF NATURE

The search for authority does not stop with finding that equality was a source for rights. Beyond equality lay another source—nature. Just as the right to equality was the source of other rights, so nature was an authority for the right to equality.[1] In this chapter we are concerned with nature only as an authority for rights and although it would be impossible to conduct an accurate survey, it is no exaggeration to suggest that nature was one of the two or three most frequently cited sources during the American Revolution. If we look at the arguments of individual writers rather than official petitions and resolutions, natural law is the source most clearly identified as an authority. James Otis called it the "origin" and "author" of rights. James Wilson said that "God and nature had given" people rights, and John Dickinson thought that rights "are created in us by the decrees of Providence."

We must be careful not to make too much of our facts. To say that nature was one of the authorities cited for the validity of rights is quite different from saying that nature defined rights, determined which rights were enjoyed by British subjects, or provided for the enforcement of rights. The chief utility of nature as a source of rights was not to claim rights but to give them an authority independent of human creation. "Kings or parliaments could not *give* the *rights essential to happiness*,"

Dickinson explained. "We claim them from a higher source—from the King of kings, and Lord of all the earth. . . . They are born with us; exist with us; and cannot be taken from us by any human power, without taking our lives."[2]

Nature was also cited as the authority for particular rights such as the right to taxation by consent, and for all-embracing rights such as the right to "liberty." Even Alexander Hamilton, in an uncharacteristically extreme argument, succumbed to the ease of attributing liberty—and therefore, rights—to the authority of nature.[3] Another, less frequently utilized, aspect of natural-law authority for rights was that there was no higher authority. It was the highest source and created rights not only beyond the reach of positive law, but also rights against positive law. "Resolved," some North Carolina freeholders voted in 1774, "That those absolute rights we are entitled to as men, by the immutable Laws of Nature, are antecedent to all social and relative duties whatsoever." We may think the notion of such a right farfetched, but the notion was not unique in the eighteenth century. Even elected legislative bodies went off the constitutional deep end. "The natural Rights of the Colonists" were the same as those "of all Mankind," the Massachusetts House boasted three years before the revolutionary controversy began. "The principal of these Rights is to be 'free from any superior power on Earth, and not to be under the Will or Legislative Authority of Man, but to have only the Law of Nature for his Rule'." Although statements such as this have received much attention from constitutional historians, they were not common during the American Revolution. Their rhetoric was striking, but the constitutional principle was fantasized and void of any practical application.[4]

Natural Rights

There were several theories explaining why nature was a constitutional authority for rights. One was God—John Selden thought the law of nature "the law of God"—or "God and Nature," with or without revelation.[5] Another was the state of nature itself or the "*residuum* of natural liberty, which is not required by the laws of Society to be sacrificed to public convenience"—that is, the rights people had possessed when living in nature before governments were formed. Closely related to that concept was the theory that natural rights were those rights belonging to man as man, rights to which you were entitled from your God-given nature, and which could be deduced from the great plan of nature. A final definition was reason. Natural law was reasonable—remarkably, also a favorite description of lawyers for common law—it was law "founded in Natural Reason."[6] There were, in addition, three attributes often mentioned as part of natural law that were also associated with natural rights. They were that natural law and therefore natural rights were universal, immutable, and inalienable.[7]

A point deserving attention from students of the American Revolution is that few British civil rights came within any of these meanings. Certainly they were not universal. Few people in other countries enjoyed the right of representation, to taxation by consent, to jury trial, to judges at tenure of good behavior, and not everyone had the right to petition. The possession of property may have existed in the state of nature, but not the right to security in property. The fact is that few British civil rights fit any of the eighteenth-century definitions of natural law. It is possible there was only one right that everyone agreed was natural, the right to self defense.

Much was claimed for natural rights in the eighteenth century; they were boasted of and cherished. But if we read carefully what was said, those rights turn out to be broad generalities, with the exception of self-defense. Robert Hall may have been as specific as any eighteenth-century political theorist, yet he did not get much more concrete than asserting that the fact "can scarcely be doubted" that "there are *natural rights*."

> Every man must have a natural right to use his limbs in what manner he pleases, that is not injurious to another. In like manner he must have a right to worship God after the mode he thinks acceptable; or in other words, he ought not to be compelled to consult any thing but his own conscience. These are a specimen of those rights which may properly be termed *natural*.

Hall's "rights" were ideals, not actualities, the shared platitudes of mankind, not standards for controlling governmental conduct that can be translated into legal rights. Yet they are no less precise than what every other eighteenth-century exponent of natural rights came up with when providing working specifics. Even William Paley in his important treatise on moral and political philosophy was no more detailed. He knew what natural rights were —"Natural rights are such as belong to a man, although there subsisted in the world no civil government whatever"— but he defined none in a way that a lawyer could have enforced. "*Natural rights* are, a man's right to his life, limbs, and liberty; his right to the produce of his personal labour, to the use, in common with others, of air, light, water. If a thousand different persons, from a thousand different corners of the world, were cast together upon a desert island, they would from the first, be every one entitled to these rights." At least Paley, unlike Hall, did not mention the right to worship.[8]

There is a lesson in the fact that few imperialists disputed American whig claims to natural rights. But what lesson? It could be that the concept of natural rights had such a hold on eighteenth-century legal thought every one knew that they had validity and that the colonists possessed them. Or it could have been the opposite: everyone knew natural rights were so nebulous, why quarrel about them? There were, however, a small number of imperial officials and ministerial writers who questioned colonial whig citation of the authority of nature and natural rights. Their criticisms are worth considering as their constitutional arguments were based on legal principles that delineate the only viable authority for natural law. Anthony Bacon, a member of Parliament who had run a store in Maryland, was talking correct eighteenth-century constitutional law when he pointed out that natural rights "have no meaning: for men are born members of society, and consequently can have no rights, but such as are given by the laws of that society to which they belong. To suppose any thing else, is to suppose them out of society, in a state of nature." John Lind is also of interest as he was one of several ministerial pamphleteers who, in an apparent effort to weaken the appearance of the American whig constitutional argument, tried to make the British believe that American whigs claimed natural rights rather than constitutional rights. "The terms of *natural* and *inherent* rights . . . are to my understanding, perfectly unintelligible," Lind wrote. "The *Citizen* is to look for his *rights* in the laws of his country." Lind's legal principle explains why ministerial writers made such efforts to persuade people in the mother country that Americans based their claim to rights on nature, not on the constitution, custom, or positive law. There was little support among eighteenth-century legal theorists for the proposition that nature could be authority for converting natural rights into positive rights. It was for that reason the revolutionary controversy was concerned with positive constitutional rights, not abstract natural rights.[9]

THE IRRELEVANCY OF NATURAL RIGHTS

We are dealing in this chapter only with the authority for rights and with natural rights. As a result, the great bulk of the evidence and argumentation dealing with the irrelevancy of natural law to the pre-revolutionary controversy is not pertinent to this discussion. Here we are limited to evaluating the significance of natural rights to the American whig constitutional case. Only three points need be raised: (1) that nature (like natural law in the wider context) was almost always cited as alternative authority for rights; (2) that, in the context of rights, natural law was equated with British constitutional and positive law and with English common law; and (3) natural rights based on the authority of nature only, and not also said to be positive, were not a factor in the revolutionary debates.

It is possible to find in political pamphlets and anonymous newspaper articles claims made to rights on the authority of nature alone. They are not found in official colonial petitions, resolutions, or declarations. Rather, just as claims to natural law are stated in the alternative to claims to constitutional and charter law, so claims to natural rights stated alternative authority. An example that cites only one alternative was a resolve passed by the Lyme, Connecticut, town meeting in 1766, saying that the colonists possessed a natural right to rights, that is "an inviolable Right by the God of Nature, as well as by the English Constitution, (and is unalienable even by ourselves) to those Principles and Immunities which by the Execution of the Stamp Act we shall be forever stript and deprived." The authority for this right to rights is nature, true enough, but it is also the British constitution. The authority of nature, in other words, is an alternative authority, as it is in dozens of similar resolutions where natural law is cited as the authority for rights along with common law, prescription, grant, purchase, contract, or custom. Even in the Massachusetts resolves of 1765, containing what may be the strongest statement about natural law made by any colonial assembly, the claim is to constitutional rights with nature the authority for those rights.[10]

At every important occasion when the American whig leadership gathered to claim rights and state grievances, nature was rejected as the sole authority of rights. The only exceptions would be the Boston Declaration of 1772 and the preamble of the Declaration of Independence — just the preamble, the rhetorical flourish, and not the indictment or substantive part that contains neither natural law nor natural rights. An instance occurred in the committee for states rights, grievances, and means of redress of the first Continental Congress. The debate, which has been frequently printed and is well known, turned on two points, according to John Adams. The first point was, "Whether We should recur to the Law of Nature, as well as to the British Constitution and our American Charters and Grants. Mr. Galloway and Mr. Duane were for excluding the Law of Nature. I was very strenuous for retaining and insisting on it, as a Resource to which We might be driven, by Parliament much sooner than We were aware." The resolutions that resulted from this debate were the Declaration of Rights of the first Continental Congress. They have often been cited either as an instance of colonial whig reliance on natural rights or as a mixture of natural and other kinds of rights. In the Declaration's preamble, Congress claimed as the authority for the rights being declared, "the immutable laws of nature, the principles of the English constitution, and the several charters or compacts." But if the rights themselves are examined, not the preamble, it will be found that not one right is asserted that was not either a constitutional right or a right derived from the authority of custom, the original contract, the migration purchase, or the second original contract. The authority of nature was cited to reinforce the authority for positive or what can be called nonnatural rights. Such was the norm of colonial whig claim to rights. Nature was mentioned either as alternative authority or as rhetorical flourish. Natural law did not provide the rights themselves. We should not be surprised. Much as the English-speaking peoples of the eighteenth century were attuned to natural law, they knew there were practical limits preventing the ideal from becoming positive reality. "Liberty is the natural birthright of mankind," Arthur Young observed in 1772, "and yet to take a comprehensive view of the world, how few enjoy it!"[11]

The fact of the matter is that the American whigs did not in any official petition or resolution claim a natural right that was not already extant in British constitutional theory or English common law.[12] If we wish to see a natural right stated independently of positive authority it is necessary to look at proposals made by individuals to assemblies, conventions, or congresses, not to what those bodies adopted. William Henry Drayton, for example, urged the Continental Congress to claim on the authority of nature a natural right to the protection of certain constitutional or fundamental "claims, rights and liberties." "That the Americans, are of natural right entitled, to all and singular those inherent though latent powers of Society, necessary for the safety, preservation and defence of their just claims, rights and liberties herein specified; which no contract, no constitution, no time, *no climate* can destroy or diminish." The "claims, rights and liberties" mentioned by Drayton were all constitutional or fundamental law. It appears that he is saying that there was a natural right to the preservation of positive rights. It is probable that Drayton's right was never claimed by an official American representative body.[13]

THE MYTHOLOGY OF NATURAL RIGHTS

A question is posed by what has just been stated. If English and British constitutional law formulated the rights that American whigs claimed in the controversy with Great Britain, why does so much of the historical literature say that Americans were motivated by a natural-rights theory? Why is it sometimes said that colonial whigs abandoned their defense of the "rights of Englishmen" and, during the final stages of the quarrel, depended solely on natural rights?[14]

One explanation is carelessness. Some writers have assumed that every time the word "natural" was used, the colonists were inventing or redefining a right from nature. Or, when the words "covenant," "compact," or "contract" are encountered, it is not asked whether reference is to the social contract, or to the original contract, and it is taken for granted that natural law is being discussed.[15] There are also some scholars who have translated every claim to rights into a claim to a natural right, even the rights to trial by jury and to taxation by consent. In other words, rights that in the eighteenth century were peculiar to the British are, in the twentieth century, transmuted into natural rights.[16] It has, for example, been said that James Otis "appealed to the law of nature to make what he conceived to be a constitutional argument against the taxation of the American colonies. He began with the claim that the colonists 'are free born British subjects'" and hence "entitled to all the natural, essential, inherent and inseparable rights of our fellow subjects in Great-Britain."[17] Thus an appeal to equality of rights between the American and British peoples is an appeal to nature. It may be, of course, depending on how natural law is defined. The criterion, however, must be how Otis defined it. A claim to constitutional rights in the eighteenth century cannot now be metamorphosed into natural law just because we no longer understand the eighteenth-century British constitution.

One problem with eighteenth-century definitions must be cleared up now for some of the doctrines of positive law that are discussed in the following chapters — consent, contract, prescription, purchase, custom — have occasionally been labeled natural law. Usage must be examined closely. The word "contract" had several constitutional meanings and they must be distinguished if we are to know whether a natural or a positive legal authority was being cited. If people in the eighteenth century spoke of the "social contract," they were most likely referring to natural law. When the reference was to one of the "original contracts," the authority was always constitutional or fundamental law, never nature.

Constitutional terms were used more loosely in the eighteenth century than they are today. Rights stood on a more theoretical basis and the precision of definitions provided today by judicial interpretation was less common. Words still had meaning, however, and there is no doubt that people in the eighteenth century distinguished between natural rights and positive rights possessed by contract or prescription. In 1735 the *Craftsman*, Bolingbroke's newspaper, attacked theorists of Robert Brady's school who wrote that the institution of Parliament was not immemorial, that "*Liberty* and *Property* are not our antient Inheritance, but of very modern Date," and who implied that "*the People of England by our* antient Constitution, *were* SLAVES by LAW ESTABLISH'D." These legal arguments were based on historical conclusions that the *Craftsman* could not accept, yet in rejecting them, the newspaper's editor was somewhat sloppy in applying concepts. "[A]s *long Possession* gives a Title in Law, or at least enforces it, even in Cases of *private Property*, so the *publick, Rights of Mankind* acquire Strength by *long Prescription*; and if to This We add *particular Compacts with our Governors*, they become our *legal* as well as our *natural Rights*." The rival *Daily Gazetteer* had a field day criticizing the *Craftsman's* careless compounding not just of positive rights with natural rights, but of authorities for positive rights as authority for natural rights.

> 'Tis plain, *by publick Rights*, he means *natural Rights*; for, immediately after, he calls them *Natural*, as distinguish'd from *Legal*. But, can *natural Rights* acquire Strength by *Prescription?* No, surely: They are the same *Yesterday, to Day*, and *for Ever*: They are established in the *unalterable Nature* of Things; and are neither stronger nor weaker *by Time*: They are *the only Foundation* of all just Authority; and, *the sole Reason* for all Laws: Whatever are the Rights of Men *in this Age*, were their Rights *in every Age*; for, Rights are independent of *Power*.

What the *Craftsman* says was the eighteenth-century understanding. Rights founded in contract, custom, usage, or prescription were positive rights, not natural rights.[18]

It is necessary to pay close attention to precisely what was said and a survey of revolutionary political and legal arguments reveals that the term "natural rights" was used in several varying ways. Sometimes, but not often, we find it referring to absolute, inalienable rights above the whim and caprice of governmental discretion, as when Earl Camden told the House of Lords "that the natural right of mankind, and the immutable laws of justice, were clearly in favour of the *Americans*." It is believed that no colonial legislative body ever used the term in this sense, certainly not to claim the existence of rights independent of positive law.[19]

The most common mention of natural rights occurred when claiming rights or a right on the authority of nature as an alternative authority in conjunction with one or more other authorities. As with most arguments employing alternatives it could be expressed many ways.[20] Perhaps the most common was to derive the authority for rights from a combination of nature, the constitution, contract, and equality.[21]

The argument has been made that the American Revolution began on a "potentially ambiguous note" because the Continental Congress's Dec-laration of Rights appealed simultaneously to "the immutable laws of nature, the principles of the English constitution, and the several char-ters and compacts." The truth is there was little substantive difference between natural rights and positive rights. To dissect a natural right was to find a British right and it was natural because the British possessed it. What the constitution did not confer was not natural. That was why the Pennsylvania Assembly could boast that the colony's constitution "is founded on the natural Rights of Mankind, and the noble Principles of *English* Liberty, and therefore is, or ought to be, perfectly free." The same was true for common law. Indeed, the rights that British subjects on both sides of the Atlantic claimed to possess in the eighteenth century are a curious mirror of British constitutional law and English common law. "The rights of men are *natural* or *civil*," James Otis noted. "The natural absolute personal rights of individuals are so far from being opposed to political or civil rights that they are the very basis of all municipal laws of any great value." Or, as a London writer said in 1775, "Civil rights are, or ought to be, a confirmation of natural rights, as far as the free subordination of society can admit." Both men were correct except for putting the cart before the horse. Natural rights were the reflection, not the essence; they were the confirmation, not the source, of positive rights.[22]

CHAPTER TWELVE

RIGHTS AS PROPERTY

When he delivered law lectures at Cambridge University during the nineteenth century, Frederick William Maitland defined the law of equity. "What is Equity?" he asked. "In the year 1875 we might have said 'Equity is that body of rules which is administered only by those Courts which are known as Courts of Equity'." Since, however, courts of equity had been abolished "we are driven to say that Equity now is that body of rules administered by our English courts of justice which, were it not for the operation of the Judicature Acts, would be administered only by those courts which could be known as Courts of Equity."[1] In other words, to define the law of equity, one must know the business of the courts administering equity. What then was equity? The law of equity was the law administered by those courts empowered to administer equity. It is doubtful if Maitland, who was both a common lawyer and a historian, would, as a historian, have uttered such a statement. As a lawyer, he was more at home with circular definitions; circularity characterized common-law definitions. A good sample was the eighteenth-century definition of property provided in chapters 3, 4, and 5: property was the right of possession which could not be appropriated except with the consent of the possessor or the possessor's representative.

If historians find the circular explanation unsatisfactory it may be be-

cause, unlike Maitland, they are not lawyers and do not share the lawyer's preference for the functionally empirical even at the expense of the
theoretically precise. That reason is one explanation why the eighteenth-
century emphasis on property has sometimes been misinterpreted. Another reason is the twentieth century's intellectual prejudice against
elevating the material to a civil right. The thought has been that when
seventeenth-century English and eighteenth-century Americans defended
their right to property, they were speaking as a governing class seeking
to protect their private holdings, both personal and real. Sometimes they
were, and it is important not to ignore that fact.[2] But in legal terminology, "property" was not necessarily the object itself, but the right and
interest or domination lawfully held over the object; it was a species of
title, inchoate or complete, legal or equitable, corporeal or incorporeal,
tangible or intangible, visible or invisible, real, personal, or contractual.
In constitutional terminology, by contrast, property generally referred
to the object but the object was quite intangible, a legal abstraction. Most
commonly, when used in revolutionary constitutional debates, as well
as during earlier English constitutional crises of the seventeenth century,
"property" referred to rights of all kinds. "By this definition," Howard
Nenner points out, "it would be meaningful to speak of a man's property
in his life, his liberty, and his religion. This, certainly, was what Petyt
intended when he wrote that men 'had a right and Property in their lives
and Estates' and what Hale intended when he wrote that 'Every man
hath an unquestionable property in his own life and in his own self'."
There is no better example of what was meant than the right of being
taxed only by representation. And with it, we again encounter the circularity of legal definition. The right to be taxed only by yourself or your
representative was, the *New London Gazette* asserted, "a fundamental
birth-right-privilege." In other words it was owned, it was a constitutional right that was property. But it was also a constitutional right that
defined the constitutional definition of property, for "if we have not this
right, we have no property: Nothing to have and hold, which we can call
our own."[3]

It is necessary to continue to stress both the English constitutional background to the American Revolution and English legal vocabulary. Because some past observers have failed to consider either, they have fallen
into the error of thinking either that the colonial case against parliamentary taxation concerned property rights in a corporeal sense only, or that
the revolutionary era was divided into an early period involving property rights, followed by another in which personal rights were threatened.[4] To the extent that it divides personal property from personal rights,
that dichotomy is misleading, and it is misleading because personal rights

were personal property. The same constitutional tradition was on the line whether Parliament attempted to tax the colonies for purposes of raising revenue or sought to try criminal cases at vice admiralty without a jury. To be deprived of tangible assets by taxation without representation had much in common, constitutionally speaking, with being tried for a criminal offense without a jury. Both could be an unconstitutional taking of property, and the property taken would not be the tax assessed or the judicial penalty imposed, but the right to be taxed without consent and the right to be tried by a jury of peers.

The Vocabulary of Property

The legal vocabulary came naturally to eighteenth-century Americans out of seventeenth-century English constitutional controversies. The language of property, as employed by common lawyers, was accepted idiom in popular political discussion because when property was mentioned, the questions were generally constitutional.[5] "Have the two Houses [of Parliament] a strict right & property to lay upon the people what Taxes they shall judge meet?" the royalist jurist David Jenkins asked in 1648, using the concept of property to question the power of government. "Have the parliament a *right* to take from the lowest of the subjects the smallest privilege which he inherits, unless forfeited by law?" Nicholas Ray asked in 1765, reversing the ownership and vesting the property in the subject. In both instances, "property" served as a restraint on government power. It was called property because the operating concept was ownership. "[T]he political rights of the people are INSEPARABLY connected with the right of property," the *Remembrancer* for 1776 noted. So, too, were their constitutional rights.

There were numerous ways to express the concept of property ownership in rights, but always they seem to have been words lifted from the vocabulary of the common law. "Freehold" was one word. Sir George Moore made a rather floral use of it when telling the House of Commons "that our Liberties are our Freehold, and the fairest Flower that groweth in the Garden of the Commons: and, if they be once nipped, they will never grow again." Another word was "estate." To say that people had an "estate" in their rights was so common it would be redundant to quote an example. Unique enough to justify quotation, however, is a sentence written by Sir John Hawles demonstrating the flexibility of constitutional language by making the noun a verb. Hawles wrote of "the true Liberties and Priviledges which every *English man* is Justly Intituled unto, and Estated in by his Birth-right."[6]

The language was the language of the Inns of Court, removed from Westminster Hall and tossed about in the political arena. We must be on guard, however, not to think of it as a rhetorical tactic adopted by popularizers seeking to prop up ideas with the camouflage of technical jargon. Common lawyers used the same language in the same context. They, too, thought of rights as property, and they did so in their professional as well as political writings. Blackstone employed the imagery of property in his *Commentaries*, describing "the rights of persons" as things that "belonged" to them, and Sir Joseph Jekyll, future Master of the Rolls, told the House of Lords during the Sacheverell impeachment trial, that "the People have a Right to the Laws and the Constitution," a right of which they could be "dispossessed" by arbitrary principles.[7]

The talk, moreover, went beyond saying such things as "[o]ur property in the Constitution"; that the government "endowes the subject with" "liberties and infranchisements"; of claiming a "private interest" in fundamental rights; or of calling Magna Carta "the grand title deed, by which we hold our properties, our liberties, and our lives."[8] It was also substantive, for the tenure in which a right was reported to be held indicated judgments about the constitutional strength and viability of that right. When a right was said to be in villeinage or held at will, it was very precarious. In common-law parlance the least secure real tenures were the unfree villeinage or the holding known as tenant at will. The same was true for constitutional rights. Rights in danger of governmental abuse were rights held at will. Sir Edward Coke said that if people became tenants at will of liberty all rights would be open to royal encroachment. "For a freeman to be a tenant *at will* of his liberty," Coke was quoted in 1766, "I will never agree to it." John Dickinson said just about the same when warning that if the "intolerable acts" closing the Port of Boston, changing the charter of Massachusetts Bay, and removing trial of certain offenses from the colonies to England, succeeded, it could be said of the Americans "that they hold their lives, liberties, and properties, by the precarious tenure of the Will of others."[9]

There were two words of ownership used more frequently than any others to describe the authority of rights as property. One word was "birthright," the second was "inheritance." "We have a right to petition; that is the birth-right of Englishmen," the lord mayor of London boasted in 1770. "I am restored to my birthright, to the noble liberties and privileges of an Englishman," a future lord mayor, John Wilkes, announced on being released from king's bench prison. Birth was a source, an authority for rights. The British were said to have a right to liberty "from birth." A person owned British rights just by being born British. William Penn entitled one of his pamphlets, published in 1687, *The Most Excel-*

lent Privilege of Liberty & Property Being the Birth-Right of the Free-born Subjects of England.[10]

"Inheritance" was the other common ownership word, and it may be that, along with "contract," "purchase," and "charter," it was the authority most frequently cited by American whigs to explain why they possessed rights. "Inheritance" appears so frequently in the pages of this study that it warrants slight discussion. It was not a different concept, but another way of stating ownership of rights acquired at birth. The right of liberty provides a good example of a right inherited. "Liberty . . . is your Inheritance," Charles Lucas told Dubliners, claiming for the Irish an inheritance the English had long considered their own special legacy. "The Common Law hath so admeasured the Kings Prerogative, as he cannot prejudice any man in his inheritance, and the greatest inheritance a man hath is the liberty of his person, for all others are accessary to it," Coke had told the Petition of Right Commons. Liberty, Penn agreed, was the "inestimable Inheritance that every Free-born Subject of England is Heir unto by Birthright." At a time when the Council of the North still maintained extensive judicial jurisdiction, curtailing common-law rights in the northern marches of England, Edward Hyde, the future Lord Clarendon, attacked that prerogative court by speaking not of inequality or discrimination, but of heirs disinherited of their inheritance. "What hath the good *Northern* People done," he asked, "that they, and they alone of all the People of this happy Island, must be disinherited of their Birthright, of their Inheritance? For Prohibition, Writs of *Habeas Corpus*, Writs of Errour, are the Birth-right, the Inheritance of Subjects."[11]

Hyde linked the two words birthright and inheritance and the combination made constitutional sense. Both terms referred to the same single authority for rights, their ownership as property. It was common practice to mention the two together, much as if they were a legal formula for pleading rights or for securing rights. "FREEDOM, the natural Right of *Englishmen*, is our *Birthright*, our *Inheritance*," a London newspaper exclaimed in 1775, "it was handed down to us by our Ancestors, and *sealed* often with their BLOOD."

To speak of an inherited birthright in rights was an old, established — one might almost say *inherited* — method of pleading to the constitutional merits. "[T]he liberties, franchises, privileges, and jurisdiction of parliament are the ancient and undoubted birthright and inheritance of the subjects of England," the English Commons reminded Charles I in 1628. Thirteen years later, the Irish Commons claimed "their Birthright and best Inheritance" in a protest against Strafford's regime, and sixteen years after that it was the interregnum Commons protesting to Oliver Cromwell that their "liberties and privileges" were "the birth-right and inheritance of the people."

Defending the same property in rights the colonists used the same pleadings. In 1764, before the Stamp Act was introduced into the House of Commons, Virginia's Council and burgesses protested that it would deprive them of their right to taxation by consent, and based their claim to that right solely on ownership: that they had acquired it by long customary possession and that it was their "invaluable Birthright, descended to them from their Ancestors." Eleven years later, loyalists in Anson County, North Carolina, relied on the same inheritance, the same ownership of rights, to protest the colonial whig course of events. "We are truly invigorated with the warmest zeal and attachment in favour of the British Parliament, Constitution and Laws, which our forefathers gloriously struggled to establish, and which are now become the noblest birthright and inheritance of all Britannia's Sons."[12]

THE TENURE OF RIGHTS

There was very little discussion in the seventeenth or eighteenth centuries about the tenure in which rights were held as property. A casual reading of the literature leads to the conclusion that the title was in severalty. When we go behind the words for the substance, however, there is an implication that it was in common—that is, a concurrent ownership. One of the most frequently stated rules about property in rights was that the ownership, although it could, in individual cases, be forfeited for crime after conviction by due process of law, could not voluntarily be surrendered. One reason for that rule, it seems, was because the personal ownership in the rights was shared by the collective group and no individual could jeopardize them by becoming less free or enjoying fewer rights than his fellow subjects. Even more persuasive were the frequent references to protecting the rights of generations yet unborn, the future British heirs of the inheritance, implying they had property claims on the rights, certainly to their preservation, and therefore possessed a concurrent ownership in them. Stephen Johnson, a Connecticut clergyman, was one of the few commentators to identify a type of concurrent title when he spoke somewhat vaguely of holding rights "jointly." During the Stamp Act crisis he cited John Locke for the proposition that people could not surrender liberty, and explained: "But, if we had a right to do it, by the law of nature, yet, in a state of government, and as members of a free community and kingdom, we cannot do it; because, in this state, we hold our liberties and privileges jointly, in common with the rest of our fellow subjects; and therefore cannot give them up, without betraying the liberty and privileges of the community and kingdom to which we belong." Taking the other perspective and arguing that not only the individual but also the corporate body could not surrender liberty and civil rights even to the sovereign, Francis Gregor did not use the terms "joint" or "common." He seems to have been a lawyer, as he was editing an edition of Fortescue, first published in 1737 and reissued in 1775. Saying that neither the single citizen nor entire society could contract away liberty and civil rights, Gregor argued that "the Right of the whole Nation is made up of an Union of the Rights which every particular Person who composes it had in and of himself; and if no particular Person has a Right to procure his own Harm, neither can a whole Nation have any such Right."[13]

But what is the answer to the question asked by the author of *Licentiousness Unmask'd*. "By what tenure do we now hold our liberty?" It may be that the common-law writer Capel Lofft provided the only direct answer. "Every inhabitant of England," he wrote in a 1777 tract defending American whigs, "is seized, per my et per tout, in parcel and in whole, as joint tenant with every other inhabitant of those liberties to which all have one title, indefeazible but by his own act."

Although too little was said about the title to rights for a definitive rule of law to be stated, a cautious conclusion would be that ownership in rights was vested in individuals less as severalty than as tenancy in common. The larger estate in which the common interests were held was vested in society. Two points seem reasonably certain. Society owned as trustee, holding its property in rights for the benefit of the commonance. Second, society must not be confused with governmental power; the concept of rights ownership was a theory of constitutionality limiting power.[14]

CHAPTER THIRTEEN

PROPERTY IN RIGHTS

For seventeenth-century English and eighteenth-century Americans to speak of civil rights as private property or an inheritance was not merely a convenience of expression, a borrowing of words from the common law that, passing into everyday use and becoming idioms, lost their legal connotations. Nor was it a figure of speech, an analogy drawn to physical inheritances received from lineal ancestors or to material things to which a citizen became entitled at birth. When pamphleteers, politicians, or lawyers spoke of receiving liberties by birthright or of inheriting rights, they were thinking of intangible but real items actually obtained at birth and of real ancestors from whom one could inherit. If there was a difference, it was of degree, not of kind. A personal civil right claimed as a birthright or an inheritance, although truly property in the same sense as was land, chattels, and inchoate obligations, was a higher kind of property as it was a species of civil liberty and personal rights. John Cartwright expressed the idea when he quoted a "protest" against suspension of statutes. "A greater inheritance," he said, "descends to every one of us from right, and the *laws*, than from our parents." A paragraph attributed to Lord Chancellor Somers was even more explicit. The two types of inheritance, he agreed, were the same in kind but not degree.

As the subjects of the King are born to lands and other things, so
are they born to inherit and enjoy the laws of this realm, that so every
man have an equal benefit by law. It is therefore called common right,
and is a greater inheritance to every man than that which descends
to him as heir, from his parents. Because thereby his goods, land,
wife, children, his body, life, honor, and estimation are protected
from injury and wrong. This common right is called the law of the
subject, and the judges are sworn to execute justice (as my Lord *Coke*
says) according to law and custom of *England*. All which do prove
how justly the laws are called the great inheritances of every subject, and the inheritance of inheritances, without which inheritance
we have no inheritance.[1]

It might be thought that by the era of the American Revolution, seven
decades after the Glorious Revolution and the advent of parliamentary
supremacy, the concept of property in rights would have degenerated
into a mere popularization, no longer used to explain constitutional reality.
But to suppose that as fact is to suppose that by 1760 parliamentary supremacy was understood to mean parliamentary sovereignty. It may have
in actual constitutional practice, but not yet in popular constitutional
theory. Since people, including many lawyers, still believed that British
government was not arbitrary, they still believed there were constitutional
limits on legitimate power, one of which was the restraint inherent in
the notion that rights were owned by the people and protected as property. Edmund Burke believed it, or at least sounded as if he did. "By a
constitutional policy, working after the pattern of nature," he asserted,
"we receive, we hold, we transmit our government and our privileges,
in the same manner in which we enjoy and transmit our property and
our lives. The institutions of policy, the goods of fortune, the gifts of
providence, are handed down to us, and from us, in the same course and
order." The same constitutional metaphor was repeated by Jean Louis
De Lolme, the Swiss student of British government and author of the
leading treatise on constitutional law to be published during the revolutionary era. Rights for the British were "an inheritance," he wrote. "[T]his
right of inheritance is expressed in English by one word, (*birth-right*) the
same as that which expresses the King's title to the Crown."[2]

De Lolme was explaining why lawyers conceptualized rights as property. That is the issue to which this chapter is addressed. First two minor
if obvious points should be gotten out of the way: that the property-in-
rights concept was not a legal fiction and was not natural law. At least,
eighteenth-century constitutional theorists who utilized the concept did
not think it a fiction. Rights were incorporeal, but still property. To say
they were owned was no more a legal fiction than to say today that to

sell a copyright is to transfer ownership, or to say that a chose in action is property. Moreover, it was not natural law. Sometimes it is mistaken for natural law, perhaps because property as authority for rights is an authority distinct from the sovereign's command, and, for legal positivists in the twentieth century, any source of law other than the command of the sovereign appears to be natural law. That, of course, could be one meaning of natural law if one chooses to adopt a definition that would make international law and all primitive laws "natural" as well. That was not the eighteenth-century meaning. Then, property as authority for rights was positive, much like the authority of custom, prescription, the original contract, or the sovereign's command. Charles Yorke, son of Lord Chancellor Hardwicke and himself momentarily lord chancellor in 1770, made a scholarly and convincing legal argument that the right of inheritance could not exist at natural law in the sense of law in the state of nature, but had to come from positive law. In the other meaning of natural law — natural to humans and, therefore, universal — the concept of inherited property rights in civil rights was probably also thought not to exist. "Ask an Englishman what makes him so tenacious of his laws and privileges? and he will answer, Because they are his birth-right," John Collier observed in another legal treatise. "But ask him, if the like privileges are not the birth-right of a Turk, or a negro slave in Jamaica? 'tis a hundred to one but he hesitates for an answer; and when he does answer, the odds are as great, but he replies in the negative." It remained, however, for Edmund Burke, a nonlawyer capable of using a double legal expression, "entailed inheritance," to provide the best evidence that the property-in-rights concept was not thought to be natural law. He did so when stating why rights held as property were secure. The explanation lay in part with the alternative which could not be secured: natural rights. The positive was superior to the speculative. That realization was why, in a nation without a written constitution or a tribunal empowered to resolve legal and constitutional disputes, people attempted to preserve liberty and to avoid arbitrary govenment by "considering their most sacred rights and franchises as an *inheritance.*"

> In the famous law of the 3d of Charles I. called the *Petition of Right,* the parliament says to the king, "Your subjects have *inherited* this freedom," claiming their franchises not on abstract principles "as the rights of men," but as the rights of Englishmen, and as a patrimony derived from their forefathers. Selden, and the other profoundly learned men, who drew this petition of right, were as well acquainted, at least, with all the general theories concerning the "rights of men," . . . [but] they preferred this positive, recorded, *hereditary* title to all which can be dear to the man and the citizen, to that

vague speculative right, which exposed their sure inheritance to be scrambled for and torn to pieces by every wild litigious spirit.

. . .

You will observe, that from Magna Charta to the Declaration of Right, it has been the uniform policy of our constitution to claim and assert our liberties, as an *entailed inheritance* derived to us from our forefathers, and to be transmitted to our posterity; as an estate specially belonging to the people of this kingdom without any reference whatever to any other more general or prior right. By this means our constitution preserves an unity in so great a diversity of its parts. We have an inheritable crown; an inheritable peerage; and an house of commons and a people inheriting privileges, franchises, and liberties, from a long line of ancestors.[3]

THE PROPERTY IMPERATIVE

The conceptualization of rights and liberties as individual property inherited and possessed was not a phenomenon appearing only during constitutional crises, such as the English Civil War, the Glorious Revolution, or the American Revolution.[4] It was simply the way rights were explained, a theory of antithesis between the authority of kings and the personally owned rights of the subject. The concept was inherited from an idealization of the medieval constitutional system in which law was neither public nor private, but the sum of all the people's subjective rights, a law making it one of the highest duties of rulers to protect their subjects' rights. The law was the king's and it was also the people's, it was their possession and also the protection of all they possessed including their other rights. Thus, property was antecedent to government, although not to law which created government and endowed kings with the right to rule, a right that also was property, owned by the king as a privilege as long as the law was held inviolate.[5]

The argument was both simple and subtle. The authority of the monarch was, in a manner of speaking, "lowered" to the status of a property right. It was, in other words, on the same level as the rights of the people and to restrain and limit the power of the Crown, one right of property was set against another. Translated from the metaphor of property to legal doctrine, the constitutional rule was summarized by Bishop Burnet when he reversed the usual emphasis on the people's rights and focused attention on those of the king.

Subjects are only bound to render to Princes that which is *theirs*: That is, the Rights which are vested in them by Law, Custom, and

Constitution, and no more. And if we are only bound to render them that which is *theirs*, then if they should demand that which is not *theirs*, but is by the most express Provisions that are possible, still *ours*; such as the Liberty of our Person, the Property of our Estate, and the Observance of our Laws, we are certainly not bound to render these; because in a Constitution like ours, no Prince can say they are *his*.[6]

There were people in Great Britain during the second half of the eighteenth century who would have carried the concept of property beyond the limits of what was understood to be the constitutional doctrine. One example is the writer who would have made even the king's prerogative part of the people's rights through property.[7] Another is George Rous who claimed that "[t]he public rights of the community are the *property* of the *People alone* — every power of Government is a *trust* delegated by the People, and its extent prescribed by the terms of delegation."[8] The trouble is that this law was no longer law when Rous wrote in 1791. Still, the concept of property in rights retained throughout the second half of the eighteenth century a strong grip on the constitutional vision and was advanced not as a means of securing private gain against society but of limiting the legitimacy of governmental power. In no other constitutional controversy was this theory more convincingly argued than in the American Revolution. It may even be that, together with the British reform movement to extend the franchise, the American Revolution was the last occasion when the property-in-rights authority was a significant topic in constitutional debate.

Historians may wonder how the concepts of seventeenth-century revolutionary England were taken whole into the American revolutionary controversy, not only 3,000 miles, but 130 years away. Lawyers have no difficulty. For them law has a timeless dimension, and physical, chronological, and geographical circumstances do not change legal principles. In the theory of law, American whigs had no problem adapting the seventeenth-century English argument of property in rights against Stuart kings and applying it to their own times and conditions. In the remainder of this chapter we will consider how they worded their case.[9]

THE AMERICAN LANGUAGE

Americans inherited both the concept of rights as a species of property and the language — the language of law — with which to explain rights. "By the British Constitution, our best inheritance," the Continental Congress resolved, "rights, as well as duties, descend upon us."[10]

The language may have been borrowed but it was not figurative. Americans really seem to have believed they had inherited rights and that those rights were truly property. "[W]hen persons have entered into a civil combination, and are become a body politick, at their decease, they leave all their civil privileges to their descendants," William Patten assured people in Plymouth County, Massachusetts Bay, when celebrating repeal of the Stamp Act. "[W]e of this Generation may say too with *St. Paul*, that we are free born, born to Liberty," another New England clergyman had exclaimed in the Connecticut election sermon of 1759, "our Fathers died and went off the stage, with a chearful Hope, of transmitting their Privileges to the latest Generation." The Philadelphia physician Benjamin Rush seems to have thought rights not only property, but concrete property, for he depicted them not just held in trust but "deposited" with society's lawmakers for safekeeping.[11]

American whigs not only inherited their manner of conceptualizing rights, they also inherited all of the common-law terms the British employed to describe the ownership of rights. "Title" was a common word. The colonists, Increase Mather announced in 1689, had a "Title to the Common Rights of Englishmen." They were not limited to a legal title either, for, as a New Yorker pointed out during the revolutionary debate, Americans had "an equitable Title to those Privileges for which We contend." The title was held in several tenures. One was "unalienable," "vested in the people," according to the New Jersey lower house. The title was almost a vested right in itself, a Rhode Island governor believed, since the people "do not hold those rights as privileges granted them, but possess them as inherent and indefeasible." Another American claim was in common. "British privileges," the Boston town meeting asserted, "we hold in common with our fellow subjects who are natives of Britain." A third, of course, was possession. The colonists, Delaware's House of Assembly voted, had "been in Possession of, and now are entitled to, all the inherent Rights and Liberties of his Majesty's Subjects in Great-Britain, or elsewhere."[12]

The most peculiarly common-law term Americans employed to explicate ownership of rights was "seisin." Technically seisin referred to the right of possession or, better still, the right to possess and to enjoy the fruits of a property: "enjoyment" in the sense meant by a writer in 1765 when urging the freeholders of South Carolina to elect representatives "who will use their best endeavours to *preserve, support and defend the enjoyment of every* CONSTITUTIONAL LIBERTY, RIGHT *and* PRIVILEGE *that has been handed down to us by our* FOREFATHERS, *and which we* CLAIM *as* BRITISH SUBJECTS." The legal principle was that Americans were seized of their liberty, rights, and privileges and could not, except by law, be disseized of them. The people of Connecticut, having "a property in their own estate," that colony's House of Representatives resolved, "are not to be disseized of their liberties or free customs, sentenced or condemned, but by lawful judgment of their peers."[13]

THE AMERICAN INHERITANCE

In the last chapter there was a sampling of the rights the eighteenth-century British claimed as their property. To obtain an indication of how extensive they were, there is no need to run down the entire list; a brief survey should do the job. Just as the privileges of the House of Commons were the "undoubted birthright and inheritance of the subjects of England," so the people's right to petition was "their birth right and inheritance."[14] Not only did the citizen have a birthright to "general freedom and security," but "[h]e hath also by birthright a property in the English constitution."[15] Having a birthright in the constitution meant that the British had a birthright in government by consent, that is "[a] Government by King, Lords, and an Assembly representative of the People is the birthright of every Englishman."[16] To make that claim was much like saying that just about every British constitutional right was inherited property owned as a birthright.

There is only one further point of British background to be mentioned. It has already been noted that the Bill of Rights codified the concept of owned, inherited rights. The idea also had judicial sanction. Chief Justice John Holt, in a landmark constitutional decision, ruled that the right of an elector to his vote was property of which the elector could not be divested save by judgment at common law. The concept that the privilege of voting was a property right would give future British reformers incredible difficulty. To extend the franchise to all British citizens, they had to disenfranchise some of the boroughs, a manifestation of power too arbitrary for many eighteenth-century constitutionalists who equated rights with property. "It is a little paradoxical," John Almon protested, "to demand a franchise for those who never enjoyed it, and deny the exercise of it in those who have supposed it to be an inheritance. It is holding liberty at the will of another, which Sir Edward Coke says 'is a tenure not to be found in all Littleton'."[17]

There is no need to run down a list of the rights Americans claimed as their property for they are more or less all of the rights discussed in other chapters of this study. They included, of course, the birthrights of trial by jury at the venue and to representation,[18] as well as the inheritance of English common law, British liberty, and the constitution.[19] It would be more profitable to illustrate how colonial whigs argued the concept of property in rights by considering briefly a right that is otherwise not a topic of this volume, the right to taxation by consent, a right that is more fully discussed in the volume dealing with Parliament's authority to tax the colonies.

There was no other right, privilege, franchise, or liberty claimed by the colonial whigs that relied more on the concept of personal inheritance, and not on speculations deduced from nature, than the doctrine that for taxation to be constitutional it had to be by consent. Hence, taxation by consent is the best right with which to summarize the birthright argument. First, we must distinguish between two constitutional rules that may appear similar, but were quite different. One is the constitutional maxim that no property owner could be deprived of that property by taxation unless the tax was imposed by the owner's consent or the consent of the owner's representative. The second is that the right not to be taxed without the consent of the owner of property or the owner's representative was a property right.

The doctrine of taxation only by consent was as old as England's ancient constitution. In theory that meant that it had always been the constitutional rule. "[B]y the Laws and Statutes of this Realm," the Commons declared in 1628, "the free Subjects of *England* do undoubtedly inherit this Right and Liberty, not to be compel'd to contribute any Tax, Tollage, Aid, or to make any Loans not set or impos'd by common Consent, by Act of Parliament." Later, granting an annual revenue to Oliver Cromwell as lord protector, the House prayed "that it be declared and enacted, that no charge be laid, nor no person be compelled to contribute to any gift, loan, benevolence, tax, tallage, aid, or other like charge without common consent by act of parliament, which is a freedom the people of these nations ought by the laws to inherit." Similar words were used to describe the exact same right as it existed in Great Britain during the revolutionary era. The right not to be taxed except by consent, it was said in London the year the Stamp Act passed, was secured to every member of the community "and will continue his birthright as long as that constitution shall remain inviolate, and in its full vigor."[20]

The extension of the doctrine to America had been inevitable and just as inevitably it was expressed in the colonies as it had been in the mother country: as an inheritance. One ground on which it was theorized was as the inheritance by the settlers of America and their descendants of a right to inherit—"this right was born with, and so inherent in them, that nothing but some actual crime, which attainted their blood, could deprive them of it."[21]

Finally, it may be noted that the right to be taxed only by consent need not be claimed directly as property. It could be held incidental to ownership of another right, such as the right to equality. According to that theory the property that was acquired by birthright was the right to equal treatment, and an incident of the tenure enjoyed in the right of equality was the right to taxation by representation.[22]

No matter the property interest stressed, joinder of the question of Parliament's authority to tax with the constitutional principle that liberties and civil rights were personal property led to but one conclusion. It was that under the British Constitution the right to be taxed only by personal consent or the consent of an elected representative was a "sacred Birthright and most valuable Inheritance" belonging to American as well as British subjects. That reason was why a Philadelphian, eight days after the Stamp Act became law, wrote that "[t]he burden of the tax is not the point; it is the laying it upon us, as we apprehend, unconstitutionally, a submission to which will be giving up our birthright, and entailing slavery on our posterity."[23]

THE IMPORTANCE OF PROPERTY

There was no other authority for rights, except the original contract and its special American variations, that had so strong a hold on the colonial whig constitutional imagination as the authority of rights being the concurrent and personal property of the people. Because the right to property itself was so hallowed and absolute, the "propertyness" of rights gave rights much of their immutability. It also provided rights with much of their aura of constitutional defensibility, vesting in the people yet another right — the right to preserve their rights by force and even rebellion against constituted authority. On the day that the Stamp Act became operative, the *Boston Evening-Post* reprinted an argument from the *New-London Gazette* warning that the rights Americans "had in possession" were about to be "superceeded and vacated by the act." Yet, because they were owned in possession they could not constitutionally be superseded or vacated, certainly not voluntarily.

> [I]f these be our rights, they are ours to have and to hold, to possess and defend against all claimants whatsoever. They are indefeasible rights; we cannot yield them up; nor can they be taken away from us. — Were we so base, we could not yield them up, because they are the birth-right inheritance of our children, to which they are born; and so are our's to hold, but not to give up; nor can any claimants rightfully take them from us: this would make them rights and no

rights, or our's, and not our's at the same time: for such claimants
could take them away, only, on account of their having a better right
to them than we.

Before we dismiss the argument as extreme American rhetoric, it is
well to keep in mind that the people's right to defend their property in
rights was very much part of the constitutional language of contemporary London. "[I]f then we applaud our ancestors for obtaining such liberties for us, at a time when all the rights of Englishmen were trampled
upon, and despotism had trodden down the laws," the earl of Chatham
exclaimed in the House of Lords shortly before the Battle of Lexington,
"surely we cannot, in reason, deny that portion of liberty (so hardly and
honourably obtained) to our own brethren — brethren by the same common parent, and who are unquestionable heirs of the same glorious inheritance." As theory, the right to defend property in rights had almost
universal acceptance. Even so ardent an imperialist as William Knox
conceded that the colonists owned it and should exercise it. His words
were mostly rhetoric, yet are important to the extent that he was giving
lip service to a constitutional argument he felt he could not deny. Unable to say the colonists did not possess the right to resistance, Knox attempted to limit it to a right against the monarch, saying it had never
been a right against the legislature. "The common law of England is,
I grant, the rightful inheritance of every British subject," Knox wrote,
"and protects his property and person from violence or impositions, which
might be attempted by authority of the prerogative of the crown; and
whenever such attempts are made, the colonists will, I hope, assert their
consanguinity to Englishmen, and apply to the British parliament for
redress."

Colonial whigs would have none of Knox's argument. They would have
been willing to ask Parliament for redress against the Crown, but there
was no occasion. The king was not threatening them, Parliament was,
and Knox's common law did not protect the colonists from Parliament.
His common law was subject to the will of Parliament. From the colonists' perspective the right to defend their property in rights had to be as
good against Parliament as against the Crown or it was no right. "When,"
the Massachusetts Provincial Congress told the voters of that colony, "a
People entitled to that freedom which your ancestors have nobly preserved, as the richest inheritance of their children, are invaded by the
hand of oppression, and trampled on by the merciless feet of tyranny,
resistance is so far from being criminal, that it becomes the Christian
and social duty of each individual."

The concept holds one more surprise. The question whether the time had come to resist could be answered by using property terms such as "interest" and "inheritance." Commenting on the Battle of Lexington, "an American" told the inhabitants of New York, "Let every *American* consider what interest have we in *George* the Third, or what inheritance have we in the Parliament of *Great Britain*."[24]

CHAPTER FOURTEEN

THE AUTHORITY
OF MIGRATION

One authority for rights has been overlooked by most constitutional studies of the American Revolution. Quite often it is not even recognized as authority, yet it was cited from the very beginning to the very conclusion of the revolutionary debate. In fact, if we take Patrick Henry's Virginia resolutions opposing the Stamp Act to be the start of the colonial side of the controversy, then this claim of authority was the very first American defense made. "*Resolved*," the preamble of Henry's resolutions provided, "That the first Adventurers and Settlers of this his Majesty's Colony and Dominion of *Virginia* brought with them, and transmitted to their Posterity, and all other his Majesty's Subjects since inhabiting in this his Majesty's said Colony, all the Liberties, Privileges, Franchises, and Immunities, that have at any Time been held, enjoyed and possessed, by the people of *Great Britain*." Rights were claimed in that opening statement of the colonial whig argument, and the first authority mentioned for those rights was not the constitution or equality, but migration.[1]

There were various explanations for the migration claim. The simplest, stated by the first Continental Congress and Georgia's Commons House of Assembly, was that the migrants had enjoyed certain rights in the mother country and had not lost them in passage. They resolved, "That, by such emigration, they by no means forfeited, surrendered, or lost any of those rights, but that they were, and their descendants now are, entitled to the exercise and enjoyment of all such of them as their local and other circumstances enable them to exercise and enjoy." Or as the attorney general of Quebec told a Montreal jury when opening a capital prosecution, "every Set of *English* Planters, upon their first occupying and settling a new Colony, have carried with them the Laws of *England* then in Force at the Time of their leaving it to go to the new Colony."[2] Another way of expressing the theory was in terms of property, to think of rights as part of the baggage the migrants transported to the New World. It "followed" from the principles of the British constitution, New York's General Assembly explained to the House of Lords, "that the Colonists carried with them all the rights they were entitled to in the country from which they emigrated." That is, they brought with them at migration, the Pennsylvania General Assembly pointed out, "those constitutional Rights and Liberties which were inseparably annexed to their Persons," and those rights were "now vested in their Descendants, as an Inheritance the most important and valuable."[3]

A third variation was to stress what was called "the nature of their emigration," to argue that the first settlers did not come to enjoy fewer rights than they had possessed in England, but had anticipated obtaining if not more rights at least the same rights better secured. In chapter 17, the American migration contract will be discussed. It might be thought to be the same argument to authority as the migration itself. But the contract was based either on the assurance, real or implied, that the migrants would enjoy English rights in the new settlements or on their reliance that they would. Here the probative fact is not promise, real or implied, or reliance on promise, but expectation without even an implied promise. As Governor Stephen Hopkins pointed out, "there would be found very few people in the world, willing to leave their native country, and go through the fatigue and hardship of planting in a new uncultivated one, for the sake of losing their freedom."[4]

THE SIGNIFICANCE OF MIGRATION

The migration principle was not an important authority for colonial rights. It would not merit extended discussion but for three considerations: (1) it has not been given any weight by the constitutional historians of the American Revolution; (2) it was not *sui generis* to colonial whigs but was an old, established doctrine in British constitutional theory; and (3) it was taken seriously by defenders of parliamentary authority during the revolutionary controversy. Moreover, there was a negative significance to the principle: but for its implications the supporters of imperial rule might have argued that the first settlers, on leaving England, had separated themselves from their civil rights. "Any privileges the colonists have lost," one argument went, "they must have lost either by the bare act of *emigration*, or by some *agreement* or surrender." Colonial whigs had to assert the migration principle, if for no other reason than to avoid that conclusion.[5]

The supposition is only a guess, but it seems likely that the migration principle has been ignored by constitutional historians because they have not recognized that it was a legal argument. Perhaps the fact would have been more apparent had they paid attention to British and Irish political literature, which contained much about the migration theory applied to the Saxons invading England and the English settling in Ireland. As early as 1643, Philip Hunton was contending that the Saxons "no doubt continued the freedome they had in Germany. . . . Who sets not here the antiquity of our Liberties and frame of Government? so they were governed in Germany, and so here to this day, for by transplanting themselves, they changed their soyl, not their manners and Government." During the very years of the American controversy, two non-Englishmen searching for the roots of British liberty, an Irish common-law professor, Francis Stoughton Sullivan, and Gilbert Stuart, a Scottish historian trained in Scots law, wrote almost identical statements about the migration of Saxon rights. "The Saxons brought along with them into Britain their own customs, language, and civil institutions. Free in Germany, they renounced not their independence, when they had conquered."[6] More to the point, Thomas Jefferson thought, was that there never had been "any claim of superiority or dependence asserted over them by that mother country from which they had migrated." To demonstrate the difference between that independence and what parliamentary supremacy purported for the colonies, the *Gentleman's Magazine* printed a mock proclamation by Frederick the Great, in which the Prussian king claimed the very rights over the United Kingdom that Parliament was asserting over the colonies, and on the same authority—the imperial contract as executed in the Seven Years War.

> Whereas it is well known to all the world, that the first German settlements made in the island of Britain were by colonies of people, subjects to our renowned ducal ancestors . . . and that the said colonies have flourished under the protection of our august house, for ages past . . . and yet have hitherto yielded little profit to the same: And whereas we ourself have in the last war fought for and defended the said colonies, against the power of France, and thereby enabled

them to make conquests from the said power in America; for which we have not yet received adequate compensation.

Asserting that Prussia was entitled to repayment, the proclamation imposed taxes on "the said colonies in Britain," forbade manufacturing in them, and ordered that felons convicted of capital offenses in Prussia be transported "into the said island of Great-Britain, for the better peopling of that country."[7]

A second point revealed by British literature is that whatever American whigs said about the migration principle the Irish said as well. Consider the following sentence, published in 1775, and which is practically the same, word for word, with dozens that are cited further on in this chapter: "They who quit their native Country, to seek a Settlement in Some other Part of the World, take with them wherever they go, as their Birth Right, the Laws of their native Country, and a Power to exercise them in their full Extent; unless they go into Territories of some other State, that will not suffer them to retain their own Laws." This quotation is from a pamphlet published in Dublin, dealing with "the Rights of [the] Colonists and Planters" of Ireland. It had nothing to do with the American crisis. Interestingly, as early as 1738, Samuel Madden, like his uncle, William Molyneux, a champion of Irish rights, had applied the migration principle to the Anglo-Irish by drawing an analogy to the American colonists. "[M]ay not the children of those Englishmen, who have planted in our colonies in America," he asked, "be as justly reckoned Indians and savages, as such families, who are settled here, can be considered and treated as mere Irishmen and aliens?"[8]

We may not expect it, but the migration principle was taken seriously by critics of the American whigs. Some attempted to turn it around, saying the colonists were barred from complaining of a constitutional inequality when it was of their own making. "If the condition of the colonists of America, in respect of taxation, is unfavourable, who is to blame?" William Barron asked. "Did they not voluntarily subject themselves to this disadvantage, when they emigrated?" A New Englander, writing in a Boston newspaper, thought the answer was yes. "[W]ho bro't us into these circumstances," he wrote, also referring to the taxation issue, "our ancestors, ourselves, they or we came voluntarily; if we return to Great Britain we shall remove the difficulty, but we chose to remain here, which subjects us to this inconvenience and shall the constitution bend to our partialities, or shall not we acquiesce in the voluntary inconvenience."[9]

An even stronger criticism came from observers who believed that migration made no difference, that in the 1770s the British constitution meant parliamentary supremacy, setting the rule for British subjects no matter where they traveled in the Empire. "It must be granted," Lord Mansfield told the House of Lords of the first English settlers of North America, "that they migrated with leave as colonies, and therefore from the very meaning of the word were, are, and must be subjects, and owe allegiance and subjection to their mother country." He meant, of course, subjection to Parliament, and conveniently did not mention that at the time of settlement Parliament had been neither supreme or sovereign in English government. It was supreme in the British government of the 1760s, however, and, for imperial lawyers such as Mansfield, that fact overrode all American whig arguments about migration rights. He could not contemplate the question in any way other than from the perspective of sovereignty. The first colonial settlers had been subjects of the sovereign power and migration did not alter their condition, a condition of absolutes, not relatives. Mansfield's version of the constitution contained no measure for taking into account changed circumstances, or even the drastically revised meaning of sovereignty as it had evolved over the last century and a half. The American whig legal perspective was attuned more to seventeenth-century constitutional thought and customary rights. When *Junius* reached a conclusion similar to Mansfield's and remarked that the migration of the original Americans "deserved no praise," Arthur Lee answered by citing usage following settlement. "We are not setting up any new claim, but opposing it in you," he wrote, asserting a constitutional theory quite at odds with Mansfield's legislative sovereignty. "We are exclaiming against your invasion of those rights which are essential to the existence of freedom, against the infringement of those privileges which we have enjoyed and exercised for more than a century."[10]

The Right of Migration

A legal doctrine was cited both to nullify the migration principle and to implement it. The rule, borrowed from Roman law, was that a country conquered in war was at the will and pleasure of the conqueror and had to accept whatever laws and privileges the conqueror decreed. The reverse side of the rule was that countries not conquered but settled by the British received the English common law unaltered. A factual dispute running throughout colonial history had been whether British North America had been settled or conquered. The colonists were continually asserting that, except for New York and Jamaica, they were never conquered, sometimes arguing that if anyone had been conquered it had been the Indians and they, the settlers, had been the conquerors. "Some of the Plantations, 'tis true, came to *England* by Conquest. But must the Conquerors themselves be look't upon as a conquered People," the Barbadian Edward Littleton asked in 1689. "It were very strange, if those that bring Countries under the Dominion of *England*, and maintain the possession, should by so doing lose their own *English* Liberties."[11]

Three different concepts should be kept distinct. The first concerns which laws the first settlers carried with them. The generally accepted rule was that they took only so much English law as was applicable to their situation and the conditions of an infant colony. The other two concepts deal with rights and must not be confused. The first is the right of British migrants going from the home kingdom to a settled, not conquered, territory, to carry with them the common law and constitutional rights. Although there were lawyers who questioned special applications of this right, there was remarkably uniform authority supporting the right.[12] A second distinct right was the right to migrate. This right rested on less convincing grounds and whether it was a right that had been owned by English people in the seventeenth century was quite important due to the argument that if there was no such right, then migration was an "indulgence" granted to the first settlers on terms set by the government. One of the terms could have been that the settlers did not carry with them English rights or only those rights that the sovereign permitted.[13]

There was language in official statements issued by some colonial assemblies at the time of the Stamp Act indicating that migration was thought to have been a governmental indulgence. The words, however, were ambiguous, not a clear admission either that permission was needed for migration or that it had been accepted with conditions attached. What can be asserted is that, as the revolutionary controversy intensified, arguments changed and the idea of migrating with permission ceased to be mentioned. It is sometimes said that Richard Bland and Thomas Jefferson resolved the issue by postulating a natural right of all people to emigrate. That supposition is nonsense. The natural right of migration was neither an American original nor a radical doctrine but one that long had been a staple in the legal literature of Europe. Burlamaqui stated the principle just as absolutely as Jefferson, even adding that "the subjects of a state cannot be denied the liberty of settling elsewhere, in order to procure the advantages which they do not find in their native country."[14] The trouble is that the right was natural, not positive, and may not have existed at common law. During the decades of the original settlements, the earl of Strafford maintained that the right did not exist in England and at that time the king had authority to issue the writ of *ne exeat regno* restraining any person or group from departing the country.[15] By the second half of the eighteenth century, the law was less clear. The writ was probably limited to issue on petition of private persons seeking to keep parties to a civil action within a court's jurisdiction, and Parliament had assumed jurisdiction in the area, passing legislation forbidding named persons, such as the South Sea directors, from quitting the Kingdom. Thomas Pownall, writing about the North America colonies, stated positively there was no right to migrate, and Francis Plowden, writing about British rights, was just as positive that there was.[16] The better view is that there was no positive right, but there was an implied right by acquiescence of the government. Whether or not that acquiescence carried conditions, restricting the other rights or curtailing what law the settlers carried with them, was the issue in dispute, not whether there was a natural right of migration.

THE EXPECTATION OF MIGRATION

The American whig contention that one authority for their rights was the migration itself must be briefly summarized. The principle was generally stated as an assumed, obvious fact, one not likely to be disputed.[17] The physical image was of the first settlers carrying their rights with them in the passage across the Atlantic. There were even explanations of how they did it. One was that the first settlers had possessed rights in England and, on leaving, simply took them along just as they took their other movable property.[18] A second, more legal explanation was that rights had not been affected by migration as it was a constitutionally neutral undertaking. Going from the European part of the Empire to the American part was, in constitutional law, no different than going from London to Dover.[19] A third explanation was the theory that common law followed the subject, for, as counsel argued in *Dutton* v. *Howell*, when "Subjects of *England*, by Consent of their Prince, go and possess an uninhabited desert Country; the Common Law must be supposed their Rule, as 'twas their Birthright, and as 'tis the best, as so to be presumed their Choice; and not only that, but even as Obligatory, 'tis so."[20]

In a number of legal opinions, counsel to the board of trade as well as the attorney and solicitor generals of England advising the Privy Council, had upheld the doctrine that some but not all law had been carried to the New World by the migration. "The Common Law of England, is the Common Law of the Plantations," Richard West ruled in 1720. "Let an Englishman go where he will, he carries as much of law and liberty with him, as the nature of things will bear."[21] That, of course, was the factual dispute. How much did the nature of things bear? The British position, never clearly defined, was basically that no matter what rights migrated to the colonies, they were subject to parliamentary supremacy.

American whigs, by contrast, not only claimed all rights existing in the mother country but derived from the migration itself additional rights or, at least, extra protection for rights. The material arguments on which the whigs based this claim can be reduced to three themes: the expectation of migration; the purpose of migration; and the equality of migration.

The expectation theme assumed that the early settlers thought about rights and would not have come to North America had they known that Parliament would claim the supremacy it started to claim in 1764. "If this had been the doctrine formerly," Christopher Gadsden thought, "the sons of Britain would have been thinly, very thinly, scattered on this side [of] the Atlantic ocean. It might indeed have been *then* fixed on, *very properly*, as a place to transport her [Britain's] convicts to, but surely no free men, on such conditions, would have ever thought of coming to America." John Dickinson may have taken the argument the furthest, contending that the migration expectation placed colonial rights beyond the reach of Parliament.[22]

A corollary principle to the expectation thesis was that rights derived from the authority of migration were property inheritable by progenies. The first settlers had brought "as inherent in their Persons, all the Rights and Liberties of natural-born Subjects within the Parent State," New Jersey's Assembly told George III. Now those rights and liberties were "vested in the People of this Colony."[23]

THE PURPOSE OF MIGRATION

One way — perhaps the most persuasive way — to prove the expectation of the first settlers was to learn their purpose for migration. It was, an agent for Massachusetts explained to a secretary of state, for "the preservation" "of the priviledges of Englishmen" "intire and uncontrouled" that "the Forefathers of the present inhabitants preferr'd an inhospitable desart to their native Soil."[24] The first settlers were both driven "from their native land" by "the effect of tyranny and oppression,"[25] and left voluntarily "not only to enlarge the *British* Empire and extend its Commerce, but to enjoy that perfect Security of Liberty to which they were entitled as *British* Subjects in their native Land."[26] The archloyalist, Thomas Hutchinson, even claimed that "[t]he first planters of the Massachusetts Colony removed to America, expecting there to enjoy civil and religious liberty to a GREATER DEGREE than their fellow-subjects at that time enjoyed it in England."[27] There were a number of political theorists who agreed with Hutchinson, saying that although the first settlers were primarily interested in preserving "all the civil Rights and Liberties of British Subjects," they anticipated enjoying those rights to a fuller perfection. That was especially true in the area of law, as one objective of the migration was to become "freed from the Oppression of ecclesiastical Courts, as well as from some particular Customs, Tenures, and Usages, which by the common and Statute Law were confined to certain Districts in England."[28]

This historical argument was used by whigs to support a legal conclusion so important that writers on the imperial side felt it necessary to dispute the factual evidence.[29] It was irrelevant whether aspects of either side's history were inaccurate or were a partial selecting of favorable evidence that ignored contrary data, for it was not history but law that was in dispute. It was at best forensic history, if history at all, and was not intended to prove a historical lesson but to support a legal conclusion. That conclusion appeared obvious to John Erskine, a Scottish theologian. "Trade was the object of England in encouraging colonies," Erskine wrote. "A love of freedom was the chief motive of the adventurers. They must therefore have been idiots, if they had become Colonists, on condition that every shilling they gained might lawfully be taken from them, and armed men set over them to govern every action." It may be that some constitutional theorists would have pushed the argument further, saying that, due to the purpose of the migration, Americans were entitled to more than British rights: that the migration had added to the privileges they owned. "We have, indeed, been told," a political writer for London's *Gentlemen's Magazine* observed, "that having fled to that country from oppression, their migration, as it argued in them a love, so it gave them a title to freedom superior to their fellow subjects who remained at home."[30]

THE EQUALITY OF MIGRATION

The theory that the migration was authority for "superior" rights was not an American doctrine. More modest in their constitutional pretensions, colonial assemblies employed the migration principle not to create rights but to support their claim to existing rights. They primarily used the migration principle to reinforce the right to an equality of rights with the British people. As both New Jersey and North Carolina legislators told George III, "The subjects thus emigrating, brought with them, as inherent in their persons, all the rights and liberty of natural-born subjects within the parent-state."[31] The principle that the migration was an authority for equality of rights was stated many times by official American bodies, perhaps never more fully than by the Assembly of Jamaica, a colony that did not rebel. The "settlers of the first colonies" of North America had been the equals of their fellow English subjects, the Assembly resolved. "[T]herefore the people of England had no rights, power, or privilege, to give to the emigrants; as these were, at the time of their emigration, possessed of all such rights, equally with themselves."[32]

Again, we have encountered a constitutional contention that was neither new nor *sui generis* to the American controversy. The equality of the Irish with the British had often been pleaded on the authority of the migration principle.[33] Stated in its strongest form, the principle would have made the migration itself an authority for equal rights. That, at least, was the view of a Scottish writer who contended that "certain natural, unalienable, and exclusive rights, privileges, and exemptions, are annexed to emigration, although the emigrants continue to acknowledge a subjection to the mother-state." American whigs did not reject this theory of rights by annexation to migration, but they did not claim it, either. Like the assertion that migration was authority for superior rights, it went beyond the constitutional position they were defending. It was sufficient for their case to have the authority of migration prop up the right to an equality of rights, as the New Hampshire lower house argued on telling the king that the early settlers "bro't over with them their Natural allegiance to the Crown of England with an inseperable unalienable Right to all that Protection of their Liberty and Property to which all Liege Subjects of the British Empire are Intituled."[34]

CHAPTER FIFTEEN

THE MIGRATION PURCHASE

We are not quite done with the migration concept. It was important in one other respect, one also involving disputes of fact leading to a conclusion of constitutional law. The initial argument came from the imperial side of the debate, when defenders of parliamentary supremacy claimed that the American colonies were in Great Britain's debt, as the mother country had financed their settlement, furnished their populations, and protected them from foreign enemies. This debt provided Great Britain with constitutional justification both to tax the colonies and, for purposes of imperial supervision, to exercise some police power curtailing what would otherwise be autonomous American civil rights. The colonies answered the taxation part of this argument by pleading the settlement and commercial contracts, contending that the constitution provided methods of paying London other than by submission to parliamentary rule. To defend their claim to rights, they also cited the facts of migration, most particularly the theme that the migration was a purchase by which they had resecured title to the rights they possessed.

The facts of the migration purchase were summarized by the second Continental Congress, in "the declaration of the causes for taking up arms."

Our forefathers, inhabitants of the island of Great-Britain, left their native land, to seek on these shores a residence for civil and religious freedom. At the expense of their blood, at the hazard of their fortunes, without the least charge to the country from which they removed, by unceasing labour, and an unconquerable spirit, they effected settlements in the distant and inhospitable wilds of America, then filled with numerous and warlike nations of barbarians.— Societies or governments, vested with perfect legislatures, were formed under charters from the crown, and an harmonious intercourse was established between the colonies and the kingdom from which they derived their origin. The mutual benefits of this union became in a short time so extraordinary, as to excite astonishment. It is universally confessed, that the amazing increase of the wealth, strength, and navigation of the realm, arose from this source; and the minister [William Pitt], who . . . directed the measures of Great-Britain in the late war, publicly declared, that these colonies enabled her to triumph over her enemies.

The doctrine of constitutional law following from these facts was that American civil and religious rights had been secured by purchase. In an extreme statement of the theory, the people of Gloucester, Massachusetts, thought the migration alone, without conferring benefits on Britain, was enough to complete the purchase. "[T]he first settlers of this country," they voted, "left their native land and came into this, when a wild uncultivated wilderness, inhabited by no human creatures except Savages, and suffered extreme hardships, risqued their lives and spent their fortunes to obtain and secure their civil and ecclesiastical liberties and privileges. . . ."[1]

The Cost of Migration

The factual dispute needs little summary. Imperialists maintained that the settlement of North America had been costly to the mother country in population lost, protection offered, and various services rendered, most particularly financial. That settlement debt gave Great Britain a claim on the colonies, including constitutional authority to enforce repayment. The American answer was that no colonies except Georgia and Nova Scotia had received any aid, neither monetary nor military, at the time of settlement. New York had been obtained from the Dutch in exchange for Surinam and those three instances, whigs said, were the only financial claim Great Britain had on the colonies except for assistance in war and protection for their trade at sea, two items Americans paid for by permitting Parliament to regulate trade under the commercial contract.[2] "Nor have these colonies since [the conquest of New York], been any expence to the crown, either for support of their governments, or inhabitants," Connecticut's Moses Mather contended in a frequently repeated argument. "And the Americans have had no enemies but what were equally the enemies of Great-Britain; nor been engaged in any war, but what the nation was equally engaged in, except the wars with the Indians; which they carried on and maintained themselves."[3]

That twentieth-century historians have resolved the disputed facts on one side or the other[4] is irrelevant. Once again it is important to realize that what looks like an argument about historical data and its interpretation did not concern history. The dispute was about law. It is quite probable that the question of fact might easily have been resolved had it not been for the conclusion of law it supported. To sustain the conclusion that they favored, people prejudged the factual question and there could never have been agreement about the history even had history been pertinent. After all, resolution of the facts would have been of no importance except for the constitutional principle each side sought to establish. Yet the argument about historical facts — better called forensic facts — is important to keep in mind, for it explains why certain statements were phrased in the wording that they were. An example is Joseph Warren's 1775 Boston Massacre oration:

> The crown of England looked with indifference on the contest; our ancestors were left alone to combat with the natives. Nor is there any reason to believe, that it ever was intended by the one party, or expected by the other, that the *grantor* should defend and maintain the *grantees* in the peaceable possession of the lands named in the patents. And it appears plainly, from the history of those times, that neither the prince, nor the people of England, thought themselves much interested in the matter. They had not then any idea of a thousandth part of those advantages which they since *have*, and we are most heartily willing they should *still continue* to reap from us.

Warren's argument would have made little sense had London not been claiming it was owed a settlement debt. Why did he bother saying that the mother country owed the colonies no protection and why did he admit that Great Britain was entitled to unanticipated "advantages" from the commercial contract? These questions would have had no point had Warren been reciting history rather than arguing facts supporting the migration purchase of rights.[5]

There is no need to go further into the factual dispute. It is the legal conclusion that interests us. From the historical record, as they interpreted it, American whigs drew two constitutional conclusions. The first was that the colonies owed Great Britain nothing "for any defence or protection from the first planting the country to this moment, but on the contrary, a balance is due to us from our exertions in the general cause." The second is the one that concerns us, as it raised the topic of this chapter, the migration purchase. It was articulated by the town meeting of Wallingford, Connecticut, during the Stamp Act crisis. "[I]t appears from ancient records and other memorials of incontestable validity," Wallingford voted, "that our ancestors with a great sum purchased said township: at their only expence, planted, with great peril possessed and defended the same." Or, in a more elaborate form, the claim was to a purchase that became inheritable property. That claim was made eight years later in the famous Suffolk resolves. "[W]hereas this, then savage and uncultivated desert, was purchased by the toil and treasure, or acquired by the valor and blood of those, our venerable progenitors, who bequeathed to us the dear bought inheritance, who consigned it to our care and protection; the most sacred obligations are upon us to transmit the glorious purchase, unfettered by power, unclogged with shackles, to our innocent and beloved offspring."[6]

THE PHYSICAL PURCHASE

Again, a point must be made that has been made before, a point that probably could be ignored if it were not so often assumed that the American revolutionaries originated many of their constitutional arguments. Few were original with them and that is certainly true for the legal concept of purchased rights. It came straight out of British constitutional thought. The English had often talked of purchasing liberties and rights. The 1648 declaration of the county of Dorset called "our Liberties" the "purchase of our ancestors' blood," and in 1768 a pamphleteer called on his fellow Britons to defend "their liberties, which their fore-fathers purchased with seas of blood."[7]

The American case was expressed in exactly the same terms as the British but generally referred to different facts. A Londoner writing in 1764 about "that sacred English liberty, handed down to us by our ancestors, at the expence of their blood and treasure,"[8] was referring to the English civil wars, to the struggles by Parliament against the prerogative, and to individuals such as John Hampden and Algernon Sidney. Americans claimed to be heirs of the same legacy, and of another, more recent purchase. That special, colonial, migration purchase was argued on three distinct sets of facts. Two were physical purchases, one from the Indians and the other by hardship. The third was a value-added purchase, by which Americans had increased the wealth, strength, and glory of the British Empire.

The purchase from the aboriginal natives was the least important, but still significant to the constitutional argument. Colonial whigs generally made two contentions: (1) the original settlers, not the British government, made the purchase; and (2) the transaction had not only been for the soil but "with it the jurisdiction of the country."[9]

The chief American whig claim of purchasing rights was not by money from the natives but by the physical difficulties of migration. Even if the colonists did not have a right to liberty in some other way, John Adams wrote, "our fathers have earned it and bought it for us, at the expence of their ease, their estates, their pleasure and their blood." They had done it by the migration, the people of Salem were told, "they undautedly exposed themselves to every kind of hardship, and bravely met death in the high places of the field, that they might secure to you a quiet possession of those rights and liberties, which as men, as Englishmen, and as Christians, they knew you were entitled to." The first settlers relied on having these rights acknowledged in return for the migration. It may be because of their reliance that some whigs argued that the greater the hardship or the greater the suffering they endured, the stronger their tenure in the rights purchased. They had, in John Dickinson's words, "*purchased an inheritance . . . at a prodigious price.*"[10]

The constitutional theory may not be fully persuasive, but the argument was seriously made and deserves to be seriously evaluated. It is simply wrong to say that when New England towns passed resolutions reciting the dangers and bravery of the first generation that they were boasting that "their ancestors had been heroes." They were, rather, explaining an authority — purchase — upon which they based part of their constitutional claim to civil rights. It is for that reason that clergymen preached of "dearly purchased privileges," of "valuable, dear-bought rights," of "liberties" that "our fathers dearly bought" and that "descend to us in a patrimony purchased at their expense," and of "the dear bought patrimony of our pious, noble spirited ancestors, which they have procured for us, at an immense cost of treasure and blood." One newly settled town in Maine stated the legal theory with sufficient clarity to show that the purpose was to maintain property and rights. Other communities might argue that they had inherited rights from forebears who had settled a howling wilderness,

> But the People of this Town of Gorham have an Argument still nearer at hand: Not only may we say that we enjoy an Inheritance purchased

by the Blood of our Forefathers, but this Town was settled at the
Expence of our own Blood! We have those amongst us, whose Blood
streaming from their own Wounds watered the Soil from which we
earn our Bread! Our Ears have heard the infernall Yells of the native
Savage Murderers — Our Eyes have seen our young Children welter-
ing in their Gore, in our own Houses. . . .

The General Court of Massachusetts stated the legal theory explicitly in
1764 when it issued a "Brief State" of the "Exertions and Expences" of
Massachusetts "in the common Cause." The statement was made for one
purpose only, the legislators explained. It was not to boast or gain advantage, or to obtain new grants. "They desire only that the Privileges their
Ancestors purchased so dearly, and they have never forfeited, may be continued to them."[11]

These colonists were boasting of rights purchased, not of ancestors to
be admired. That was what a writer in the *Gentlemen's Magazine*, most
likely not an American, meant when he told Lord North that the colonists had rights "to purchase which their forefathers endured the greatest distress, and lived content in unfrequented woods, divested of all the
comforts and necessaries of life." That was also what the town of Concord meant, just over a year before it was the scene of battle, when its
voters spoke of "the sole purchase, and glorious product of the heroic
Enterprises of the first Settlers of these American Colonies."[12]

THE VALUE-ADDED PURCHASE

"Purchase" was one word describing how Americans had acquired title
to their rights or how they established the authority for claiming those
rights. A second word was "compensation." "These rights belong to us,"
an American wrote of British liberties, "we may claim them in compensation for the most substantial services done to the mother country." A
third word was "consideration." "[T]he Colonists," Pennsylvania's House
of Assembly pointed out, "have paid a valuable Consideration to the
Crown for the said Charter and Laws, by planting and improving a Wilderness, far distant from their Mother Country, at a vast Expense, and
the Risk of many Lives from the savage Inhabitants, whereby they have
greatly encreased the Trade and Commerce of the Nation, and added
a large Tract of improved Country to the Crown, without any Aid from,
or Expence to, *Great-Britain* in the said Settlement."[13]

The value-added argument repeated the migration-purchase facts with
the additional claim that by settling the colonies, Americans of every

generation had increased the dominions, strength, and wealth of the mother country. As early as 1691, Increase Mather asserted that it had been understood that a consideration — or, at least, an expectation — for enriching Great Britain would be the preservation of colonial rights.[14] Expectation was one argument for establishing the consideration. Another was payment — that Americans had earned the rights they possessed. They had done so, the New York Assembly resolved, "by giving an almost boundless Extent to the *British* Empire, expanding its Trade, increasing its Wealth, and augmenting that Power which renders it so formidable to all *Europe*."[15]

There were two other arguments that are of interest, the first because of the man who made it, Thomas Hutchinson. An important way that the colonies had added to the value of the mother country, Hutchinson pointed out, had been their contributions to the defeat of France. He thought the wars against the French strengthened American claims to having paid for an equality of rights. The second argument, made by New Jersey's House of Representatives, attributed the increased wealth that Great Britain received from the colonies not to territory, trade, or victory in warfare, but to the fact that Americans possessed the rights that they did. It was because Americans enjoyed the rights they did that Britain enjoyed its prosperity.[16]

Exponents of imperial rule rejected these arguments. It was beside the point, they said, that Great Britain had reaped benefits from the colonies. What else could be expected? "It should be considered that the object of colonization is not merely to form new towns, which shall call us the Mother country; but to extend our *commerce*, our *resources*, our means of *wealth* — of *Empire*, upon our own terms. If this is not done, our title to America is a *vain name*, and nothing more." There were also imperialists who rejected outright the historical argument on which the value-added purchase was premised, and assumed a history opposite to the one American whigs assumed. The colonies, Samuel Johnson insisted, "were settled under English protection; were constituted by an English charter; and have been defended by English arms." There were, of course, imperialists who knew history better than Johnson. They accepted the American whig argument of facts but did not think the American conclusion of law followed from those facts. "The risques, *they say, they have run in making their settlements* cannot, as they pretend, be admitted as done with a view of *serving the mother country*," one writer observed.[17] John Gray's answer was more to the point, and might have been sustained had the question whether the value-added purchase was an authority for American rights been argued in a court competent to rule on the imperial constitution. "The conditions of that tenure," Gray

contended, "are no ways altered on account of the hardships and difficulties which the first settlers had to struggle with, any more than the
unexpected difficulties and disappointments that miners meet with, give
them a fuller right or title to the ore when found, than they had originally from their lease."[18]

CHAPTER SIXTEEN

THE ORIGINAL CONTRACT

Language is again the focus of our attention. "Contract" was another word that was used on both sides of the Atlantic; we must ask why it was used and what it meant. "Contract" was one of the most common and useful terms employed by people in the eighteenth century to express thoughts about constitutionalism and to describe the limits on government. A political commentator, seeking ways to remove placemen and pensioners from Parliament, defined the British constitution as if it had come out of contractarian theory and not from immemorial custom. "[T]he constitution of England," he suggested, "is nothing more than a solemn compact between king and people, for the mutual happiness and support of both." In New York, Alexander Hamilton used the same word but made a much broader statement of constitutional principle when he wrote that "the origin of all civil government, justly established, must be a voluntary compact between the rulers and the ruled."[1]

There are puzzles surrounding the term "contract" in the historical literature. One is why its use is so often referred to as Lockean or why the notion that government rests on a contract between the governors and the governed should be called a whig principle. Neither Locke nor the whigs originated it. In law it can be traced through English history to Anglo-Saxon times. On being sentenced to death, Charles I was reminded that as king he had been bound by "a contract and a bargain," and Parliament based the forced abdication of James II on the grounds that he had violated the "original contract." Perhaps the thought is that Locke popularized among Americans the idea of a contract, not that he originated it. Even so, it is not clear why the notion is Lockean rather than common law or constitutional. It had been a basic legal doctrine of the English constitution long before John Locke was born.[2]

Another puzzle is why so many students of the American Revolution who tell us that the concept of contract had significance in the revolutionary debates treat the distinction between the contracts as if it were of no importance, seldom telling their readers whether they are discussing the social contract or the original contract. No eighteenth-century lawyer wishing to be understood would have ignored the difference and eighteenth-century commentators on contract theory wrote distinctly enough that the two are kept separate in most writings.

The social contract is not the original contract; the two are quite different. Sir William Blackstone was one of many participants in the revolutionary argument who denied there was such a thing as a social contract, but accepted the original contract as a demonstrable source of constitutional authority. The same was true for those colonial whigs who bothered to mentioned the social contract. Gordon Wood was correct when he observed that "this Lockean notion of a social contract was not generally drawn upon by Americans in their dispute with Great Britain, for it had little relevance in explaining either the nature of their colonial charters or their relationship to the empire."[3] What Wood could have added was that there was probably no notion more relevant to those questions than the original contract.

Most eighteenth-century political writers are clear. When we read them we know which contract they mean. Quite often they draw the distinction.[4] The fact that the difference was universally understood increases the puzzle about Locke, as Locke is one of the few writers who is said to have confused the two contracts into one or to have interpreted the original contract more as a trust deed than an exchange of reciprocal promises.[5]

The social contract is the supposed agreement under which people depart from the state of nature and enter into society. Sometimes called the "contract of society," it was described by Burlamaqui as the first covenant "by which each individual engages with all the rest to join for ever in one body, and to regulate, with one common consent, whatever regards their preservation and their common security."[6]

The original contract, the only one of these two contracts of importance to the revolutionary controversy, was the agreement about the nature, the limits, and the location of legitimate power. "In fine," Burlamaqui added, "when once the form of government is settled, there must be another covenant, whereby after having pitched upon one or more persons to be invested with the power of governing, those on whom this supreme authority is conferred, engage to consult most carefully the common security and advantage, and the others promise fidelity and allegiance to the sovereign." It has also been called the contract of government, the contract of submission, and the governmental contract. In law the most apt description would be the constitutional contract. In the eighteenth century, however, with a uniformity uncharacteristic of that age, it was always called the original contract.[7]

THE THEORY OF CONTRACT

The original-contract theory is of absolute importance for understanding the constitutional controversy leading up to the American Revolution. It was not, however, of equal significance to every issue. On the question of Parliament's authority to tax the colonies, it was of some significance but not much. By contrast, there was no doctrine of more importance to the whigs' case against Parliament's authority to legislate for the colonies. The reason is that the original contract was a legal theory limiting the legitimate power of the state. That also explains why it has some bearing on the question of the authority for rights. Rights existed not only as positive possessions, but as restraints on government. Yet the original contract is by no means as important to rights as to coercive lawmaking, and does not merit the same analysis and extensive discussion it must receive in a volume on the constitutionality of parliamentary legislation. What is said in this chapter is directed solely at contractarian authority for rights. It is a much less extensive body of material than that relating to the original contract as a limitation on the sovereign command. Even so, the authority of the original contract is of great interest, for there was no other authority for rights so uncomplicated and such a direct authority for civil rights. "Let it be observed, that the *privileges* we claim are not the *grants* of *Princes*," someone wrote of Irish rights in 1783, "they are ORIGINAL *rights*, conditions of the original CONTRACTS, coequal with *prerogative*, and coeval with our *government*." An author considering the rights of the British against the East India Company stated the same authority as one of four alternatives. "[T]he innate rights and privileges of Englishmen," he wrote, are "the rights to which all men are entitled by the laws of nature, and of which Englishmen are in possession by the constitution of the government, by national compact and the laws of civil society."[8]

The emphasis of the original-contract theory was on the protection of rights by limiting government rather than on the creation of rights. The very idea of the contract restrained power. That was why, Elisha Williams claimed in a 1744 New England pamphlet, no power over religious matters could be entrusted to the civil magistrate "by any original Compact which is truly supposed the Foundation of all civil Government." By the original contract, John Dickinson said, writing legislative instructions, the prerogative could "not intrench any farther on our *natural* liberties, than is expedient for the maintenance of our *civil*." Dickinson was quoting Sir William Blackstone, who believed the British king confined by constitutional bounds so certain "that it is impossible he should ever exceed them, without the consent of the people, on the one hand; or without, on the other, a violation of that original contract, which in all states impliedly, and in ours most expressly, subsists between the prince and the subject."[9]

The theory was that, as the king received no more power than stipulated by the contracting parties, he could have "no right to abet tyranny, or usurpation on the rights of the people." The same was true for Parliament. It could "never be legally authorised by this constitution to enact such statutes as are subversive of those rights, which, by the laws of nature, and of the social compact of Englishmen they are entitled to enjoy." James Iredell, a future United States Supreme Court justice, also interpreted the original contract as a severe check on power, and, applying the concept to the colonies, thought the check itself a right. "*Our original Contract*," Iredell wrote, "stipulates Sovereignty on the one side; Liberty on the other. That happy kind of Monarchy, which reserves just power enough to the Crown to make it useful and respectable, but not enough to enable it to despise the people whom it governs, was instituted in America."[10]

Legal theorists of the eighteenth century, unlike their counterparts in the twentieth century, did not make the existence of a long list of rights a test of liberty. People were free if not subject to arbitrary government. There were, however, at least three rights essential to nonarbitrary government. To be free, people had to possess the rights of trial by jury, due process of law, and some form of representation through which "consent" could be expressed. What the eighteenth century did stress rather than specific rights were tests of "good" or "right" or "legal" or "just" or "legitimate" government. The primary test was that government not be "arbitrary." A secondary test was that it be based on contract. One definition of "just" government was that it had been created by contract. "[A]ll Government of Right originates from the People, is founded in Compact only, and instituted solely for the Good of the Whole," the Delaware Declaration of Rights provided in 1776. "[A]ll legal Government," John Dickinson added that same year, "must be founded on express or implied Compact." A government by compact, the preacher of Connecticut's 1738 election sermon had exclaimed, "is the most Ordinary and the most Regular Government." The original contract was something "which in the very Nature of free Governments must be supposed," a "Freeholder" told the *Maryland Gazette* ten years later.[11]

It was commonly expressed theory that the only two bases for legitimate rule were compact and conquest. The legal explanation was that people on entering into society and then forming government, with first the social and then the original contracts, do so to retain natural rights. Hence, the contract is formed to maintain and secure rights, not to abridge them, and cannot be other than a basis for limited, nonarbitrary, and therefore "legitimate" government.[12]

The Reality of Contract

There were always constitutional commentators who thought the concept of contract to be historical and legal nonsense.[13] There were others who seem to have thought the existence of the original contract could be historically proven.[14] This argument need not concern us, for whether the contract was fact or fiction, its importance to this study is limited to its authority for the existence of rights independent of sovereign power. And that is the point, for if we ask what the eighteenth-century legal mind believed, we will find that historical proof was irrelevant; constitutional acceptance was what mattered. Whether or not the original contract was a historical fiction, it was a constitutional reality. And, because of the need to protect rights, it was real. William Paley, for one, knew both that the original contract was a fiction and that there were constitutional rights that the people possessed.

> But the truth is, that in the books, and in the apprehension of those who deduce our civil rights and obligations *a pactis*, the original contract is appealed to and treated of as a reality. Whenever the disciples of this system speak of the constitution; . . . of laws being constitutional or unconstitutional; of inherent, unalienable, inextinguishable rights, either in the prince, or the people; or indeed by any laws, usages, or civil rights, as transcending the authority of the

subsisting legislature, or professing a force and sanction superior to what belong to the modern acts and edicts of the legislature, they secretly refer us to what passed at the original convention.[15]

Theory must be cited to explain theory. The law needed the original contract if jurisprudence was to define limited government. The "whole Scheme" of the British constitution would have "been one monstrous Absurdity, unless an *original Contract* had been supposed," the *Craftsman* argued. "They have been blinded therefore by Ignorance, or Passion, or Prejudice, who did not always see that there is such a Thing necessarily, and in the very Nature of our *Constitution*; and that They might as well doubt whether the Foundations of an ancient, solid Building were suited and proportion'd to the Elevation and Form of it, as whether our *Constitution* was establish'd by *Composition* and *Contract*." The original contract was the "very nature" of the constitution, an anonymous author observed, because when people "put themselves under their several respective Forms of Government, . . . there is a Tacit Contract suppos'd in the very nature of the Trust itself. . . . [S]o where-ever any Government is, this Tacit Contract is necessarily suppos'd to go along with it, as being founded in the very nature of the thing." The purpose of the original contract was, therefore, what Samuel Johnson in 1683 had called the "National Covenant." It told a man that he lived in England rather than in Turkey, and "whether he and his Children were born Freemen or Slaves."[16]

THE TERMS OF THE CONTRACT

Of all Europe's peoples, the English probably knew their contract best. They had enforced it enough times, most recently against James II.[17] They could trace its terms from the pledge of King Canute that he would rule by the laws of Edgar, to the coronation oath of George III. "The coronation oath importeth on the part of the king, a public *solemn recognition of the fundamental rights of the people*," the *London Magazine* claimed in 1765, the year of the Stamp Act. A discussion of the contract's stipulations, written by a colonist during the era of the American Revolution, comes from John Tucker's Massachusetts election sermon for 1771. Tucker was describing the British government as colonial whigs wanted it to be.

Its constitutional laws are comprized in *Magna-Charta*, or the great charter of the nation. This contains, in general, the liberties and privileges of the people, and is, *virtually*, a compact between the King and them; the reigning Prince, explicitly engaging, by solemn

oath, to govern according to the laws: — Beyond the extent of these
then, or contrary to them, he can have no rightful authority at all.

Tucker was speaking of the original contract, the constitutional contract
of the British government. He was not talking about the American variation of the contract, the original colonial contract (which will be introduced in the next chapter), which was the instrument most colonists referred to when they wrote about contract.[18]

Tucker was a bit unusual in one respect. He found the terms of the
original contract in one document, Magna Carta. Other constitutional
commentators did the same, taking Magna Carta as the model for implied terms, not citing it for its specific provisions, an English constitutional tradition that will be discussed in chapter 19. It was seldom,
however, that Magna Carta, the Petition of Right, or any other English
constitutional document was said to be the contract. If anything revealed
the stipulations of the contract, it was not any of the great landmarks
of English liberty but the Coronation Oath. And even then the conditions were not negotiated but rather the contract was made, as Josiah
Tucker pointed out, when the king "took a solemn Oath to govern his
People according to Law; and when they on their Parts expressed their
Consent to his Accession to the Throne by loud Huzzas, and Shouts of
Joy." The promise to govern by the law was a general pledge, yet more
specific than it would be if made today. It meant not just statutes promulgated — due process and the rule of law — but rule by established custom, a right to governance restrained by usage. Custom and usage were
identified not only by the past social and legal practices of the English
and Scottish nations, but by the tenured rights of the people. Put another
way, the terms of the original contract were found by the same method
as the constitution of Great Britain and the common law of England were
found: by custom.[19]

CHAPTER SEVENTEEN

THE ORIGINAL
COLONIAL CONTRACT

The doctrine that the terms of the original contract were found in governmental usage provides one explanation why English constitutional history does not contain chapters about contract renegotiations, renewals, amendments, or novations. The revolutionary settlement enacted by Parliament when bestowing the throne on William and Mary was, in constitutional theory, evidence of constitutional custom, not a new original contract. The one new original contract postulated in British constitutional lore was the contract made by English settlers emigrating to Ireland or to the American colonies. This contract can be called by several names: the migration contract, the settlement contract, the second original contract, the original American contract, or the original colonial contract.

When considering this second original contract it is well to keep in mind certain distinctions. Not every claim to usage or to contract is a claim related to the original colonial contract. When the people of Richmond County, Virginia, asserted the right to be taxed only by a local assembly, and based their claim on the authority of "Charter, natural Justice, and constant Usage, ever since their first Settlement in America," they cited three distinct authorities for rights, none of which was a contract unless they meant the charter to be evidence of the original colonial contract. When the first Continental Congress told the British people that the colonists claimed the "same fair inheritance" of rights as did they, "guarantied by the plighted faith of government and the most solemn compacts with British Sovereigns," it was citing the authority of contract, but the original contract, not the second or original colonial contract. When, however, the voters of Westerly, Rhode Island, said that their ancestors had migrated to New England "upon express conditions that all their natural, civil, and religious rights and privileges should be secured to them and their heirs forever," they were relying on the authority of the original colonial contract.[1]

What the voters of Westerly meant was explained by Massachusetts' Samuel Cooke. The original colonial contract, Cooke said, consisted of the conditions "which their fore-fathers, the first occupants made, and asserted as the terms of their removal with their effects, into this wilderness." Even more, these conditions were obligatory, Virginia's Richard Bland wrote, elaborating on the constitutional theory. "[T]he Terms of the Compact must be obligatory and binding upon the Parties; they must be the Magna Charta, the fundamental Principles of Government, to this new Society; and every Infringement of them must be wrong, and may be opposed."[2]

Once more we are encountering what was the constitutional norm for American whigs, a legal argument that was not *sui generis*, but well established in the polemics of imperial legal debate. The Irish had been making it for years. In 1775, at a time when all attention was focused on the original American contract, a pamphlet was printed in Dublin reminding readers that the first English emigrants to Ireland had made a compact with the Crown retaining their civil rights under the English constitution. The original colonial contract was not even a new argument in North America. It had been pleaded in the colonies following the New England rebellion against the prerogative taxation imposed by Governor Edmund Andros. John Palmer, the most competent common lawyer in Andros's administration, defended prerogative taxes on grounds that North America was conquered territory and subject to prerogative decrees. Edward Rawson, answering Palmer, denied the fact of conquest, and countered with the original colonial contract, stating it in terms close to those asserted by American whigs eighty years later.

> [T]here was *an Original Contract* between the King and the first Planters in *New-England*, the King promising them, if they at their own cost and charge would subdue a Wilderness, and enlarge his Dominions, they and their Posterity after them should enjoy such

Priviledges as are in their Charters expressed, of which that of not
having Taxes imposed on them without their own consent was one.[3]

Rawson is not as clear as we would wish. It may be that he would
have limited the original colonial contract to rights stated or implied in
the colonial charters. If so, his rule of construction was narrower than
that adopted by most Americans who considered the question. They
would have found the terms of the contract in a much wider range of
evidence — actual statements made by or on behalf of the Crown, the conditions of migration, the understanding, expressed or implied, of the emigrants, and subsequent government practice and legal custom. From the
twentieth-century perspective, this proof appears difficult to obtain and
easily challenged on grounds of relevancy or directness. The eighteenth-
century constitutional mind apparently thought any of the contracts readily proven. "However difficult," James Wilson wrote, "it may be in other
states, to prove an original contract, consisting in any other manner, and
on any other conditions, than are naturally and necessarily implied in
the very idea of the first institution of a state; it is the easiest thing imaginable to prove it in our constitution and to ascertain some of the material
articles of which it consists." Wilson was referring to the original contract in British constitutional law. Daniel Dulany, Jr., thought it was even
easier to prove the original colonial contract. "The Origins of other Governments," he explained, "is covered by the Veil of Antiquity, and is
differently traced by the Fancies of different Men; but, of the Colonies,
the Evidence of it is as clear and unequivocal as of any other Facts."[4]

The Implied Colonial Contract

Perhaps Wilson and Dulany were unusual in thinking the original contracts easily proven. They were not, however, unusual in thinking there
had been contracts. Almost everyone who mentioned the subject accepted
the doctrine of the original contract. What they disagreed about was
whether the contract was real or implied, and what its provisions were.
It is impossible to say whether more Americans thought the contract real
rather than implied, or whether many even thought about the question
or thought the answer to be of significance. Whether real or implied,
it was the same contract, for the terms were deduced from the same evidence. Still, the legal premises were somewhat different, as were the arguments proving the contract. The two theories should be discussed
separately, taking the implied contract first.

James Iredell, like Wilson a future United States Supreme Court justice, formulated one of the best explanations for implying the original colonial contract.[5] The provinces of British North America, he wrote, were

> Colonies planted originally by men emigrating from their own country, where they unhappily feared freedom was near losing its existence, in search of this desired blessing among woods and deserts, which they thought preferable to all kinds of ease and luxury enjoyed by a humiliating tenure; increased by the surprising industry of the first settlers, and by the blessing of Providence, to an amazing degree, and come at length to enjoy a pretty comfortable state of maintenance, secured to them, as they fondly hoped, by sanctions of a most sacred and inviolable nature. In these possessions they long lived easy and happy, flattering themselves that they should be permitted to enjoy freely property procured for them by the severe labor and virtue of their ancestors, and that the valuable blessings of the British Constitution, bestowed on them by their charters, would never be infringed.

The two elements creating the implied contract were encouragement by the Crown and reliance on the part of the emigrants. "[T]hese colonies," the Stamp Act Congress told George III, "were originally planted by subjects of the British crown, who, animated with the spirit of liberty, encouraged by your Majesty's royal predecessors, and confiding in the public faith for the enjoyment of all the rights and liberties essential to freedom." The Congress was saying that there were two aspects to the royal encouragement. The first was the encouragement itself, which was given in anticipation of reaping the benefits of the migration. Maryland, for example, had been settled by people whom its Lower House of Assembly claimed had been "encouraged by the Crown to transplant themselves hither, for the Sake of improving and enlarging It's Dominions; which . . . has been in a great Measure obtained."[6]

The second aspect of the royal encouragement cited by the Stamp Act Congress was the settlers' confidence in the "public faith" of the mother country. The migrants, the Massachusetts House said, came to North America with royal consent, "which we humbly apprehend involves the consent of the nation." This consent, of course, was also implied, a writer for the *Boston Evening-Post* explained. "If we suppose the King to act in behalf of the whole English nation, which having, by laws of its own making conferred that office upon him, is bound to abide by, and acknowledge his actions in their behalf, as their own; then there will be an implied contract virtually subsisting, between the King & the nation

on the one part, & the adventurers for settling the colonies, on the other."
That was an American whig argument, not a British one. By the 1760s,
the king no longer possessed authority to bind the nation in this way. In
1630, when Massachusetts was settled, it may be that he had had authority, but that was irrelevant in British legal thinking. Constitutional principles were applied anachronistically. To judge in 1765 the constitutionality of actions that had occurred in 1630, the law of 1765 was applied,
not the law of 1630. If the king could not bind the nation in 1765, he
could not have bound it in 1630. It did not matter that at that time the
Crown generally barred Parliament from colonial affairs. According to
the legal theory of 1765, consent of the nation had to come from Parliament, either by direct vote expressing or implying consent or by some
legislation implying acquiescence in the king's actions.[7]

The second element implying the original colonial contract was the
expectation of the migrants. The probative fact was not just that they
had left home to settle a new empire, but that they did so with specific
expectations. The freeholders of Roxbury, Massachusetts, argued that the
first settlers "seated themselves in this howling wilderness, that they might
here quietly enjoy Liberty Civil and Religious." A contention made over
and over was that the first settlers had thought in terms of contract, and
of implied offer and acceptance. Surely, the argument went, they would
not have ventured "their lives and estates in this *desert* land without some
security against any encroachment on this *inestimable part* of their mother
constitution." The implied fact was drawn from a conclusion some constitutional commentators thought undeniable. "[W]hat Englishmen in
their right Wits," both Edward Rawson and Increase Mather had asked
in the 1690s, would have come over to North America "if their Reward
after all must be to be deprived of their *English Liberties?*" Three-quarters
of a century later, in 1776, following passage of the Declaratory Act in
which Parliament promulgated its authority to bind the colonies by legislation "in all cases whatsoever," a New Hampshire newspaper asked the
same question. "Can any body believe, that our ancestors came over to
America upon the terms of Britain's binding them by law (or having a
right to do so) in all cases whatever, or that since being here, they or
their posterity have at any period of time, made so foolish and wicked
a bargain?"[8]

The probative fact that was argued was that the first settlers would
not have migrated but for the expectation. The legal principle cited to
make the fact binding was reliance. To encourage settlement, the government either had held out the prospect of enjoying English rights, or had
said nothing, implying that English rights would be enjoyed. In terms
of law, the expectation had been an inducement for migration, the first

generation of Americans and those who came in later years had acted on that inducement, and the contract had been executed.[9]

The original migration or settlement was the consideration paid by the colonists. "[I]n consideration of settling the desart," Philip Livingston explained, the king promised "that he would protect the settlers and their dependents, in the enjoyment of their natural rights."[10] The consideration also was put in terms both of *quantum meriut* and of equity, that is, of fairness. The *quantum meriut* theory was that Great Britain had gained more by letting people seeking security of rights migrate than keeping them at home and in that way received a benefit in payment for the migration. The equity consideration was based on a sense of fair play: "[F]or *Britain* to have reduced her children to a more abject state of slavery, for having exposed themselves to every hardship in a foreign clime to promote her interest, than they would have been exposed to if they had remained inactive at home, would have been so flagrant an act of injustice, as would have effectually prevented our ancestors from undertaking so meritorious a service."[11]

A special American form of consideration for the implied original colonial contract was the migration purchase discussed in chapter 15. It was mentioned as consideration by Pennsylvania's House of Representatives when speaking of the colonists having "paid a valuable Consideration to the Crown for the said Charter and Laws," and by Connecticut's Assembly when it said that Charles II had, "in Consideration of such Purchase," promised that the settlers and their descendants "should have, and enjoy, all Liberties, and Immunities of free and natural Subjects."[12]

A final consideration said to have been part of the implied original contract was mutual promises. This was seldom mentioned, as it was difficult for most people to think of promises being exchanged by implication. It was, however, stated as the consideration by at least one writer in a New England newspaper, who is worth quoting not so much for this theory of consideration, as for his detailed explanation of the implied original colonial contract.

> [T]he implied contract I take to be this—That if the adventurers will hazard their lives and properties in acquiring, according to the rules of justice, possessions in the desart regions of America, far remote from their native land, and encounter all the difficulties and dangers necessarily attending such an enterprise, that then the King and the nation will support and defend them in those possessions: They paying due allegiance to his Majesty, and holding the lands of him upon stipulated conditions; and that they shall lose no part of their natural *rights, liberty and property*, by such removal; but that they, *and all their posterity for ever, shall as fully and freely enjoy them, to*

all intents, constructions, and purposes whatsoever, as if they and
every of them were born in England.[13]

THE TAXATION STIPULATION

The right to be taxed by consent illustrates the *implied* original contract in operation. At the height of the Stamp Act crisis a Bostonian wrote
that the act "is universally esteemed here as arbitrary and unconstitutional, and as a breach of charter and compact between K[ing] and subject." The word "universally" was not an exaggeration. If there was any
stipulation that every whig believed was in the implied contract, it was
that taxation would be by consent. "The principal privilege implied," the
Massachusetts House asserted, "is a freedom from all taxes, but such as
they shall consent to in person, or by representatives of their own free
choice and election."

The voters of the New Hampshire town of Dover raised a question not
often considered. With whom had the first migrants made the original
contract? The answer that it had been made with the Crown, they
thought, was enough to prove the unconstitutionality of parliamentary
taxation. "And as it doth not appear that any Parliaments have been Parties to any Contracts made with the European Settlers in this once howling Wilderness, now become a pleasant Field, we look on our RIGHTS too
dearly bought to admit them now, as Tax-Masters, since we have Parliaments of our own."[14]

CHAPTER EIGHTEEN

THE REALITY OF CONTRACT

The suggestion has been made that the contract, whether the social contract or the original contract, was a "hypothetical" or "metaphorical" mode of argument with no historical or factual validity, that its value lay in its rhetorical or polemical utility, permitting theories about the origins of authority to be framed in terms of some principle such as consent. This analysis has much merit, but it fails to explain the concepts of eighteenth-century whigs. True, some whigs may have thought the contract a convenient metaphor, a way of postulating governmental legitimacy in terms similar to popular sovereignty without seeming to deny either the reality of obligarchic hegemony or the fiction of monarchical rule. But there were many more whigs — very many more — who thought the original colonial contract a provable fact, an actual institution that may not have been negotiated and signed at a specific moment in time, but that explained the current arrangement of constitutional power.[1]

It would be a mistake to be skeptical. Whigs could believe in the reality of the original colonial contract more easily than we can. They had a factual basis, a historical event, with which to locate it. That event was the migration of the first settlers, an event about which it was reasonable to postulate the notion of offer and acceptance between ruler and ruled, or the notion of people assuming the future guarantee of the rights they had possessed since birth. But even more important was the way the eighteenth-century British thought about government. Contract was simply the concept every educated person was conditioned to use when expressing ideas concerning basic constitutional principles. Writers slipped into the language effortlessly, not only because it was how they formulated arguments but also because they knew it was how the readers whom they were addressing thought about government. Both sides of almost every political or constitutional dispute might argue in terms of contract. Just as American whigs premised their claim to rights on their original contract, imperialists countered with answers applying the contract against them.[2]

There were persuasive reasons for saying that the original contract was an actual contract. One was that people thought of government as a trust. If the rulers were entrusted with authority for the benefit of those they ruled there had to be "an *implied* Covenant," Josiah Tucker pointed out. "For every Trust implies a Covenant, or Condition of some Kind, or other, according to the Nature of the Case." Another reason was that the obligations of the original contract were so clear and ascertainable that its existence could not be doubted. Think of the confidence Pennsylvania's Provincial Congress must have felt about the clarity of the contract when claiming that the contract's terms were not only certain but certain enough to restrain unconstitutional government activity. A final reason why the original contract was accepted as an actual, binding document is that it *had* to be real. In a legal environment without a written constitution and in which people were frightened of arbitrary government, there was almost no alternative to the reality of contract except arbitrary government. This truism was stated innumerable times during the eighteenth century. The technique was simple and can be demonstrated by considering one example. "[W]e in *America* have a just Claim to the *hereditary Rights of British* Subjects," A *Freeholder* wrote the *Maryland Gazette* in 1748. "In consequence of this, I say, that our *Constitution* is plainly an *original Contract* betwixt the *People* and their *Rulers*; and as many Jests as have been broke on this Expression, we might safely venture to defy the warmest Stickler for arbitrary Power to produce any one Point of Time, since which we know any Thing of our *Constitution*, wherein the whole Scheme of it would not have been one monstrous Absurdity, unless an *original Contract* had been suppos'd."[3]

Perhaps the best evidence we could wish for of the aura of reality with which eighteenth-century political theorists thought of the original contract would be to find its specific provisions discussed as if they were actually written down and could be quoted. There is an abundance of such evidence, some of which has already been mentioned. An argument made by Lord Lyttelton in the House of Lords is worth careful consideration. "They went out subjects of Great Britain," he said of the first settlers, "and unless they can shew a new compact made between them and the parliament of Great Britain (for the king alone could not make a new compact with them) they still are subjects to all intents and purposes whatsoever." It is significant not only that Lyttelton assumed that the answer to fundamental constitutional issues, even one so important as parliamentary supremacy, could be found in the contract, but also that writers on the colonial whig side of the dispute answered his rule of law with counter legal principles based on the same assumptions. "Should it be said," one wrote in 1775, "that the Colonists were subjects of the Crown of *England*, and members of that State before their emigration, and therefore must continue so unless they can show that they are discharged by some express agreement; it may be answered, that their compact as members of that State was, in the nature of it, limited to their continuance in that Realm, and consequently was discharged by their emigration." These remarks deserve to be compared. Lyttelton said that to sustain their constitutional argument Americans had to produce the original colonial contract, something he believed they had not done. The whig writer, without conceding that the second contract, the original colonial contract, had not been proven, contended that the first settlers, by the very act of migration, were released from their obligations under the original British contract, and they were released from that contract because that was what the contract itself provided.[4]

Perhaps as persuasive of the reality of contract as arguments about what the contract said are arguments about which side had the burden of proof and how that proof was to be established. Sir William Draper used this approach when saying something very much similar to Lyttelton, but instead of demanding that the original American contract be produced, he may have accepted the existence of the contract, placing on the colonial whigs the burden of proving its specific terms. "If the State upon their departure had promised them any particular Immunities," he wrote of the first migrants, "they would be in the right not to submit to any Taxes levied upon them in breach of such a promise. Let them produce this promise, or they must still remain subject to our Taxation." The voters of the Massachussetts town of Bellingham disagreed. The correct rule should be the exact opposite, they claimed. Great Britain was asserting the right to tax; it therefore was the party with the burden of proof, a burden that could not be sustained "by ambiguous Words, that may be taken either Way, nor by dark Riddles, nor by Explanation made on one Side of the Question only: But such Compact must be plain and easily understood, it being of such vast Consequence." For the Bellingham voters, the contract was real and from that reality they knew which side should have the burden of proof. With their certainty about the actuality of the contract, they made the burden both specific and heavy. "Is there any such Compact between the Parliament of Great-Britain and our Predecessors, or the General Court of this Province; when was it made, in what Year, or in what King's Reign, or in what Book is it recorded?"[5]

THE SPECIFICITY OF CONTRACT

Writing in 1777 on Canadian affairs, Francis Maseres, former attorney general of Quebec and an official in the English judiciary, outlined the constitutional consequences resulting from the fact that eighteenth-century lawyers perceived the original contract to be real. "[A]ll civil powers are ultimately founded on compacts," he explained, "and every *question of right* will, if traced to its fountain-head, appear to be in reality *a question of fact*, that is, an inquiry concerning an ancient fact, to wit, the intention of the parties between whom the question arises, or of their ancestors and predecessors, at a time when the case, concerning which it has arisen, began to exist." That was why lawyers could think the original contract a reality. For them the constitution was real and so was the contract, for the contract was very close to being the constitution. In fact, some of those who wrote about the contract in the eighteenth century equated it with the constitution. The correspondent to the *Maryland Gazette* just quoted was one; another was the earl of Abingdon. In a magazine article entitled "Great Outlines of the English Constitution," Abingdon asked, rhetorically, what the constitution is. "I would say, that *Constitution* signified *Compact*," Abingdon answered. "I define *Constitution* then to be, those *Agreements* entered into, those *Rights* determined upon, and those *Forms* prescribed by and between the members of any society in the first settlement of their union, and in the frame and mode of their government."[6]

The original colonial contract seems to have been real even to Governor Thomas Hutchinson, who asserted that "[t]he agreements made with the Subjects who went into the Colonies were known to all the world." What was known? Another New England governor furnished one answer. "Before their departure," Stephen Hopkins wrote of the first settlers, "the terms of their freedom, and the relation they should stand in to the mother country, in their emigrant state were fully settled; they were to remain subject to the king, and dependant on the kingdom of Great Britain. In return they were to receive protection, and enjoy all the rights and privileges of freeborn Englishmen."[7] Hopkins says what is pertinent for us:

among the various terms of the original contract, the stipulations generally singled out and mentioned with specificity were the rights of the
people.

The voters of Roxbury, Massachusetts, boasted that their ancestors "had
the promise of a King for himself and Successors, that they and theirs
should enjoy all the Liberties and Immunities of natural-born Subjects
within the Realm of England." It was a specific promise made for a specific purpose. "Our ancestors," the governor and Company of Rhode Island told George III, "removed and planted here under a royal promise,
that, observing and fulfilling the conditions enjoined them, they and their
children after them forever, should hold and enjoy equal rights, privileges and immunities with their fellow subjects in Britain."[8] For that
specific promise the king received specific consideration. It was an exchange of promises, according to Gilbert Burnet, bishop of Salisbury, who
told Increase Mather that the first settlers "promised the King to inlarge
his dominions on their owne charges, provided that they and their posterity after them might enjoy such and such priviledges." Mather did not
have to be told these facts; he knew them well. "[T]hese original compacts," he wrote, "were made and entered into by the King, not only for
himself, but expressly for his heirs and successors on the one part, and
the colonies, their successors and assigns on the other."[9]

Mather used the term "expressly," as did other writers when describing
the original colonial contract. The terms had been "expres[s]ly stipulated,
between the King and People."[10] Some participants in the revolutionary
debates even knew when the original contract had been negotiated. Samuel Adams said it occurred "[i]mmediately after their Arrival here" when
the first settlers "solemnly recogniz[e]d their Allegiance to their Sovereign in England, & the Crown graciously . . . declared them & their Heirs
for ever entitled to all the Libertys & Immunitys of free & natural born
Subjects of the Realm." Nine years later an anonymous writer was just
as sure that the transaction had occurred on the other side of the Atlantic, although he thought the terms were the same as Adams described. His
confidence in being able to envision the scene is truly wonderful. "[I]t was
the same thing as if both King and people had assembled upon the sea
shore, and the one had sworn to govern them according to the laws of the
land, and the other to obey him in *America* as subjects within the realm."[11]

THE CONTRACT OF PROMISE

An important reason why commentators could write so confidently
of the terms of the original colonial contract was that the facts of the

contract were found in subsequent governmental custom. The way Great Britain had governed the colonies for 150 years was evidence not just of colonial customary rights but of the original contract. As a result, the terms of the contract could be proven not only by prior expectation, but also by subsequent government conduct, not only in the contract of promise, but in the custom of contract.[12] One aspect of the constitutional proof — the reliance of the early settlers on retaining English rights — has been previously mentioned, but a new element deserves notice. The element we saw before was settler expectation. The new element is royal enticement. For in addition to the claimed fact of an actual reliance on an implied promise, there was the assertion of an actual reliance on an actual promise.

This real promise, real acceptance, and real contract were stated many times in the eighteenth century, often in contexts having nothing to do with the revolutionary controversy and even in courts of common law. Perhaps the most interesting way to introduce it is to consider a source in which we might not expect to find the real contract cited. A pamphlet that contemporaries attributed to George Grenville, but which was more probably written for Grenville by Thomas Whately, locates the source of the contract in "[t]he Encouragement given to Settlement" by specific promises of the British government to recent settlers. These promises were both assurances that the settlers' property would be protected from Indian and European enemies — promises implied from various activities such as the stationing of imperial troops in Florida and Quebec — and assurances that constitutional rights would be preserved, a promise explicitly promulgated in various royal proclamations issued following the French and Indian War. The assurance of military protection had been an important inducement attracting settlers, but "the most powerful Inducement" was the king's public assurance that "Liberties and Properties" would be secured by the British constitution. The terms of the inducement, specifically stated in the proclamations, were representative government and the benefit of English laws, promises intended to entice settlers. Although long, it is necessary to quote the germane part of one proclamation as found by special verdict of a petite jury in the leading constitutional case dealing with the original colonial contract, *Campbell* v. *Hall*. The litigation concerned rights in the recently conquered colony of Grenada.

> [W]hereas it will greatly contribute to the speedy settling [of] our said new governments that our loving subjects should be informed of our paternal care for the security of the liberties and properties of those who are and shall become inhabitants thereof; we have

> thought fit to . . . [have] given express power and direction to our
> governors . . . [to] call general assemblies within the said governments
> respectively, in such manner and form as is used and directed in those
> colonies and provinces in America, which are under our immediate
> government. . . . And in the mean time and until such assemblies
> can be called as aforesaid, all persons inhabiting in, and resorting
> to our said colonies, may confide in our royal protection for the en-
> joyment of the benefit of the laws of our realm of England.[13]

The proclamation was an actual, concrete promise. The condition on
which the emigrants later were said to have relied was clearly stated and
widely publicized. The expectation that the proclamation would be said
to have aroused was not only deduced by hindsight, it also had been anticipated. The year after the proclamation was issued, a New Englander
predicted that the "happy effects of his Majesty's wisdom" would "doubt-
less contribute, vastly to enlarge the present foundation of the British empire in this western hemisphere." What should not be thought is that the
proclamation was unique in the contractarian argument. The colonists
cited other specific, real, stated incitements held out not only to recent
emigrants but also to the first settlers. Promises had been made by the
king, the Maryland Assembly resolved, referring to the proprietorship
granted to Lord Baltimore by King Charles I, "for the Encouragement
for People to Transport themselves and families in to this Province." These
promises, stated in the Charter, included "all Libertys Franchises and
privileges of this our Kingdom of England." There were similar induce-
ments in the other colonial patents that will be considered in the next
chapter, dealing with the Charter contract. The terms were both stated
and inferred, for the promise of "Libertys Franchises and privileges" was
generally stated and the encouragement to settle was implied.[14]

One other feature should be mentioned. Even the important factual
aspect of the encouragement contract — the prior, explicitly stated
inducement — was not necessary to make the contract binding. The essential point to be proven was the encouragement. That was the probative
fact of this category of the original colonial contract in the same way
that reliance or expectation had been of the category discussed in chapter 17. Encouragement could be implied just as could reliance, although
it was done much less frequently due to the charters and proclamations
that could be quoted for specific promises.[15]

A final point should be made, if for no other reason than that it has
been made in regard to every other authority for rights discussed so far,
and not to make it might leave the impression that the encouragement
contract was an exception to the general rule. It is, of course, that the

theory of the encouragement contract was not *sui generis* to the American colonies. It had been stated before in English law, especially in regard to Ireland. In 1719, for example, the Irish House of Lords claimed that a "Compact" made with the Crown and confirmed by succeeding kings, "proved a great Encouragement, to many of the *English* to come over and settle themselves in *Ireland*, where they were to enjoy the same Laws and Liberties, and live under the like Constitution, as they had formerly done in the Kingdom of *England*."[16]

The Proclamation Contract

The theory of the encouragement contract was stated in terms both of promise and expectation by a South Carolinian in 1764. "[I]f," he contended, "there is a right in the subject derived to him from the laws and constitution of his country, and that right confirmed and established to him by the crown, as a condition and encouragement to him to transport himself abroad, it is not in the power of the crown afterwards, to limit, retrench, or abridge that right, by any subsequent instruction or declaration whatever, and nothing but his own act and consent can deprive him of it."[17]

At first glance, the South Carolinian's constitutional theory seems extreme, at least if he meant to extend it to Parliament as well as to the Crown. It was probably not valid law, yet it was not extreme for the time it was made. An instance of the theory being applied is provided by the Quebec Act of 1774, a statute designated one of the "intolerable acts" by American whigs, because it extended the borders of Canada down into the backcountry of the older colonies, restricted the right of trial by jury, introduced government by appointed council rather than by representation, and permitted the Catholic clergy to retain some of their former status. It is illustrative of the range of the original-contract concept that both Lord Chatham and Earl Camden claimed that the Quebec Act violated the contract, but that they were referring to different contracts. For Chatham the contract could be deduced from all the statutes of supremacy from the time of Henry VIII "down to this day." These statutes, taken together, formed "a clear compact, that all establishments by law are to be Protestant." One part of the Quebec Act violated that compact. For Camden the contract that was breached was the proclamation promising representative government and guaranteeing British rights. These promises, Camden claimed, had been "fulfilled in every other province, excepting that of Quebec, to which many settlers had been allured by this proclamation, who, by a most disgraceful violation of the royal faith, were since, with the rest of that province, subjected to the civil laws of France, and to the despotism of a governor and a dependent council, instead of being allowed an assembly, and laws made 'by the representatives of the people', as they were solemnly promised."[18]

Almost every person opposing the Quebec Act cited the proclamation contract.[19] The factual argument was best stated by the British settlers themselves. "[U]pon the faith of your sacred Majesty's Royal Proclamation," or stated more strongly, "induced by your Majesty's paternal care for the security of the liberties and properties of your subjects," or, in eighteenth-century terms, stated even more strongly, "induced to venture their Property in the said Province on the Faith of his Majesty's Proclamation, and other Promises solemnly given," they "did come and settle ourselves in the said Province . . . whereby the value of the Land, and wealth of its inhabitants are more than doubled." Yet what is the result? "[W]e find," despite the royal "promises" that they would enjoy "the benefit of the laws of the realm of England, until assemblies should be called therein," that, due to the Quebec Act, "we are deprived of the franchises granted by your Majesty's royal predecessors, and by us inherited from our forefathers."[20]

The constitutional argument was rejected. The Quebec Act was a statute passed by Parliament and, therefore, valid despite the proclamation contract. Yet — and this is important — the contractual argument was not irrelevant to lawyers. A revealing exchange occurred in the House of Commons during the debate on the Quebec Bill. On the administration's side was Attorney General Edmund Thurlow, one of the strongest spokesmen for maintaining parliamentary sovereignty over the colonies. He had no doubt Parliament had authority to govern them all, including Quebec, on any terms it thought fit to lay down. If anyone should be expected to dismiss the proclamation contract as irrelevant it would have been Thurlow. Instead, he rejected the argument that the proclamation prohibited passage of the Quebec Bill not on grounds that the proclamation was not a contract, but by questioning the opposition's interpretation of the contract. "He condemned in very harsh terms the advisers of the proclamation, and the imperfect, improper manner in which it was drawn up. He denied however, that it contained any such assurance as that contended for by the gentlemen on the other side. He said, that no such encouragement should have been given; that it was impolitic to hold out any benefits to the natural born subjects of this country to emigrate thither from hence, or to go from the other Colonies." The attorney general was answered by Sergeant John Glynn, a leading barrister and member of the opposition, who argued several of the important constitutional cases of the day against the government, notably the general-warrants litigations. Glynn, reading the facts differently from the way Thurlow interpreted them, contended that the proclamation was a contract. "He observed, that whatever contrary opinion might be maintained, it was his, that all conquests, as soon as made, vested in the King, Lords, and Commons; but that, until the two latter interfered, the King, as actual representative of the whole, was justified in making such regulations as he might think proper, so that they were not actually repugnant to the laws or constitution. The latter not being the case of the Proclamation, he thought the nation in every respect bound to fulfil every thing promised by that solemn engagement."[21]

THE RULE OF *CAMPBELL* v. *HALL*

In 1766, long before the Quebec Act debate, Lord Mansfield had described to the House of Lords his understanding of how colonial constitutions had evolved. "Some things were done by instructions from the secretaries of state," he explained, "other things were done by order of the king and council, and other things were done by commissions under the great seal. It is observable, that, in consequence of these establishments from time to time, and of the dependency of these governments upon the supreme legislature at home, the lenity of each government in the colonies has been extreme towards the subject; and a very great inducement it has been to people to come and settle in them."[22] Mansfield's statement is a remarkable instance of how complicated imperial constitutional law could be. He was claiming a very high supremacy on behalf of Great Britain, a supremacy not just of Parliament over the colonies but of the prerogative as well. No colonial whig could have sat still and accepted his argument that colonial constitutions were to be found in administrative instructions to the governors, orders in council, and the wording of commissions issued under the Great Seal. Mansfield's constitutional authorities were about as far from the concept of government by the authority of contract, consent, and inherent rights possessed by the people as they could get, yet, inadvertently, he conceded the chief factual proof of the proclamation contract. Despite the autocratic origins of power, Mansfield admitted, colonial government was lenient, a condition he described as an "inducement" for settlement.

Mansfield's argument is of interest for a second reason. Since the constitutionality of the proclamation contract could not be tested in a court of law against a statute such as the Quebec Act because there was no judicial tribunal competent to hear the case, the constitutional issue had to be resolved in Parliament and contested in debates between Thurlow and Glynn, for once Parliament acted there was no appeal. There was, however, one occasion when the proclamation contract was made an issue in constitutional litigation—in the court of King's Bench, Lord Chief Justice Mansfield presiding. The case was *Campbell* v. *Hall* and the colony involved was Grenada, like Quebec recently captured from the French and subject to the king's 1763 proclamation.

Grenada had not only been covered by the proclamation promising representative government and other rights, but British subjects had also migrated there, some actually claiming they did so in reliance on the proclamation's promise. One, for example, cited his rights under the proclamation contract when protesting London's allowing Roman Catholics to vote in the newly incorporated colonies. "I have a considerable property [in Grenada]," he protested, "which I was induced to purchase upon the faith of the King's proclamation, assuring me that I should enjoy all the benefits of the laws of the realm of England, one of which is an absolute disqualification of all persons professing the Romish religion, to hold any offices of trust or emolument under the British government."[23]

London, of course, disagreed with this interpretation of the proclamation contract, although Thomas Whately, writing on behalf of the ministry, admitted that "Assurances" had been given that "a Constitution similar to that of *Great Britain*, shall be formed" in Grenada, a promise that should have excluded Catholic electors. As a matter of law, however, it was immaterial whether anyone acted on contractarian expectations or what those expectations were. It was also of no legal significance that it was understood to be fact, sometimes reiterated in the London press, that on the strength of the proclamation "numbers of his Majesty's protestant subjects from divers parts of his dominions resorted to Grenada in full confidence that they should enjoy all the benefits of the laws of the realm of England." Since Catholics had been granted the franchise by act of Parliament, the question whether a constitutional contract had been broken could not be raised in a court of common law.[24]

The constitutional premises were different, however, when the alleged violation of the proclamation contract did not arise from a parliamentary statute. That was the situation in *Campbell* v. *Hall*. At issue was a customs duty imposed by letter patent that also continued a poll tax from the era when the island had been under French rule. In other words, the litigation concerned taxes promulgated by the Crown rather than parliamentary taxation. The plaintiff, Alexander Campbell, a British subject who had purchased a plantation on Grenada three months before the king's proclamation, sued to recover the amount he had been assessed on the grounds that prerogative taxes were illegal.

Several constitutional issues were in contention, including the doctrine of conquest, the powers of prerogativism, and the proclamation contract. "The substance" of the proclamation, one of the plaintiff's counsel argued, was "a recital of the benefit naturally resulting to the British empire from a system of colonization in Grenada; and in order to invite the natural subjects of that country . . . to settle there, it repeatedly assures them that a constitution as soon as possible shall be formed in exact conformity and representation of the English government." Also appearing for the plaintiff, Sergeant Glynn argued that even had the people of Grenada, under the doctrine of conquest, been subject to prerogative taxes as a conquered people, "the king, by his proclamation, has concluded himself from this right." Arguing for the government and supporting the legality of the tax, Attorney General Thurlow took the same strong stand for parliamentary supremacy he took in the House of Commons. The king, he contended, had not imposed the tax on his own authority, but as an agent acting on behalf of Parliament. "By the subordinate authority to the Lords and Commons (which I consider as being as much subordinate with regard to the dominions acquired to the king, as with regard to the state and dominions of the state here), the king regulates the government, and requires imposts from the country, in such manner as he sees requisite." Making an alternative argument, Thurlow also sought to distinguish the proclamation on its facts. It did not promise all British constitutional privileges, as the plaintiff contended. "The proclamation might convey the English laws," he suggested, "but not the political and constitutional system in general in this kingdom."[25]

Delivering the opinion for a unanimous court, Lord Mansfield held for the plaintiff. Quoting the entire proclamation, Mansfield interpreted it as a promise made by the government and accepted by British emigrants to Grenada. "With what view is the promise reciting the comission actually given?" he asked. "To invite the settlers; to invite subjects. Why? The reason is given. They may think their liberties and properties more secure when they have a legislative assembly." After all, Mansfield pointed out, the governor and council existed at the king's pleasure, and if there were no elected assembly, the Crown, by removing the governor and council, could at will change "the constitution," making civil rights insecure. "Therefore that assurance is given them for the security of their liberties and properties, and with a view to invite them to go and settle there after this proclamation that assured them of the constitution under which they were to live." Taking into consideration the proclamation, together with a second similar proclamation and the governor's commission, which also had been publicized, Mansfield ruled that "the king had immediately and irrevocably granted to all who did or should inhabit, or who had or should have property in the island of Grenada — in general

to all whom it should concern — that the subordinate legislation over the
island should be exercised by the assembly with the governor and council, in like manner as in the other provinces under the king." As a result,
even though the king had constitutional authority to levy taxes on a conquered country such as Grenada, because the taxes had been decreed after
the proclamation had been promulgated, the taxes were "contrary to and
a violation" of the proclamation "and therefore void."[26]

The holding, based on unique facts, was not an important precedent
in imperial constitutional law. Still, *Campbell* v. *Hall* is significant because it demonstrates that the original colonial contract, in its special
form of a prior promise to induce settlement, could be an enforceable
contract, and that it was a contract in positive, not natural, law. The
supposition is, and it can remain only a supposition, that had there been
a supreme judicial tribunal to which American colonists could have appealed, as Alexander Campbell had been able to appeal, the original colonial contract would have posed a constitutional issue that the court would
have been compelled to resolve. *Campbell* v. *Hall* was also significant
because of the discussion it generated during the months leading up to
the American Revolution. Mansfield's ruling permitted writers, lawyers,
and speakers sympathetic to the American whig argument to cast doubt
on the validity of the government's constitutional doctrine that the colonies were subject to parliamentary supremacy. An example is Lord Camden. As usual, when defending the side of liberty and civil rights, Camden exaggerated, but the decision in *Campbell* v. *Hall* helped to give the
exaggeration constitutional plausibility. Pretending to cite the doctrine
that Mansfield had laid down, and ignoring — at least in the reported version of his speech — the fact that it rested on the wording of the proclamation, Camden told the House of Lords that *Campbell* v. *Hall*

> clearly proved, that in all accessions of territory to the crown, the
> king is constitutionally entrusted, and required to extend to his new
> subjects, the laws of England, and the benefit of a constitution simi-
> lar to that of our own country — that he can give no less than those
> rights and privileges which by the common law, as well as by the
> Act of Settlement, are declared to be "the birthright of every British
> subject."[27]

CHAPTER NINETEEN

THE EVIDENCE
OF CHARTER

There were colonial whigs so certain the original contract of migration was real that they could quote norms of construction for its interpretation — norms the original settlers formulated to guide later generations. "We have ever supposed our Charter the greatest security that could be had in human affairs," the voters of Weymouth, Massachusetts, lamented shortly before the Stamp Act was to become operative. "This was the sentiment of our forefathers — they have told us that they should never have left the land of their nativity, and fled to these ends of the earth, triumph'd over dangers, encountered difficulties innumerable, and suffer'd hardships unparallel'd, but for the sake of securely enjoying civil and religious liberty, and that the same might be transmitted safe to their posterity."[1]

Weymouth equated the contract with the colonial charter, something quite different from what we have seen in the last two chapters. In fact, the importance of charter in colonial whig constitutional theory was not as a separate authority for rights — that is, that rights were created by charter or were defined by the terms of a charter. Indeed, it might be debated whether charters were thought to be authority at all. Charters were valued primarily as evidence of rights — they were not thought documents originating or guaranteeing rights — yet there is no gainsaying that they were regarded as significant by people on both sides of the Atlantic during the era of the American Revolution.[2] In the American legal vocabulary of civil rights, the word "charter" was often an adjective modifying the noun "rights." A common description of colonial rights was to call them "charter rights." Charles Chauncy in 1747 referred to "the *civil charter-rights* of this people," and in 1765 the voters of Rowley condemned the Stamp Act as "an invasion upon our charter rights and privileges."[3]

THE CONTRACT OF CHARTER

For historians of today the most striking aspect of charter in terms of eighteenth-century law, an aspect quite forgotten in the twentieth century, was its association with the original colonial contract. For some constitutional commentators, admittedly a relative few, the charter was the contract. Late in the seventeenth century Bishop Burnet told Increase Mather that "there was a greater Sacredness in the CHARTER OF NEW-ENGLAND, than in those of the [municipal] Corporations in ENGLAND; For those were only Acts of Grace, whereas the CHARTER of NEW-ENGLAND was a *Contract* between the KING and the *First Patentees*."[4] The thought was continually turning up in the literature of the American Revolution. Henry Goodricke, opposing colonial whig claims to rights, wrote that "[t]he Charters implied the original compact," Thomas Jefferson referred to "the original charter of compact granted to S[i]r Walter Ralegh" in 1584, Joseph Galloway called William Penn's Frame of Government "his *Covenant* with the People," and Joseph Hawley told his fellow colonists to take comfort from the fact that "we have the deed of compact, the Charter-rights in our own hands." James Iredell was more extreme than most whigs when, in a moment of careless expression, he equated the charter not only with the original colonial contract but with the constitution as well. "I have always been taught, and, till I am better informed, must continue to believe," Iredell wrote in the *North Carolina Gazette* in 1773, "that the constitution of this country is founded on the provincial charter, which may well be considered as the original contract between the King and the inhabitants."[5]

Theory was consistent. The contract of charter was said by eighteenth-century writers to have been negotiated in exactly the same way that they said the original colonial contract had been negotiated. To recruit settlers and obtain what proved to be "a great emolument to the British crown," the government "stipulated to secure" the migrants "natural, civil and religious rights, both to them and their posterity, by charter." As a document existed, the terms of the contract did not always have to be speculated from settler expectations or implied from subsequent custom. Some provisions were spelled out in the charter or could be inferred from specific language.[6]

In the literature of the revolutionary debates, we encounter certain words used over and over to explain why charter entailed both an offer from the Crown and an acceptance by the first settlers. One word was "condition." Colonial charters were said to be "the Condition upon which our Ancestors originally settled this Country," or they were the "express Condition, of set[t]ling Colonies for the Benefit of the Crown."[7] A second operative word was "faith." It was said either that the migrants "went out upon the faith of the King's charters," that is, "under the faith of charters, which promised them the enjoyment of all the rights of *Englishmen*,"[8] or that because of the charter "the royal Faith is plighted to protect & defend us his American Subjects, in the free & full Enjoyment of each and every Right & Liberty enjoyed by his Subjects in Great Britain."[9] Daniel Dulany, Jr., summed up the factual theory, citing charter not just as evidence of a real contract negotiated but as proof that an offer had been made and accepted. "[T]hey entered into a compact with the crown," he wrote of the first settlers,

> the basis of which was *that their privileges as English subjects should be effectually secured to themselves and transmitted to their posterity*. And as for this purpose precise declarations and provisions formed upon the principles and according to the spirit of the English *constitution* were necessary, CHARTERS were accordingly framed and conferred by the crown and accepted by the settlers.[10]

For some colonies the sequence of events was different. They were the ones that received their charters after settlement rather than before, and that fact meant that the legal theory as to why the charter was a binding contract had to be altered. An example is Connecticut, which was settled from Massachusetts, adding new territory and wealth to the Empire at no expense to the central government. It was "in consideration thereof" that the settlers "obtained a charter from King Charles the Second." That contract was less an offer and acceptance than a payment for services rendered. "The Powers and Privileges granted by this Charter were properly the Purchase of the People," the Connecticut government argued in 1764. "[T]here really were valuable Considerations which were proper Foundations" for the Charter, and the people of the colony regarded the Charter "as the Purchase of their Ancestors, as a gracious and royal Reward of the Merit and Services of their Forefathers, and as one of the best Inheritances they left to their Children." That the Connecticut charter had been granted almost three decades after settlement and in its preamble said that the settlers had increased imperial trade and wealth, added

> Weight and Strength to the Title on which the Claim of the Colony to the Rights, Immunities, and Franchises therein granted and confirmed are founded, for here are the Considerations of large Sums of Money advanced, Conquest made at the Expence of the Blood and Treasure of the Planters, eminent publick national Services performed and to be performed, and all to the Enlargement of the King's Dominions and for the Increase of the national Commerce, which the Charter is a clear and full Evidence of.

As much as any other colonial charter, the charter obtained by the people of Connecticut had been "granted that they should have and enjoy all the liberties and immunities of free and natural subjects born within the realm of England."[11]

THE RIGHTS OF CHARTER

No matter whether a charter was negotiated by offer and acceptance or given for services rendered, the theory that it was a contract provided American whigs with stronger arguments for defending it than had it been a one-sided grant from the Crown. The charter that Massachusetts had received from William and Mary, the colony's council told Governor Thomas Hutchinson, "contained certain Rights and Privileges granted to this People as an Inheritance." Any infraction of those rights "would be unjustifiable and in Violation of the mutual Compact." From this constitutional perspective, in addition to all the other authority for American civil rights, there was also what the Connecticut town of Pomfret called the "solemn Charter Compact." Seen in terms of the contractual theory, this authority followed from the fact that the charter had been negotiated on such a high level of government, for such inestimable consideration, which had been paid beyond any imaginable expectation, "that it ought to be kept Sacred and Inviolated by each Party and . . . cannot in any Respect be varied or altered by one Party only, without a most Criminal Breach of Faith."[12]

The argument that charters should be honored because they were executed contracts of the most solemn nature was as far as American whigs went in contending that the colonial charters provided constitutional support for their rights. In sermons or pamphlets written by private individuals, there are claims or suggestions that charters were an authority for rights,[13] but not in official statements issued by whig representative bodies. The most that they claimed was that rights had been obtained "by several charters of compact from the crown" or that the British constitution "was covenanted to us in the charter of the province." More typical were assertions making charters authorities of lesser standing than constitutional or fundamental, such as the Pennsylvania's Assembly equation of its charter with mere statute law when it said that the charter was "of the same Validity, with respect to the Rights thereby granted to the People here, as the Laws and Statutes of *England*, with regard to the Privileges derived under them, to the People of *England*."[14]

Even the Boston town meeting, a body tending to make more extreme claims than other whig groups, did not say that charter was the authority for rights and perhaps did not think of it as an alternative authority for rights. There were, Boston said, charter rights — rights identified by charter — but it is not clear if the voters thought these rights rested on the authority of charter alone. It was the task of the legislature, the town meeting resolved, to maintain "the invaluable rights and privileges of the province . . . as well those rights which are derived to us by the royal charter, as those which being prior to and independent on it, we hold essentially as free born subjects of Great Britain." The constitutional principle, a writer for the *London Magazine* explained, was that rights existed "of a higher nature than royal grants and charters, rights superior to, and independent of them."[15]

Two South Carolinians summed up the most generally held attitude about the relationship between the colonial charters and civil rights. The rights that Americans claimed equally with the British, William Henry Drayton wrote, were "of infinitely more importance, than the Colony Charters from the Crown." And Christopher Gadsden warned that "confirmation of our essential and common rights as Englishmen may be pleaded from charters safely enough; but any further dependence upon them may be fatal."[16] Charters were too vulnerable to be the authority for rights; if charter was the authority, then the rights would be equally vulnerable.

There were legal reasons for not making much of the authority of charter. One was the weakness of the contract argument. "The assertion that these charters are not charters, but *Pacta conventa*, is brim-full of absurdity," Allan Ramsay pointed out, "the whole sovereign power could not, by the nature of things, enter into any indefeasible compact of that sort."[17] Ramsay's law may or may not have been valid in the seventeenth century when most of the charters were issued, but it was constitutional law when he wrote in 1769, and it was the later law that would have decided the matter could the question have been put to a judicial test. A second reason was that not every colony had a charter. Plymouth, one of the earliest colonies, and Quebec, one of the last, never had charters, nor did Georgia, as it had been settled under parliamentary authority and not by grant of the Crown. The charters of Maryland and Pennsylvania had been granted to their proprietors, not to the settlers. A third reason not to depend on charter for rights was the risk of the counter argument that if rights came from charter they were limited by charter. "The colonies have no rights independent of their charters; they can claim no greater than those give them," Martin Howard had argued during the Stamp Act crisis. "What were the privileges originally granted by the crown to the colonies?" John Lind asked. "A review of the charters is the only means of answering this question."[18] The fourth reason was the most important. Charters could not secure rights, for they were revocable. They were not immutable, they were not organic acts, they were vague grants of power to municipal corporations which the superior legislative authority could alter, revise, amend, or revoke at any time. Subject to the sovereign's whim and caprice, charters offered little protection for civil rights.

In 1773 the voters of Petersham, Massachusetts Bay, recalled that the original charter of the province — a "compact between our forefathers and Great Britain"— had been voided by James II. Later, after the Glorious Revolution, the people of the colony received a new charter "which abridged them of many, very many, valuable and reasonable rights which were contained in the former, without any colour of right." The loss of rights by seizing one charter and granting a new one may have occurred only once to Massachusetts, but it was legal,[19] a fact demonstrated in 1774 when the "intolerable acts" were passed and the power of revocation was exercised a second time.

The Probativeness of Charter

We must not allow conclusions of law to mislead us about conclusions of history. The fact that colonial charters were mutable does not mean they had no role to play in imperial constitutional law. On the question of colonial rights they had a probative, evidentiary significance. They were, after all, written and served, Governor Hopkins pointed out, as "the authentic evidence of the conditions" that the first settlers "removed upon." Even more, they were the sole public documents connecting the colonies with the mother country. "The Charters," Joseph Hawley maintained, "from their subject matter and the reality of things, can only operate as the evidence of a compact between an *English* King and the *American* subjects; their running in the style of a grant is mere matter of form, and not of substance." Hawley would have interpreted a charter quite generally: as a "royal assurance that those rights which adhered to them [the first settlers] as men, and their Constitution confirmed to them as *Englishmen*, should not be invaded." Richard Henry Lee had that rule of evidence in mind when he described the charter as "confirming" to the migrants "and their Posterity forever, all the Franchises privileges and immunities of the free people of England they left behind them." The same is true of Maryland's Stamp Act resolutions, in which the lower house of Maryland voted that "the said Charter is Declaratory of the Constitutional Rights and Privileges of the Freemen of this Province."[20]

Just what that evidence revealed was a matter of dispute. Daniel Dulany, Jr., exaggerated greatly when he boasted that to secure rights charters had been so precisely drafted that "all the Doubts and Inconveniencies which might have arisen from the Application of general Principles to a new Subject, were prevented." In truth, one of the great difficulties with charters was vagueness. They contained specifics regarding trade and the imperial connection, but little concerning rights. About the most that could be taken from them were broad generalities, such as the Rhode Island legislature's claim that by its charter the colony "is declared and entitled to all the Privileges and Immunities of natural born Subjects, to all Intents and Purposes, as if they had been abiding and born within the Realm of England." Certainly it was not possible to get more out of charters than did Governor Hopkins when he wrote:

> By all these charters, it is in the most express and solemn manner granted that these adventurers, and their children after them forever, should have and enjoy all the freedom and liberty that the subject in England enjoy; that they might make laws for their own government suitable to their circumstances, not repugnant to, but as near as might be agreeable to the laws of England; that they might purchase lands, acquire goods, and use trade for their advantage, and have an absolute property in whatever they justly acquired.[21]

It would be misleading to be too negative. The lesson of this chapter is not that charters were unimportant to the revolutionary dispute about the authority for colonial civil rights. Rather, what must be understood is the reason why charters were not important: they were not embryo constitutions or documents espousing democratic principles; they did not contain guarantees about freedom of speech, press, religion, or assembly. Instead, charters were seventeenth-century instruments concerned at the most with property rights, the security of property, and jury trials. What importance charters had was not as substance but as symbols. People thought of them as they thought of another charter, an ancient English charter, permitting American whigs to frame an argument for colonial rights within one of the strongest, most persistent dogmas of English constitutionalism: the tradition of Magna Carta embodying the fundamental constitutional concept that individuals had rights limiting the power of government.

At the height of the Stamp Act crisis, when the leaders of Great Britain were beginning to realize that Americans would not permit the stamp tax to be collected, William Pitt was taking the waters at Bath. Pitt was ill, yet told a member of Parliament that he planned to return to London to fight for repeal of the Stamp Act and "stand by the colonies in their rights of Charter and Magna Charta."[22] Pitt's constitutional context— Magna Carta—was one in which many other—perhaps most—British legal and political writers viewed colonial charters: they were equated constitutionally with Magna Carta.[23] The analogy had been implicit in the legal attitudes of the early settlers such as John Winthrop, and had been explicitly stated by Increase Mather during the late seventeenth century when he labeled the second Massachusetts charter "the *Magna Charta* of *New England*."[24] The Connecticut charter, the House of Representatives of that colony resolved in 1765, stood "upon the same Basis with the grand Charters and Foundations of English Liberty."[25] The Stamp Act passed that year was understood by many Americans to have breached the colonial charters in the same constitutional sense that King John had breached ancient charters granted by his predecessors—breaches of law provoking the resistance that eventually forced John to grant Magna Carta.[26] The historical similarity was an essential part of the American whig constitutional cognition. "If our charter rights are infring'd," a New Englander told the *Boston Gazette* in 1767, "we cannot be 'tame spectators,' of it any more than our brethren would be of a breach of Magna Carta."[27]

The constitutional theory that colonial charters were confirmations of fundamental British civil rights was deftly employed by Benjamin Franklin when examined at the Bar of the House of Commons in support of the motion to repeal the Stamp Act. As agent for Pennsylvania, Franklin had to explain an embarrassing clause in Pennsylvania's charter that seemingly sanctioned parliamentary taxation. He relied on the authority of Magna Carta. "I know," Franklin conceded, that "there is a clause in the charter, by which the King grants, that he will levy no taxes on the inhabitants, unless it be with the consent of the assembly, or by act of Parliament." "How then," he was asked,

> could the assembly of Pennsylvania assert, that laying a tax on them by the stamp-act was an infringement of their rights?
>
> A. They understand it thus; by the same charter, and otherwise, they are intitled to all the privileges and liberties of Englishmen; they find in the great charters, and the petition and declaration of rights, that one of the privileges of English subjects is, that they are not to be taxed but by their common consent. . . .
>
> Q. Are there any words in the charter that justify that construction?
>
> A. The common rights of Englishmen, as declared by *Magna Charta*, and the petition of right, all justify it.[28]

Franklin's constitutional theory might be dismissed as unsound or speculative law were it not so much within the spirit of one of the strongest traditions of English constitutional law: Lord Coke's metamorphosing Magna Carta from a medieval adjustment of feudal power into a constitutional document restraining arbitrary power. The provisions of King John's charter were less significant than the instrument itself. That explains why we should concentrate on the concept of constitutional evidence. Magna Carta was evidence that English and British government had never been arbitrary. The same constitutional role belonged to colonial charters. They were prized, John Dickinson believed, as "evidential of rights and immunities belonging to all the King's subjects in America."[29] Even when specific terms of a charter were cited, discussed, or argued in the eighteenth century, they were not the main exhibit in evidence. It was the general grant, not specifics, that mattered. "[T]he said rights and immunities are recognized and confirmed to the inhabitants of this colony by Royal Grant and Charter," Connecticut's lower house claimed. There was no need to be more detailed. The colonial charters, just by the fact that they had been issued, were evidence that Americans were entitled to British constitutional rights.[30]

"If," a writer asked in the *New London Gazette* just after the Stamp Act was to become operative, "our privileges by charter, and of the common law in full, so sacredly made over to us, under royal hand and seal; and even now graciously allowed us, must be sovereignly taken away; what have we to trust to, but sovereign rule, and arbitrary power?" One answer was voted by the General Court of Massachusetts Bay a few days later when it resolved that there could be no constitutional trust except by continuing the practice of adhering to the *status quo* of charter.[31]

The argument was not new. It had shifted from seventeenth-century

Stuart England to eighteenth-century Hanoverian America, from Coke's ideal of Magna Carta to colonial charters, yet remained the same. British constitutionalism defined the rights claimed by American whigs, rights that the Connecticut legislature said they held "as Englishmen, and which are if possible, rendered more sacred and indefeasible by the royal Grant and Charter."[32] The charter was evidence of the colonial constitutional case. It was not the case itself.

CHAPTER TWENTY

THE COLONIAL
GRIEVANCES

The topic of the evidence of charter completes the survey of the various authorities on which the civil rights of the people depended in eighteenth-century British constitutional theory. Before turning to our final questions — what issues the possession of rights raised in the revolutionary controversy and how the American defense of rights contributed to the coming of the Revolution — another subject — colonial grievances — merits brief discussion.

Grievances are the other side of rights. Not every expression of grievance in the eighteenth century alleged a right violated, but generally that was the rule. It was the practice of the opponents of the British administration to state their opposition less by proposing alternative programs than by reciting grievances. The technique had been standard procedure in English and Irish constitutional government since the days of Coke and James I. That tradition explains why the English Bill of Rights was cast in the same legal form as the American Declaration of Independence, an indictment of the king by counting the grievances of the people.[1] During the age of the American Revolution, the political literature of Great Britain was top-heavy with carefully but extravagantly phrased lists of grievances. A short example is John Wilkes's answer to the Carmarthen grand jury in 1771. "We have scarcely a Right which they have not in-

vaded," he wrote of the "venal" House of Commons that had expelled
him from membership. "Without any Account they have voted away the
Property of the People . . . violated the Rights of Election, usurped the
legal Powers of Juries, imprisoned our Fellow-subjects, under the Pretence
of their Privileges [of Parliament] contrary to Law, refused even to en-
quire into the foulest Murders, because perpetrated by the Connivance,
at least, of Administration."[2] In the retrospect of the constitutional government that emerged in Great Britain in the nineteenth century, these
charges may strike us as exaggerated. If so, we would be missing the point.
Eighteenth-century readers on both sides of the Atlantic understood the
technique of grievances. The usual method was not just to complain of
governmental measures actually taken, but to warn of more dire consequences yet to come if constitutional vigilance was not strengthened. "In
other countries," Edmund Burke explained, "the people, more simple and
of a less mercurial cast, judge of an ill principle in government only by
an actual grievance; here they anticipate the evil and judge the pressure
of the grievance by the badness of the principle. They augur misgovern-
ment at a distance, and snuff the approach of tyranny in every tainted
breeze."[3]

That tactic, the British opposition tactic of claiming civil and political
rights by stating grievances, made a minor but valuable contribution to
the American whig side of the constitutional controversy leading up to
the American Revolution. Among people supporting colonial whigs in
the mother country were antiministerial members of the Houses of Parliament who frequently employed that tactic, revealing to us what they
understood to be American complaints. In November 1775, at a time when
a British army was besieged in Boston, the Antigua-born Richard Oliver,
a London West Indies merchant and alderman for Billingsgate, moved
in the House of Commons that George III be asked

> who were the original authors and advisers of the following mea-
> sures, before they were proposed by parliament: The taxing Amer-
> ica without consent of its assemblies, for the purpose of raising a
> revenue; for the extending the jurisdiction of the courts of admiralty
> and vice-admiralty; for taking away the charter of the province of
> Massachusett's Bay; for restraining the American fishery; for exempt-
> ing murderers from trial in America; for transporting accused colo-
> nists to England to be tried for offences committed in America, and
> more especially for establishing popery and despotism in Canada.

This series of charges, as well as similar ones, should be seen from two
perspectives: both as a listing of British grievances and a schedule of

American rights. "They," the London Common Council inveighed against the ministry, "have established numberless unconstitutional Regulations and Taxations in our Colonies; they have caused a Revenue to be raised in some of them by Prerogative; they have appointed Civil Law Judges to try Revenue Causes, and to be paid from out of the Condemnation Money." The lord mayor, aldermen, and livery protested the "intolerable acts" in language at least as extreme as any employed by colonial assemblies. The Boston Port Act was described as "the most merciless policy, of starving our fellow subjects into a total surrender of their liberties, and an unlimited submission to arbitrary government." The Massachusetts and Quebec Acts were condemned as measures taking away "chartered rights" "in order to deprive the people of every legal exertion against tyranny of their rulers; the habeas corpus act, and trial by jury have been suppressed, and French despotic government, with the Roman catholic religion, have been established by law over an extensive part of your majesty's dominions in America." Saying that Americans should have liberty equal to that of the British, the London officials concluded:

> It is therefore with the deepest concern, that we have seen the sacred security of representation in their assemblies wrested from them, the trial by jury abolished, and the odious powers of excise extended to all cases of revenue: the sanctuary of their houses laid open to violation at the will and pleasure of every officer and servant of the customs; the dispensation of justice corrupted, by rendering their judges dependent for their seats and salaries on the will of the crown; liberty and life rendered precarious by subjecting them to be dragged over the ocean, and tried for treason or felony here, where the distance making it impossible for the most guiltless to maintain his innocence, must deliver him up a victim to ministerial vengeance; soldiers and others in America have been instigated to shed the blood of the people, by establishing a mode of trial which holds out impunity for such murder.[4]

We should not wonder that British opposition and colonial whigs raised the same American grievances. They believed, after all, that they were defending the same constitutional tradition. But there was a discernible difference in tone. As the British were attacking the ministry, their complaints tended to be colored by political considerations. To them the evil was less the actual destruction of individual rights than a supposed ministerial conspiracy to impose arbitrary rule. The American assemblies and other colonial whig bodies, by contrast, never forgot that their complaint was not political but constitutional. Their wording tended to be less belligerent and more legal. The difference can be seen by reaction to the "intolerable acts." The London Common Council as just quoted called the Boston Port Act "merciless," a plot to starve Bostonians into accepting "arbitrary government." The Bostonians themselves focused attention on the question of law and legality, voting that "the late acts of the British parliament, for blocking up the harbor of Boston, and for altering the established form of government in this colony, and for screening the most flagitious violators of the laws of the province from a legal trial, are gross infractions of those rights, to which we are justly entitled by the laws of nature, the British constitution, and the charter of the province." Similarly, where the Londoners had complained that British "soldiers and others in America have been instigated to shed the blood of the people, by establishing a mode of trial which holds out impunity for such murder," the Continental Congress, also with exaggeration but with attention on procedural consequences, complained that persons indicted for murder in Massachusetts could be sent "to another colony, or even to Great-Britain for trial, whereby such offenders may escape legal punishment."[5]

The argument is not that every statement of grievance by American whig bodies raised constitutional questions. There were exceptions and the various differences should be kept in mind. Some grievances were constitutional and concerned colonial civil rights; this type of grievance was the one most commonly raised. By contrast, there were stated grievances that had the appearance of raising civil-rights issues but did not. An example comes from Franklin's examination at the bar of the House of Commons when he was asked why Americans had become discontented with Parliament. He mentioned a number of statutory impositions including "the restraints lately laid on their trade, by which the bringing of foreign gold and silver into the Colonies was prevented." An even stronger statement on this question, one that seemed to connect trade grievances with colonial rights, was made by the people of Pomfret, Connecticut, when they resolved, "That we have ever unmolestedly enjoyed (except some grievious Acts of Trade, &c.) our just Rights and Privileges, as the true born Sons of Liberty, until the oppressive and detestable Stamp Act." The grievance was about the "Acts of Trade," but it was not a constitutional grievance, for the colonists acknowledged Parliament's constitutional authority to regulate their trade. "[W]hatever the Colonies have suffered in their Commerce from Some Acts of Trade," an anonymous London pamphlet noted in 1766, "they have never pretended that their Rights were infringed by them." What they did complain about— what Franklin probably meant—was how Parliament sometimes exercised its constitutional power of regulation. That was a complaint about policy, not authority, a political not a constitutional grievance. Quite similar was a grievance raised by the first Continental Congress: "The charges of usual offices have been greatly encreased, and new, expensive, and oppressive offices have been multiplied." That, too, was a legislative grievance, not a rights grievance.[6]

A final category of grievances distinguishable from the others consists of those raised by individuals rather than by official colonial institutions. Franklin published an example in the *London Chronicle* when protesting "the most cruel insult that perhaps was ever offered by one people to another, that of emptying our gaols into their settlements."[7] This grievance, like legislative grievances and governance grievances, may have contributed in individual cases to the coming of the American Revolution. It is from a collection of such irritants that dissatisfaction with British rule grew. But these grievances were not concerned with rights and were not part of the constitutional controversy about rights that led to the Revolution.

The American Complaints

Like American whig claims to rights, American whig assertions of grievances remained constant and consistent throughout the revolutionary era. This fact does not mean that as time went on the list of grievances did not grow. But new grievances were not added to the whig bill of indictment because the whig case expanded, but because British policy introduced grievances that previously had not existed. This fact was especially true of legislative grievances. Rejecting Lord North's conciliatory proposal of 1775, which would have eliminated all forms of parliamentary taxation of the colonies except requisitions, Virginia's lawmakers pointed out that even if the grievance of direct taxation for revenue was resolved, the colonies would still have the grievances of (1) the Massachusetts "intolerable acts," (2) New England Fishing Acts, (3) Quebec Act, (4) statutes enlarging the jurisdiction of admiralty courts, (5) parliamentary laws permitting trial of criminal offenses away from the venue, and (6) standing armies. The first three were new grievances, created by the "coercive acts" of 1774 passed in reaction to the Boston Tea Party. At about the same time, New York's General Committee presented that colony's lieutenant governor with a list of eight grievances: (1) taxation without representation, (2) vice-admiralty, (3) trial by vicinage jury, (4) recent restraints on commerce, (5) Port of Boston Act, (6) Massachusetts Government Act, (7) Quebec Act, and (8) the military occupation of Boston. The last five were new grievances growing out of the legislation of 1774 and its enforcement.[8]

The most comprehensive lists of grievances were compiled in 1774 and 1775, a series of colonial lists leading up to the final one in the Declaration of Independence. Because most governors avoided calling assemblies into session, there are few legislative lists of grievances. Much of what we have take the form of instructions to Continental Congress delegates chosen by other kinds of whig bodies, such as congresses and conventions. The result is our loss as the few lists we have that were compiled by legislatures are the outstanding source available for understanding the grievances of the American Revolution. New Jersey's is the most unique, as it discusses in detail the new grievances of legislation and governance — for example, that an army general had been appointed governor of Massachusetts Bay — as well as summarizing all the rights grievances. The New York lists — there are two — are even more valuable, for the question put to the members of the Assembly was whether a specific complaint constituted an American grievance, and the available legislative records reveal that each answer was seriously weighed. These three documents deserve close scrutiny in any analysis of legislative and governance grievances. For purposes of understanding what the colonial assemblies thought were grievances about civil rights it is more useful to quote from a statement by Connecticut's General Assembly. It is to be found not in a petition to the king or an address to the people, but in the preamble of a militia statute enacted in the wake of the Battle of Lexington. Connecticut was preparing for war and in the preamble the legislators explained why the colony was about to fight. They recited the fact of "a sacred compact . . . secured by a Royal Charter," of "rights, liberties and immunities" that had been "the birthright of our brave, virtuous and religious ancestors," who "chose to leave their pleasant seats and all their happy prospects in their native country," tamed "a howling wilderness," and "at the expence of their ease and safety of their blood, their treasure and their lives, transplanted and reared the English constitution in these wilds upon the strong pillars of civil and religious liberty."

> And whereas since the close of the last war the British Parliament claiming a power of right to bind the people of America by statute in all cases whatsoever, hath in some acts expressly imposed taxes upon them, and in others, under various pretences but in fact for the purpose of raising a revenue, hath imposed rates and duties payable in these Colonies, established a Board of Commissioners with unconstitutional powers, and extended the jurisdiction of Courts of Admiralty not only for collecting said duties but also for the tryal of causes merely arising within the body of a county.

> *And whereas* in consequence of other statutes, judges who before
> held only estates at will in their offices have been made to depend on
> the crown alone for their salaries, and standing armies kept in time
> of peace; and it has been lately resolved in Parliament that by force
> of a statute made in thirty-fifth year of the reign of King Henry the
> eighth, colonists may be transplanted to England and tryed there upon
> accusations of treasons and misprisions, or concealment of treasons,
> committed, or alledged to be committed, in the Colonies; and by a
> late statute such tryals have been directed in cases therein mentioned.

The preamble concluded with the grievances of the Massachusetts "intolerable acts," the Quebec Act, the New England Fishery Act, that colonial petitions "have been treated with contempt, or passed by in silence,"
and the military activities in Boston that had led up to the recent fighting
at Lexington and Concord. "[A]ll which acts and measures have relation
to all the British Colonies in the principles from which they flow, and
are evidently intended to force or terrify them into a submission to Parliamentary taxation, or at least a surrender of their property at the pleasure of the British Parliament." The Connecticut Assembly, the preamble
concluded, "wish for no new rights and privileges, and desire only to
preserve their antient constitution as it has been understood and prac-
tised upon from the beginning."[9]

The Continental Congress, the body that spoke for all the assemblies,
and the single official voice for American grievances, compiled several
lists of complaints, ranging from the Continental Association of 1774 to
the Declaration of Independence of 1776.[10] Many of Congress's grievances
had to do with legislation, such as the Massachusetts acts and the charge
that commerce was burdened with oppressive restrictions, or with governance, such as the appointment of the military commander-in-chief as
governor of a colony and the dissolution of assemblies on instructions from
London. Most of the grievances, however, were concerned with rights.
Just what rights Congress thought were in jeopardy can be summarized
by considering two of its statements of grievances, both issued during October 1774, the Declaration of Rights and a petition to the king. Com-
bining the documents and including only the complaints pertaining to
rights as they have been defined in this book, the Continental Congress's
"rights grievances" were:

> The judges of Admiralty and Vice-Admiralty courts are impowered
> to receive their salaries and fees from the effects condemned by them-
> selves. The officers of the Customs are impowered to break open and
> enter houses without the authority of any civil magistrate founded
> on legal information.

The judges of courts of common law have been made entirely dependent on one part of the legislature for their salaries as well as for the duration of their commissions.

Humble and reasonable petitions from the representatives of the people have been fruitless.

The several acts of [Parliament] which impose duties for the purpose of raising a revenue in America, extend the power of the admiralty courts beyond their ancient limits, deprive the American subject of trial by jury, authorise the judges certificate to indemnify the prosecutor from damages, that he might otherwise be liable to, requiring oppressive security from a claimant of ships and goods seized, before he shall be allowed to defend his property; and are subversive of American rights.

Both houses of Parliament have resolved that colonists may be tried in England for offences alleged to have been committed in America by virtue of a statute passed in the thirty-fifth year of Henry the eighth; and in consequence thereof attempts have been made to enforce that statute. A statute was passed in the twelfth year of Your Majesty's reign directing that persons charged with committing any offence therein described in any place out of the realm may be indicted and tried for the same in any shire or county within the realm, whereby inhabitants of these colonies may, in sundry cases by that statute made capital, be deprived of a trial by their peers of the vicinage.[11]

These were the basic American grievances stated by all whig bodies in 1774 and 1775. In some of the statements issued by provincial congresses or county conventions, one grievance might be stressed more than others but always the same core of fundamental rights was repeated and its protection was demanded as a condition for remaining in the Empire. They were the grievances of taxation without representation, of trial without jury or jury trial outside the venue, of the dependence on the Crown by the judiciary for both salary and tenure, and the jurisdiction exercised by the courts of vice-admiralty.

CHAPTER TWENTY-ONE

THE ADMIRALTY GRIEVANCE

It may not have seemed to the congregation of Boston's Second Baptist Church that they had much reason for thankfulness when John Allen, preaching the annual thanksgiving sermon, recited a homily of grievances Americans shared. "See your danger," Allen urged. "[Y]our constitution is declining—your liberties departing, and not content with this, they now attack the *life*, the soul and *capitol* of all your liberties—to chuse your judges, and make them independent upon you for office or support, and erect new courts of admiralty to take away by violence, the husband from his family, his wife, his home, his friends, and his all, through a scene, less joyful than *Pluto's* horrid kingdom. To be confin'd, and tried for his life, by the accusation of a negro."

Allen exaggerated the horribles individuals might experience from the vice-admiralty, but he did not exaggerate the priority American whigs gave the vice-admiralty grievance. Next to taxation without representation, the voters of Boston resolved, "the Jurisdiction of the Admiralty, are our greatest Grievance." The complaint was that vice-admiralty threatened rights. "[W]e look upon our natural Rights to be diminished in the same Proportion, as the Powers of that Court are extended," the inhabitants of Providence voted. They were not making a peculiarly American complaint. Whigs and common lawyers in the mother country would

have voiced the same grievance. "[T]he Vice-Admiralty Court is an institution that should astonish and alarm us," a letter writer told London's
Public Ledger in 1765, "it being such an one as in its nature must prove
destructive to commerce, and appears inconsistent with freedom. . . .
[A]nd yet we find it a hardship to which two millions of British subjects
have become actually subjected."[1]

The purpose of this chapter is to explain what the Connecticut House
of Representatives meant in 1774 when it cited as a grievance the colonial vice-admiralty system, saying it was a constitutional innovation, un-
precedented, arbitrary, imperial, "highly dangerous to the liberties of his
Majesty's *American* subjects, contrary to the great Charter of *English*
liberty, and destructive of one of their most darling rights, that of trial
by juries."[2]

The Procedural Grievances

The vice-admiralty court was not new in the colonies. It had been introduced in the seventeenth century and had long been a minor grievance related primarily to parliamentary supremacy and local control over
government. These were not serious or constitutional complaints because
the vice-admiralty was a trade court, enforcing the Navigation Acts, a
matter Americans acknowledged to be within the constitutional discretion of Parliament. With the Sugar Act of 1764 and the Stamp Act of
1765, new, constitutionally objectionable authority was added to the
jurisdiction. The Sugar Act contained procedural innovations to protect
customs officers from civil liability in local colonial courts. The Stamp
Act was even more a break with precedent: an internal tax for purposes
of revenue unconnected with trade, yet prosecuted at vice-admiralty. The
purpose was to avoid trial before American juries, a fact increasing the
grievance as violation of either act was quasicriminal, meaning that colonists were denied trial by jury in prosecutions resulting in the imposition
of penalties. Moreover, in the case of the Stamp Act the alleged offense
arose "on Land — within the Body of a County — as remote from Admiralty
Jurisdiction on every constitutional Principle, as a Suit on a Bond, or an
Ejectment for a Freehold."[3]

The Sugar Act was less a departure from constitutional norms than
the Stamp Act, but one of its provisions provided the colonists with sensitive political grievances. It created a new vice-admiralty court, located
at Halifax, Nova Scotia, far from the established centers of commerce.
The court had concurrent jurisdiction with the traditional provincial vice-
admiralty courts and might have been unobjectionable had not choice

of forum been at the discretion of the prosecutor or informer. That choice could mean, the Massachusetts legislature pointed out, that "many persons, however legally their goods may have been imported, must lose their property, merely from an inability of following after." As a result, the voters of Cambridge argued when discussing enforcement of the Stamp Act, "The Distributor of the Stamps, or Mr. INFORMER, have a Sovereignty over every Thing but the Lives of the People, since it is in their Power to summon every one they please to *Quebec, Montreal* or *Newfoundland,* to answer for the pretended or real Breaches of this Act."[4]

The grievance did not prove serious. Few cases — perhaps only one — were removed from the older colonies to Halifax, and with the Townshend Statutes of 1767 Parliament again altered the admiralty jurisdiction by providing for four courts — in Boston, Philadelphia, and Charleston, as well as Halifax. But perceptions were more important than actualities. Colonial whigs had a judicial grievance reminding people of former English constitutional grievances, now virtually eliminated in the mother country, against the high commission and other church courts. They also had a legislative grievance, as the vice-admiralty statutes demonstrated both the potential of Parliament's claim to legislative supremacy, and Parliament's potential insensitivity to American rights.[5]

Other aspects of the vice-admiralty jurisdiction also were grievances. The owner of a ship or goods seized by the customs service had to post a heavy bond before being permitted to contest the seizure. The burden of proving that alleged contraband was not subject to duty or not in violation of the Navigation Acts was on the claimant "and not upon the officer who shall seize or stop the same: any law, custom, or usage to the contrary notwithstanding." Costs were assessed against the owner even when trial ended in acquittal.[6] And the grievance about which Americans most complained, "if the judge of admiralty will certify that there was probable cause of seizure, no action shall be maintained by the claimant though his goods on trial appear to be ever so duly imported and liable to no sort of forfeiture, and he hath been forced to expend ever so much in the defense of them." Again, the colonists were being treated unequally for, as Oxenbridge Thacher pointed out in the first important pamphlet on law of the American Revolution, the "last regulation is in the act peculiarly confined to America."[7]

THE CIVIL-LAW GRIEVANCE

There was a reverse side to the grievance of trial without a jury — the grievance of trial by a single judge. "[I]n this Vice Admiralty Court," Ar-

thur Lee explained, "a *King's judge holding his place during pleasure,
and receiving his money* . . . from the condemnations in his Court *determines all causes,* between the Crown and the subject *without a Jury*."[8]
There were three serious objections to the single judge presiding at vice-admiralty. First, he was a "King's judge," appointed by London to enforce the imperial trade laws and serving at pleasure. Second, he was
paid in part by fees received by the court and by a share of the condemnations he decreed. And third, he was a civil-law, not a common-law,
judge. Together, these three aspects of the admiralty jurisdiction were
said to encourage condemnations and deprive Americans of any likelihood of fair trial.[9] In addition, there was a fourth, more subtle grievance: there was no appeal from vice-admiralty "to the quarter sessions
as in *England*" where appeal was allowed, "so that no redress is to be
expected; or, if to be obtained, can be worth the expence of procuring."
The complaint was not just about equality with the English or about
the right to have a lower-court judgment reviewed, but that in England
appeal was to the quarter sessions which meant review at common law.
There was no common law in colonial vice-admiralty, either at first instance or on appeal, a much more serious grievance in the eighteenth
century than might be thought today. "[W]e are obliged," the people of
Newburyport complained, "to submit to a Jurisdiction naturally foreign
to" the British constitution, "where the Laws of Justinian are the Measure of Right, and the Common Law, the collected Wisdom of the British Nation for Ages, is not admitted." The law of Justinian was Roman
law or civil law, a law associated with arbitrary government, not with
liberty, and one more indication of Parliament's willingness to accord
unequal protection to American rights. "Unlike the *antient Barons,* who
answered with one voice 'We will not that the Laws of England be
changed, which of old have been used and approved'," the Boston town
meeting lamented, "the Barons of *modern* Times seem to have answered,
that *they* are willing those Laws should be changed, with Regard to
America, in the most tender Point and fundamental Principle!"[10]

It would be difficult to document this grievance and evaluate what
it meant in practical terms. Aside from two undoubted defects of civil-law procedure (no juries and the rule placing the burden of proof on defendants rather than prosecutors), there were no serious, substantive objections that could be raised against the jurisdiction. There were features
to the vice-admiralty jurisdiction that many Americans had found acceptable before the revolutionary controversy commenced, notably *in rem*
proceedings. Moreover, most of the judges appointed to the court were
trained in common law and, because they were generally unfamiliar with
civil law, they probably applied common-law procedure. It seems likely

that a good deal of the colonial antagonism was based not on specifics but on general features associated with a civil-law tribunal — the fact they were being treated unequally and the fact that the civil law had long been equated with arbitrary government and, in popular British mythology, was thought to be the antithesis of common law, the law of liberty. The real grievance against vice-admiralty, then, was that it presaged an increase of prerogative law, the one branch of British law with which the civil law was traditionally linked in English constitutional thought. The introduction of civil law to try "offenses and matters done at land is a great and dangerous breach of the constitution," William Bollan warned, writing on the topic of British elections in 1769. "Attempts have been made in times past to introduce the civil law; the rack which now lies in the tower was brought in for a begin[n]ing of it, but these attempts were repelled by our ancestors."[11] It was as much the image as the reality that caused alarm, as much the history as the present menace that was the grievance. Because of the dark reputation civil law had in English history — its association with the courts of Star Chamber and High Commission — the whig press could mount exaggerated yet convincing attacks on the vice-admiralty jurisdiction. Colonists had heard stories of the oath *ex officio mero* which the civil-law courts of England once administered to parties and, by asking any questions the judges pleased, trapped people into incriminating themselves. There was, for that reason, a degree of credibility to "John English's" conjecture of the ordeal awaiting Samuel Adams should the customs commissioners sue him for libel in admiralty. Once Adams was sworn he could expect questions that had nothing to do with the matter at bar. "Pray Sir," he would be asked, "when did you kiss your maid Mary?—Where? and in what manner? Did you lay with her in a barn? or in your own house?"[12] We might think the scenario farfetched, but people who believed that the Star Chamber once asked those questions of seventeenth-century defendants might well be apprehensive that vice-admiralty would ask them of eighteenth-century Americans.

THE INEQUALITY GRIEVANCE

The American whig grievance comprehended by more people than any other must have been the jury-trial grievance. And little wonder, for the right and the grievance were the reverse sides of the same coin and jury trial was the major element in the admiralty grievance.[13]

Because security of property was at stake, the jury-trial grievance concerned liberty as liberty was defined in the eighteenth century. Although there were, to be sure, penal aspects to vice-admiralty judgments, they did not involve life and limb. It was property that was libelled. Property was insecure, Virginia's House of Burgesses pointed out, "where Trial by Jury, the surest Support of Property, is denied." It was difficult to over-state the grievance, although Governor Stephen Hopkins may have done so when complaining that, due to the Sugar Act, Americans "hold all their mercantile property upon no better tenure than the will of revenue officers, and of the admiralty judge." If it was an exaggeration, it was one that many whigs feared might in time become reality.[14]

A second vice-admiralty grievance that no whig thought could be ex-aggerated was the inequality grievance. The colonists were "deprived of that firmest barrier of English liberty, *the trial by Juries*; at the same time that our fellow subjects in Great-Britain enjoy the Benefit of it in its full extent," the voters of Salem, Massachusetts, complained to their representative in the General Court. "The deprivation of such an essen-tial privilege, & so partial a distinction, cannot but awaken the jealosy of every American."[15]

Imperialists protested that the colonial whigs had their law wrong. There was nothing unequal in the vice-admiralty jurisdiction. "Offences against the Excise Laws, and against one or more late Acts of Trade, are determined without a Jury in England," Thomas Hutchinson argued. "I recollect no cases in which trials by Juries are taken away in America, by Acts of Parliament, except such as are tried in the Courts of Admir-alty, and these are either for breaches of the Act of trade, or trespasses upon the King's woods." The argument, which was often repeated, had validity, as some British taxes, not just in Scotland but in England and Wales, were prosecuted before judges without juries. One major instance besides the excise was stamp duties, a part of the American grievance that Hutchinson had not mentioned as the American Stamp Act had been repealed before it could be enforced in any court.

Colonial whigs answered that these British similarities did not miti-gate their inequality grievance against vice-admiralty. Hutchinson's argu-ment was an accurate appraisal of the comparative constitutional situa-tions only in one respect. Americans were being treated equally with the Scots as all Scottish judges were civilians, but civil law, not common law, was the law of Scotland and not a grievance there. In England, judges presiding over the juryless cases were common-law jurists, sitting in common-law courts, bound by common-law procedure. Vice-admiralty in England was limited to transactions on the seas and, unlike the colo-nies, was not extended to matters arising on land. "There is this great essential difference between" the two countries, Thacher pointed out, "in Great Britain no jurisdiction is given to any other than the common law courts; there too the subjects are near the throne, where, when they are oppressed, their complaints may soon be heard and redressed; but with respect to the colonies, far different is the case!" Hugh Baillie, Scots lawyer and admiralty judge for Ireland, who believed the important fact was how questions of property were tried, thought the Americans had the best of the argument. Just because English courts of admiralty could try some matters without juries did not mean they would ever be allowed to try cases involving property without juries, "and yet this is the thing complained of in *America*, that they are deprived of the privilege of English subjects, by being deprived of having their properties tryed by juries as in *England*."[16]

The inequality grievance against vice-admiralty was one of the most serious constitutional contentions leading to the American Revolution. It had been present throughout the entire controversy, somewhat latent as early as 1764 before the Stamp Act was passed, and still an issue in 1774 when the Pennsylvania Provincial Congress drafted the list of grievances that it expected the Continental Congress to demand that Parliament remedy. Of eight items raised, the one dealing with vice-admiralty was directed exclusively at the inequality grievance. Parliament was not asked to give up the jurisdiction; rather, it was told to renounce its claim to the authority of enacting "statutes giving the courts of Admiralty *in the colonies* greater power than courts of Admiralty have *in England*."[17]

THE DUTY OF RIGHTS

Eighteenth-century constitutional theory imposed duties on the British people; one was the duty to transmit, preserve, and defend rights. William Pitt, the earl of Chatham, referred to this duty when he told the House of Lords in 1774 "that the principal towns in *America* are learned and polite, and understand the constitution of the empire as well as the noble Lords who are in office; and consequently, they will have a watchful eye over their liberties, to prevent the least encroachment on their hereditary rights." Three months later a majority of North Carolina's convention concluded that it was time for Americans to shoulder that duty, urging the Continental Congress "to take such measures as they may deem prudent to effect the purpose of describing with certainty the rights of *Americans*; repairing the breaches made in those rights; and for guarding them for the future."[1]

We are so accustomed to thinking the North Carolina resolution representative of American thought in the age of the American Revolution that it is well to draw back and remind ourselves that what was being expressed was a hackneyed British constitutional value. "As at present we live under a government, the most perfect in *Europe*," a London writer of 1766 explained in a typical example of the sentiment, "it is the indispensible interest and duty of every true *Briton* to maintain those privileges, which have been conveyed to us from our ancestors, through so many generations, inviolable; upon which all our temporal (and in a great measure our eternal) happiness, safety, and well being depends." There was little to fear as long as the British people were vigilant and vigilance was their civic habit. Should they become apathetic they would cease to be British, a second London pamphlet explained three years later. "If the people of *England* shall ever come to be in so benumbed a state, as not to feel, and to shew they feel, any real invasion of their essential rights and privileges, the body politic must then be far advanced in a general mortification, that can end in nothing less than the death of Liberty."[2]

Although not likely, it was possible for even the vigilant British to become "benumbed" by a sense of security. "The Rights of the People are never in greater danger than when they least suspect them so to be," a barrister contended in 1768. "If they are lulled into a security, the enemy is ever watchful to seize the opportunity. Commendable, therefore, is the employment of those who are upon guard, to sound the alarm whenever the enemy approaches." The message was that the constitution alone could not guarantee rights. Citizens had to mount guard and maintain a watch on the very institutions that sheltered them from arbitrariness. "From these examples," Britons were warned in 1769, "we may learn, that we shall not be secure against danger, merely by keeping up the antient form of our Government, as we received it from our Ancestors. We must retain its virtue and essence. Let us therefore *contend earnestly for the* constitution *once delivered to us*; and with its outward form, study to preserve its inward vigour, and not suffer any of our Rights to been [*sic*] croached upon or invaded."[3]

THE DUTY TO TRANSMIT

The duty to defend rights was entailed on the possessors of rights not only by the tenure of ownership but by inheritance. In part, it was a matter of honoring and repaying the forebears who had bequeathed the legacy of rights. "Should we, or any succeeding age, despise our *liberty*, so dearly bought, what do we, but trample upon our fathers dust, and disturb the ashes of our godly ancestors, who purchased this land for us at so great expense?" Amos Adams asked, preaching the 1768 thanksgiving sermon at Roxbury, Massachusetts. The North Carolina Convention six years later thought the duty was not just to transmit, but if possible to improve and not to disgrace the heritage of those to whom so much was owed.

> [I]t is the duty, and will be the endeavour of us as *British Americans*, to transmit this happy Constitution to our posterity in a state, if possible, better than we found it; and that to suffer it to undergo a change which may impair that invaluable blessing, would be to disgrace those ancestors, who, at the expense of their blood, purchased those privileges which their degenerate posterity are too weak or too wicked to maintain inviolate.

The duty, then, could be rationalized, or made even stronger by tying it to the migration purchase. People "should keep a jealous eye" on their rights, Charles Chauncy asserted in the 1747 Massachusetts election sermon, "and think no cost too much to be expended, for the defence and security of them: Especially, if they were the purchase of wise and pious ancestors, who submitted to difficulties, endured hardships, spent their estates, and ventured their lives, that they might transmit them as an inheritance to their posterity."[4]

The duty owed to ancestors to preserve gifts they had bequeathed was a concept American whigs shared with fellow whigs in Great Britain. In 1768 a London pamphleteer commenting on the Wilkes controversy urged his readers "to shew themselves Britons, and to stand up in defence of their birthright; their liberties, which their fore-fathers purchased with seas of blood, to entail upon their posterity."[5]

Both Chauncy and the British pamphleteer expressed a similar thought: that after purchasing rights, the ancestors had entailed those rights on their descendants. That vesting gave rise to a second explanation why there was a duty to defend rights, for with the transmission of rights from the former generation came the duty to transmit them to the next generation. "Our Rights are our own to keep but not to relinquish," the whig divine Samuel Johnson observed, for "we are but Tenants for Life; and as they were Transmitted to us by our Forefathers oftentimes sealed with their Blood, so we ought to leave them, Dry at least, to our Posterity." The concept was expressed in a variety of ways in both America and Great Britain. In New Jersey, people in Essex County spoke of "the [uncalculable] priviledges of Englishmen [that] have not only been handed down to us, but committed to our Care & improvement, as well for our own, as the felicity of our remotest posterity." Further south, Richard Henry Lee urged Virginians "to hand down to your children, the liberty given you by your fathers." Across the Atlantic, in the previous decade, John Shebbeare had told Britons to "deliver the Constitution to your Sons as you received it from your Fathers," and the author of the *Guide to Rights* argued that as "our great and generous Forefathers" took care to secure "every Man in the quiet Possession of his Rights, Liberties and Properties; I think it incumbent upon us, who are their Successors, to be very watchful over so precious a Jewel, and to take Care that so glorious an Inheritance may descend whole, and intire to our Posterity."[6]

The obligation owed to posterity was another theory why the living generation had a duty to transmit rights, a duty that had nothing to do with a debt inherited from ancestors. Today's people, who enjoy rights and who will be followed by heirs entitled to the same happiness, have a duty to leave their progeny happiness comparable to their own. John Dickinson explained the principle in instructions written for Pennsylvania legislators.

> No infamy, inequity, or cruelty, can exceed our own; if we, born and educated in a country of freedom, entitled to its blessings, and knowing their value, *pusillanimously* deserting the post assigned to us by Divine Providence, *surrender* succeeding generations to a condition of wretchedness, from which no human efforts, in all probability, will be sufficient to extricate them: the experience of all states mournfully demonstrating to us, that when arbitrary power has been established over them, even the wisest and bravest nations that ever flourished have, in a few years, degenerated into abject and wretched vassals.[7]

Even William Blackstone said that the British had the duty of transmission. "The protection of the LIBERTY of BRITAIN," he wrote in the best summary of the doctrine, "is a duty which they owe to themselves, who enjoy it; to their ancestors, who transmitted it down; and to their posterity, who will claim at their hands this the best birthright, and noblest inheritance of mankind."[8]

THE DUTIES TO PRESERVE AND DEFEND

It may be that no set of resolutions or any individual writer said that the duty to transmit rights was either constitutional or legal, but there can be no doubt that that was what people thought.[9] A New Englander argued in 1739 that it was the living generation's duty to posterity "to preserve" rights "entire, without suffering the least Breach to be made on them."[10] The operative concept in that statement was "preservation." For rights to be transmitted, they first had to be preserved "without diminution or abridgement,"[11] a duty that might require positive steps to be taken. "[W]e are determined, for ourselves and posterity," the whig committee of Virginia's New Kent County voted in resolutions that were repeated up and down the Atlantic seaboard, "to support and maintain the rights and privileges of British subjects, which we are entitled to, against all tyrannical attempts whatever."[12]

The British thought of the duty to preserve rights as an active, practiced part of their constitution. "It is the peculiar privilege of this country, in all matters of concernment to the state," someone wrote in the *Gentleman's Magazine* for 1765, "to communicate our sentiments to the public, to give out the alarm where we see danger to the safety of our constitution, and to warn our fellow citizens of their approaching fate." The duty in Great Britain generally was said to go much further. In *An Historical Essay on the English Constitution*, published in London in 1771 and again in 1776, the author (either Obadiah Hulme or Allen Ramsay), said that the duty mandated active, coercive defense of rights by "using every legal remedy." We must not be misled by the adjective "legal" in the expression "legal remedy." One aspect of British constitutional rights was the right to resist even the government's invasion of them. Should the government invade rights, the invasion would be "unlawful" and resistance to the invasion "lawful." Bass Crosby, lord mayor of London, was speaking of a "legal remedy" when he told the inhabitants of Farringdon Without that to preserve rights he would oppose even the authority of Parliament. "The frequent Invasions which have been made on the Rights and Liberties of this Country," he wrote while confined in the Tower of London for resisting the House of Commons, "demand the strenuous Opposition of every honest Friend of Liberty and Law."[13]

In a series of charges to South Carolina grand juries, William Henry Drayton drew the final legal conclusion possible, saying that the duty was not just to the constitution and personal rights, but to the law as well, and that it might be illegal to neglect the duty. As heirs of English emigrants, Carolinians had received rights from "a parentage," Drayton told the jurors, and had given authority to laws by consenting to their operation. It followed that "by your not executing what those laws require, you would weaken the force, and would shew, I may almost say, a treasonable contempt of those constitutional rights out of which your laws arise, and which you ought to defend and support at the hazard of your lives."[14]

Drayton said that the duty to defend rights gave a legality to the "hazard" of life. Other whigs acted on that legality. It was, the committee of Chester County, Pennsylvania, voted a month after the Battle of Lexington, "the indispensable duty of all the freemen of this County" to take up arms "to defend our liberty, property, and lives, against all attempts to deprive us of them." Certainly not everyone in Great Britain, but many people, including some in high office, understood that it was "law" the Americans acted on and understood the legal principles on which colonial whigs relied, because they were British principles supposedly as old as the English constitution. The Americans, London's Common Council told King George, "ought to enjoy peace, liberty, and safety," and "whatever power invades these rights ought to be resisted." The legal theory of the duty to defend rights was based on the ownership of rights and explained in 1694 by Samuel Johnson as a revolution principle. "[T]he Rights of the Nation being Invaded, may be Defended; for otherwise they are No Rights," Johnson wrote. This legal theory was frequently voiced in the House of Commons during debates on American affairs. For illustration it would be useful to quote a tory rather than a whig, Charles Manners, marquis of Granby, member for Cambridge University, and future duke of Rutland. Two weeks before the Battle of Lexington, speaking against the bill that would have restrained the commerce of all the colonies except New York and Georgia, he justified American resistance: "If the peaceable part of mankind must tamely relinquish their property and their freedom, and submit to the yoke of the oppressor, merely to avoid the imputation of rebellion, where are your inherent and indefeasible rights, the glory and the boast of Englishmen?"[15]

CHAPTER TWENTY-THREE

THE EXIGENCY OF RIGHTS

Just as it contained fundamental rights, so also eighteenth-century British constitutional law contained their opposites, fundamental grievances, and these too were part of the American constitutional case leading to the Revolution. To say some rights were fundamental is not to say that there was a scale of importance to rights on which some were considered more fundamental or "higher" than others. The distinction, rather, was that some rights were less imperiled than others and that threats to rights were not all the same. The colonists would never have rebelled over denial of petition if that was the only right taken from them. Denial of the right to petition would not have aroused concern when the public press was uncensored and every petition was published. People knew that petitions were being read and, therefore, whether or not petitions were officially received, their chief function was served. The right to be taxed only by consent was different. It was too fundamental in British constitutionalism to be overlooked when in jeopardy. It could, however, be ignored when not in danger, as with the Tea Act at the time when dutied tea was not being landed and taxes were not being collected, or with the Sugar Act, when its terms were perceived as ambiguous and there was disagreement as to whether it was a tax measure or a trade regulation.

Eighteenth-century constitutional theory required that some rights, once threatened, be defended: rights essential to the contemporary definition of liberty, rights without which the British constitution could not exist. Some of these were factors in the revolutionary controversy. Taxation by consent was a right American whigs had to defend, even at the risk of war, as they showed when, in all but one of their seaports, they prevented the landing of East India tea. Another was the right to trial by jury. Americans were denied this right in very special circumstances, all of them pertaining to revenue cases. In fact, the colonial grievance of trial by jury was so closely associated with the grievance of parliamentary taxation for purpose of revenue, that, as a practical matter, it is difficult to separate the two grievances, and to imagine how the trial-by-jury grievance alone could have produced rebellion. Moreover, jury trial was denied not by abolishing the right to a jury but by shifting special types of cases from common law to the vice-admiralty court, which sat without juries. Thus, although the substantive grievance may have been the denial of a jury, the constitutional grievance was the extension of the admiralty jurisdiction. The complaint had to be stated against the jurisdiction, and, as a result, the jury grievance was encompassed within the admiralty grievance. This was a matter of verbal expression that may not have affected the constitutional substance but did alter the appearance of constitutional grievances. An example is provided by the last New York petition of grievances complaining that Parliament had extended "the Courts of Admiralty beyond their ancient limits, giving them a concurrent jurisdiction, in causes heretofore cognizable only in Courts of Common Law, and by that means depriving the *American* subjects of a trial by Jury." The right to trial by jury was more fundamental than the right not to be tried at vice-admiralty, and, next to parliamentary taxation for purposes of revenue, Americans thought it their most serious "rights" grievance. Yet, because of the way the issue was wrapped up in another, it was not always stated in a form that expressed its constitutional importance.[1]

Quite different was the other jury grievance: change of venue. That could be stated in terms of constitutional survival, terms delineated by the Massachusetts House of Representatives when it condemned the "dockyards" act as "a measure repugnant to justice, highly derogatory to our rights, and shakes the very foundation of our constitution by not only depriving the American subjects of the very important right of juries from the vicinage but subjects them to be transported from their friends and neighbours to be tried in a distant country beyond the seas, in any county in Great Britain." A constitutional grievance could not be more strongly stated than that. To say it "shakes the very foundation" of constitutional law is to label it an intolerable grievance. And yet the venue complaint turned out to be less a grievance about rights than about abortive parliamentary power. It was more symbolic than real, symbolic of what Parliament threatened in curtailing or abolishing American rights, rather than a demonstrable threat to trial by jury. If that fact seems questionable, recall the *Gaspee* affair. Parliament might enact a statute but that statute was little more than a theoretical grievance if it could not be enforced, and, as the burning of *Gaspee* proved, the imperial government could not enforce the dockyards statute in North America. London needed the cooperation of local officials before colonists could be removed from the vicinage of the crime to an English county for trial. Rhode Islanders burned the revenue cutter *Gaspee* and the colony's officials knew who burned it, but no one was sent to Britain for trial. The statute's only effect on the course of events was as a grievance, and to the extent it was a grievance it helped the cause of militant American whigs. It made no contribution to the substance of imperial rule.[2]

More clearly identified as a separate grievance, unconnected with the issue of parliamentary supremacy, was the grievance of a dependent judiciary. Judicial salaries and appointments were matters both enforceable by the British Crown and of significance to every colony, although the grievance differed from colony to colony. Until the Massachusetts "coercive legislation" of 1774, the constitutional grievance did not include royal appointment of judges. In some colonies, such as Massachusetts, judges had been appointed locally, and had quite often been natives, such as Thomas Hutchinson who was chief justice of the colony before becoming governor. In other colonies, one of which was South Carolina, judges had been appointed by the Crown and generally were placemen sent from London to preside over local provincial courts. These differences in the process of judicial selection were well established in the imperial constitution, long part of the customary colonial constitutions, and did not contribute to the revolutionary controversy. What had been judicial grievances even before the 1760s had been the tenure of office enjoyed by judges. This grievance would always have been a serious irritant in imperial relations, especially as Americans became more jealous of their right to enjoy equal rights with the British, but it is doubtful if judicial tenure alone could have precipitated a constitutional crisis. In any case, after passage of the Townshend duties and the Massachusetts "coercive acts," the grievance of judicial tenure was subsumed by the larger constitutional issue of parliamentary supremacy. First, the Townshend legislation introduced the question of judicial salaries, as the revenue from the duties was to pay colonial judges, even some appointed locally. Next, in 1774, the Massachusetts government statute took the election of councilors from the House of Representatives and vested their appointment in the Crown, with the result that Massachusetts judges, who now were appointed by the governor and Council, held their offices at the pleasure of London. The new grievance for the people of Massachusetts, Arthur Lee pointed out, was "the Violation of their Security in the due Administration of Government and of Justice, by rendering the Governor and Judges *totally* dependent on the Crown." The mayor, aldermen, and livery of London charged that this judiciary grievance could be applied to all the colonies, for "the Dispensation of Justice" had been "corrupted, by rendering their Judges dependent, for their seats and salaries, on the will of the Crown." The grievance still related to judicial independence, tenure, and salaries, but, because of the manner in which the salary and appointment innovations had been promulgated, the grievance shifted from one about rights and the authority of governance to parliamentary supremacy. According to the Suffolk Resolves, Massachusetts citizens had to determine which command was constitutional: the old command of local provincial law with judges dependent on both the legislature and the Crown, or the newer command of Parliament with judges dependent on the Crown alone. "[S]o long as the justices of our superior courts of judicature . . . are appointed, or hold their places by any other tenure than that which the charter and the laws of the province direct, they must be considered as under undue influence, and are, therefore, unconstitutional officers, and as such, no regard ought to be paid to them by the people."[3]

THE SEARCH-WARRANT GRIEVANCE

Two other "nongrievous" grievances deserve mention because of their great importance to the controversy over rights in the American Revolution and to future American constitutional law. One was the right of homeowners not to have soldiers quartered in private residences and the other was the right of property owners to be secure against unreasonable searches and seizures conducted by government agencies. Both of these rights and their violation by the British provided colonial whigs with some of their most emotional arguments. Moreover, legends about violations of these rights have entered the folklore of the American Revolution, with tales of an arbitrary militarism intruding on personal privacy, leading to demands that protections be included in the federal Bill of Rights. Article 3 of the Bill of Rights prohibits quartering troops in time of peace and article 4 restricts searches to warrants issued for probable cause. Even today, civil libertarians surround both articles 3 and 4 with a mythology about the British army being forced on colonial homeowners and of British soldiers in the colonies smashing down warehouse doors in search of contraband goods.

A twentieth-century civil libertarian who compared the federal Bill of Rights to the British statutes regarding quartering troops in eighteenth-century North America might well find more to praise in the imperial laws. The Bill of Rights prohibits quartering troops in private homes in peacetime; the two parliamentary statutes controlling the British army in the colonies forbade billeting soldiers in private houses in war as well as peace. Quarters had to be found in inns, livery stables, alehouses, victual houses, and houses of wine retailers, by the terms of the first statute, and uninhabited houses, outhouses, barns, "or other buildings" under the quartering law of 1774 (one of the "intolerable acts" that precipitated the Revolution). More to the point, the two statutes were practically unenforceable. Sensitive to American rights, the House of Commons had made certain the military could not abuse its authority by making the British army subject to local whig control. Troops not only were not quartered in private colonial houses, officers also encountered legal difficulties in finding any housing. The quartering acts were a grievance only because Parliament had enacted them, not for what they provided or how they affected colonial personal rights.[4]

Search warrants were much more a British grievance than an American grievance during the 1760s. General warrants issued by executive authority without judicial supervision were a grievance the colonies did not share with the mother country. For one thing, the secretary of state executed them and there was no comparable officer in America. For another, general warrants were used to identify persons responsible for printing libelous material, a meaningless pursuit in the colonies where printers could not be prosecuted since juries would not indict or convict for seditious publication. Why then were search warrants a colonial grievance? The answer is that they were a vicarious grievance. It must be suspected that the American apprehension about government searches came from reading British publications — blanket, unqualified condemnations of the grievance by the British press and the common-law bar. Due in part to the fact that the issue came to the public's attention as a result of the government's effort to prosecute John Wilkes, no other legal topic received so much publicity in the mother country during the revolutionary era, or was scrutinized in so many pamphlets. Searches by executive rather than judicial authority were condemned by a wide range of political and legal opinion, including the administration's chief lawyer, Lord Chief Justice Mansfield. "The messenger, under this warrant," Chief Justice Camden explained in *Entick* v. *Carrington*, "is commanded to seize the person described, and to bring him with his papers to be examined before the secretary of state." If such a warrant was legal, Camden warned, "the secret cabinets and bureaus of every subject in this kingdom will be thrown open to the search and inspection of a messenger, whenever the secretary of state shall think fit to charge, or even to suspect, a person to be the author, printer, or publisher of a seditious libel." The warrant, the chief justice ruled in *Leach* v. *Money*, was illegal, as "our law holds property so sacred, that no man can set his foot on his neighbor's close without his leave." Or, he should have added, without the leave of Parliament, for had there been a statute authorizing them, general warrants would have been upheld.[5]

The British cider excise statute was also of some importance in educating Americans about search-and-seizure rights, even though the excise did not apply to the colonies. It imposed on Great Britain a tax that raised constitutional issues remarkably similar to those raised by the Stamp Act. The cider excise statute was repealed as a result of opposition similar to the opposition that forced the Stamp Act repeal. When the cider excise was first enacted, dissentient lords protested its search-and-seizure implications. Houses, they complained, "are made liable to be entered and searched at pleasure. We deem this to be not only an intolerable oppression, affecting private property, and destructive of the peace and quiet of private families; but . . . [also] 'a badge of slavery'." The lord mayor, aldermen, and Commons of London also used the term "badge of slavery" when petitioning against the act on the grounds that it exposed "private houses to be entered into, and searched at pleasure, by persons unknown." Opposition was aroused not by the tax, but by the constitutional grievance. Anticipating American whig arguments two years later against the Stamp Act, people in Cullompton, Devonshire, told the lord mayor of London that excise laws "strike at the fundamentals of our constitution, and have ever been looked upon as most grievous and oppressive." The assessment was not on the sale of cider but on its consumption at the farm where it was manufactured. The law, therefore, did not affect nonagricultural places, especially London, yet London's court of Common Council led the opposition, on grounds that the act "is inconsistent with those principles of liberty, which have hitherto distinguished this nation from arbitrary governments."[6]

Such language must not be dismissed as the sloganeering of opposition rhetoric. Rather, it was conventional constitutional thought, reflecting the way most Britons wished to see themselves and the society in which they lived. Moreover, the sanctity of private homes was a measure of constitutional conduct that even supporters of the excise conceded to be the legal ideal when they defended the search-and-seizure powers not on the grounds of constitutionality but on the justification of necessity. The extent to which that constitutional criterion represented contemporary constitutional wisdom and constitutional standards can be grasped by considering the strong words and decisive law applied by the Privy Council the next year, disallowing a New Hampshire law protecting deer. The purpose of the legislation was good, the Privy Council admitted, and perhaps even necessary, "but the Powers therein given are very extraordinary and totally inconsistent with the Principles of this [British] Constitution." The objectionable part of the act was the authority New Hampshire vested in the deer keepers appointed to enforce the law.

> [T]hey to have full Power to search all Places, and to open all Doors and Chests, or other Places locked or concealed where they have reason to suspect the Flesh or Skins of any Deer killed at such unseasonable times to be hid. . . . That the Power of searching given by this Clause is so very extensive, that it is unsafe to be entrusted with any one, as no Information upon Oath is required, nor the Warrant of any Civil Magistrate made necessary, nor indeed is the having in possession any such Flesh or Skins created an Offence by this or any other Act, nor any Penalty thereon inflicted, and yet this Act is to supersede all other Methods of Prosecution for killing Deer.[7]

By the ideals of British constitutionalism, the New Hampshire statute was too sweeping, but it was no more sweeping than the search powers of the cider excise law. Nor was it much more drastic than another parliamentary enactment that did apply to the colonies, and that the whigs made a constitutional grievance, the writ of assistance authorizing entry into private homes and places of business by customs officers seeking evidence of undutied goods. In this instance, the warrant was in the statute and the writ was a judicial document allowing the customs man to commandeer the assistance of a local peace officer. The writ was issued to the official for his career, not on the evidence of suspected lawbreaking, and could be used to search any premises as neither locations nor individual suspects had to be identified. The writ, in other words, resembled a general search warrant, an objection raised against the British version of the writ by a London writer in 1771.

> The powers which our statute law gives to the officers of the customs are still more grievous than those given to the officers of the excise. By virtue of a *general warrant* from the exchequer, called a Writ of Assistance, which they have not scrupled to give to the meanest custom-house officer who will pay for it, that officer has power to order a constable to attend him, and to enter any house, to break open any doors, to seize whatever customable or prohibited goods

he finds, and to lodge them in the king's warehouse; and, if within a certain time the owner does not claim them, and prove that they have paid the duties they ought to have paid, they are forfeited.

Objectionable as this power was in Great Britain, it was even more grievous in the colonies, Boston's *Journal of the Times* contended in an article explaining the constitutional argument to American readers. "If such power was in the least degree dangerous there," the *Journal* said of Great Britain, "it must be utterly destructive to liberty here. For the people of England have two securities; against the undue exercise of this power by the crown, which are wanting with us. In the first place if any unjustice is done there, the person injured may bring his action against the offender, and have it tried before independent judges who were *no parties in committing the injury.—Here* he must have it tried before dependent judges, being the men who granted the writ."[8]

The complaint was partly the familiar one of equality of treatment between peoples and partly the vice-admiralty grievance. There was, in addition, the particular grievance that writs of assistance were general warrants. "The Officers of the Customs," the Continental Congress and the New Jersey House of Representatives complained, "are empowered to break open and enter houses, without the authority of any Civil Magistrate, founded on legal information." The lord mayor, aldermen, and livery of London raised the same objection — that writs of assistance were general warrants — when saying of the colonists that "the sanctuary of their Houses [is] laid open to violation, at the will and pleasure of every Officer and Servant in the Customs."[9]

The writ-of-assistance grievance was largely a matter of constitutional theory. For Americans, writs of assistance were grievous because they were authorized by Parliament and were yet another potential threat to rights posed by Parliament's claim to legislative supremacy. The writ, however, was never a real threat or practical grievance. Writs of assistance were not issued in any American government except Massachusetts, New York, and perhaps New Hampshire. The judges of other colonies refused to grant them. In New York the writ was not renewed and in New Hampshire, if ever granted, may not have been used.[10] Only in Massachusetts are there cases in which the customs service attempted searches under authority of the writ, and they are meaningless as grievances. Because of the conditions of local provincial law, officers could enter premises only with permission of the owner. As Daniel Malcom proved in 1766 when the comptroller of the Port of Boston, the deputy collector of the port, and the deputy sheriff of Suffolk county attempted to search his cellar, any whig could prevent imperial officers from utilizing the writ.[11] Local law was simply stronger than the law of Parliament in Massachusetts. It was probably stronger in New Hampshire as well.

Search and seizure was a grievance, and it was important. However, it was a grievance mainly because of American knowledge of the general warrants controversy in Great Britain. It was not a grievance about British rule in the colonies. The writ of assistance was not a cause of the American Revolution and was mentioned as a grievance to strengthen the whig case, not because it was of any practical significance. It may have contributed to the Bill of Rights, but as a constitutional grievance it would not have led to separation from the mother country.

CHAPTER TWENTY-FOUR

THE ISSUE OF RIGHTS

Many scholars have doubted that the grievance of rights and the defense of rights were issues leading to the American Revolution, even though much evidence must be disregarded to conclude that rights were not an issue. Contemporaries said rights were an issue over and over again. It cannot be said that colonial whigs successfully explained to the British people their constitutional grievance about rights. What can be said is that there were many individuals in the mother country, a very high percentage of those who wrote pamphlets and newspaper articles about the question, who understood that the controversy had much to do with constitutional rights. Some of the strongest defenders of American rights were British — people who surely believed rights were an issue. It is not surprising, and little should be made of the fact, that the antiadministration publicist Catharine Macaulay and people of her political and constitutional persuasion claimed that the colonial controversy was about rights. The British government, Macaulay charged, "attempted to wrest from our American colonists every privilege necessary to freemen; — privileges which they hold from the authority of their charters, and the principles of the constitution." What is worth thinking about is the fact that there were also anti-American publicists, such as John Wesley, who acknowledged that the colonial controversy involved security of rights.

Wesley wrote pamphlets strongly rejecting the American constitutional case, even plagiarizing some of the misrepresentations published by Samuel Johnson, yet, in a letter to the secretary of state for the colonies, Wesley conceded a point that he publicly did not admit in his pamphlets: that Americans were motivated by rights. "All my prejudices are against the Americans," Wesley told Lord Dartmouth, "for I am an High Churchman, the son of an High Churchman, bred up from my childhood in the highest notions of passive obedience and non-resistance; and yet in spite of all my rooted prejudice, I cannot avoid thinking (if I think at all) that an oppressed people asked for nothing more than their legal rights and that in the most modest and inoffensive manner which the nature of the thing would allow."[1]

THE RIGHTS INSTRUCTIONS

"I wish most sincerely with you," Benjamin Franklin wrote Joseph Galloway from London, "that a Constitution was form'd and settled for America, that we might know what we are & what we have, what our Rights and what our Duties in the Judgment of this Country as well as in our own." It is evidence of how much people thought that rights were an issue in contention that Franklin's wish was repeated over and over in the 1770s. The first order of business for restoring harmony within the Empire, it was said, was to settle the matter of rights, privileges, and grievances on a permanent, constitutional foundation. "[T]he Extent of the Rights which the Colonies ought to insist upon," a subcommittee of the Massachusetts Committee of Correspondence wrote to the Viriginia committee in October 1773, "is a Subject which requires the closest Attention and Deliberation; and this is a Strong Reason why it should claim the earliest Consideration of, at least, every Committee; in order that we may be prepared, when time and Circumstances shall give to our Claim the surest prospect of Success." The Massachusetts committee thought the right time would be when Britain became involved in a "general War." Once that happened, colonial assemblies should "withhold all kinds of Aid" from the mother country "until the Rights and Liberties which *they ought to enjoy* are restored, and secured to them upon the most permanent foundation."[2]

A suitable occasion did not occur. Great Britain's next war was with the colonies. To learn what colonial assemblies thought were rights issues, therefore, we must dissect credentials voted by assemblies instructing delegates to the Continental Congresses and examine congressional resolutions. Instructions were a well-established practice in the colonies, especially in New England where town meetings routinely instructed lower-house representatives on business they wanted conducted in the assembly. The purpose of instructions, the town of Rowley explained to its representative during the Stamp Act crisis, was "to prevent all unwarrantable suspicions that might arise hereafter, and to leave upon record a lasting testimony to posterity, that we do not quietly, and for no consideration, give up our and their inestimable Rights as British subjects."[3] The assemblies and conventions that instructed delegates to the Continental Congress not only were telling their representatives what policies they wanted enacted, they were also setting the agenda and even defining the authority of Congress, a body that had no constitutional power except what was delegated to it by the colonies.

The Pennsylvania Assembly's instructions were typical. They concentrated on the issue of rights and made resolution of that issue the key to the restoration of constitutional harmony.

> Resolved, That there is an absolute necessity that a Congress of Deputies from the several Colonies . . . form and adopt a plan for the purposes of obtaining redress of American grievances, ascertaining American rights upon the most solid and constitutional principles, and for establishing that Union & harmony between Great Britain and the Colonies, which is indispensably necessary to the welfare and happiness of both.

North Carolina, which addressed its instructions to the entire Congress, not just to its delegates, authorized the Congress "to take such measures, as they may deem prudent, to effect the purpose of describing with certainty the rights of Americans, repairing the breaches made in those rights, and for guarding them for the future from any such violations done under the sanction of public Authority." Massachusetts instructed its delegates "to deliberate and determine upon wise and proper measures, to be by them recommended to all the Colonies, for the recovery and establishment of their just rights and liberties, civil and religious, and the restoration of union and harmony between *Great Britain* and the Colonies, most ardently desired by all good men." The most specific instructions on rights may have been provided by New Hampshire. First, New Hampshire instructed its delegates "to extricate the Colonies from their present difficulties; to secure and perpetuate their rights, liberties, and privileges, and to restore that peace, harmony, and mutual confidence which once happily subsisted between the parent country, and her Colonies." Later, New Hampshire delegates were sent additional instructions, telling them to use the rights grievance to formulate a solution to the imperial controversy. The New Hampshire General Court wanted a constitutional solution based on both precedent and established institutions, for the delegates were also told to "consider the principles of the British constitution, the rights, liberties and immunities essential to all colonies and peculiar to each, how far the natural civil or charter rights of all or any may have been or are infracted or infringed."[4]

Although assembly instructions are our most important evidence for the emphasis colonial whigs expected the Continental Congress to place on rights, hundreds of less important groups, representative and *ad hoc*, spoke out in 1774. Just as for years town meetings in the north had been calling on representatives "to keep the strictest watch over our essential, constitutional rights & privileges," so, after passage of the Massachusetts "intolerable acts" introduced a new, more menacing dimension to the imperial controversy, grand juries and county conventions to the south also called for a stand in defense of colonial rights. An example is a meeting of George Washington's Fairfax County, urging the Continental Congress to "concert a general and uniform plan for the defence and preservation of our common rights, and continuing the connection and dependence of the said Colonies upon *Great Britain*, under a just, lenient, permanent, and constitutional form of Government." A North Carolina county convention called for a continentwide agreement to stop importing British products "till the just Rights of the said Colonies are restored to them, and the cruel Acts of the British Parliament against the Massachusetts Bay and Town of Boston are repealed."[5]

Obeying its instructions, the first Continental Congress made rights and grievances a main order of business. "It is necessary," James Duane told his fellow delegates three days after the Congress convened, "that the first point, *our Rights*, should be fully discussed and established upon solid Principles: because it is only from hence that our Grievances can be disclosed; & from a clear View of both that proper Remedies can be suggested and applied." Duane's plan was followed. In its "Declaration and Resolves" of 14 October 1774, the Congress first defined the authority for American rights, next stated some of the rights the colonies claimed, and then made demands for the preservation or restoration of those rights. The authority for rights, set forth in the initial four resolutions, was limited to the migration, to the migration inheritance, and to British constitutional principles, including the doctrine of consent. The "immutable laws of nature" were mentioned in the preamble. The next five resolutions detailed the rights grievances and, although by now familiar, are worth repeating to show what rights the Congress, with instructions from every part of the continent and over a month of debate, thought important enough to be reiterated. They are surprisingly general, and must be read in the context of the decade-long imperial controversy. The claim to common law, for example, covered the vice-admiralty grievance. The eighth and ninth counts reflect particular grievances of 1774. The right to assembly had been threatened for the first time in colonial history by the Massachusetts "intolerable acts," and the recent military occupation of Boston would not have been possible had Great Britain not maintained a standing army in North America.

> 5. That the respective colonies are entitled to the common law of England, and more especially to the great and inestimable privilege of being tried by their peers of the vicinage, according to the course of that law.
>
> 6. That they are entitled to the benefit of such of the English statutes, as existed at the time of their colonization; and which they have, by experience, respectively found to be applicable to their several local and other circumstances.
>
> 7. That these, his majesty's colonies, are likewise entitled to all the immunities and privileges granted and confirmed to them by royal charters, or secured by their several codes of provincial laws.
>
> 8. That they have a right peaceably to assemble, consider of their grievances, and petition the King; and that all prosecutions, prohibitory proclamations, and commitments for the same, are illegal.
>
> 9. That the keeping of a Standing army in these colonies, in times of peace, without the consent of the legislature of that colony in which such army is kept, is against law.

The only right claimed that could be labeled "new," in the sense that it previously had not been identified, was the assertion that the colonies were entitled to "immunities and privileges . . . secured by their several codes of provincial laws." Just what the right was is debatable. The resolution seems to say that a source of authority for colonial rights was local, colonial legislation. Put another way, it could mean that Congress was claiming that the citizens of a colony were entitled to any right that the assembly declared to be an "immunity and privilege." Read from its most extreme interpretation, this claim of authority for rights could have prevented accommodation with Great Britain, as it would have made the colonial legislators the final arbiters of rights. That interpretation would be incorrect, however, if the alleged right is placed in the context of imperial constitutional law. Legislation in all but two colonies was subject to veto by appointed governors, and the statutes of all the colonies, including Connecticut and Rhode Island, had to be approved by the Privy

Council. The colonies did not quarrel with these imperial checks. They were constitutional and were never a grievance in the revolutionary controversy. The Crown could, therefore, disallow any claim of immunities and privileges that London felt went too far. In terms of law, that meant the Continental Congress was not asserting colonial autonomy to declare civil rights, but was reiterating the American whig doctrine that whatever authority the imperial government possessed to restrain expansion of colonial rights belonged constitutionally to the Crown's prerogative and not to Parliament.[6]

The issue of rights was much the same at the second Continental Congress as it had been at the first. South Carolina's Provincial Congress appointed delegates "with full power to concert, agree upon, direct and order such further measures as in the opinion of the said Deputies, and the Delegates of the other *American Colonies* . . . shall appear to be necessary, for the recovery and establishment of *American* Rights and Liberties, and for restoring harmony between *Great Britain* and her Colonies." Maryland's delegates to the second Congress, instructed after the Battle of Lexington, were told to seek "a happy reconciliation of the differences between the Mother Country and the *British* Colonies in *North America*, upon a firm basis of constitutional freedom." There was no need to be more specific as the convention had "confidence in the wisdom and prudence of the said Delegates, that they will not proceed to the last extremity, unless, in their judgments, they shall be convinced that such measure is indispensably necessary for the safety and preservation of our liberties and privileges."

When the second Continental Congress met, it continued to assert — as the first Continental Congress had asserted — that the imperial crisis concerned rights and that Americans were fighting to preserve rights they had always possessed; they were not contending for new rights or for the authority to create new rights.

> In our own native land, in defence of the freedom that is our birthright, and which we ever enjoyed till the late violation of it; for the protection of our property, acquired solely by the honest industry of our forefathers and ourselves, against violence actually offered, we have taken up arms.[7]

Perhaps we should be suspicious about taking people at their word, and look instead for the hidden motivations that lay behind what, to a more cynical and more secure age, have the appearance of being platitudes of political propaganda. But if we are willing to believe that people meant what they said, or at least expected their contemporaries to accept their arguments as sincere, then we must admit that to some immeasurable but extensive degree the fighting that broke out in April 1775 had much to do with the issue of rights. People not only said so over and over, they also claimed their actions were motivated by the belief that rights were in danger. In its last petition to George III, voted less than a month before British troops marched to Concord, the New York General Assembly spoke for much of the continent when it said, "we wish only to enjoy the rights of *Englishmen*, and to have that share of liberty, and those privileges secured to us, which we are entitled to upon the principles of our *free and happy Constitution*."[8]

THE SERIOUSNESS OF RIGHTS

It cannot be said that as large a percentage of people in Great Britain as in North America understood that the issue of rights had been one of the causes of the war. But a large percentage of the British population did and a larger percentage of the reading public had the fact thrust at them almost daily in newspapers, pamphlets, and occasional printed sermons. Certainly anyone who kept up to date on parliamentary affairs had to have been aware of the issue, so often were rights mentioned either in debate or petitions. In February 1775, for example, London merchants protested the New England fisheries and trade bill on the grounds of rights, claiming that, if enacted, the legislation would aggravate American grievances.

> [A]mong the other grievances of which our fellow-subjects in *America* so generally complain, is of their being deprived of Trial by Jury, in particular cases, and the extension of the jurisdiction of Admiralty Courts; which grievances your Petitioners, with much concern find are not only continued, but extended by the present Bill, and they think it their duty to represent to the Honourable House, that it is their firm opinions that the disquietude which universally prevails in the minds of their follow-subjects in *America* will not be removed unless lenient measures be pursued, and their grievances redressed.

Perhaps the best evidence that people in the mother country believed American whigs were serious about rights are the various peace plans offered by the administration, discussed in chapter 25, and the peace plans moved by antiadministration members of Parliament, discussed in chapter 26. All British plans treated rights and grievances as matters that had to be resolved if Americans were to be persuaded to return to the Empire.[9]

Did many Americans share the whig consensus that their rights were in danger? Did many even understand or care about those rights? Although quantitative answers will always elude us, there are facts that can be noted even if they cannot be weighed. One of the most impressive is the remarkable agreement of whig values from colony to colony and throughout the transatlantic English-speaking world. But even were that agreement undisputed among historians, its existence raises other unanswerable questions. Was it limited to a small intellectual elite? How far among the inarticulate did the agreement spread? Did the average colonists understand what their leadership was saying about constitutionalism, liberty, and rights? We may quote the numerous pamphlets, sermons, and letters to newspapers, but we will never know how many readers they had or if they were comprehended by more than a few.[10] However, we know what the whig spokesmen were saying and that their leadership, whether by force of persuasion or by blind deference, was being followed. Understood or not, whig ideas carried the day and the values on which whig arguments were based were the values of the English common-law tradition of rights.

Another immeasurable but historical fact is the popular acceptance of the whig rights ideology implied in the resolutions of town meetings, town committees, and county conventions. We must be struck not only by the consistency of arguments but by the uniformity of grievances. One would surely expect to find local differences; that, for example, some of the seaports would have made the writ of assistance a constitutional complaint. None did, and a plausible explanation would be that people knew it was never a serious element in the revolutionary controversy about rights. By contrast, town after town spoke out on the more distant and more constitutionally sophisticated grievance of judicial dependence. The annual Boston town meeting for 1772 gathered at a time when the only imperial tax for revenue — the tax on tea — was not being collected and, as a constitutional issue, was dormant. The chief matters in immediate controversy were that Governor Hutchinson was justifying executive decisions on the grounds that he was following instructions sent him by the ministry in London, and that he and other colonial officials were to be paid their salaries by the British Crown rather than by Massachusetts taxpayers. If ordinary people did not understand that these were rights issues we would not expect to find them raised at the meeting. These grievances, however, were the main business of the day. In what would have seemed extreme, even meaningless, language if the topic was not considered constitutionally important, the voters of Boston told their representatives:

[W]e think it our Duty at such a Time as this, when the very Being
of our Constitution is so dangerously attack'd, to express to you . . .
the Sense we have of the Oppressions which we suffer. No People were
ever in Circumstances more truly alarming than those in which the
People of this Province now are. [They raised the grievance that parliamentary governance and taxation made them slaves.] We are especially under the most uneasy Apprehensions from the repeated Re-
fusals of our Governor to accept of an honorable Support from the
People; and we have the highest Reason to believe that a Part of the
very Money unjustly taken from us, is applied to support him in a
State of Independence upon the People over whom he presides. If
this is the Case, our Situation is truly deplorable. The same Oppressions of which we so justly complain, are made the Support of the
Man, who ought to exert his utmost Power to obtain a Redress of
our Grievances.

These words, of course, were written for the voters by their leaders. They
did not concoct them, however, in hidden conclave, but as a committee
elected by the meeting. It is too glib to say the voters were following their
"betters." Among their betters were Thomas Hutchinson, Andrew Oliver,
and Jonathan Sewall, whose leadership they rejected. The committeemen who wrote these words wrote them for a constituency. Today we
may find the words "slavery," "oppression," and "alarming" overstatements
of the constitutional situation. The committeemen thought differently.
If these words did not reflect their own views — and they did — then they
used them because they reflected the views of their constituency, and they
expected that constituency to adopt them — which it did.

A few months earlier, Samuel Cooper, pastor of Boston's Brattle Square
Church, told former Governor Thomas Pownall about an incident in
which ordinary people displayed sensitivity to an abstract aspect of the
rights issue that we would be unwise to dismiss without consideration.
Governor Hutchinson had politicized the annual thanksgiving proclamation by asking prayers of thanks "for the *Continuance of our Privileges*,"
Cooper explained, underlining the objectionable words for emphasis.

This was deem'd by the People an open Insult upon them, and a pro-
phane Mockery of Heav'n. The general cry was, we have lost our
Most essential Rights, and shall be commanded to give Thanks for
what does not exist. Our congregations applied to the several Ministers in Town praying it might not be read as usual, and declaring
if we offer'd to do it, they w'd rise up and leave the Chh. . . . Had
the Ministers inclined it was not in their Pow'r to read it, a circumstance w'ch never before [took] Place among us. It was read only

in Dr Pemberton's Church, of which the Governor is a Member. He
did it with confusion, and Numbers turn'd their Backs upon him and
left the Chh in great indignation. . . . I mention these circumstances
so particularly in Confidence and because nothing has of late occur'd among us from which you may so well Judg[e] of the Sentiments of the People.

Pownall was familiar with the objectionable phraseology. When governor he had urged in his own thanksgiving proclamations thankfulness
to God for supporting "Us in our Civil and Religious Rights and Liberties." Although the prayer about rights had been "a customary clause"
in thanksgiving proclamations, Cooper pointed out, it "has been omitted
ever since the Stamp Act." On thanksgiving day, he added, some of the
clergy planned "to give Thanks of the Privileges we enjoy, and implore
of the Almighty God the restoration of w't we have lost."

Joseph Warren, a member of the committee that drafted Boston's extreme language of 1772 about Hutchinson's salary from the Crown, had
no doubt as to two facts: (1) that rights were an issue; and (2) that rights
were an issue that people understood. "It is the united voice of America
to preserve their freedom, or lose their lives in defence of it," he told Josiah Quincy in a private letter five months before the Battle of Lexington. "Their resolutions are not the effects of inconsiderate rashness, but
the sound result of sober inquiry and deliberation. I am convinced that
the true spirit of liberty was never so universally diffused throughout all
ranks and orders of people, in any country on the face of the earth, as
it now is through all North America."[11]

CHAPTER TWENTY-FIVE

THE CAUSATION OF RIGHTS

Urging colonial assemblies and conventions to distribute among the people the constitutional arguments and statements of principle of the American whig cause, the Continental Congress contended that "the more our right to the enjoyment of our ancient liberties and privileges is examined the more just and necessary our present opposition to ministerial tyranny will appear." Georgia's Provincial Congress did not need persuasion. "[W]e are truly sensible," it had resolved five months earlier, "how much our safety and happiness depend on a constitutional connection with Great Britain, and that nothing but the being deprived of the privileges and natural rights of Britons could ever make the thought of a separation otherwise than intolerable." Two months before that, whigs of New York County, writing to the mayor and Corporation of London, had drawn the same conclusion. Referring to the right of security in property as "[t]his exalted blessing," they claimed to be "resolutely determined to defend with their blood, and transfer it uncontaminated to their posterity."[1]

These whig bodies were saying that rights were worth fighting for. That is, they were saying what the governor of Connecticut said, explicitly and directly, to the secretary of state for the colonies. "[I]t is our duty," Jonathan Trumbull wrote, and "we should be highly culpable if we should not claim and maintain the constitutional rights and liberties derived to us as men and as Englishmen, as the descendants of Britons and members of an empire whose fundamental principle is the liberty and security of the subject." It was as members of that Empire that they would fight, for under the migration contract they were entitled to the "rights and liberties" not of Americans but Englishmen. "Would the plains of British America have been the temptation to the poor of Europe, had not Great Britain established liberty there, and opened that part of the world for the helpless and distressed?" an anonymous London writer asked in 1775. "The French, the Spanish, and Portuguese American colonies," he pointed out, "certainly contain vacant room enough for all the poor who have emigrated from Europe, and enjoy an asylum in British America." A sort of answer to the question had been voted the previous year by the people of Bristol, Rhode Island. "Instead of exploring another asylum," they resolved, "we are determined to join with our brethren on the Continent in all Lawful measures to Defend our rights and privileges in this good land which our fathers have transmitted to us, their posterity."[2]

Defending rights gave American whigs a peculiar perception of their constitutional and political stance. Taking up arms against the British Parliament did not make them disloyal to the British king. "Are we in *real rebellion* against our lawful sovereign? Have we risen up in opposition to his *just and salutary* laws, and *without sufficient reason* cast off his government?" a regiment beseizing Boston was asked a month after the Battle of Bunker Hill. "We not only *think* but *know*," they were told in answer, "that our privileges civil and sacred, and our property are all at stake, and that we are loudly called upon to defend them at the *risk* of *life*."[3] The reason why Marblehead voted military training, the town meeting explained, was that local men "may soon be called forth to assist in defending the Charter and Constitution of the Province, as well as the Rights and Liberties of all America." They would be fighting "with the greatest reluctance," a whig preacher told a Delaware congregation on the day appointed by Congress for fasting and prayer, "because we cannot maintain our freedom with any other sacrifice than that of our blood."[4]

Easy as it is to find such quotations among American whigs, it is even easier to find them in the literature of the British opposition. "[N]othing but dire necessity compelled the colonies to take up arms," the duke of Grafton told the House of Lords. "We are the aggressors," the earl of Chatham agreed. "We have invaded them. We have invaded them as much as the Spanish Armada invaded England." David Hartley, the man who would be assigned the task of negotiating the Treaty of Paris with the United States, repeated the argument over and over in the House of Com-

mons, where he directly confronted Lord North with the charge that
North's policies had left British America no option but to seek redress
by extralegal means.

> You have condemned them unheard, you have subverted all their civil
> rights, you pensioned their judges, you garble their injuries, you con-
> trol the free debates of their assemblies, you confiscate their char-
> ters, you take their property by violence from them; and, when they
> petition or complain, you tell them that these are pretended griev-
> ances; yet these are the grievances which they seek redress of under
> arms.[5]

Hindsight was not the only perspective of the British opposition. A few,
such as Edmund Burke, had possessed the foresight to remember that
arms were the last refuge of the English when denied what they believed
were their rights. Before the first battle was fought, at a time when the
quiet countryside of Massachusetts' Middlesex County had not yet heard
the drums of civil war, Burke warned the Commons that security of rights
and equality of rights were the twin bonds of British constitutionalism.

> My hold of the Colonies is in the close affection which grows from
> common names, from kindred blood, from similar privileges, and
> equal protection. These are ties, which, though light as air, are as
> strong as links of iron. Let the Colonies always keep the idea of their
> civil rights associated with your government; — they will cling and
> grapple to you; and no force under heaven will be of power to tear
> them from their allegiance. But let it be once understood, that your
> Government may be one thing, and their Privileges another; that
> these two things may exist without any mutual relation; the cement
> is gone; the cohesion is loosened; and every thing hastens to decay
> and dissolution.[6]

THE MOTIVATION OF RIGHTS

Some British political leaders and commentators interpreted the American controversy differently, believing that colonial grievances about rights
were a false issue, advanced by the whigs to gather popular support, hiding the real cause of discontent, whether it was the trade laws, independence, or nationalism.[7] More important for our understanding of the
motivations of American resistance are the doubts of historians, alluded
to in the last chapter, protesting that to say that rights or principles motivated colonial rebellion, threatens "to reduce the revolutionary move-

ment to a static and conservative defense of existing ideals and traditions."[8] A lawyer might answer that American whigs did not claim to defend existing ideals but to defend *threatened* rights, and say that the historical question to answer is whether those rights, in fact, were threatened. A historian's answer would seek a broader, less technical perspective as, for example, one offered by Ian Christie. "It is an act of faith, not a process of historical investigation," he wrote, "which dismisses the enormous, overwhelming masses of contemporary evidence demonstrating the urgency and vital nature of the arguments about constitutional principle as merely a smoke-screen for the operation of economic interest."[9]

The "overwhelming masses of contemporary evidence" to which Christie refers are too vast to be summarized here. The best that can be done is to point out some highlights that have to do with the controversy about rights. The British administration, for example, always acted on the premise that it was confronted not by a nationalist movement or by economic discontent, but by grievances about rights. A preliminary piece of evidence is that all of the literature of the revolutionary debate was concerned with the constitutional dispute and seldom, very seldom, raised nonconstitutional questions. If the pamphlets were "a smoke-screen," what was the purpose? The only persons one could wish to fool would belong to future generations. Contemporaries were addressed to be persuaded. A writer who pleaded constitutional issues might personally be motivated by economic or nationalistic considerations, but that he mentioned only constitutional factors indicates he believed the constitution was what motivated the people for whom he wrote. The entire literature of the Revolution is addressed to persons who were assumed to care about jury trial and government by constitutional consent. Many of the disputants were aware that others might wonder if their arguments should be taken at face value, whether their concern for rights motivated their writings or their words were a screen hiding another purpose. One of these was the brilliant, well-educated Pennsylvania physician and scientist, Hugh Williamson. Williamson witnessed the Boston Tea Party and carried the news to London where he gauged the anger of British reaction. He wrote a pamphlet to persuade whigs in the mother country that Americans were sincerely motivated by fear that their rights were in jeopardy. His words were chosen to make that point about rights and to make it to that audience.

> When we see men diligent in pointing out secret causes of public complaints, or labouring to place them to some account which the parties do not avow, we are apt to suspect a want of candour in the enquirer, or an absence of real and obvious grievance in the persons

complaining. If the Americans had gone out of the way to seek for some grievance, if they had gone back to revive some ancient claim, or discuss some doubtful theorem, then indeed we might have said that the ostensible cause was not the true one, and that they sought for something which they did not avow. Nothing of this sort has happened to the Americans. Their complaints immediately followed the injuries they had received; the injuries were not trifling or imaginary, they were gross and palpable, they lay in the very road and must have been removed, else the miserable colonists must have stumbled and fallen into the very pit of despotism.[10]

It is difficult to find direct statements from either side of the revolutionary debates denying that economics had anything to do with the controversy. The thought just did not occur to those people. From their perspective, if material gain or well-being were more highly valued than rights, it would have been unthinkable for the colonies to quarrel with the mother country. Both sides believed that, under imperial rule, Americans were prosperous and blessed above other peoples in worldly goods and a stable standard of living. It was "a land of milk and honey, and wherein we may eat bread to the full," a whig clergyman exclaimed in satisfaction, "no part of the habitable world can boast of so many natural advantages as the northern part of *America*." "There are no people on earth more secure from the humiliating effects of poverty," a loyalist clergyman agreed. In fact, Americans enjoyed such an enviable economic position that some foreigners found the Revolution a puzzle. A Frenchman, who did not understand the constitutional grievance and probably did not appreciate the importance in which the English-speaking world held civil rights, wrote:

> Had the Americans submitted to the easy taxes imposed upon them, they would have continued the happiest people under heaven—They were free.—They enjoyed an advantageous trade; they had no enemies but the winds and waves. By their unnatural rebellion, they have lost their commerce, they are exposed to all the horrors of a civil war. . . .[11]

American whigs both agreed and disagreed with the Frenchman. They agreed that they had been prosperous and that their rebellion had cost them their commerce. They disagreed that had they submitted to Parliament's easy taxes they could have remained the happiest people under heaven. They would have been happy in material goods, perhaps, but would have lost their property in rights. They knew that British imperial policy, even the navigation acts, were not costly to them. Of the twenty-

seven grievances alleged in the Declaration of Independence, only one
can be said to raise an economic issue. In fact, so far were American whigs
from thinking the controversy anything but constitutional, we never find
them noticing the fact. About the closest an official whig body came to
stating that colonial whigs put preservation of constitutional rights ahead
of their economic prosperity was contained in a message from the Continental Congress to the Assembly of Jamaica. "We are resolved to give
up our commerce, that we might preserve our liberty," the Congress wrote.
If the historian seeks more explicit evidence, it is necessary to turn to a
rare letter in which comparative values were weighed, as in one written
by John Dickinson. "Our Towns are but brick and stone, and mortar and
wood; they, perhaps, may be destroyed; they are only the hairs of our
heads; if sheared ever so close, they will grow again. We compare them
not with our rights and liberties." Dickinson concluded with a wonderful sentence, summing up the relative weight American whigs gave to
the security of the law over material security. "We worship as our fathers
worshipped, not idols which our hands have made." This was no smoke
screen. It was written for the private eyes of one of the continent's most
dedicated, committed, and militant whigs, Arthur Lee.[12]

We need not be surprised that American whigs believed their cause
constitutional and idealistic, but what of American loyalists? The two
most prominent were Thomas Hutchinson and Joseph Galloway, both
of whom thought that the revolutionary controversy concerned constitutional law and, to some extent, constitutional rights. They differed from
the whigs in their priorities, placing material stability ahead of speculative apprehensions about imperial threats to rights. "I am not desirous
of a change in the constitution," Hutchinson told a friend. "If we could
be prudent—I think I may say only silent—we might save the country
and retain the rights we contend for." Galloway wrote as if the controversy was entirely constitutional and civil war could be avoided if the
constitutional grievances were resolved.[13]

The controversy was also thought to be constitutional and to involve
rights by many who viewed it from the perspective of imperial officials.
Time and again the commander-in-chief, General Thomas Gage, and
the royal governors reported to London that the roots of American discontent were constitutional. "There are three Fundamentals on which
the People in this Country endeavour to Establish the Political Doctrines
they have promulgated within these few Years," the general told the British secretary at war. "These are *Charter Rights, British Constitution*, and
the Laws of God and Nature." It might be protested that Gage misunderstood the whig's constitutional case, but, then, so did some whigs. The
pertinent fact is that people on both sides of the controversy knew that

ideas and values were at stake, not that they comprehended every aspect of the constitutional debate. Consider something that the secretary of state, Lord Dartmouth, wrote to the royal governors a month before the Battle of Lexington. The king, he explained, was encouraged "from having seen that, admidst all the intemperance into which a people, jealous of their liberties, have been unfortunately misled, they have nevertheless avowed the justice, the equity, and the propriety of subjects of the same State contributing, according to their abilities and situation, to the Public Burdens." Reading this statement from an official document promulgating imperial policy for North America, we may be struck by the wishful thinking. We should also be struck by the fact that both the king and the secretary of state understood the Americans to be "a people, jealous of their liberties."[14]

It is sometimes forgotten that the government of Great Britain officially acknowledged that a prime cause of the American Revolution had been a disagreement about rights. To restore peace to the Empire, the Houses of Parliament enacted, and the king signed into law, two "conciliatory" statutes. The first abrogated for all time in the future all British claim to the right of taxing the colonies. The second appointed peace commissioners to treat with Americans about rights. The intent of the legislation, the preamble explained, was "the quieting and extinguishing of divers Jealousies and Apprehensions of Danger to their Liberties and Rights, which have alarmed many of his Majesty's Subjects in the Colonies . . . and for a full Manifestation of the just and gracious Purposes of his Majesty, and his Parliament, to maintain and secure all his Subjects in the clear and perfect Enjoyment of their Liberties and Rights." The commissioners were authorized to negotiate

> concerning any Grievances or Complaints of Grievances, existing or supposed to exist, in the Government of any of the said Colonies, Provinces, or Plantations respectively or in the Laws and Statutes of this Realm respecting the same . . . and concerning any other Regulations, Matters, and Things, necessary or convenient for the honour of his Majesty, and his Parliament, and for the common Good of all his Subjects.

Even if in 1775 the rulers of Britain had not understood that American whigs were serious about rights, they surely understood that when they enacted this legislation. Searching for a constitutional formula to return the colonies to the Empire, they acknowledged that grievances had to be redressed. It was a matter, as the duke of Richmond told the House of Lords, of treating "Englishmen in America like Englishmen in Great Britain."[15]

THE MOTIVATION OF CONSTITUTIONALISM

"You may be advocates for liberty, so am I, but in a constitutional and legal way," Governor James Wright told Georgia's Commons House of Assembly in January 1775. The Commons House answered that whigs also advocated the constitutional and legal way, but for any way to be constitutional, Americans had to "enjoy all the rights and privileges of *British* subjects, as fully and effectually, in all respects, as the inhabitants of *Great Britain* do; and to that end, it now appears highly necessary that the constitutional rights of his [majesty's] *American* subjects may be clearly defined and firmly established, that so they may hold those inestimable blessings on such a footing as will unite the mother country and the Colonies by a reciprocation of benefits, on terms consistent with the spirit of the Constitution." These imperial and constitutional antagonists were referring to the same constitution. As the two sides prepared for war there was a unity of ideals; each was motivated by loyalty to the constitution. In the same town on the same day that Governor Wright addressed the Commons House, Georgia's Provincial Congress convened. "[L]et us convince our enemies," the Congress was urged in the opening sermon, "that the struggles of America have not their rise in a desire of independency, but from a warm regard to our common constitution."[16]

It does not do to be cynical when the people we seek to understand were not. If we are to comprehend why American rebels against George III insisted that they were not rebels we must recapture a way of thinking about law that made the Parliament — today's sovereign — the rebel, a rebel against the constitution or the sovereignty of law. There is a subtlety and complexity to English constitutional law, expressed by both the government of Great Britain and whigs in British North America, which allowed colonial whigs and parliamentary imperialists, even at the moment of armed conflict, to appeal not only to law and constitutionalism, but to the same law and the same constitutionalism. Appreciating the legal heritage of the timeless, unchanging body of English constitutional principle permits us not only to realize why Americans were not concocting novel theories about natural law, but why they could believe that, when resisting the mandates of Parliament, they were not rebelling against, but were defending the British constitution.

"We do, with the greatest sincerity, assure your Majesty," the New Jersey Assembly told George III in February 1775, "that our complaints do not arise from a want of loyalty to your royal person, or a disposition to withdraw ourselves from a constitutional dependence on the *British* Crown; but from well grounded apprehensions that our rights and liberties are intimately affected by the late measures," meaning the "intolerable acts" passed by Parliament to punish Boston and Massachusetts Bay. For the New Jersey Assembly to make that claim, its members had to think of rights as legal entities existing independently of the will and command of Parliament — as property, as an inheritance, as a mandate of the original contract or the migration purchase. In other words, rights were constitutional in the seventeenth-, not the nineteenth-century's meaning of "constitution." To be loyal to that constitution and to defend the rights of that constitution did not make one disloyal to Parliament, as Parliament too was constitutional. There would be no conflict, the New York General Assembly told the House of Commons, if Parliament was loyal to the constitution, that is, to the constitution as it was interpreted by American whigs.

> We harbour not an idea of diminishing the power and grandeur of the mother-country, or lessening the lustre and dignity of parliament; our object is the happiness which, we are convinced, can only arise from the union of both countries. To render this union permanent and solid, we esteem it the undoubted right of the colonies to participate of that constitution whose direct end and aim is the liberty of the subject.[17]

It would be an oversimplification to end this argument with only American evidence. The same motivation of constitutionalism could, and sometimes was, cited as motivation for the British side of the civil war. After all, the British thought the same eighteenth-century thoughts as did American whigs, and also said that the conflict was about law and rights. As with the colonists, the law was English and British law, and the rights were British rights. "At all events," Ambrose Serle noted in a pamphlet published in 1776, "we Britons know for what we contend; but the Americans (excepting their republican demagogues) know not. We stand up only for our constitution, and to keep it from being split into parts for an easy destruction by external foes."[18]

THE REDRESS OF RIGHTS

Today we may no longer understand the many proposals made to solve the imperial crisis about rights. One problem is that most were, at least by twentieth-century standards, too imprecise to set guidelines for either legislative solution or constitutional settlement. It is impossible to guess what program the Delaware Assembly wanted implemented when it instructed its delegates to the second Continental Congress:

> That you do adhere to those claims and resolutions made and agreed upon at the last meeting of the Congress; yet, for the restoration of that harmony with the Parent State . . . you may, on your parts, yield such contested claims of right as do not apparently belong to the Colonists, or are not essentially necessary to their well being.

Two years later, on the other side of the Atlantic and the other side of the controversy, John Hinchcliffe, Bishop of Peterborough, told the House of Lords that the way to restore harmony was to "convince the colonies (hitherto they have had no means to be convinced of it) that parliament is really disposed to attend to and redress their grievances." Why Americans should trust the institution of Parliament over which they held no check, even if completely convinced of the good intentions of the Parliament then in session, the bishop did not say.[1]

These broad arguments would hardly be worth quoting were they not representative of most solutions offered to the rights controversy. There is a vast literature from the revolutionary period, in pamphlets and parliamentary motions, that does not bear analytical examination. The few detailed plans for resolving rights can be quickly summarized; they fall into two categories: (1) comprehensive plans (discussed in the next section); and (2) solutions to single grievances or single solutions to all grievances.

The simplest solutions dealt with one or two grievances. The easiest of these were grievances about rights that had been altered recently or were applied differently in the colonies than in English law. An example is the vice-admiralty grievance; there was virtual unanimity as to how it should be redressed. Even the most militant colonial whigs did not demand that the jurisdiction be abolished. It should, rather, be restored to "its *constitutional* bounds" or what the people of Boston termed the court's "*proper Element.*" That is, confine the jurisdiction "to transactions *upon the seas*," "according to the antient English Statutes." Most of the British peace plans submitted to Parliament would have solved the vice-admiralty grievance in this way. The bill of "conciliation" offered by former Secretary of State Henry Seymour Conway, for example, provided that "the powers of the Admiralty, and Vice-Admiralty Courts, be restrain'd within their ancient limits, and the trial by jury, in all civil cases, where the same may have been abolished, restored."[2]

Another species of the single solution to the rights controversy was the blanket solution, redressing all or most grievances, not just one. An example of this technique would have repealed all objectionable parliamentary legislation. That scheme may have been the favorite American solution to the imperial crisis, premised on a constitutionally naive belief that, once constitutionally threatening statutes were null and void, the imperial constitution could revert to where it had been before Parliament claimed authority to legislate internally for the colonies. The usual formula was to ask for a "return" to the law of 1763. That was the most frequently suggested and simplistic of the solutions proposed to the grievance against imperial legislative authority or parliamentary supremacy, and evaluation of its merits is best left to a constitutional history dealing with that topic. Less often it was suggested as an answer to the rights controversy, as, for example, by New York's General Assembly.

> We claim but a restoration of those rights which we enjoyed by general consent before the close of the last war; we desire no more than a continuation of that ancient government to which we are intitled by the principles of the British constitution, and by which alone can be secured to us the rights of Englishmen.[3]

Equality was a second general or blanket solution frequently proposed. "[O]nly grant us the liberty you enjoy," Americans insisted, "and we shall always remain one people," but the problem was how to establish equality within a constitutional theory of a sovereign Parliament in which some of the equals were not represented. At the first Continental Congress, John Rutledge proposed extending to the colonies all English and British statutes enacted since the first migration that secured the "rights and Liberties of the Subject." That legislative scheme would have overcome some aspects of the inequality grievance, but at the cost of implying parliamentary power to create and therefore abolish rights. The New York General Assembly seems to have tried to avoid that dilemma when it modified the equality solution by telling George III, "Your Majesty's *American* subjects have hitherto been in a state of infancy, and till lately have submitted implicitly, and without repining, to the authority of the parent state. They have now reached the period of maturity, and think themselves entitled to their birth-right, an equal participation of freedom with their fellow-subjects in *Britain*." When these words were being considered, Colonel Philip Schuyler moved a substitute. "Although your Majesty's *American* subjects have, in some instances, submitted to the power exercised by the parent state, they nevertheless conceive themselves entitled to an equal participation of freedom with their fellow-subjects in *Britain*." The substitute was rejected by a vote of fourteen to nine and the original language was adopted. We are not told why, but from the perspective of constitutional law the only difference between them was that the substitute conceded more inherent authority to Parliament than did the original.[4]

The Redress of Grievances

Few of the many schemes advanced by individuals and members of Parliament to resolve the imperial crisis mentioned rights in general. Once the fighting started most people of opinion in Great Britain forgot about the "rights" grievance. Attention primarily was focused on the issues of taxation and parliamentary supremacy. If those two controversies could be resolved, it was generally assumed, the conflict would end. As a result, every plan put forward for bringing the North American colonies back into the Empire dealt with taxation and only a few mentioned rights. Even those that did consider rights did not take them up as a general grievance, but rather attempted to resolve disputes about individual rights such as trial by jury or the vice-admiralty grievance. Of the comprehensive peace plans — a more accurate description would be plans for constitutional reformation — that were presented to Parliament, four proposed solutions to the controversy over rights. One, of course, was the administration's conciliatory statutes (quoted in the last chapter), which authorized the peace commissioners of 1778 to discuss grievances with the Americans and assure them that both king and Parliament would "maintain and secure" all British subjects "in the clear and perfect Enjoyment of their Liberties and Rights." None of the other three plans were adopted, yet they are worth brief summary both because of what they reveal of British thinking about the rights grievance and because of the three men who drafted them. The first was by David Hartley who would be Britain's plenipotentiary to the Paris Peace Treaty. The second was introduced by Henry Seymour Conway, secretary of state in charge of colonial affairs during the Stamp Act crisis. The third, actually several plans offered at different times, was sponsored by William Pitt, earl of Chatham, who enjoyed the greatest respect accorded to any member of Parliament by American whigs.[5]

Hartley's proposal was constitutional nonsense, and deserves our attention for that very reason. No one worked harder or spoke or wrote more often for the cause of Anglo-American peace than did David Hartley. He opposed the legislation that led to war and he opposed the war, offering eight motions for reconciliation, all of which were defeated. He wanted to restore the colonies to the constitutional customs they had enjoyed before 1763 and, if unity could not be established on the principles of the old imperial constitution, he would have recognized American independence and joined the two countries by integrating their commerce. He was, therefore, the person we might expect to advance the most comprehensive scheme guaranteeing colonial rights within the Empire. Instead, his rights solution was as inefficacious as Lord North's conciliatory statutes.

Hartley's best effort occurred during the debate on the conciliatory bills, when he moved that the king

> instruct the commissioners appointed to treat, consult, and agree upon the means of quieting the disorders now subsisting in certain of the colonies, plantations, and provinces of North America, to establish, as a fundamental, previous to any treaty, and from which they shall not have liberty to depart, that all persons, born either in Great Britain, Ireland, or the colonies, provinces, and plantations of North America, shall be considered as natural born subjects, and enjoy all rights and privileges as such, throughout all the said dominions in common, in the manner heretofore accustomed.

That was it, there was nothing more. Hartley would have combined the equality solution with the return-to-1763 solution and would have asked Americans to trust future Parliaments. There were no constitutional mechanisms proposed for securing rights or keeping the sovereign from again altering the privilege of jury trial or taking property without the consent of the governed.[6]

General Conway's "Bill for Conciliation with the Colonies," although proposing security for rights no more immutable constitutionally than Hartley's, had the merit of being a more specific reformation. First, Conway spelled out the source of rights, providing "[t]hat the Colonies in America are justly entitled to all the privileges, franchises, and immunities, granted by their several charters and constitutions; and that the said charters or constitutions ought not to be invaded or resumed, unless for misuses, or some legal ground of forfeiture." Conway identified a specific source for rights — the charters — but what did he mean by their "constitutions"? Perhaps he was referring to the proprietary grants of Maryland and Pennsylvania. Conway undoubtedly thought he was being definite. Hartley would have recognized American rights as those to which the colonists had been "accustomed." Conway's location of rights in charters has the appearance of greater notoriety and identification, but it may be wondered if he had ever read a charter. They said little that could be construed as rights, except for the mandate that laws and customs were to be similar to the laws and customs of "England," a mandate that by rules of loose construction can be read as codifying the right to an equality of rights with the British people. There was little else in charters to quiet the revolutionary controversy over rights. Most, for example, mentioned the admiralty jurisdiction, but said nothing about limiting it to maritime matters or restricting it from hearing questions traditionally within the purview of common law. The provision that charters "ought not to be invaded or resumed" may have been intended by Conway to secure rights, but under the British constitution that security depended on the goodwill of Parliament. Parliament was the final judge, and if there was doubt whether a statute "invaded" or "resumed" a charter right, Parliament only had to insert a clause saying there was no invasion or resumption and the question was constitutionally resolved. Conway apparently would also have left it to parliamentary discretion whether a charter had been "misused" and whether there was "some legal ground for forfeiture."

Conway also offered a solution to American grievances. It had the merit of identifying the grievances with specificity but in attempting to provide security against future grievances was as constitutionally inept as his location of rights in colonial charters. First, he would have repealed all statutes and parts of statutes about which Americans complained. Conway wanted to correct nonstatutory as well as statutory grievances by having Parliament mention colonial petitions and remonstrances and declare that the demands for redress made in those petitions and remonstrances were granted.

> That immediately upon the conclusion of any treaty of conciliation between Great Britain and America, all those rights, principles, and immunities, which were demanded by the several associated Colonies in their Petitions and Memorials to the King, and to the two Houses of Parliament, (and particularly in the Petition of the Congress to the King of the 8th of *July*, 1775, and in the Memorial of the Colony of New-York to the House of Lords of the 25th of *March*, 1775; and in the Representation and Remonstrance of the General Assembly of the said Colony of New-York, to the House of Commons of the same date,) be, and are hereby declared to be conceded, and confirmed on the part of Great Britain.[7]

Assuming that the cited petitions contained all the grievances that Americans wanted redressed, this clause would have satisfied the political demands of American whigs about grievances, but it would not have satisfied them constitutionally. The constitution was not changed. The grievances had been created because Parliament insisted that, as sovereign, it had the authority to enact them into law. They would have been removed only because Parliament, again asserting supremacy, repealed them. In both instances, Parliament exercised power of internal legislation that American whigs denied it possessed constitutionally. The ultimate grievance was parliamentary supremacy and Conway would have accentuated that grievance — the legislative or supremacy grievance — to redress "rights" grievances.

Lord Chatham moved at least two comprehensive bills and offered one motion to redress American grievances. His immediate concern was to end taxation and to prevent the administration from employing troops in Massachusetts Bay "to violate and destroy the just rights of the people." His ultimate purpose, however, was to maintain parliamentary supremacy and his plan is chiefly of interest in a study of Great Britain's claim to the constitutional authority of legislating internally for the colonies. The present discussion is limited to Chatham's proposals guaranteeing rights within the constitutional context of legislative sovereignty vested in a body in which Americans were not represented.

Chatham's first bill was truly comprehensive, for it sought to clarify ambiguities in the imperial constitution, not just to restore rights. It began, for example, by denying that Americans were entitled to a right they

claimed and in the Declaration of Independence had stated to be a grievance. The colonies, the bill provided, did not have the right to consent
to keeping a standing army in their midst. An army was constitutional
if Parliament consented to it and could legally be sent anywhere within
the Empire that the Crown directed. "Nevertheless," the bill provided
in a clause devoid of any constitutional meaning except good intentions,
"in order to quiet and dispel groundless jealousies and fears, be it hereby
declared, that no military force, however raised, and kept according to
law, can ever be lawfully employed to violate and destroy the just rights
of the people."

Chatham next turned to the jury grievance, including the vice-
admiralty grievance. His bill provided

> that the powers of Admiralty and Vice-Admiralty courts in America
> shall be restrained within their ancient limits, and the trial by jury,
> in all civil cases, where the same may be abolished, restored: and
> that no subject in America shall, in capital cases, be liable to be in-
> dicted and tried for the same, in any place out of the province wherein
> such offence shall be alleged to have been committed, nor be deprived
> of a trial by his peers of the vicinage; nor shall it be lawful to send
> persons indicted for murder in any province of America, to another
> colony, or to Great Britain, for trial.

In the reported debates, which are not complete, nothing is said about
the jury provision. Earl Gower, however, raised the administration's set
objection to the vice-admiralty solution, insisting "that the Act of Navigation would be of no avail, would be no more than a dead letter, if the
laws for establishing the admiralty courts were repealed; for to talk of
laws for restricting and regulating their commerce without the means
of enforcing and executing them, was a mere mockery of reason and common sense."

Gower's objection may have been misdirected. Whether it was or not
depended on what Chatham intended by restraining "within their ancient limits" vice-admiralty courts. If those words meant the same as
American whigs meant by them, the admiralty jurisdiction still would
have enforced most aspects of the Navigation Act and laws of trade. It
would, of course, have been confined to matters arising on the seas and
no longer employed to enforce internal revenue statutes. But in another
part of his bill, Chatham renounced Parliament's authority to tax without colonial consent for purposes of revenue, making that aspect of vice-
admiralty's jurisdiction no longer needed.

Chatham compromised on the only other colonial grievance he thought important enough to redress, the judiciary grievances. He confirmed to the imperial government two of the constitutional powers it had recently asserted and gave American whigs one of the rights they claimed. Judges were to be appointed and paid by the Crown, but their tenure would be as colonial whigs wanted—"as his Majesty's judges in England, *quamdiu se bene gesserint.*" Chatham concluded with a general statement of policy, not implementing the equality solution, but turning instead to constitutional custom. Chatham wanted Parliament to declare

> that the colonies in America are justly entitled to the privileges, franchises, and immunities granted by their several charters or constitutions; and that the said charters or constitutions ought not to be invaded or resumed, unless for misuser, or some legal ground of forfeiture.

It is certain that the Continental Congress would not have accepted Chatham's bill had it been enacted into law. Whether it could have been made the basis for negotiations will never be known as it was rejected by the House of Lords by a vote of 61 to 32. Virginia's House of Burgesses thought it could have been useful, noting that the bill "differed but in a few points" from demands stated on behalf of the colonies by the Continental Congress. "Lord *Chatham's* bill, on the one part, and the terms of Congress on the other," the burgesses told the royal governor, "would have formed a basis for negotiation, which a spirit of accommodation on both sides might, perhaps, have reconciled." It would have taken more than a spirit of accommodation, however. American whigs would have had to rekindle a feeling of constitutional trust in Parliament they had long since lost.[8]

Chatham's second attempt to restore the Empire, offered two years later, was less comprehensive but directed entirely at the issue of rights. It was a motion to end the war "upon the only just and solid foundation, namely, the removal of accumulated grievances." The administration was still insisting that the only terms for peace were the "unconditional submission" of the Americans, terms Chatham knew could never be obtained. "I do therefore affirm," he told the lords, "that instead of exacting unconditional submission from the colonies, we should grant them unconditional redress. We have injured them; we have endeavoured to enslave and oppress them. Upon this clear ground, my lords, instead of chastisement, they are entitled to redress. A repeal of those laws, of which they complain, will be the first step to that redress." A year before the administration was to codify some of this plan in its conciliatory statutes, the earl of Chatham sponsored the "1763" solution. "I wish for a repeal of every oppressive act which your lordships have passed since 1763," he explained. "I would put our brethren in America precisely on the same footing they stood at that period." Opposing the motion, Earl Gower complained that "it was worded in so vague and indistinct a manner, that it was impossible to know what set of measures it described, under the general charge of grievances; whether it meant as well those in which his lordship acted so distinguished a part, as those which followed or preceded them." Answering, Chatham again made it clear that he was thinking not only of the statutes such as the Massachusetts "intolerable acts," which precipitated the war, but of all parliamentary enactments that, colonial whigs charged, violated their rights. "I mean to convey, under the words 'accumulated grievances,' every thing which has passed in parliament relative to America since the year 1763."[9]

A few months later Chatham tried again. He had failed with his plan for specific redress of identified grievances and he had failed with the "1763" solution. Now he lent his prestige to the "equality" solution. Parliament, Chatham pleaded, should confirm to the Americans "those immutable rights of nature, and those constitutional liberties, to which they are equally entitled with ourselves. . . . I say, my lords, the rights and liberties to which they are equally entitled with ourselves, but no more."[10] Chatham wanted Americans equal to the British but his equality of rights was different from the equality of rights that they had been demanding since 1765. He wanted equality of rights under Parliament. They wanted equality of rights under the constitution. It was, however, a constitution that no longer existed in Great Britain if Chatham was correct, and Parliament was sovereign as well as supreme.

CHAPTER TWENTY-SEVEN

CONCLUSION

None of Chatham's plans could have been accepted by the Continental Congress; perhaps no plan would have been. None of Chatham's plans would have been constitutionally successful; perhaps any plan would have failed. The task may have been constitutionally impossible by 1778, yet in 1774 the task had not appeared difficult. North Carolina's convention told its deputies to the Continental Congress that it was prepared to resist British constitutional encroachments "until we obtain an explicit declaration and acknowledgment of our rights."[1] They probably did not realize it — most Americans did not realize it — but the North Carolinians were asking for constitutional guarantees that were constitutionally unobtainable.

It may be that Americans had no choice but to reach for the constitutionally unreachable. In February 1778, the House of Commons was debating the administration's conciliatory bills. John Aubrey, member for Aylesbury, supported the bills but urged Lord North to resign immediately so some other person could lead the government during the peace negotiations. Would the Americans "ever sheath the sword without sufficient security against the injuries they have complained of being repeated?" Aubrey asked the Commons. Were the Americans not justified

in declining any negociation with men, who, having thus laid the
foundation of the war in perfidiousness, have built upon it with cru-
elty? I cannot, therefore, flatter myself with the hopes of reconciling
America with the proposed Bill. Those privileges and immunities
for which the Americans have ventured their lives and fortunes, they
will not, now [that] the hazard is so nearly over, trust for a moment
in the hands they have just rescued them from.[2]

Aubrey's question — how could Americans, once they returned to the
Empire, obtain security that their grievances would not be repeated —
explains why no peace plan could be completely and constitutionally
sufficient. The question was either constitutionally unanswerable or had
to be answered in the negative. Although the claim may seem too extreme to credit, the fact is that under the British constitution, after 1774,
perhaps even after 1765, Americans could not return to their former constitutional status and still enjoy the constitutional security of which Aubrey spoke.

If it was possible to establish constitutional security for rights under
the eighteenth-century British constitution, no one explained how it could
be accomplished. In one respect that may not be surprising. After all,
the British constitution was not only the best in the world, it was the
finest that could be devised by human ingenuity, and even the friends
of the colonies in Parliament believed Americans should be happy to come
again under its clement shelter if only Lord North's administration could
be voted out of office. There was a time when colonial whigs would have
trusted that constitutional arrangement. Events between 1765 and 1774
taught them that, at least for them, even the best constitution was not
secure enough. In 1765 the administration of George Grenville had forever altered American constitutional perceptions by imposing a constitutional innovation that American imperialists as well as American whigs
had supposed impossible and most continued to think unconstitutional:
internal taxation for the purpose of raising revenue. In 1766 the administration of the marquis of Rockingham had repealed the tax, implying,
but not saying explicitly, that the colonies would not again be taxed for
the purpose of revenue. In 1767, under the administration of William
Pitt, Charles Townshend, chancellor of the exchequer, had proposed new
revenue-raising taxes on the colonies and Parliament had enacted them.
On 13 May 1769, the earl of Hillsborough, secretary of state for the colonies, wrote the colonial governors on behalf of the duke of Grafton's administration that it would introduce no new taxes for the purpose of
revenue, a pledge that some members of the opposition and some American whigs professed to believe renounced the claim of right to tax. Fi-

nally, in 1773, the administration of Lord North passed the East India Tea Tax, an external duty intended to raise revenue. The point is not that this succession of contradictory constitutional signals taught colonial whigs they could not put their faith in British politicians. The lesson of these contradictions was that American rights seemed less secured under the present British constitution than they had been before 1765. The constitutional dilemma was parliamentary sovereignty. It was not that Rockingham and Parliament had acted unconstitutionally by implying there might be no further colonial taxes after repeal of the Stamp Act, or that Hillsborough made an unconstitutional promise when pledging on behalf of the cabinet a matter properly within the constitutional jurisdiction of Parliament. The dilemma was that one British Parliament, no matter how solemnly its honor was committed, could not bind subsequent Parliaments. One session of a Parliament could not even bind another session of the same Parliament.

For participants in the American revolutionary dispute, the dilemma was complicated by the conflict between two definitions of the British constitution. One constitution was the old English constitution of customary powers, with rights secured as property, both inherited and inherent, from the arbitrary capriciousness of government power. The other was a newer British constitution — the emerging constitution of the nineteenth century — of sovereign command and of arbitrary parliamentary supremacy. The conflict between the two can be caught in the thinking of James Duane at the first Continental Congress. "It is now," he told his fellow members of the committee on rights, "essential to place our Rights on a broader & firmer Basis to advance and adhere to some solid and Constitutional Principle which will preserve Us from future Violations — a principle clear & explicit and which is above the Reach of Cunning, & the Arts of oppression." Duane was thinking of the constitution of parliamentary command when he sought security from "future Violations"; he was thinking, that is, of that new emerging constitution of parliamentary sovereignty. After all, he was saying that American rights had to be put "above the Reach" of arbitrary power, and under the British constitution of 1774, that meant "above the Reach" of parliamentary supremacy. The constitutional question, of course, was how that goal could be accomplished, and it is on this issue that those seeking a solution to the imperial crisis encountered the constitutional dilemma.

What is interesting about Duane is not that he saw that there was a problem; everyone saw that there was a problem. It is his answer that is of interest, for it not only shows that he did not understand the depths of the problem, it also delineates the constitutional dilemma that the revolutionary disputants faced. John Adams, another member of the committee, reported that Duane found the constitutional security for American rights in the second original contract. "Upon the whole," he wrote, Duane was "for grounding our Rights on the Laws and Constitution of the Country from whence We sprung, and Charters, without recurring to the Law of Nature—because this will be a feeble Support. Charters are Compacts between the Crown and the People and I think on this foundation the Charter Governments stand firm." Duane apparently spoke from a written text for we have his own version of what he said. "I shall only observe that their Charters are to be esteemed as Compacts," he told the committee, referring to the colonies, "that they have long been acquiesced in, and if exceptionable in their origin can not now be violated but by oppression." Duane also appealed to the British constitution, to the fact that it ordained a limited monarchy, and to the familiar tradition that it was "a free Constitution." "But if the Subject is bound by a Law to which he does not assent, either personally or by his Representative, he is no longer free but under an arbitrary power, which may oppress or ruin him at pleasure." Duane may not have realized that he was describing two constitutions, the old constitution in which rights existed independent of sovereign will and pleasure, and the newer constitution in which the "arbitrary power" of parliamentary command could, at its pleasure, "oppress" the subject by ignoring "rights." In the nineteenth century, the British would no longer use the word "oppress" in this context. In 1774, it was a word that still had constitutional meaning in London almost as much as in Philadelphia. In that fact lay the dilemma making security of rights almost a constitutional impossibility. None of the statesmen, politicians, and lawyers searching for a solution devised a usable plan because they thought of Parliament in the old way, and not as a sovereign of arbitrary will and pleasure. Duane's solution made much more sense to the generation of 1774 than it would have to John Austin and the British of 1850. The first migrants had made a contract with the king, he argued, and they owned rights that could not be forfeited or altered by moving from one part of the Empire to another.

> The priviledges of Englishmen were inherent. They were their Birth right and of which they cou[l]d only be deprived by their free Consent. Every Institution legislative and Juridical, essential to the Exercise & enjoyment of these Rights and priviledges in constitutional Security, were equally their Birth right and inalienable Inheritance. They cou[l]d not be with held but by lawless oppression and by lawless oppression only can they be violated.[3]

Duane's solution can be understood only in the context of the two constitutions. He relied entirely on the old customary constitution of inherited and inherent rights vesting at birth. It was the Cokeian constitution in which law was a right, not a command, and, because law, not Parliament, was sovereign, it made constitutional sense to speak of Parliament's command as "lawless oppression."

If Parliament was now sovereign, and if rights were or soon would be whatever Parliament said they were, Duane's solution was no solution. It was based on the constitution that restored Charles II to the throne, the constitution for which Americans were about to fight. The question historians must address is whether the people of 1774 did not know that the constitution was no longer the same, or knew the constitution had changed but did not want to admit it, for to do so meant admitting that they were governed by arbitrary power. We can be certain that they had a sense of difference, conscious of if not articulating the fact that Parliament could enact and declare to be "law" what Duane called "lawless oppression." The particular "oppression" to which he referred was probably the Massachusetts "intolerable Acts," especially the act closing the Port of Boston. The debate on passage of the Port of Boston Act had turned partly on three issues: (1) whether Parliament had to give Boston and Massachusetts a hearing before punishing them; (2) whether people innocent of the Tea Party could be punished along with those who had thrown the tea into Boston Harbor; and (3) whether a judgment of guilt without trial on the facts was constitutional. The majority of Parliament, by the very act of voting for the Boston Port bill, had ruled that the sovereign's command could not only abrogate the right to trial by jury and substitute legislative judgment for that of common law, but could appropriate private property on the sole ground of the sovereign's discretionary will and pleasure.

There were two ways in which the constitutional dilemma could be stated. One approach was to ask "whether the frame and model of the British constitution is such, as practically to admit of securing to the colonies the same political rights and privileges with the mother country." That is, how, under a constitution of arbitrary command, can a collective group of subjects, separated geographically, have security and equality of rights when all the commands emit from a representative body in which they share not an iota of the representation? From the narrow perspective of the newer constitution of sovereign command, the answer was that there could be no constitutional assurance of security and equality. The real issue was sovereignty. "A paltry tax upon tea, a particular insult, a single act of violence or sedition, was not the true ground of the present dispute," Earl Gower told the House of Lords. "It was not this tax, nor that Act, nor a redress of a particular grievance; the great question in issue is, the supremacy of this country, and the subordinate dependence of America." The security and equality of American rights, therefore, had to be entrusted to the good faith and fair dealing of Parliament.[4]

The second way of thinking about the constitutional dilemma was procedurally. The question became how, under the British constitution of the late eighteenth century, to secure rights in the seventeenth-century meaning of English fundamental law. The dilemma then would not be equality within an Empire governed by the discretionary commands of one part of that Empire, but to reestablish security of rights under a constitution that only recently had changed from a constitution of the sovereignty of customary or fundamental law to the sovereignty of arbitrary legislative command. It is an issue that some legal theorists of Great Britain have been raising in the late twentieth century. The procedure they seek to devise is called "entrenchment." The problem is how to "entrench" fundamental rights in a constitution of parliamentary supremacy — that is, how to promulgate a right and secure it from invasion by a later Parliament. The objective is not to make rights constitutionally inviolable as in American law, but to secure them from parliamentary invasion unless invasion is sustained by a vote higher than a simple majority (two-thirds or three-fourths). The answer seems to be that rights cannot be entrenched in twentieth-century British law. The question the American Revolution posed was whether it was possible to entrench them in the British constitution of 1775.

It cannot be said that no members of Parliament comprehended the problem. If some did, however, comprehension did not help them find the answer. The evidence that has survived indicates that only two members made proposals that had the potential of becoming solutions. One, with perhaps half an answer, was James Luttrell, member for Stockbridge. "[I]t was for liberty they fought, for liberty they died," he said of American whigs in the Commons debates of December 1777. "An American Magna Charta is what they wisely contend for; not a Magna Charta to be taxed by strangers, a thousand leagues distant . . . but if constitutional freedom was secured to America, every victory might then gain over some worthy friends to our cause."[5]

Luttrell's solution can be described either as medieval or modern. It was medieval in that it would have harked back to the constitutional settlements between the Crown and the feudal barons, and guaranteed American rights by resuscitating the fundamental-law concept of Magna Carta, giving to either the people of British North America or to each colony, he does not say which, an American Magna Carta. It was modern in that he may have been thinking of what was to become the American method of guaranteeing rights against the sovereign, the written constitution. But how an American Magna Carta could be promulgated under the eighteenth-century British constitution, Luttrell did not say. He may have known the problem and he did offer an answer of sorts. There is no evidence, however, that he gave any thought to how that answer could be implemented. The obvious procedure, the most viable one under the British constitution, would have been to pass the American Magna Charta through the two Houses of Parliament as a bill to be signed into law by the king. But what would prevent tomorrow's Parliament from repealing the fundamentals today's Parliament had promulgated? It was the same constitutional problem as before. The security of American rights could be guaranteed only by fundamental law, but fundamental law could no longer exist in a constitution of sovereign parliamentary supremacy.[6]

We must return to a supposition that should be obvious but has not been commented on by students of the American Revolution. Luttrell and his generation were not accustomed to thinking through the questions of constitutional procedure and concluding that they faced twentieth-century problems of entrenching rights. The prevailing legal theory was still based on the concepts of the old English constitution: limited government, customary restraints, and inherited birthrights beyond the discretionary power of legislative authority. The constitutional bugbear that stirred most constitutional fears remained as it had been throughout British history, arbitrary power. Lawyers, statesmen, and politicians, reluctant to acknowledge that arbitrary power had crept into British constitutionalism, were unwilling to come to grips with the possibility that the threat of arbitrary power lay at the center of the imperial crisis. There seems to be no other explanation for the incredible fact that just one member of Parliament offered a solution to the constitutional dilemma, that is, how to implement entrenchment, and that solution went unnoticed, was undebated, and was not seriously considered.

That solution, the only solution that seems to have been proposed to the dilemma of securing American rights under a constitution of parliamentary supremacy, was offered by William Pitt, earl of Chatham. The House of Lords was debating how to phrase an address of thanks to the king. Asserting, as he always did, that "I will never consent to the American claims of sovereignty," Chatham wanted Parliament to surrender a small part of its sovereignty: its sovereignty over American rights. He moved that the House supplicate George III to end hostilities in North America, and assure him that the lords would

> cheerfully co-operate with the magnanimity and tender goodness of his Majesty for the preservation of his people, by such explicit and most solemn declarations and provisions of fundamental and irrevocable laws, as may be judged necessary for ascertaining and fixing for ever, the respective rights of Great Britain and her colonies.

Chatham had a glimpse of the constitutional problem. To secure American rights the constitution required "fundamental and irrevocable laws." He even had a procedure for identifying those laws. "It may be said, who shall offer, and where will be the security on either hand for a faithful performance," he explained. "To this I answer, not by any declarations of right here, or assertions of it there, but barely by operative acts here, consented to, acknowledged and ratified by the several assemblies in America."[7]

Those words are all we have.[8] Chatham seems to have said nothing more about his plan. Indeed, we are left to wonder if it was a developed, thought-out plan, or just another fleeting moment in Pitt's great career, an idea occurring to him during parliamentary debate, an aside that he tossed out and no one caught. The only member of the House to support Chatham either missed the procedural solution or did not understand it. "His doctrine is for fundamental and irrevocable laws, and not for acts of parliament, destructive of fundamental and irrevocable laws," the earl of Abingdon said. "Such acts are the laws of tyrants, and not the acts of a free and limited government. The legislature of this country cannot deprive America of life, liberty, and property; and yet all this, in subversion of our constitution, is attempted." If Abingdon understood that Chatham was groping for a way to reestablish fundamental law in the new constitution of parliamentary command, he did not understand the constitutional dilemma itself. The constitution of which he spoke was not one for which a procedure entrenching rights had to be devised. It contained fundamental rights. It was a constitution that Parliament could not "subvert," a constitution "of a free and limited government," in which fundamental law already existed protecting American rights from Parliament for, as he said, Parliament could not "deprive America of life, liberty, and property."[9]

If we cannot be certain of all aspects of Chatham's plan, we at least know its principal constitutional concept. It was a notion of constitutional devolution or a procedural technique constitutionally related to devolution. The procedure was not the devolution often talked about in today's Great Britain, delegating some of Parliament's authority in local affairs to regional Welsh and Scottish assemblies. The legal substance was similar to devolution, but the procedure was closer to the constitutional practice adopted by Canada in 1982 after the Canadian Supreme Court ruled that the federal government's formula for entrenching a charter of rights into Canada's constitution was legal but constitutionally questionable. To quiet constitutional doubts about its entrenchment scheme, Ottawa sought to establish the charter through a consensus of the provinces, obtained by a national conference of elected officials.

Chatham faced the same problem that Canada would face — constitutional entrenchment — but his procedure seems more closely related to the amendment mechanism adopted by the American Constitution of 1789. Chatham would have entrenched American rights into the imperial constitution by having Parliament pronounce a right fundamental. The endorsement of each American assembly was then sought, an endorsement, it would appear, lifting parliamentary enactment above ordinary legislation to the degree of fundamental law. The consent Chatham sought, therefore, was formally legislative, obtained from existing constitutional lawmaking institutions, and, in terms of eighteenth-century legal thought, more "constitutional" than the executive, not legislative, Canadian political consensus.

It is evident that Chatham's fleeting thought was to create rights. His sole object was to solve the dilemma of entrenching fundamental rights in the imperial constitution. As far as can be determined, Chatham gave no attention to the procedural question of how security for fundamental rights would be maintained or whether those rights were fundamental only against the British Parliament, not against colonial assemblies. There is no point in discussing the ramifications of the issues that had to be resolved. Instead, a hint of the dimensions of just one of these issues — how fundamental should fundamental rights be made — can be gleaned by considering one aspect of the Canadian compromise.

Legal thought in twentieth-century Canada, like legal thought in nineteenth-century Great Britain, rejected the American notion that fundamental rights had to be absolutely secured from legislative invasion. The legislatures of Canada are permitted to override some of the guarantees in the Canadian Charter of Rights. Both Parliament and provincial legislatures are empowered to set aside "fundamental" freedoms, by incorporating a "notwithstanding" clause in ordinary legislation. Canadian rights, therefore, are more secure than British rights but not fundamental or "constitutional" in the American meaning of the concept, as they are not rights that can be vindicated fully against the government. Although the Canadian solution of the entrenchment dilemma moved Canadian rights somewhat closer to the American doctrine of constitutional rights, it is not a complete break with the nineteenth-century British constitutional tradition in which no rights are secure against Parliament, and in which Parliament is the instrument of politics, controlled by the ministry in power, not by the rule of law.

The question left unanswered by Lord Chatham's plan, the only proposal for securing American rights that seems to have been raised in a House of Parliament, includes more than the issue of how entrenched or how fundamental rights were to be. Were they to be as constitutionally secure as today's British rights, Canadian rights, or American rights? If they were to be secured rights, there was the further matter of the procedure for securing them. It is inconceivable that American whigs would have accepted Chatham's entrenchment mechanism and left this question unanswered. Writing their own constitutions they soon would demonstrate their concern with entrenching rights constitutionally even beyond the reach of themselves; beyond the power of the majority to abrogate. In 1777 they may not have known how to accomplish the feat. When experience, joined with experiment and necessity, demonstrated the utility of the independent judiciary guided by the concept of the rule of law, a new constitutional consensus would emerge. The instruments — the independent judiciary and the rule of law — were inherited from the ideals of the old English constitution, but the constitutional consensus was an American consensus; it would never be a British consensus.

Finally, there is the question whether British legal thought could have tolerated Chatham's plan. It would have created a constitutional anomaly quite untidy even for that most untidy of legal systems, the common law. For had Parliament and the colonial assemblies entrenched American rights in the imperial constitution, they would have made American rights more secure than British rights. American rights would have been entrenched against Parliament in the imperial constitution, but British rights would have remained mutable, subject to parliamentary will and pleasure under the British constitution.

There is an important lesson to be drawn from these questions about entrenchment. It is not the obvious lesson about the difficulties Chatham would have encountered implementing his plan. The lesson, rather, is that no plan could have secured fundamental rights sufficiently under the eighteenth-century British constitution to quiet the apprehensions of American whigs. Constitutional thought in the English-speaking world was at a crossroads, and Americans were drawing forever apart from their fellow subjects of George III. The British were looking ahead to a constitution of parliamentary command, in which government was entrusted with arbitrary power and civil rights were grants from the sovereign. What remained was to make the sovereign more representative of society, so that government, even though arbitrary, would be government by consent. The Americans were looking backward, not to government by consent but to government by the rule of law, to the constitution of John Hampden and the shipmoney controversy, to a sovereign that did not grant rights but was limited by rights, a sovereign that was, like rights, created by law, the guardian of civil rights. What remained was to devise an instrument to limit government when it threatened rights, so that rights, not government, would be secured.

One month before British troops and New England farmers faced each other in the town of Lexington, the governor of Connecticut asked the British secretary of state for the colonies why parliamentary sovereignty and fundamental rights could no longer coexist. "*British* supremacy and *American* liberty are not incompatible with each other," the governor believed. "They have been seen to exist and flourish together for more than a century. What now renders them inconsistent?"[10]

They were inconsistent both because the British constitution was altered and because the constitutional premises on which American rights had rested had changed. The security of rights under the old constitutional system had been custom. People had, by inheritance, a right of property in trial by jury, and the legal fact of inherited right was proven by unaltered immemorial custom. At one time custom had established the right to trial by jury by proving that the Crown could not take it away. In more recent times, custom had come to show that Parliament would not take that right away. For Americans, everything changed when Parliament invaded their right to trial by jury in revenue matters and their right to trial at the vicinage for certain crimes. The premises on which the right rested were forever different. The authority of custom, of ownership, of inheritance was destroyed. The right to trial by jury existed at the grace and favor of the sovereign's restraint. Even if Parliament repealed all its statutes on jury trial and restored matters to where they had been by constitutional custom, the right would never regain its former security. Trial by jury was now a grant, and no longer an inherent right. Once Parliament exercised sovereignty and shattered custom, the right was not a fundamental secured right in the sense that "fundamental secured right" was understood by Sir Edward Coke, John Hampden, Algernon Sidney, and American whigs.

American whigs began their resistance in 1765 in the belief that Parliament was acting unconstitutionally. They went to war in 1775 in the belief that they were fighting to defend the British constitution, not rebelling against it; they were, in fact, doing both. They were defending the constitution of limited government and of property in rights that once had been the English constitution. They were rebelling against the constitution of arbitrary power that the British constitution was about to become.

ACKNOWLEDGMENTS
SHORT TITLES
NOTES
INDEX

ACKNOWLEDGMENTS

Research for this study was supported by a fellowship grant from the John Simon Guggenheim Memorial Foundation and by a Huntington Library–National Endowment for the Humanities Fellowship. Leave from teaching duties at New York University School of Law was provided by the Filomen D'Agostino Greenberg and Max E. Greenberg Faculty Research Fund at the School of Law, and by Norman Redlich, dean of the School of Law. Thomas Mackey, Cornelia Dayton, and Maura Doherty verified citations and text. The manuscript benefited from the attention of a distinguished group of legal historians: Norman Cantor, William E. Nelson, and the student members of the New York University School of Law Colloquium in Legal History. A final debt of gratitude is owed to Robert Middlekauff, Martin Ridge, and the marvelous staff of the Huntington Library in San Marino, California. There is no finer institution at which to pursue the elusive study of eighteenth-century Anglo-American constitutionalism. It is not the books and manuscripts alone that make the Huntington special. There are the long walks with history among the cactus and the coyotes. It was on one walk, somewhere between the Japanese and Australian gardens, that Robert Smith of East Montana State in Billings first brought to my attention the important study written by Franklin Pierce on the eighteenth-century right to public facilities. It was down by the lily pond that Pat Smith suggested that Mrs. Franklin Pierce may have been the first American to identify it as a fundamental right.

New York University School of Law

SHORT TITLES

In citing works in the notes, short titles have generally been used. Works frequently cited have been identified by the following short titles:

Abercromby, "De Jure"
> James Abercromby, "De Jure et Gubernatione Coloniarum, or An Inquiry into the Nature and the Rights of the Colonies, Ancient, and Modern." ca. 1780. HM 518, Huntington Library, San Marino, Calif.

Abingdon, *Thoughts on Burke's Letter*
> Willoughby Bertie, earl of Abingdon, *Thoughts on the Letter of Edmund Burke, Esq; to the Sheriffs of Bristol, on the Affairs of America.* 6th ed. Oxford, [1777].

Account of Stamp Act Congress
> *Authentic Account of the Proceedings of the Congress held at New-York, in MDCCLXV, On the Subject of the American Stamp Act.* n.i., 1767.

Acherley, *Britannic Constitution*
> Roger Acherley, *The Britannic Constitution: or, the Fundamental Form of Government in Britain.* 2d ed. London, 1727.

Acts of the Privy Council
> *Acts of the Privy Council of England. Colonial Series. Vol. IV.* A.D. *1745–1766. Vol. V.* A.D. *1766–1783.* Edited by James Munro. 1911, 1912.

Adams, *"Braintree Instructions"*
"Instructions of the Town of Braintree to their Representative, 1765, *Massachusetts Gazette and Boston News-Letter* (10 October 1765): 2–3.

Adams, *Historical View*
Amos Adams, *A Concise, Historical View of the Difficulties, Hardships, and Perils Which attended the Planting and progressive Improvements of New-England with A Particular Account of its long and Destructive Wars, Expensive Expeditions, &c.* London, 1770. Published earlier in Boston.

Adams, *Legal Papers*
Legal Papers of John Adams. Edited by L. Kinvin Wroth and Hiller B. Zobel. 3 vols. Cambridge, Mass., 1965.

Adams, *Religious Liberty*
Amos Adams, *Religious Liberty an invaluable Blessing: Illustrated in Two Discourses Preached at Roxbury Dec. 3, 1767. Being the Day of general Thanksgiving.* Boston, 1768.

Adams, *Works*
The Works of John Adams, Second President of the United States. Edited by Charles Francis Adams. 10 vols. Boston, 1856.

Adams, *Writings*
The Writings of Samuel Adams. Edited by Harry Alonzo Cushing. 4 vols. New York, 1904–08.

Addresses of the Common Council
Addresses Presented from the Court of Common Council to the King, On his Majesty's Accession to the Throne, and on various other Occasions, and his Answers. Resolutions of the Court . . . Instructions at different Times to the Representatives of the City in Parliament. Petitions to Parliament for different Purposes. . . . Agreed to between the 23d October, 1760, and the 12th October 1770. London, [1770].

Addresses and Petitions of Common Council
Addresses, Remonstrances, and Petitions; Commencing the 24th of June, 1769, Presented to the King and Parliament, from the Court of Common Council, and the Livery in Common Hall assembled, with his Majesty's Answers: Likewise the Speech to the King, made by the late Mr. Alderman Beckford, When Lord Mayor of the City of London. London, [1778].

Aldridge, "Paine and Dickinson"
A. Owen Aldridge, "Paine and Dickinson," *Early American Literature* 11 (1976): 125–38.

[Allen,] *American Alarm*
[John Allen,] *The American Alarm, or the Bostonian Plea, For the Rights and Liberties, of the People, Humbly Addressed to the King and Council, and to the Constitutional Sons of Liberty, in America.* Boston, 1773.

Allen, *American Crisis*
> William Allen, *The American Crisis: A Letter, Addressed by Permission to the Earl Gower, Lord President of the Council, &c. &c. &c. On the present alarming Disturbances in the Colonies.* London, 1774.

[Allen,] *Beauties of Liberty*
> [John Allen,] *An Oration, Upon the Beauties of Liberty, or the Essential Rights of the Americans. Delivered At the Second Baptist Church in Boston, Upon the last Annual Thanksgiving.* 3d ed. New London, Conn., 1773.

Allen, *Magistracy an Institution*
> James Allen, *Magistracy an Institution of Christ upon the Throne. A Sermon preached in the Audience of His Excellency William Shirley, Esq; the Honourable His Majesty's Council and House of Representatives of the Province of the Massachusetts-Bay in New England, on the Day of Election of Councellors for said Province.* Boston, 1744.

[Allen,] "To Council and House"
> [John Allen,] "To the honourable the People's Council, and House of Representatives, of the Province of the Massachusetts-Bay," printed in [Allen,] *American Alarm.*

[Allen,] *Watchman's Alarm*
> [John Allen,] *Watchman's Alarm to Lord N[ort]h's, or The British Parliamentary Boston Port-Bill Unwrapped. Being an Oration on the Meridian of Liberty; Not to inflame but to cheer the Mind: or as an Apple of Gold in the Pictures of Silver for the mourning Captives in America. With some Observations on the Liberties of the Africans. By the British Bostonian.* Salem, Mass., 1774.

[Almon,] *Free Parliaments*
> [John Almon,] *Free Parliaments: or, a Vindication of the Parliamentary Constitution of England: in Answer to Certain visionary Plans of Modern Reformers.* London, 1783.

American Archives
> *American Archives, Fourth Series. Containing a Documentary History of the English Colonies in North America From the King's Message to Parliament, of March 7, 1774, to the Declaration of Independence by the United States.* Vols. 1 and 2. Washington, 1837.

American Gazette
> *The American Gazette. Being a Collection of all the Authentic Addresses, Memorials, Letters, &c. Which relate to the Present Disputes Between Great Britain and her Colonies. Containing also Many Original Papers Never Before Published.* London, 1768.

"Americanus," *Letter to Freeholders*
> "Americanus," *A Letter to the Freeholders and other Inhabitants of the*

Massachusetts-Bay, relating to their approaching Election of Representatives. [Newport, R.I.,] 1739.

[Anderson,] *Free Thoughts*
[James Anderson,] *Free Thoughts on the American Contest.* Edinburgh, 1776.

Andrews, "Acts of Trade"
Charles M. Andrews, "The Acts of Trade," in *The Cambridge History of the British Empire: Volume I, The Old Empire From the Beginnings to 1783.* Edited by J. Holland Rose, A. P. Newton, and E. A. Benians. Cambridge, 1929, pp. 268–99.

Andrews, *Settlements*
Charles M. Andrews, *Our Earliest Colonial Settlements: Their Diversities of Origin and Later Characteristics.* New York, 1933.

Annual Register 1764
The Annual Register, or a View of the History, Politics, and Literature, For the Year 1764. London, 1765.

Anon., *Abuse of Standing Parliaments*
Anonymous, *The Abuse of Standing Parliaments, and the the Great Advantage of Frequent Elections. In a Letter to a Noble Lord.* London, [1750?].

Anon., *Application of Political Rules*
Anonymous, *An Application of some General Political Rules, to the Present State of Great-Britain, Ireland and America. In a Letter to the Right Honourable Earl Temple.* London, 1766.

Anon., *In Behalf of the Constitution*
Anonymous, *A Speech in Behalf of the Constitution, Against the Suspending and Dispensing Prerogative &c.* London, 1767.

Anon., *British Liberties*
Anonymous, *British Liberties, or the Free-born Subject's Inheritance; Containing the Laws that form the Basis of those Liberties, with Observations thereon; also an Introductory Essay on Political Liberty and a Comprehensive View of the Constitution of Great Britain.* London, 1766.

Anon., *Case of Great Britain*
[Gervase Parker Bushe or George B. Butler,] *Case of Great Britain and America, Addressed to the King, and Both Houses of Parliament.* 3d ed. Boston, [1769].

Anon., *Case of Presbyterians*
Anonymous, *The Case of the Scotch Presbyterians, of the City of New-York.* New York, 1773.

Anon., *Civil Liberty Asserted*
Anonymous, *Civil Liberty Asserted, and the Rights of the Subject De-*

fended, Against the Anarchial Principles of the Reverend Dr. Price. London, 1776.

Anon., *Compleat View*
Anonymous, *A Compleat View of the Present Politicks of Great-Britain. In a Letter from a German Nobleman, to his Friend at Vienna.* London, 1743.

Anon., *Conduct of a Gentleman*
Anonymous, *The Conduct of a Rt. Hon. Gentleman in resigning the Seals of his Office justified, by Facts, and upon the Principles of the British Constitution. By a Member of Parliament.* 2d ed. London, 1761.

Anon., *Conduct of Mansfield*
Anonymous, *A Short Examination into the Conduct of Lord M[ans]f[iel]d, through the Affair of Mr. Wilkes.* London, 1768.

Anon., *Confutation of Sherlock*
Anonymous, *A Confutation of sundry Errors in Dr. Sherlock's Book concerning Allegiance.* [London, 1691].

Anon., *Considerations upon the Act*
Anonymous, *Considerations Upon the Act of Parliament Whereby a Duty is laid of six Pence Sterling per Gallon on Molasses, and five Shillings per Hundred on Sugar of foreign Growth, imported into any of the British Colonies.* Boston, 1764.

Anon., *Considerations on the Addresses*
Anonymous, *Considerations on the Addresses Lately Presented to His Majesty, on Occasion of the Loss of Minorca. In a Letter to a Member of Parliament.* 2d ed. London, 1756.

Anon., *Considerations on the Imposition*
Anonymous, *Considerations on the Imposition of 4½ per Cent. Collected on Grenada, and the Southern Charibbee Islands, by Virtue of His Majesty's Letters Patent, Under Pretence of the Prerogative Royal, Without Grant of Parliament.* London, 1774.

Anon., *Considerations on Information*
Anonymous, *Considerations on Proceedings by Information and Attachment. Addressed to the Members of the House of Commons. By a Barrister at Law.* 2d ed. London, 1768.

Anon., *Considerations upon Rights of Colonists*
Anonymous, *Considerations Upon the Rights of the Colonists to the Privileges of British Subjects, Introduc'd by a brief Review of the Rise and Progress of English Liberty, and concluded with some Remarks upon our present Alarming Situation.* New York, 1766.

Anon., *Constitutional Answer to Wesley*
Anonymous, *A Constitutional Answer to the Rev. Mr. John Wesley's Calm Address to the American Colonies.* London, 1775.

Anon., *Constitutional Considerations*
Anonymous, *Constitutional Considerations on the Power of Parliament to Levy Taxes on the North American Colonies*. London, 1766.

Anon., *Constitutional Right*
Anonymous, *The Constitutional Right of the Legislature of Great Britain, to Tax the British Colonies in America, Impartially Stated*. London, 1768.

Anon., *Court of Star Chamber*
Anonymous, *The Court of Star Chamber, or Seat of Oppression*. London, 1768.

Anon., *Critical Review of Liberties*
Anonymous, *A Critical Review of the Liberties of British Subjects. With a Comparative View of the Proceedings of the H[ous]e of C[ommon]s of I[relan]d, against an unfortunate Exile of that Country; who, in contending for the Rights and Liberties of the Publick, lost his own*. 2d ed. London, 1750.

Anon., *Defence of English History*
Anonymous, *A Defence of English History, Against the Misrepresentations of M. de Rapin Thoyras, in his History of England, Now Publishing Weekly*. London, 1734.

Anon., *Defence of Resolutions*
Anonymous, *A Defence of the Resolutions and Address of the American Congress, in Reply to Taxation no Tyranny*. London, [1775].

Anon., *Dialogue between High and Low*
Anonymous, *A Dialogue Between Jack High and Will Low; Proper for the Perusal of those who have a Right to Choose Members for the ensuing Parliament*. London, 1710.

Anon., *Divine Rights*
Anonymous, *The Divine Rights of the British Nation and Constitution Vindicated*. London, 1710.

Anon., *Easy upon Government*
Anonymous, *An Essay upon Government, Adopted by the Americans Wherein, The lawfulness of Revolutions, are Demonstrated in a Chain of consequences from the Fundamental, Principles of Society*. Philadelphia, 1775.

Anon., *Evidence of Common and Statute Laws*
Anonymous, *The Evidence of the Common and Statute Laws of the Realm; Usage, Records, History with the Greatest and Best Authorities Down to the 3d of George the IIId, in Proof of the Rights of Britons Throughout the British Empire. Addressed to the People*. London, 1775.

Anon., *Examination of the Legality*
Anonymous, *A Candid Examination of the Legality of the Warrant Issued*

by the Secretaries of State For Apprehending the Printers, Publishers, &c. of a late Interesting Paper. London, 1764.

Anon., *Examination of Rights of Colonies*
Anonymous, *An Examination of the Rights of the Colonies, Upon Principles of Law.* London, 1766.

Anon., *Fact without Fallacy*
Anonymous, *Fact Without Fallacy: or, Constitutional Principles Contrasted with the Ruinous Effects of Unconstitutional Practices.* London, 1793.

Anon., *Fair Trial*
Anonymous, *A Fair Trial of the Important Question, or the Rights of Election Asserted; Against the Doctrine of Incapacity by Expulsion, or by Resolution: Upon True Constitutional Principles, the Real Law of Parliament, the Common Right of the Subject, and the Determinations of the House of Commons.* London, 1769.

Anon., *Fatal Consequences*
Anonymous, *The Fatal Consequences of the Want of System In the Conduct of Public Affairs.* London, 1757.

Anon., *Foundation of British Liberty*
Anonymous, *The Foundation of British Liberty; Proving the indisputable Right of every Englishmen to the Common Laws of the Land, for the Protection of his Person and Property: In a Letter from a Gentleman in the Country to his Friend in London.* London, 1768.

Anon., *History of George III*
Anon., *The History of the Reign of George the Third, King of Great-Britain, &c. to the Conclusion of the Session of Parliament Ending in May, 1770.* London, 1770.

Anon., *History of Lord North*
Anonymous, *The History of Lord North's Administration, to the Dissolution of the Thirteenth Parliament of Great-Britain.* London, 1781.

Anon., *Inquiry into the Nature*
Anonymous, *An Inquiry into the Nature and Causes of the Present Disputes Between the British Colonies in America and their Mother-Country; and their reciprocal Claims and just Rights impartially examined, and fairly stated.* London, 1769.

Anon., *Judgment of Whole Kingdoms*
Anonymous [generally attributed to Lord Somers or to Daniel Defoe], *The Judgment of Whole Kingdoms and Nations, Concerning the Rights, Power, and Prerogative of Kings, and the Rights, Privileges, & Properties of the People.* 12th ed. Newport, R.I., 1774.

Anon., *Justice and Necessity of Taxing*
Anonymous, *The Justice and Necessity of Taxing the American Colonies*

Demonstrated. Together with a Vindication of the Authority of Parliament.
London, 1766.

Anon., *Late Occurences*
Anonymous, *The Late Occurences in North America, and Policy of Great Britain, Considered.* London, 1766.

Anon., *Legality of Impressing Seamen*
Anonymous, *An Essay on the Legality of Impressing Seamen.* London, 1777.

Anon., *Legality of Putting Soldiers to Death*
Anonymous, *An Enquiry into the Legality of Putting Soldiers to Death by Sentence of a Court-Martial in Time of Peace.* Dublin, 1771.

Anon., *Letter*
Anonymous, *A Letter to the People of Pennsylvania*, reprinted in Bailyn, *Pamphlets*, pp. 257–72.

Anon., *Letter to Cooper*
Anonymous, *A Letter to the Rev. Dr. Cooper, on the Origin of Civil Government; in Answer to his Sermon, Preached before the University of Oxford, on the Day appointed by Proclamation for a General Fast.* London, 1777.

Anon., *Letter on Corruption*
Anonymous, *A Letter to the People of Great Britain, on the present alarming Crisis. Pointing at the most eligible Means for limiting the Number of Place-Men and Pensioners, in Parliament, and putting an end to Bribery and Corruption; to obviate the Dangers which now threaten this Kingdom.* London, 1771.

Anon., *Letter to Freeholders* (1742)
Anonymous, *A Letter to the Freeholders and other Inhabitants of this Province, qualified to vote for Representatives in the ensuing Election.* [Boston, 1742.]

Anon., *Letter to Freemen of New York*
Anonymous, *A Letter to the Freemen and Freeholders of the Province of New-York, Relating to the Approaching Election of Their Representatives.* New York, 1750.

Anon., *Letter to a Member*
Anonymous, *A Letter to a Member of Parliament. Concerning the present State of Affairs at Home and Abroad.* London, 1740.

Anon., *Letter to North Concerning East-India*
Anonymous, *A Letter to the Right Honourable Lord North, &c. &c. &c. on the Present Proceedings Concerning the East-India Company.* London, 1773.

Anon., *Letter to North on East-India Bill*
Anonymous, *A Letter to the Right Honourable Lord North on the East-India Bill now depending in Parliament.* London, 1772.

Anon., *Letter to People of Great Britain*
Anonymous, *A Letter to the People of Great-Britain, in Answer to that Published by the American Congress.* London, 1775.

Anon., *Letter to Robert Morris*
Anonymous, *Letter to Robert Morris, Esq. Wherein the Rise and Progress of our Political Disputes are Considered. Together with some Observations on the Power of Judges and Juries as relating to the Cases of Woodfall and Almon.* London, 1771.

Anon., *Liberty in Two Parts*
Anonymous, *Liberty in Two Parts.* London, 1754.

Anon., *Licentiousness Unmask'd*
Anonymous, *Licentiousness Unmask'd; or Liberty Explained.* London, n.d.

Anon., *Magna Charta Opposed to Privilege*
Anonymous, *Magna Charta, Opposed to Assumed Privilege: Being a complete View of the Late Interesting Disputes between the House of Commons and the Magistrates of London.* London, 1771.

Anon., *Means of Reducing the Rebels*
Anonymous, *Reflections on the Most Proper Means of Reducing the Rebels, and What Ought to be the Consequence of Our Success.* London, 1776.

Anon., *Middle Line*
Anonymous, *The Middle Line: Or, An Attempt to Furnish Some Hints for Ending the Differences Subsisting between Great-Britain and the Colonies.* Philadelphia, 1775.

Anon., *Narrative of Lords of Ireland*
Anonymous, *A Narrative of the Proceedings of the Lords of Ireland. In the Years 1703 and 1719, In Consequences of the Attempts made at those Periods by the Lords of Great Britain to Enforce their Authority in this Kingdom.* Dublin, 1782.

Anon., *National Mirror*
Anonymous, *The National Mirror. Being a Series of Essays on the Most Important Concerns: But Particularly those of the East-India Company.* London, 1771.

Anon., *Necessity of Repealing the Stamp Act*
Anonymous, *The Necessity of Repealing the American Stamp-Act Demonstrated: Or, a Proof that Great-Britain must be injured by that Act.* London, 1766.

Anon., *North-Country Poll*
Anonymous, *The North-Country Poll; or, an Essay on the New Method of Appointing Members to serve in Parliament.* London, 1768.

Anon., *Observations upon the Authority*
Anonymous, *Observations Upon the Authority, Manner and Circumstances of the Apprehension and Confinement of Mr. Wilkes. Addressed to Free-Born Englishmen.* London, 1763.

Anon., *Old Constitution*
Anonymous, *The Old Constitution and Present Establishment in Church and State Honestly Asserted.* London, 1718.

Anon., *Philosophical Survey of Nature*
Anonymous, *A Philosophical Survey of Nature: in which the Long Agitated Question Concerning Human Liberty and Necessity, is Endeavoured to be fully Determined.* London, 1763.

Anon., *Plain Reasons*
Anonymous, *Plain Reasons for New-Modelling Poynings' Law, in such a Manner as to assert the Ancient Rights of the Two Houses of Parliament, Without Entrenching on the King's Prerogative.* Dublin, 1780.

Anon., *Plan to Reconcile*
Anonymous, *A Plan to Reconcile Great Britain & her Colonies, and Preserve the Dependency of America.* London, 1774.

Anon., *Plea for Poor*
Anonymous, *A Plea for the Poor and Distressed, Against the Bill for granting an Excise upon Wines, and Spirits distilled, sold by Retail, or consumed within this Province &.c.* Boston, 1754.

Anon., *Policy of the Laws*
Anonymous, *An Inquiry into the Policy of the Laws, Affecting the Popish Inhabitants of Ireland, Preceded by a Short Political Analysis of the History and Constitution of Ireland, In which the Rights of Colonists and Planters are briefly mentioned . . . with some Hints respecting America.* Dublin, 1775.

Anon., *Present Crisis*
Anonymous, *The Present Crisis, With Respect to America, Considered.* London, 1775.

Anon., *Privileges of Jamaica*
Anonymous, *The Privileges of the Island of Jamaica Vindicated; with an Impartial Narrative of the Late Dispute Between the Governor and House of Representatives, Upon the Case of Mr. Olyphant, A Member of that House.* London, 1766.

Anon., *Protest of a Private Person*
Anonymous, *An Address to the People of England: Being the Protest of*

a *Private Person Against every Suspension of Law that is liable to injure or endanger Personal Security*. London, 1778.

Anon., *Remarks upon a Discourse*
Anonymous [Henry Barry?], *Remarks upon a Discourse Preached December 15th 1774. Being the Day recommended by the Provincial Congress: And afterwards at the Boston Lecture. By William Gordon, Pastor of the third Church in Roxbury*. [New York,] 1775.

Anon., *Remarks on the New Essay*
Anonymous, *Remarks on the New Essay of the Pen[n]sylvanian Farmer; and on the Resolves and Instructions Prefixed to that Essay; By the Author of the Right of the British Legislature Vindicated*. London, 1775.

Anon., *Representative of London*
Anonymous, *The Representative of London and Westminster in Parliament Examined, and Consider'd*. London, 1702.

Anon., *Right of British Legislature*
Anonymous, *The Right of the British Legislature to Tax the Colonies Considered, In a Letter to the Right Hon. Frederick Lord North*. London, [1774].

Anon., *Rights Asserted*
Anonymous, *The Rights of the People Asserted, and the Necessity of a More Equal Representation in Parliament Stated and Proved*. Dublin, 1783.

Anon., *Rights of East-India*
Anonymous, *An Enquiry into the Rights of the East-India Company, of making War and Peace; and of Possessing their Territorial Acquisitions Without the Participation or Inspection of the British Government*. London, 1772.

Anon., *Rights of Parliament*
Anonymous, *The Rights of Parliament Vindicated, On Occasion of the late Stamp-Act. In which is exposed the Conduct of the American Colonists. Addressed to all the People of Great Britain*. London, 1766.

Anon., *Rights of People to Petition*
Anonymous, *The Rights of the People to Petition, and the Reasonableness of complying with such Petitions: In a Letter to a Leading Great Man*. New ed. London, 1769.

Anon., *Second Answer to Wesley*
Anonymous [W.D.], *A Second Answer to Mr. John Wesley. Being a Supplement to the Letter of Americanus, In which the Idea of Supreme Power, and the Nature of Royal Charters, are briefly considered*. London, 1775.

Anon., *Some Fugitive Thoughts*
Anonymous, *Some Fugitive Thoughts on a Letter Signed Freeman, ad-*

dressed to the Deputies, assembled at the High Court of Congress in Phila-delphia. South Carolina, 1774.

Anon., *Spirit and Principles*
Anonymous, *The Spirit and Principles of Whigs and Jacobites Compared. Being the Substance of a Discourse delivered to an Audience of Gentlemen at Edinburgh, December 22, 1745*. London, 1746.

Anon., *State Necessity*
Anonymous, *State Necessity Considered as a Question of Law*. London, 1766.

Anon., *"Taxation no Tyranny" Considered*
Anonymous, *The Pamphlet Entitled, "Taxation no Tyranny," Candidly Considered, and It's Arguments, and Pernicious Doctrines, Exposed and Refuted*. London, [1775].

Anon., *Thoughts on Quebec Act*
Anonymous, *Thoughts on the Act for making more Effectual Provision for the Government of the Province of Quebec*. London, 1774.

Anon., *To Committee of London Merchants*
Anonymous, *A Letter To the Gentlemen of the Committee of London Mer-chants, Trading to North America: Shewing In what Manner, it is appre-hended, that the Trade and Manufactures of Britain may be affected by some late Restrictions on the American Commerce, and by the Operation of the Act for the Stamp Duty in America; as also how far the Freedom and Liberty of the Subjects residing in Britain, are supposed to be inter-ested in the Preservation of the Rights of the Provinces, and in what Man-ner those Rights appear to be abridged by that Statute*. London, 1766.

Anon., *To Freemen of Pennsylvania* (1755)
Anonymous, *To the Freemen of Pennsylvania, and more especially to those of the City and County of Philadelphia*. [Philadelphia, 1755?].

Anon., *To the Princess of Wales*
Anonymous, *Letter to Her R[oya]l H[ighnes]s the P[rinces]s D[o]w[a]g[e]r of W[ales] on the Approaching Peace. With a few Words Concerning the Right Honourable the Earl of B[ute], and the General Talk of the World*. 3d ed. London, 1762.

Anon., *To Tax Themselves*
Anonymous, *An Argument in Defence of the Exclusive Right Claimed by the Colonies to Tax Themselves; With A Review of the Laws of England, Relative to Representation and Taxation. To which is Added, an Account of the Rise of the Colonies, and the Manner in which the Rights of the Subjects within the realm were communicated to those that went to Amer-ica, with the Exercise of those Rights from the First Settlement to the Pres-ent Time*. London, 1774.

Anon., *Tyranny Unmasked*
Anonymous, *Tyranny Unmasked. An Answer to a Late Pamphlet, Entitled Taxation no Tyranny.* London, 1775.

Anon., *Vindication of the Livery*
Anonymous, *Vindication of the Petition of the Livery of the City of London, to his Majesty, as to the Charge upon the Ministry of raising a Revenue in our Colonies.* n. i., 1769.

Anon., *With Respect to America*
Anonymous, *Reflections on Government, With Respect to America. To which is Added, Carmen Latinum.* London, 1766.

Answer to a Book
His Majesties Answer to a Book, Entituled, The Declaration, or Remonstrance of the LORDS *and* COMMONS, *of the 19th of May, 1642.* n.i., 1642.

Ashton, "Tradition and Innovation"
Robert Ashton, "Tradition and Innovation and the Great Rebellion," in *Three British Revolutions: 1641, 1688, 1776.* Edited by J. G. A. Pocock. Princeton, N.J., 1980, pp. 208–23.

[Auckland,] *Principles of Penal Law*
[William E. Auckland,] *Principles of Penal Law.* 2d ed. London, 1771.

[Backus,] *Letter to a Gentleman*
[Isaac Backus,] *A Letter to a Gentleman in the Massachusetts General Assembly, Concerning Taxes to support Religious Worship.* [Boston,] 1771.

[Bacon,] *Short Address*
[Anthony Bacon,] *A Short Address to the Government, the Merchants, Manufacturers, and the Colonists in America, and the Sugar Islands, On the present State of Affairs.* London, 1775.

[Baillie,] *Appendix to a Letter*
[Hugh Baillie,] *An Appendix to a Letter to Dr. Shebbeare. To which are added, Some Observations on a Pamphlet, Entitled, Taxation no Tyranny; In which the Sophistry of that Author's Reasoning is Detected.* London, 1775.

Baillie, *Letter to Shebear*
Hugh Baillie, *A Letter to Dr. Shebear: Containing a Refutation of his Arguments Concerning the Boston and Quebec Acts of Parliament: and his Aspersions upon the Memory of King William, and the Protestant Dissenters.* London, 1775.

Bailyn, "Central Themes"
Bernard Bailyn, "The Central Themes of the American Revolution," in *Essays on the American Revolution*, edited by Stephen G. Kurtz and James H. Hutson, pp. 3–31. Chapel Hill, N.C., 1973.

Bailyn, *Ordeal*
Bernard Bailyn, *The Ordeal of Thomas Hutchinson*. Cambridge, Mass., 1974.

Bailyn, *Pamphlets*
Pamphlets of the American Revolution, 1750–1775. Vol. 1. Edited by Bernard Bailyn. Cambridge, Mass., 1965.

Baldwin, *New England Clergy*
Alice M. Baldwin, *The New England Clergy and the American Revolution*. New York, 1958.

[Bancroft,] *Remarks*
[Edward Bancroft,] *Remarks on the Review of the Controversy Between Great Britain and her Colonies. In Which the Errors of its Author are exposed, and the Claims of the Colonies vindicated, Upon the Evidence of Historical Facts and authentic records*. London, 1769.

Barker, *Essays*
Ernest Barker, *Essays on Government*. Oxford, 1945.

Barker, "Natural Law"
Sir Ernest Barker, "Natural Law and the American Revolution," in *Traditions of Civility: Eight Essays*, pp. 263–355. Cambridge, 1948.

[Barron,] *History of Colonization*
[William Barron,] *History of the Colonization of the Free States of Antiquity, Applied to the Present Contest between Great Britain and her American Colonies. With Reflections concerning the future Settlement of these Colonies*. London, 1777.

Barrow, *Trade*
Thomas C. Barrow, *Trade and Empire: The British Customs Service in Colonial America 1660–1775*. Cambridge, Mass., 1967.

[Barwis,] *Three Dialogues*
[Jackson Barwis,] *Three Dialogues Concerning Liberty*. London, 1776.

Becker, *Declaration*
Carl Becker, *The Declaration of Independence: A Study in the History of Political Ideas*. New York: Vintage Books, 1958.

Beloff, *Debate*
Max Beloff, "Introduction," in *The Debate on the American Revolution 1761–1783*, edited by Max Beloff. 2d ed. London, 1960.

Bentham, *Fragment on Government*
Jeremy Bentham, *A Fragment on Government* (1776), reprinted in Bentham, *A Fragment on Government and An Introduction to the Principles of Morals and Legislation*. Edited by Wilfrid Harrison. Oxford, 1967, pp. 1–112.

[Bernard,] *Appeal to the Public*
[Thomas Bernard,] *An Appeal to the Public; Stating and Considering the Objections to the Quebec Bill.* London, 1774.

Birdsall, "Non Obstante"
Paul Birdsall, "Non Obstante," in *Essays in History and Political Theory in Honor of Charles Howard McIlwain*, pp. 37–76. Cambridge, Mass., 1936.

Blackall, *Exeter's Answer*
Offspring Blackall, *The Lord Bishop of Exeter's Answer to Mr. Hoadly's Letter.* London, 1709.

Blackstone, *Commentaries*
William Blackstone, *Commentaries on the Laws of England.* 4 vols. Oxford, 1765–69.

Bland, *An Inquiry*
Richard Bland, *An Inquiry into the Rights of the British Colonies, Intended as an Answer to the Regulations lately made concerning the Colonies, and the Taxes imposed upon them considered.* Williamsburg, Va., 1766.

[Bland,] *Colonel Dismounted*
[Richard Bland,] *The Colonel Dismounted: Or the Rector Vindicated. In a Letter addressed to His Reverence: Containing A Dissertation Upon the Constitution of the Colony.* Williamsburg, Va., 1764.

[Blount,] *William and Mary Conquerors*
[Charles Blount,] *King William and Queen Mary Conquerors: Or, a Discourse Endeavouring to prove that Their Majesties have on their Side, against the Late King, the Principal Reasons that make Conquest a Good Title.* London, 1693.

[Bohun,] *Desertion*
[Edmund Bohun,] *The History of the Desertion, or an Account of all the Publick Affairs in England, from the beginning of September 1688 to the twelfth of February following.* London, 1689.

[Bolingbroke,] *Dissertation*
[Henry Saint John, Viscount Bolingbroke,] *A Dissertation Upon Parties; In Several Letters to Caleb D'Anvers, Esq.* 3d ed. London, 1735.

[Bolingbroke,] *Freeholder's Catechism*
[Bolingbroke, H. St. John, 1st Viscount,] *The Freeholder's Political Catechism. Very Necessary to be Studied by every Freeman in America.* New London, Conn., 1769.

[Bollan,] *Continued Corruption*
[William Bollan,] *Continued Corruption, Standing Armies, and Popular Discontents Considered; And the Establishment of the English Colonies*

in America, with Various subsequent Proceedings, and the Present Contests, examined, with Intent to promote their cordial and perpetual Union with their Mother-Country, for their Mutual Honour, Comfort, Strength, and Safety. London, 1768.

[Bollan,] *Free Britons Memorial*
[William Bollan,] *The Free Britons Memorial, to all the Freeholders, Citizens and Burgesses, who Elect the Members of the British Parliament, Presented in Order to the Effectual Defence of their Injured Right of Election.* London, 1769.

Boorstin, *Mysterious Science of Law*
Daniel J. Boorstin, *The Mysterious Science of the Law: An Essay on Blackstone's* COMMENTARIES *Showing how Blackstone, Employing Eighteenth-Century Ideas of Science, Religion, History, Aesthetics, and Philosophy, Made of the Law at Once a Conservative and a Mysterious Science.* Cambridge, Mass., 1941.

Boston Chronicle
The Boston Chronicle. (Weekly newspaper.)

Boston Evening-Post
The Boston Evening-Post. (Weekly newspaper.)

Boston Gazette
The Boston Gazette and Country Journal. (Weekly newspaper.)

Boston News-Letter
The Massachusetts Gazette and Boston News-Letter, also sometimes *The Massachusetts Gazette and the Boston News-Letter,* or *The Boston News-Letter.* (Weekly newspaper.)

Boston Post-Boy
The Boston Post-Boy & Advertiser. (Weekly newspaper.)

Boston Town Records
A Report of the Record Commissioners of the City of Boston, Containing the Boston Town Records, 1758 to 1769. 16th Report. Boston, 1886. *A Report of the Record Commissioners of the City of Boston, Containing the Boston Town Records, 1770 Through 1777.* 18th Report. Boston, 1887.

[Boucher,] *Letter from a Virginian*
[Jonathan Boucher,] *A Letter From A Virginian to the Members of the Congress to be held at Philadelphia, on the first of September, 1774.* Boston, 1774.

Bourguignon, *First Federal Court*
Henry J. Bourguignon, *The First Federal Court: The Federal Appellate Prize Court of the American Revolution, 1775–1787.* Philadelphia, 1977.

Boyer, "Borrowed Rhetoric"
  Paul S. Boyer, "Borrowed Rhetoric: The Massachusetts Excise Controversy
  of 1754," *William and Mary Quarterly* 21 (1964): 328–51

Brady, *Complete History*
  Robert Brady, *A Complete History of England, from the First Entrance
  of the Romans under the Conduct of Julius Caesar, Unto the End of the
  Reign of King Henry III.* London, 1685.

Brand, *Defence of Reeves*
  John Brand, *A Defence of the Pamphlet Ascribed to John Reeves, Esq. and
  Entitled "Thoughts on the English Government."* London, 1796.

[Braxton,] *Address to the Convention*
  [Carter Braxton,] *An Address to the Convention of the Colony and Ancient Dominion of Virginia; on the Subject of Government in general, and
  recommending a particular Form to their Consideration.* Philadelphia,
  1776.

Breen, *Good Ruler*
  T. H. Breen, *The Character of The Good Ruler: A Study of Puritan Political Ideas in New England, 1630–1730.* New Haven, Conn., 1970.

Brewer, "Wilkites and the Law"
  John Brewer, "The Wilkites and the Law, 1763–74: A Study of Radical Notions of Governance," in *An Ungovernable People: The English and Their
  Law in the Seventeenth and Eighteenth Centuries.* Edited by John Brewer
  and John Styles. New Brunswick, N.J., 1980, pp. 128–71.

Briefs of American Revolution
  *The Briefs of the American Revolution: Constitutional Arguments Between
  Thomas Hutchinson, Governor of Massachusetts Bay, and James Bowdoin
  for the Council and John Adams for the House of Representatives.* Edited
  by John Phillip Reid. New York, 1981.

[Brooke,] *Liberty and Common Sense*
  [Henry Brooke,] *Liberty and Common-Sense to the People of Ireland,
  Greeting.* London, 1760.

Brown, *Estimate of Manners*
  John Brown, *An Estimate of the Manners and Principles of the Times.* 7th
  ed. Boston, 1758.

Brown, *Revolutionary Politics*
  Richard D. Brown, *Revolutionary Politics in Massachusetts: The Boston
  Committee of Correspondence and the Towns, 1772–1774.* New York, 1976.

Browning, *Court Whigs*
  Reed Browning, *Political and Constitutional Ideas of the Court Whigs.*
  Baton Rouge, La., 1982.

Burgh, *Political Disquisitions*
> J. Burgh, *Political Disquisitions; or, An Enquiry into public Errors, Defects, and Abuses. Illustrated by, and established upon Facts and Remarks, extracted from a Variety of Authors, Ancient and Modern.* 3 vols. Philadelphia, 1775.

Burke on American Revolution
> *Edmund Burke on the American Revolution: Selected Speeches and Letters.* Edited by Elliot Robert Barkan. New York, 1966.

Burke, *Letter to Sheriffs*
> Edmund Burke, *A Letter from Edmund Burke, Esq; One of the Representatives in Parliament for the City of Bristol, to John Farr and John Harris, Esqrs. Sheriffs of that City, on the Affairs of America.* 3d ed. London, 1777.

Burke, *Revolution in France*
> Edmund Burke, *Reflections on the Revolution in France, and on the Proceedings in Certain Societies in London Relative to that Event in a Letter Intended to have been Sent to a Gentleman in Paris.* Philadelphia, 1792.

Burlamaqui, *Politic Law*
> J. J. Burlamaqui, *The Principles of Politic Law: Being a Sequel to the Principles of Natural Law.* London, 1752.

Burnet, *Divine Authority of Government*
> Tho. Burnet, *The Divine Authority of Government, with the Measure of Subjection Stated, and the Lawfulness of the Revolution Demonstrated.* London, 1726.

Burnet, *Essay upon Government*
> Thomas Burnet, *An Essay Upon Government: or, the Natural Notions of Government, Demonstrated in a Chain of Consequences from the Fundamental Principles of Society.* 2d ed. London, 1726.

[Burnet,] *Sermon at Salisbury*
> Gilbert [Burnet,] *A Sermon Preach'd in the Cathedral-Church of Salisbury, on the 29th Day of May, in the Year 1710.* London, 1710.

Burnett, *Continental Congress*
> Edmund Cody Burnett, *The Continental Congress.* New York, 1941.

Cambridge Magazine
> *The Cambridge Magazine: or Universal Repository of Arts, Sciences, and the Belle Letters.* For the Year MDCCLXIX. London, 1769.

Camden, "Speech on American Taxation"
> Lord Camden, "Speech on American taxation, House of Lords, 24 February 1766," reprinted in *The Debate on the American Revolution 1761–1783.* Edited by Max Beloff. 2d ed. London, 1960, pp. 119–24.

Campbell, *Duty of Allegiance*
George Campbell, *The Nature, Extent, and Importance, of the Duty of Allegiance: A Sermon Preached at Aberdeen, December 12, 1776, Being the Fast Day Appointed by the King, on Account of the Rebellion in America*. Aberdeen, 1777.

Campbell, *Chancellors*
John Lord Campbell, *The Lives of the Lord Chancellors and Keepers of the Great Seal of England*. 3d ed., vol. 5. London, 1849.

Candidus, *Two Letters*
Mystagogus Candidus, *Two Letters: viz. I. A Letter to the Earl of Abingdon, in which his Grace of York's Notions of Civil Liberty are Examined by Liberalis; published in the London Evening Post, November 6th, 1777. II. Vera Icon; or a Vindication of his Grace of York's Sermon, preached on February 21st, 1777*. London, 1777.

Canning, *Letter to Hillsborough*
George Canning, *A Letter to the Right Honourable Wills Earl of Hillsborough, on the Connection Between Great Britain and her American Colonies*. Dublin, 1768.

Care, *English Liberties Boston Edition*
Henry Care, *English Liberties, or the Free-Born Subject's Inheritance; Containing Magna Charta, Charta de Foresta, The Statute De Tallagio non concedendo, The Habeas Corpus Act, and several other Statutes; with Comments on each of them*. 5th ed. Boston, 1721.

Care, *English Liberties Providence Edition*
Henry Care, *English Liberties, or the Free-Born Subject's Inheritance. Containing Magna Charta, Charta de Foresta, the Statute De Tallagio non concedendo, the Habeas Corpus Act, and several other Statutes; with Comments on each of them*. 6th ed. Providence, R.I., 1774.

[Care,] *English Liberties Second Edition*
[Henry Care,] *English Liberties: or, the Free-Born Subject's Inheritance Etc*. London, 1691.

Carroll, "First Citizen"
Charles Carroll, "First Citizen," [Fourth Letter, 1 July 1773], reprinted in *Maryland and the Empire, 1773: The Antilon-First Citizen Letters*. Edited by Peter S. Onuf. Baltimore, Md., 1974.

[Cartwright,] *American Independence*
[John Cartwright,] *American Independence the Interest and Glory of Great Britain; Containing Arguments which prove, that not only in Taxation, but in Trade, Manufactures, and Government, the Colonies are entitled to an entire Independency on the British Legislature; and that it can only by a formal Declaration of these Rights, and forming thereupon a friendly*

League with them, that the true and lasting Welfare of both Countries can be promoted. In a Series of Letters to the Legislature. Philadelphia, 1776.

Cartwright, *Appeal on Constitution*
John Cartwright, *An Appeal on the Subject of the English Constitution.* Boston, England, [1797].

Cartwright, *Constitution Produced*
John Cartwright, *The English Constitution Produced and Illustrated.* London, 1823.

Cartwright, *Legislative Rights*
John Cartwright, *The Legislative Rights of the Commonalty Vindicated; or, Take Your Choice! Representation and Respect: Imposition and Contempt: Annual Parliaments and Liberty: Long Parliaments and Slavery.* 2d ed. London, 1777.

Cartwright, *People's Barrier*
John Cartwright, *The People's Barrier Against Undue Influence and Corruption: Or the Commons' House of Parliament According to the Constitution.* London, 1780.

[Cartwright,] *Take Your Choice*
[John Cartwright,] *Take Your Choice!* London, 1776.

Carysfort, *Letter to Huntingdonshire*
John Joshua Proby, 1st earl of Carysfort, *A Letter from the Right Honourable Lord Carysfort, to the Huntingdonshire Committee.* London, 1780.

[Carysfort,] *Serious Address*
[Carysfort, John Joshua Proby, 1st earl of,] *A Serious Address to the Electors of Great-Britain, on the Subject of Short Parliaments and an Equal Representation.* London, 1782.

Carysfort, *Thoughts on Constitution*
Lord Carysfort [John Joshua Proby, first earl of Carysfort,] *Thoughts on the Constitution with a View to the Proposed Reform in the Representation of the People, and Duration of Parliaments.* London, 1783.

Cato's Letters
Cato's Letters: or, Essays on Liberty, Civil and Religious, And other Important Subjects. In Four Volumes. 6th ed. London, 1755.

"Cato's Letters"
John Trenchard and Thomas Gordon, "Cato's Letters," reprinted in *The English Libertarian Heritage From the Writings of John Trenchard and Thomas Gordon in The Independent Whig and Cato's Letters.* Edited by David L. Jacobson. Indianapolis, 1965.

Chalmers, *Opinions*
George Chalmers, *Opinions of Eminent Lawyers on Various Points of English Jurisprudence, Chiefly Concerning the Colonies, Fisheries and Commerce of Great Britain*. Burlington, Vt., 1858.

[Chandler,] *What Think Ye of Congress*
[Thomas B. Chandler,] *What think ye of the Congress Now? or, An Enquiry, How far the Americans are Bound to Abide by, and Execute, the Decisions of the Late Continental Congress*. New York, 1775.

Chapman, *Burke*
Gerald W. Chapman, *Edmund Burke: The Practical Imagination*. Cambridge, Mass., 1967.

Chatham, "Speech on Quartering Act of 1774"
Earl of Chatham [William Pitt], "Speech in the House of Lords, 26 May 1774," reprinted in *The Debate on the American Revolution 1761–1781*. Edited by Max Beloff. 2d ed. London, 1960, pp. 151–56.

Chatham, *Speech of 20 November*
Lord Chatham's Speech in the British House of Lords, at the Opening of the Session, 20th November 1777, on the Debate for Addressing the Throne. [London,] 1778.

Chauncy, *Civil Magistrates*
Charles Chauncy, *Civil Magistrates must be just, ruling in the Fear of God. A Sermon Preached before His Excellency William Shirley, Esq; the Honourable His Majesty's Council, and House of Representatives, of the Province of the Massachusetts-Bay in N. England; May 27, 1747. Being the Anniversary for the Election of His Majesty's Council for the said Province*. Boston, 1747.

Chauncy, *Discourse on "the good News"*
Charles Chauncy, *A Discourse on "the good News from a far Country." Deliver'd July 24th. A Day of Thanksgiving to Almighty God, throughout the Province of the Massachusetts-Bay in New-England, on Occasion of the Repeal of the* STAMP ACT. Boston, 1766.

Christie, "Quest for the Revolution"
Ian R. Christie, "The Historians' Quest for the American Revolution," in *Statesmen, Scholars and Merchants: Essays in Eighteenth-Century History Presented to Dame Lucy Sutherland*. Edited by Anne Whiteman, J. S. Bromley, and P. G. M. Dickson, Oxford, 1973, pp. 181–201.

Christie & Labaree, *Empire*
Ian R. Christie & Benjamin W. Labaree, *Empire or Independence 1760–1776: A British-American Dialogue on the Coming of the American Revolution*. New York, 1977.

Clark, *British Opinion*
> Dora Mae Clark, *British Opinion and the American Revolution.* New
> Haven, Conn., 1930.

[Cluny,] *American Traveller*
> [Alex. Cluny,] *The American Traveller: or, Observations on the Present State,
> Culture and Commerce of the British Colonies in America, And the fur-
> ther Improvements of which they are capable; with An Account of the Ex-
> ports, Imports and Returns of each Colony respectively,— and of the Num-
> bers of British Ships and Seamen, Merchants, Traders and Manufacturers
> employed by all collectively.* London, 1769.

Cohen, "Revolution and Natural Law"
> Lester H. Cohen, "The American Revolution and Natural Law Theory,"
> *Journal of the History of Ideas* 39 (1978): 491–502.

Collection of Irish Letters
> *A Collection of the Letters which have been addressed to the Volunteers
> of Ireland, on the subject of a Parliamentary Reform.* London, 1783.

Collection of Letters
> *A New and Impartial Collection of Interesting Letters, from the Public
> Papers; Many of them Written by Persons of Eminence, On a great Variety
> of Important Subjects, which Have occasionally engaged the Public At-
> tention: From the Accession of his present Majesty, in September 1765, to
> May 1767. In Two Volumes.* London, 1767.

Collier, *Essay on Charters*
> John Collier, *An Essay on Charters: In which are Particularly Considered,
> Those of Newcastle. With Remarks on its Constitution, Customs, and Fran-
> chises.* Newcastle, 1777.

Commager, *Documents*
> Henry Steele Commager, *Documents of American History.* New York, 1934.

Commemoration Ceremony
> *Commemoration Ceremony in Honor of the Two Hundredth Anniversary
> of the First Continental Congress in the United States House of Represen-
> tatives.* House Document No. 93–413, 93d Congress, 2d session. Washing-
> ton, D.C., 1975.

Commons Debates 1628
> *Commons Debates 1628.* Edited by Robert C. Johnson, Mary Frear Keeler,
> Maija Cole, and William B. Bidwell. 6 vols. New Haven, Conn., 1977–1983.

Complete Protests
> *A Complete Collection of All the Protests of the Peers in Parliament, Entered
> on their Journals, Since the Year 1774, on the Great Questions of the Cause
> and Issue of the War between Great-Britain and America, &c. to the Pres-
> ent Time.* London, 1782.

Conference of Both Houses
> A Conference Desired by the Lords and had by a Committee of both Houses, Concerning the Rights and Privileges of the Subjects. Discoursed by Sir Dudley Digges. Sir Edward Littleton Knight, now Lord Keeper. Master Selden. Sir Edward Cooke. With the Objections by Sir Robert Heath Knight then Attorney Generall, and the Answers. 3 Apr. 4 Car. 1628. London, 1642.

Conkin, *Truths*
> Paul K. Conkin, *Self-Evident Truths: Being a Discourse on the Origins & Developments of the First Principles of American Government — Popular Sovereignty, Natural Rights, and Balance & Separation of Powers.* Bloomington, Ind., 1974.

Constitution of New Jersey (1776)
> *Constitution of New-Jersey.* Burlington, N.J., 1776.

Conway, *Peace Speech*
> Henry Seymour Conway, *The Speech of General Conway, Member of Parliament for Saint Edmondsbury, on moving in the House of Commons, (On the 5th of May, 1780).* London, 1781.

Cooke, *Election Sermon*
> Samuel Cooke, *A Sermon Preached at Cambridge, in the Audience of his Honor Thomas Hutchinson, Esq; Lieutenant-Governor and Commander in Chief; The Honorable His Majesty's Council, and the Honorable House of Representatives, of the Province of the Massachusetts-Bay in New-England, May 30th, 1770. Being the Anniversary for the Election of His Majesty's Council for the Said Province.* Boston, 1770.

Cooper, "Letters"
> Frederick Tuckerman, "Letters of Samuel Cooper to Thomas Pownall, 1769–1777," *American Historical Review* 8 (1903): 301–30.

Cooper, *Crisis*
> Samuel Cooper, *The Crisis. Or, a Full Defence of the Colonies. In which it is incontestibly proved that the British Constitution has been flagrantly violated in the late Stamp Act, and rendered indisputably evident, that the Mother Country cannot lay any arbitrary Tax upon the Americans, without destroying the essence of her own liberties.* London, 1766.

Cowell & Manley, *Interpreter*
> John Cowell and Thomas Manley, *The Interpreter of Words and Terms, Used either in the Common or Statute Laws of this Realm, and in Tenures and Jocular Customs.* London, 1701.

Craftsman
> *The Craftsman.* Vols. 13–14. London, 1737.

Cragg, *Freedom and Authority*
> Gerald R. Cragg, *Freedom and Authority: A Study of English Thought in the Seventeenth Century.* Philadelphia, 1975.

Crane, "Franklin and Stamp Act"
> Verner W. Crane, "Benjamin Franklin and the Stamp Act," *Publications of the Colonial Society of Massachusetts* 32 (1934): 56–77.

Creasy, *Imperial Constitutions*
> Sir Edward Creasy, *the Imperial and Colonial Constitutions of the Britannic Empire, Including Indian Institutions.* London, 1872.

Crisis
> *The Crisis.* (Weekly newspaper "Printed and published for the Authors by T. W. Shaw," London, January 1775–6 October 1776.)

Critical Review
> *The Critical Review: Or Annals of Literature by a Society of Gentlemen.* (Monthly magazine, London).

Cumings, *Thanksgiving Sermon*
> Henry Cumings, *A Thanksgiving Sermon Preached at Billerica, November 27, 1766.* Boston, 1767.

Daily Gazetteer
> *The Daily Gazetteer*, London, 30 June 1735 to 27 October 1735.

[Dalrymple,] *Address of the People*
> [John Dalrymple,] *The Address of the People of Great-Britain to the Inhabitants of America.* London, 1775.

Dartmouth Manuscripts
> *The Manuscripts of the Earl of Dartmouth.* Vol. 1. Historical Manuscripts Commission, 11th report, appendix, part 5. London, 1887. *The Manuscripts of the Earl of Dartmouth* Vol. 2. *American Papers.* Historical Manuscripts Commission, 14th report, appendix, part 10. London, 1895.

Davis, *Reports*
> Sir John Davis [Davies], *Les Reports Des Cases & Matters en Ley, Resolves & Adjudges en les Courts del Roy en Ireland.* London, 1674.

Day, *Two Speeches*
> Thomas Day, *Two Speeches of Thomas Day, Esq. at the General Meetings of the Counties of Cambridge and Essex, Held March 25, and April 25, 1780.* n.i., 1780.

"Declaration of 1689"
> "The Declaration of the Gentlemen, Merchants, and Inhabitants of Boston, and the Country Adjacent. April 18, 1689," reprinted in *The Andros Tracts* 1. Prince Society Publication vol. 5. Boston, 1868, pp. 11–20.

Delaware Declaration of Rights (1776)
> *A Declaration of Rights and Fundamental Rules of the Delaware State, formerly stiled the Government of the Counties of New-Castle, Kent and Sussex, upon Delaware, In Convention at New-Castle, For the Delaware*

State, Begun the 27th Day of August, 1776, and continued by Adjournment to the 21st Day of September following. Wilmington, Del., 1776.

Delaware House Minutes (1765–1770)
Votes and Proceedings of the House of Representatives of the Government of the Counties of New Castle, Kent and Sussex, upon Delaware. At Sessions held at New Castle in the Years 1765–1766–1767–1768–1769–1770. Dover, Del., 1931.

De Lolme, *Constitution*
J. L. De Lolme, *The Constitution of England, or an Account of the English Government.* London, 1775.

De Lolme, *Constitution: New Edition*
J. L. De Lolme, *The Constitution of England; or, an Account of the English Government; in which it is Compared Both with the Republican Form of Government, and the Other Monarchies in Europe.* New ed. London, 1807.

Denison, *Westerly*
Frederic Denison, *Westerly and Its Witnesses.* Providence, R.I., 1878.

De Pinto, *Letters on Troubles*
M. De Pinto, *Letters on the American Troubles; Translated From the French.* London, 1776.

[Devotion,] *The Examiner*
[Ebenezer Devotion,] *The Examiner Examined. A Letter From a Gentleman in Connecticut, To his Friend in London. In Answer to a Letter from a Gentleman in London to his Friend in America: Intitled, The Claim of the Colonies to an Exemption from Internal Taxes imposed by Authority of Parliament, examined.* New Haven, Conn., 1766.

Diary of John Adams
Diary and Autobiography of John Adams. Edited by L. H. Butterfield. 4 vols. Cambridge, Mass., 1961.

Dicey, *Introduction*
A. V. Dicey, *Introduction to the Study of the Law of the Constitution.* 8th ed. London, 1927.

Dickerson, *Acts*
Oliver M. Dickerson, *The Navigation Acts and the American Revolution.* Philadelphia, 1951.

Dickerson, "Writs"
O. M. Dickerson "Writs of Assistance as a Cause of the Revolution," in *The Era of the American Revolution*, edited by Richard B. Morris. New York, 1965, pp. 40–75.

Dickinson, *Connecticut Election Sermon*
Moses Dickinson, *A Sermon Preached before the General Assembly of the*

Colony of Connecticut, at Hartford on the Day of the Anniversary Election, May 8th, 1755. New London, 1755.

Dickinson, "Debate on Glorious Revolution."
H. T. Dickinson, "The Eighteenth-Century Debate on the 'Glorious Revolution'," *History* 61 (1976): 28–45.

Dickinson, "Letter to Inhabitants"
John Dickinson, "Letter to the Inhabitants of the British Colonies," reprinted from the *Pennsylvania Journal* of May and June 1774, in Dickinson, *Writings*, pp. 469–501.

Dickinson, *Letter to Merchants*
John Dickinson, *Letter to the Philadelphia Merchants Concerning Non-Importation, July, 1768*, reprinted in Dickinson, *Writings*, pp. 439–45.

Dickinson, *Letters*
John Dickinson, *Letters from a Farmer in Pennsylvania to the Inhabitants of the British Colonies* (1768), reprinted in Dickinson, *Writings*, pp. 305–406.

Dickinson, *Liberty and Property*
H. T. Dickinson, *Liberty and Property: Political Ideology in Eighteenth-Century Britain.* New York, 1977.

[Dickinson,] *New Essay*
[John Dickinson,] *A New Essay [By the Pennsylvania Farmer] on the Constitutional Power of Great-Britain over the Colonies in America; with the Resolves of the Committee For the Province of Pennsylvania, and their Instructions to their Representatives in Assembly.* London, 1774.

Dickinson, "Non-Importation"
John Dickinson, "An Address Read at a Meeting of Merchants to Consider Non-Importation, April 25, 1768," reprinted in Dickinson, *Writings*, pp. 411–17.

Dickinson, "Preface"
John Dickinson, "Preface [to the 1801 edition]," reprinted in Dickinson, *Writings*, pp. xiii–xx.

Dickinson, *Speech*
John Dickinson, *A Speech Delivered in the House of Assembly of the Province of Pennsylvania, May 24th, 1764* (1764), reprinted in Dickinson, *Writings*, pp. 11–49.

Dickinson, *To Barbados*
John Dickinson, *An Address to the Committee of Correspondence in Barbados* (1766), reprinted in Dickinson, *Writings*, pp. 247–76.

Dickinson, *Writings*
The Writings of John Dickinson: Political Writings 1764–1774. Edited by Paul Leicester Ford. Philadelphia, 1895.

Documents of New Hampshire
　　Documents and Records Relating to the Province of New-Hampshire, From 1764 to 1776; Including the whole Administration of Gov. John Wentworth; the Events immediately preceding the Revolutionary War; the Losses at the Battle of Bunker Hill, and the Record of all Proceedings to the end of our Provincial History. Volume VII. Edited by Nathaniel Bouton. Nashua, N.H., 1873.

Dodgson, *Assize Sermon*
　　Charles [Dodgson], Lord Bishop of Ossory, *A Sermon Preached the 3d of August, 1766. In the Catheral Church of St. Canice. By the Right Reverend Charles, Lord Bishop of Ossory. And Published at the Request of the Judges of Assize, for the Leinster Circuit.* Dublin, 1766.

[Dowdeswell,] *Address to Electors*
　　[William Dowdeswell,] *An Address to such of the Electors of Great-Britain as are not Makers of Cyder and Perry. By the Representatives of a Cyder-County.* London, 1763.

[Downer,] *Discourse in Providence*
　　[Silas Downer,] *A Discourse Delivered in Providence, in the Colony of Rhode-Island, upon the 25th Day of July 1768. At the Dedication of the Tree of Liberty, From the Summer House in the Tree.* Providence, 1768.

[Downley,] *Sentiments*
　　[―――― Downley,] *The Sentiments of an English Freeholder, on the Late Decision of the Middlesex Election.* London, 1769.

Draper, *Thoughts of a Traveller*
　　[Sir William Draper,] *The Thoughts of a Traveller Upon our American Disputes.* London, 1774.

[Drayton,] *Letter from Freeman*
　　[William Henry Drayton,] *A Letter From Freeman of South-Carolina, to the Deputies of North-America, Assembled in the High Court of Congress at Philadelphia.* Charles-Town, S.C., 1774.

[Drinker,] *Observations*
　　[John Drinker,] *Observations on the Late Popular Measures, Offered to the Serious Consideration of the Sober Inhabitants of Pennsylvania.* Philadelphia, 1774.

Duchal, *Sermons*
　　James Duchal, *Sermons Upon the Following Subject . . .* 2d ed. Vol. 1. London, 1765.

Dugdale, *Origines Juridicales*
　　William Dugdale, *Origines Juridicales, or Historical Memorials of the English Laws, Courts of Justice, Forms of Tryal, Punishment in Cases*

Criminal, Law-Writers, Law Books, Grants and Settlements of Estates, Degree of Serjeant, Innes of Court and Chancery. 2d ed. London, 1671.

[Dulany,] *Considerations*
[Daniel Dulany,] *Considerations on the Propriety of Imposing Taxes in the British Colonies, For the Purpose of raising a Revenue, by Act of Parliament* (1765), reprinted in Bailyn, *Pamphlets*, pp. 608–58.

[Dulany,] *Considerations on the Propriety*
[Daniel Dulany,] *Considerations on the Propriety of Imposing Taxes in the British Colonies, For the Purpose of raising a Revenue, by Act of Parliament.* 2d ed. Annapolis, Md., 1765.

Dulany, *English Laws*
Daniel Dulany, Senior, *The Right of the Inhabitants of Maryland to the Benefit of the English Laws* (1728), reprinted in *Johns Hopkins University Studies in Historical and Political Sciences* 21. Edited by J. M. Vincent, J. H. Hollander, and W. W. Willoughby. Baltimore, Md., 1903.

Dummer, *Defence*
Jer[emiah] Dummer, *A Defence of the New-England Charters.* London, 1721.

Dummer, *Defence of the Charters*
Jer[emiah] Dummer, *A Defence of the New-England Charters.* Boston, 1745.

Earl, "Procrustean Feudalism"
D. W. L. Earl, "Procrustean Feudalism: An Interpretative Dilemma in English Historical Narration, 1700–1725," *Historical Journal* 19 (1976): 33–51.

Einaudi, "Burke's Political Philosophy"
Mario Einaudi, "The British Background of Burke's Political Philosophy," *Political Science Quarterly* 49 (1934): 576–98.

Eliot, *Give Cesar His Due*
Jared Eliot, *Give Cesar his Due. Or, the Obligation that Subjects are under to their Civil Rulers, As was shewed in a Sermon Preach'd before the General Assembly of the Colony of Connecticut at Hartford, May the 11th, 1738. The Day for the Election of the Honourable the Governour, the Deputy-Governour, and the Worshipful Assistants.* New London, Conn., 1738.

Ernst, "Ideology"
Joseph Ernst, "'Ideology' and an Economic Interpretation of the Revolution," in *The American Revolution: Explorations in the History of American Radicalism.* Edited by Alfred F. Young. De Kalb, Ill., 1976, pp. 159–85.

[Erskine,] *Reflections on the Rise*
[John Erskine,] *Reflections on the Rise, Progress, and Probable Consequences, of the Present Contentions with the Colonies. By a Freeholder.* Edinburgh, 1776.

Essex Result
Result of the Convention of Delegates Holden at Ipswich in the County of Essex, who were Deputed to take into Consideration the Constitution and form of Government, Proposed by the Convention of the State of Massachusetts-Bay. Newburyport, Mass., 1778.

Estwick, *Letter to Tucker*
Samuel Estwick, *A Letter to the Reverend Josiah Tucker, D. D. Dean of Glocester, in Answer to His Humble Address and Earnest Appeal, &c. with a Postscript, in which the present War against America is shewn to be the Effect, not of the Causes assigned by Him and Others. But of a Fixed Plan of Administration Founded in System.* London, 1776.

Examination of Franklin
The Examination of Doctor Benjamin Franklin, before an August Assembly, relating to the Repeal of the Stamp-Act, &c. Philadelphia, [1766].

Extract of Letter to De Berdt
Extract of a Letter From the House of Representatives of the Massachusets-Bay, to their Agent Dennys De Berdt, Esq; with some Remarks. London, 1770.

Extracts from the Votes and Proceedings (Gaine)
Extracts from the Votes and Proceedings of the American Continental Congress, held at Philadelphia, 5th September, 1774. Printed in H. Gaine. New York, 1774.

Extracts from the Votes and Proceedings (Rivington)
Extracts from the Votes and Proceedings of the American Continental Congress, Held at Philadelphia, Sept. 5, 1774. Printed by James Rivington. New York, 1774.

[Ferguson,] *Brief Justification*
[R. Ferguson,] *A Brief Justification of the Prince of Orange's Descent into England, and of the Kingdoms Late Recourse to Arms.* London, 1689.

Ferguson, "Reason in Madness"
James R. Ferguson, "Reason in Madness: The Political Thought of James Otis," *William and Mary Quarterly* 36 (1979): 194–214.

Fish, *Discourse at Worcester*
Elisha Fish, *A Discourse Delivered at Worcester, March, 28th. 1775, At the Desire of the Convention of Committees for the County of Worcester.* Worcester, Mass., 1775.

Fiske, *Importance of Righteousness*
> Nathan Fiske, *The Importance of Righteousness to the Happiness, and the Tendency of Oppression to the Misery of a People; illustrated in two Discourses Delivered at Brookfield, July 4. 1774.* Boston, 1774.

[Fitch et al.,] *Reasons Why*
> [Thomas Fitch, Jared Ingersoll, Ebenezer Silliman, and George Wyllys,] *Reasons Why the British Colonies in America, Should not be Charged with Internal Taxes, by Authority of Parliament; Humbly offered, For Consideration, In Behalf of the Colony of Connecticut.* New Haven, Conn., 1764.

Fletcher, *Vindication of Wesley*
> John Fletcher, *A Vindication of the Rev. Mr. Wesley's "Calm Address to our American Colonies:" In Some Letters to Mr. Caleb Evans.* London, [1776].

[Forster,] *Answer to the Question Stated*
> [Nathaniel Forster,] *An Answer to a Pamphlet Entitled, "The Question Stated, Whether the Freeholders of Middlesex forfeited their Right by Voting for Mr. Wilkes at the last Election? In a Letter from a Member of Parliament to one of his Constituents."* London, 1769.

Forster, *Wisbeach Assize Sermon*
> John Forster, *A Sermon Preached at the Assizes held at Wisbeach, In the Isle of Ely; August 22, 1764. Before Mr. Sergeant Forster, Chief Justice of the said Isle.* Cambridge, 1764.

Fortescue-Aland, "Preface"
> John Fortescue-Aland, "The Preface" to Sir John Fortescue, *The Difference Between an Absolute and Limited Monarchy; As it more particularly regards the English Constitution,* London, 1714.

[Forthergill,] *Considerations*
> [John Forthergill,] *Considerations Relative to the North American Colonies.* London, 1765.

Foss, *Judges of England*
> Edward Foss, *The Judges of England.* 9 vols., London, 1848–64.

Foster, *Short Essay*
> Dan Foster, *A Short Essay on Civil Government, the Substance of Six Sermons, Preached in Winsor, Second Society, October 1774.* Hartford, Conn., 1775.

[Fowle,] *Appendix to Eclipse*
> [Daniel Fowle,] *An Appendix to the late Total Eclipse of Liberty.* Boston, 1756.

Fox, *Speeches*
> *The Speeches of the Right Honourable Charles James Fox in the House of Commons.* Vols. 1 and 2. London, 1815.

Franklin, *Writings*
  The Writings of Benjamin Franklin. Vol. 5. *1767–1772.* Vol. 6. *1773–1776.*
  Edited by Albert Henry Smyth. New York, 1906.

Franklin-Jackson Letters
  Letters and Papers of Benjamin Franklin and Richard Jackson 1753–1785.
  Edited by Carl Van Doren. Memoirs of the American Philosophical So-
  ciety, vol. 24. Philadelphia, 1947.

Franklin's Letters to the Press
  Benjamin Franklin's Letters to the Press, 1758–1775. Edited by Verner W.
  Crane. Chapel Hill, N.C., 1950.

Freeman Letters
  *The Letters of Freeman, Etc. Essays on the Nonimportation Movement
  in South Carolina Collected by William Henry Drayton.* Edited by Robert M. Weir. Columbia, S.C., 1977.

Frink, *Election Sermon*
  Thomas Frink, *A King reigning in Righteous, and Princes ruling in Judgment. A Sermon Preached before His Excellency Thomas Pownall, Esq.:
  Governour, the Honourable His Majesty's Council, and House of Representatives, of the Province of the Massachusetts-Bay, in New-England, May
  31, 1758. Being the Anniversary for the Election of His Majesty's Council,
  for said Province.* Boston, 1758.

Gadsden, *Writings*
  The Writings of Christopher Gadsden 1746–1805. Edited by Richard Walsh.
  Columbia, S.C., 1966.

Gage, *Correspondence*
  *The Correspondence of General Thomas Gage With the Secretaries of State
  1763–1775.* Vol. 1. Edited by Clarence Edwin Carter. New Haven, Conn.,
  1931. *The Correspondence of General Thomas Gage with the Secretaries
  of State, and with the War Office and the Treasury 1763–1775.* Vol. 2. Edited
  by Clarence Edwin Carter. New Haven, Conn., 1933.

Gallaway, *Sermon at St. Mary's*
  John Cole Gallaway, *Christianity the true Foundation of Civil Liberty:
  A Sermon Preached at St. Mary's Church in Leicester, at the Assizes held
  there August 12, 1778.* London, 1779.

[Galloway,] *Americanus*
  [Joseph Galloway,] A Letter signed Americanus, *New-York Gazette*, 15 August 1765, reprinted in Anon., *Americanus Examined, and his Principles
  Compared with those of the Approved Advocates for America, by a Pennsylvanian.* Philadelphia, 1774.

[Galloway,] *Candid Examination*
  [Joseph Galloway,] *A Candid Examination of the Mutual Claims of Great-*

Britain, and the Colonies: with a Plan of Accommodation, on Constitutional Principles. New York, 1775.

[Galloway,] *Mutual Claims*
[Joseph Galloway,] *A Candid Examination of the Mutual Claims of Great-Britain and the Colonies: with a Plan of Accommodation, on Constitutional Principles.* London, 1780.

[Galloway,] *Political Reflections*
[Joseph Galloway,] *Political Reflections on the Late Colonial Governments: In which their original Constitutional Defects are pointed out, and shown to have naturally produced the Rebellion, which has unfortunately terminated in the Dismemberment of the British Empire.* London, 1783.

Galloway, *Speech in Answer*
Joseph Galloway, *The Speech of Joseph Galloway, Esq; One of the Members for Philadelphia County: In Answer to the Speech of John Dickinson, Esq.; Delivered in the House of Assembly of the Province of Pennsylvania, May 24, 1764.* Philadelphia, 1764.

[Galloway,] *True and Impartial State*
[Joseph Galloway,] *A True and Impartial State of the Province of Pennsylvania.* Philadelphia, 1759.

Gazette & News-Letter
The Massachusetts Gazette and Boston News-Letter.

Gazette & Post-Boy
The Massachusetts Gazette and Boston Post-Boy and the Advertiser.

Gentleman's Magazine
The Gentleman's Magazine and Historical Chronicle. (Monthly magazine, London.)

Georgia Commons House Journal
The Colonial Records of the State of Georgia. Volume XIV. Journal of the Commons House of Assembly January 17, 1763, to December 24, 1768, Inclusive. Volume XV. Journal of the Commons House of Assembly October 30, 1769, to June 16, 1782, Inclusive. Atlanta, Ga., 1907.

Gibbes, *Documentary History*
R. W. Gibbes, *Documentary History of the American Revolution, Consisting of Letters and Papers Relating to the Contest for Liberty, Chiefly in South Carolina.* New York, 1855.

Goebel, "Matrix of Empire"
Julius Goebel, "The Matrix of Empire," in Smith, *Appeals to Privy Council,* at xiii–lxi.

Goodhart, *Law of the Land*
Arthur L. Goodhart, *Law of the Land.* Charlottesville, Va., 1966.

[Goodricke,] *Observations on Price's Theory*
[Henry Goodricke,] *Observations on Dr. Price's Theory and Principles of Civil Liberty and Government, Preceded by a Letter to a Friend on the Pretensions of the American Colonies, in respect of Right and Equity.* York, England, 1776.

Gordon, *Evil Speaking*
John Gordon, *The Causes and Consequences of Evil Speaking Against Government, Considered in a Sermon Preached before the University of Cambridge, at Gt. Mary's Church, on the King's Accession, Oct. 25, 1771.* Cambridge, 1771.

Gough, *Fundamental Law*
J. W. Gough, *Fundamental Law in English Constitutional History.* Oxford, 1955.

Gough, *Locke's Political Philosophy*
J. W. Gough, *John Locke's Political Philosophy: Eight Studies by J. W. Gough*, 2d ed. Oxford, 1973.

Gough, *Social Contract*
J. W. Gough, *The Social Contract: A Critical Study of its Development.* Oxford, 1936.

Gray, *Doctor Price's Notions*
John Gray, *Doctor Price's Notions of the Nature of Civil Liberty, Shewn to be Contradictory to Reason and Scripture.* London, 1777.

[Gray,] *Right of the Legislature*
[John Gray,] *The Right of the British Legislature to Tax the American Colonies Vindicated; and the Means of Asserting that Right Proposed.* 2d ed. London, 1775.

[Green,] *Observations on Reconciliation*
[Jacob Green,] *Observations: on the Reconciliation of Great-Britain, and the Colonies; In which are exhibited, Arguments for, and against, that Measure.* Philadelphia, 1776.

Greene, *Quest*
Jack P. Greene, *The Quest for Power: The Lower Houses of Assembly in the Southern Royal Colonies, 1689–1776.* Norton Library ed. New York, 1972.

Gregor, "Preface"
Francis Gregor, "The Preface" to Sir John Fortescue, *De Lauibus Legum Angliae.* New ed. London, 1775.

Grey, "Unwritten Constitution"
Thomas C. Grey, "Origins of the Unwritten Constitution: Fundamental Law in American Revolutionary Thought," *Stanford Law Review* 30 (1978): 843–93.

Griffith, *Passive Obedience*
> David Griffith, *Passive Obedience Considered: In a Sermon Preached at Williamsburg, December 31st, 1775.* Williamsburg, Va., [1776].

Guide to Rights
> A *Guide to the Knowledge of the Rights and Privileges of Englishmen.* London, 1757.

Guttridge, *English Whiggism*
> G. H. Guttridge, *English Whiggism and the American Revolution.* Berkeley, Calif., 1966.

Hacker, "The First American Revolution"
> Louis M. Hacker, "The First American Revolution," reprinted in *Causes and Consequences of the American Revolution.* Edited by Esmond Wright. Chicago, 1966, pp. 114–42.

Hale, *History*
> Sir Matthew Hale, *The History of the Common Law of England.* 2d ed. corrected. London, 1716.

Halifax, *Charles II*
> George Savile, Marquis of Halifax, *A Character of Charles the Second: And Political, Moral and Miscellaneous Thoughts and Reflections.* London, 1750.

Hall, *Apology for Freedom*
> Robert Hall, *An Apology for the Freedom of the Press, and for General Liberty.* London, 1793.

Hall, *Edward Randolph*
> Michael Garibaldi Hall, *Edward Randolph and the American Colonies 1676–1703.* Chapel Hill, N.C., 1960.

Hamilton, *Duty of Obedience to Laws*
> Hugh Hamilton, *The Duty of Obedience to the Laws and of Submission to Magistrates. A Sermon Occasioned by the Late Disturbances in the North of Ireland, Preached before the Judges of Assize in the Cathedral Church of Armagh, on Sunday, April 12, 1772.* London, 1772.

Hamilton, *Farmer Refuted*
> Alexander Hamilton, *The Farmer Refuted: or A more impartial and comprehensive View of the Dispute between Great-Britain and the Colonies, Intended as a Further Vindication of the Congress* (1775), reprinted in *The Papers of Alexander Hamilton,* vol. 1. Edited by Harold C. Syrett. New York, 1961, pp. 81–165.

Hamowy, "Jefferson and Scottish Enlightenment"
> Ronald Hamowy, "Jefferson and the Scottish Enlightenment: A Critique of Garry Wills's *Inventing America: Jefferson's Declaration of Independence,*" *William and Mary Quarterly* 36 (1979): 503–23.

Handlin, *Popular Sources*
The Popular Sources of Political Authority: Documents on the Massachusetts Constitution of 1780. Edited by Oscar Handlin and Mary Handlin. Cambridge, Mass., 1966.

Harrington, *Prerogative of Popular Government*
James Harrington, *The Prerogative of Popular Government, A Political Discourse in Two Books* (1658), reprinted in *The Political Works of James Harrington.* Edited by J. G. A. Pocock. Cambridge, England, 1977, pp. 389–566.

Hart, "Bentham and America"
H. L. A. Hart, "Bentham and the United States of America," *Journal of Law and Economics* 19 (1976): 547–67.

[Hartley,] *Appeal to Juries*
[David Hartley,] *The Right of Appeal to Juries in Causes of Excise, Asserted.* London, [1763].

Hartley, *Letters on the War*
David Hartley, *Letters on the American War. Addressed to the Right Worshipful the Mayor and Corporation, to the Worshipful the Wardens of Corporation of the Trinity-House, and to the Worthy Burgesses of the Town of Kingston-Upon-Hull.* 8th ed. London, 1779.

Hartley, *Speech and Motions*
David Hartley, *Speech and Motions Made in the House of Commons, on Monday, the 27th of March, 1775. Together with a Draught of a Letter of Requisition to the Colonies.* 2d ed. London, 1775.

Haven, *Election Sermon*
Jason Haven, *A Sermon Preached before His Excellency Sir Francis Bernard, Baronet, Governor: His Honor Thomas Hutchinson, Esq.: Lieutenant-Governor, The Honorable His Majesty's Council, and the Honorable House of Representatives, of the Province of the Massachusetts-Bay in New-England.* Boston, 1769.

Hawkins, *Life of Johnson*
Sir John Hawkins, *The Life of Samuel Johnson, LL.D.* 2d ed. London, 1787.

Hawles, *Englishman's Right*
Sir John Hawles, *The Englishman's Right: A Dialogue Between a Barrister at Law, and a Juryman.* Dublin, 1732.

Hay, "Property"
Douglas Hay, "Property, Authority and the Criminal Law," in *Albion's Fatal Tree: Crime and Society in Eighteenth-Century England.* New York, 1975, pp. 17–63.

Hazeltine, "Influence"
> H. D. Hazeltine, "The Influence of Magna Carta on American Constitutional Development," *Columbia Law Review* 17 (1917): 1–33.

Hexter, "Hobbes and the Law"
> J. H. Hexter, "Thomas Hobbes and the Law," *Cornell Law Review* 65 (1980): 471–90.

Hibernian Magazine
> *The Hibernian Magazine or Compendium of Entertaining Knowledge Containing The greatest Variety of the most Curious & useful Subjects in every Branch of Polite Literature*. (Monthly magazine, Dublin.)

[Hicks,] *Nature of Parliamentary Power*
> [William Hicks,] *The Nature and Extent of Parliamentary Power Considered; In some Remarks upon Mr. Pitt's Speech in the House of Commons, previous to the Repeal of the Stamp-Act: With an Introduction, Applicable to the present Situation of the Colonies*. Philadelphia, 1768.

Hill, *Century of Revolution*
> Christopher Hill, *The Century of Revolution 1603–1714*. Norton Library ed. New York, 1966.

Hill, *Intellectual Origins*
> Christopher Hill, *Intellectual Origins of the English Revolution*. London: Panther, 1972.

Hill, "Norman Yoke"
> Christopher Hill, "Norman Yoke," in Christopher Hill, *Puritanism and Revolution: Studies in Interpretation of the English Revolution of the 17th Century*. London, 1958, pp. 50–122.

Hill, *Puritanism and Revolution*
> Christopher Hill, *Puritanism and Revolution: Studies in Interpretation of the English Revolution of the 17th Century*. London, 1958.

Hill, *Upside Down*
> Christopher Hill, *The World Turned Upside Down: Radical Ideas During the English Revolution*. Harmondsworth, England: Penguin, 1976.

Hind, *Sermon at St. Margaret's*
> Richard Hind, *A Sermon Preached before the Honourable House of Commons; at St. Margaret's, Westminster: on Wednesday, January xxx*. MDCCLXV. London, 1765.

Hinkhouse, *Preliminaries*
> Fred Junkin Hinkhouse, *The Preliminaries of the American Revolution as Seen in the English Press 1763–1775*. New York, 1926.

Hoadly, *Sermon before Lord Mayor*
> Benjamin Hoadly, *A Sermon Preach'd before the Right Honourable the*

Lord-Mayor, Aldermen, and Livery-Men of the Several Companies of London. At the Parish-Church of St. Laurence Jewry, before the Election of the Lord-Mayor, September 29, 1705. London, 1708.

Hoadly, *Works*
 The Works of Benjamin Hoadly, D.D. Successively Bishop of Bangor, Hereford, Salisbury, and Winchester. 3 vols. London, 1773.

Hobart, *Connecticut Election Sermon*
 Noah Hobart, *Civil Government the Foundation of Social Happiness. A Sermon Preached before the General Assembly of Connecticut, at Hartford, on the Day of their Anniversary Election, May 10th, 1750.* New London, 1751.

Holliday, *Life of Mansfield*
 John Holliday, *The Life of William Late Earl of Mansfield*, London, 1797.

[Hollis,] *True Sentiments*
 [Thomas Hollis,] *The True Sentiments of America: Contained in a Collection of Letters Sent from the House of Representatives of the Province of Massachusetts Bay to Several Persons of High Ranks in this Kingdom.* London, 1768.

Hope, *Letters*
 John Hope, *Letters on Certain Proceedings in Parliament During the Sessions of the Years 1769 and 1770.* London, 1772.

[Hopkins,] *Grievances of the Colonies*
 [Stephen Hopkins,] *The Grievances of the American Colonies Candidly Examined.* London, 1766.

Hopkins, *Rights*
 Stephen Hopkins, *The Rights of the Colonies Examined* (1765), reprinted in Bailyn, *Pamphlets*, pp. 507–22.

[Hopkins,] "Vindication of a Pamphlet"
 [Stephen Hopkins,] "A Vindication of a Late Pamphlet, entitled, The Rights of Colonies examined, from the Censures and Remarks contained in a *Letter* from a Government in Halifax, to his friend in Rhode Island, just published at Newport," in *The Providence Gazette and Country Journal*, 23 February, 2 March, and 9 March 1765.

[Howard,] *Halifax Letter*
 [Martin Howard, Jr.,] *A Letter from a Gentleman at Halifax to his Friend in Rhode-Island, Containing Remarks Upon a Pamphlet Entitled The Rights of the Colonies Examined* (1765), reprinted in Bailyn, *Pamphlets*, pp. 532–44.

Howard, *Road from Runnymede*
 A. E. Dick Howard, *The Road from Runnymede: Magna Carta and Constitutionalism in America.* Charlottesville, Va., 1968.

Hudson, "Penn's *English Liberties*"
> Winthrop S. Hudson, "William Penn's *English Liberties: Tract for Several Times*," *William and Mary Quarterly* 26 (1969): 578–85.

Hume, *History*
> David Hume, *The History of England From the Invasion of Julius Caesar to the Revolution in 1688*. Vols. 5 and 6. New ed. London, 1762.

Hunn, *Welfare of a Government*
> Nathaniel Hunn, *The Welfare of a Government Considered. A Sermon Preach'd before the General Assembly of the Colony of Connecticut, at Hartford, on the Day of their Anniversary Election, May 14th, 1747*. New London, Conn., 1747.

[Hurd,] *Moral and Political Dialogues*
> [Richard Hurd,] *Moral and Political Dialogues Between Divers Eminent Persons of the Past and Present Age; with Critical and Explanatory Notes*. 2d ed. London, 1760.

Hurstfield, *Freedom, Corruption and Government*
> Joel Hurstfield, *Freedom, Corruption and Government in Elizabethan England*. London, 1973.

Hutchinson, *History* (1828)
> Thomas Hutchinson, *The History of the Province of Massachusetts Bay, From 1749 to 1774, Comprising a Detailed Narrative of the Origin and Early Stages of the American Revolution*. London, 1828.

Hutchinson, *Letters*
> *Copy of Letters Sent to Great-Britain, by His Excellency Thomas Hutchinson, the Hon. Andrew Oliver, and Several Other Persons, Born and Educated Among Us*. Boston, 1773.

[Hutchinson,] *Strictures upon the Declaration*
> [Thomas Hutchinson,] *Strictures Upon the Declaration of Congress at Philadelphia; In a Letter to a Noble Lord, &c*. London, 1776.

In Defiance of the Law
> John Phillip Reid, *In Defiance of the Law: The Standing-Army Controversy, the Two Constitutions, and the Coming of the American Revolution*. Chapel Hill, N.C., 1981.

In a Defiant Stance
> John Phillip Reid, *In a Defiant Stance: The Conditions of Law in Massachusetts Bay, the Irish Comparison, and the Coming of the American Revolution*. University Park, Pa., 1977.

"In the First Line of Defense"
> John Phillip Reid, "In the First Line of Defense: The Colonial Charters, the Stamp Act Debate and the Coming of the American Revolution," *New York University Law Review* 51 (1976): 177–215.

"In Legitimate Stirps"
John Phillip Reid, "In Legitimate Stirps: The Concept of 'Arbitrary,' the Supremacy of Parliament, and the coming of the American Revolution," *Hofstra Law Review* 5 (1977): 459–99.

"In Our Contracted Sphere"
John Phillip Reid, "'In Our Contracted Sphere.' The Constitutional Contract, the Stamp Act Crisis, and the Coming of the American Revolution," *Columbia Law Review* 76 (1976): 21–47.

In a Rebellious Spirit
John Phillip Reid, *In a Rebellious Spirit: The Argument of Facts, the Liberty Riot, and the Coming of the American Revolution*. University Park, Pa., 1979.

Independent Reflector
The Independent Reflector or Weekly Essays on Sundry Important Subjects More Particularly adapted to the Province of New-York By William Livingston and Others. Edited by Milton M. Klein. Cambridge, Mass., 1963.

"Irrelevance of the Declaration"
John Phillip Reid, "The Irrelevance of the Declaration," in *Law in the American Revolution and the Revolution in the Law: A Collection of Review Essays on American Legal History*. Edited by Hendrik Hartog. New York, 1981, pp. 46–89.

[Jacob,] *Laws of Liberty*
[Giles Jacobs,] *The Laws of Liberty and Property: Or, A Concise Treatise of all the Laws, Statutes and Ordinances, made for the Benefit and Protection of the Subjects of England*. 2d ed. London, 1734.

Jacob, *New Law Dictionary*
Giles Jacob, *A New Law-Dictionary: Containing the Interpretation and Definition of Words and Terms used in the Law*. 8th ed. London, 1762.

Jefferson, *Summary View*
Thomas Jefferson, *A Summary View of the Rights of British America Set Forth in some Resolutions Intended For the Inspection of the Present Delegates of the People of Virginia Now in Convention* (1774), reprinted in *Papers of Jefferson* 1:121–35.

Jenkins, *Lex Terrae*
David Jenkins, *Lex Terrae; or, Laws of the Land* (1647), in *Somers' Tracts* 5:98–114.

Jenkins, *Works of Judge Jenkins*
David Jenkins, *The Works of that Grave and Learned Lawyer Judge Jenkins, Prisoner in Newgate. Upon Divers Statutes, Concerning, the Liberty, and Freedome of the Subject. With a perfect Table thereto annexed*. London, 1648.

Jensen, *Revolution Within*
Merrill Jensen, *The American Revolution within America.* New York, 1974.

Johannesen, "Dickinson"
Stanley K. Johannesen, "John Dickinson and the American Revolution," *Historical Reflections* 2 (1975): 29–49.

[Johnson,] *Important Observations*
[Stephen Johnson,] *Some Important Observations, Occasioned by, and adapted to, The Publick Fast, Ordered by Authority, December 18th,* A.D. *1765. On Account of the peculiar Circumstances of the present Day.* Newport, R.I., 1766.

Johnson, *Integrity and Piety*
Stephen Johnson, *Integrity and Piety the best Principles of a good Administration of Government, Illustrated. In a Sermon Preached before the General Assembly of the Colony of Connecticut, at Hartford, on the Day of their Anniversary Election, May 10th, 1770.* New London, 1770.

Johnson, *Notes on Pastoral*
Samuel Johnson, *Notes Upon the Phoenix Edition of the Pastoral Letter. Part I.* London, 1694.

[Johnson,] *Political Tracts*
[Samuel Johnson,] *Political Tracts. Containing, The False Alarm. Falkland's Islands. The Patriot: and Taxation no Tyranny.* London, 1776.

Johnson, *Remarks on Sherlock*
Samuel Johnson, *Remarks Upon Dr. Sherlock's Book, Intituled the Case of Resistance of the Supreme Powers Stated and Resolved, according to the Doctrine of the Holy Scriptures.* London, 1689.

Johnstone, *Speech on American Affairs*
Governor Johnston[e]'s Speech on American Affairs on the Address in answer to the King's Speech. Edinburgh, [1776].

Jones, *Fear of God*
William Jones, *The Fear of God, and the Benefits of Civil Obedience. Two Sermons Preached in the Parish Church of Harwick in the County of Essex, on Sunday, June 21, 1778. And Published at the Request of the Audience.* London, 1778.

Jones, *O Strange*
Howard Mumford Jones, *O Strange New World.* New York, 1964.

Jordan, *Men of Substance*
W. K. Jordan, *Men of Substance: A Study of the Thought of Two English Revolutionaries Henry Parker and Henry Robinson.* Chicago, 1942.

Journal of Burgesses
Journals of the House of Burgesses of Virginia [vol. 10] 1761–1765, [vol.

11] 1766–1769, [Vol. 12] 1770–1772, [Vol. 13] 1773–1776 Including the records of the Committee of Correspondence. Edited by John Pendleton Kennedy. Richmond, Va., 1905, 1906, 1907.

Journal of the First Congress
Journal of the Proceedings of the Congress, Held at Philadelphia, September 5, 1774. Philadelphia, 1774.

Journal of New York Assembly (1766–1776)
Journal of the Votes and Proceedings of the General Assembly of the Colony of New-York, From 1766 to 1776 Inclusive. Reprinted in pursuance
of a joint resolution of the Legislature of the State of New-York, passed
30 April, 1820. Albany, N.Y., 1820.

Journal of the Times
Boston Under Military Rule 1768–1769 as Revealed in a Journal of the Times.
Compiled by Oliver Morton Dickerson. Reprint. New York, 1970.

Judson, Crisis
Margaret Atwood Judson, The Crisis of the Constitution: An Essay in Con-
stitutional and Political Thought in England 1603–1645. New Brunswick,
N.J., 1949.

"Junius," Junius
["Junius,"] Junius. 2 vols. London, [1772].

Jury-Man's Judgement
A Jury-man's Judgement Upon the Case of Lieut. Col. John Lilburn: Prov-
ing, By well-grounded Arguments, both to his own and every Jury-man's
Conscience. N.i., n.d.

Kammen, Rope
Michael Kammen, A Rope of Sand: The Colonial Agents, British Politics,
and the American Revolution. New York: Vintage, 1974.

Keir, Constitutional History
Sir David Lindsay Keir, The Constitutional History of Modern Britain Since
1845. 8th ed. Princeton, N.J., 1966.

[Keith,] Two Papers on Taxing
[Sir William Keith,] Two Papers on the Subject of Taxing the British Colonies in America. London, 1767.

[Keld,] Polity of England
[Christopher Keld,] An Essay on the Polity of England. London, 1785.

Kellogg, Colonial Charter
Louise Phelps Kellogg, The American Colonial Charter: A Study of English Administration in Relation thereto, Chiefly after 1688. Annual Report 1, American Historical Association for the Year 1903. Washington, D.C.,
1904.

Kenyon, "Republicanism in Revolution"
Cecelia M. Kenyon, "Republicanism and Radicalism in the American Revolution," reprinted in *The American Revolution: The Critical Issues*. Edited by Robert F. Berkhofer, Jr. Boston, 1971, pp. 3–18.

Kenyon, *Revolution Principles*
J. P. Kenyon, *Revolution Principles: The Politics of Party 1689–1720*. Cambridge, England, 1977.

Kern, *Kingship*
Fritz Kern, *Kingship and Law in the Middle Ages*. Translated by S. B. Chrimes. New York: Harper Torchbook, 1970.

Kliger, *Goths*
Samuel Kliger, *The Goths in England: A Study in Seventeenth and Eighteenth Century Thought*. Cambridge, Mass., 1952.

Knollenberg, *Growth of Revolution*
Bernhard Knollenberg, *Growth of the American Revolution*. New York, 1975.

[Knox,] *Claim of the Colonies*
[William Knox,] *The Claim of the Colonies to an Exemption from Internal Taxes Imposed By Authority of Parliament, Examined: In a Letter from a Gentleman in London, to his Friend in America*. London, 1765.

[Knox,] *Considerations on the Present State*
[William Knox,] *Considerations on the Present State of the Nation. Addressed to the Right Hon. Lord Rawdon, and the Other Members of the Two Houses of Parliament, Associated for the Preservation of the Constitution, and Promoting the Prosperity of the British Empire*. London, 1789.

[Knox,] *Controversy*
[William Knox,] *The Controversy Between Great Britain and her Colonies Reviewed; The Several Pleas of the Colonies, In Support of their Rights to all the Liberties and Privileges of British Subjects, and to Exemption from the Legislative Authority of Parliament, Stated and Considered; and the Nature of their Connection with, and Dependence on, Great Britain, Shewn Upon the Evidence of Historical Facts and Authentic Records*. London, 1769.

[Knox,] *Controversy* (Dublin Edition)
[William Knox,] *The Controversy Between Great Britain and her Colonies Reviewed; The Several Pleas of the Colonies, In Support of their Right to all the Liberties and Privileges of British Subjects, and to Exemption from the Legislative Authority of Parliament, Stated and Considered, and The Nature of their Connection with, and Dependence on, Great Britain, Shewn, Upon the Evidence of Historical Facts and Authentic Records*. Dublin, 1769.

[Knox,] *Extra Official Papers*
    [William Knox,] *Extra Official State Papers. Addressed to the Right Hon. Lord Rawdon, and the Other Members of the Two Houses of Parliament, Associated for the Preservation of the Constitution and Promoting the Prosperity of the British Empire. Volume the Second.* London, 1789.

[Knox,] *Justice and Policy*
    [William Knox,] *The Justice and Policy of the Late Act of Parliament, for Making more Effectual Provision for the Government of the Province of Quebec, Asserted and Proved, and the Conduct of Administration Respecting that Province, Stated and Vindicated.* London, 1774.

[Knox,] *Letter to a Member*
    [William Knox,] *A Letter to a Member of Parliament, Wherein the Power of the British Legislature, And the Case of the Colonists, Are briefly and impartially considered.* London, 1765.

Kramnick, *Bolingbroke's Circle*
    Isaac Kramnick, *Bolingbroke and His Circle: The Politics of Nostalgia in the Age of Walpole.* Cambridge, Mass., 1968.

Kronenberger, *Kings*
    Louis Kronenberger, *Kings and Desperate Men: Life in Eighteenth-Century England.* St. Paul, Minn., 1942.

"L.," Letter to G[renville]
    "L.," *A Letter to G. G. Stiff in Opinions, always in the wrong.* London, 1767.

Langford, *Excise Crisis*
    Paul Langford, *The Excise Crisis: Society and Politics in the Age of Walpole.* Oxford, 1975.

Langford, *Rockingham Administration*
    P. Langford, *The First Rockingham Administration 1765–1766.* Oxford, 1973.

Larkin, *Property in Eighteenth Century*
    Paschal Larkin, *Property in the Eighteenth Century with Special Reference to England and Locke.* Dublin and Cork, Ireland, 1930.

Laslett, "Introduction to Locke"
    Peter Laslett, "Introduction [and footnotes]," to John Locke, *Two Treatises of Government.* 2d ed. Edited by Peter Laslett. Cambridge, England, 1967.

Lathrop, *Innocent Blood*
    John Lathrop, *Innocent Blood Crying to God From the Streets of Boston. A Sermon Occasioned by the Horrid Murder of Messieurs Samuel Gray, Samuel Maverick, James Caldwell, and Crispus Attucks, with Patrick Carr, since dead, and Christopher Mark, judged irrecoverable, and several other badly wounded, by a Party of Troops under the Command of Captain*

Preston: On the Fifth of March, 1770, and Preached the Lord's-Day Following. London, 1770.

Leder, *Liberty*
Lawrence H. Leder, *Liberty and Authority: Early American Political Ideology 1689–1763.* Chicago, 1968.

Lee, *Appeal to Justice*
[Arthur] Lee, *An Appeal to the Justice and Interests of the People of Great Britain, in the Present Dispute with America.* 4th ed. New York, 1775.

Lee, *Arthur Lee*
Richard Henry Lee, *Life of Arthur Lee, LL.D.* 2 vols. Boston, 1829.

Lee, "Preface"
Richard Henry Lee, "Preface to Williamsburg Edition," reprinted in Dickinson, *Writings*, pp. 289–95.

Lee, *Richard Henry Lee*
Richard Henry Lee, *Memoir of the Life of Richard Henry Lee, and His Correspondence with the Most Distinguished Men in America and Europe, Illustrative of their Characters, and of the Events of the American Revolution.* 2 vols. Philadelphia, 1825.

[Lee,] *Second Appeal*
[Arthur Lee,] *A Second Appeal to the Justice and Interests of the People, on the Measures Respecting America. By the Author of the First.* London, 1775.

[Lee,] *Speech Intended*
[Arthur Lee,] *A Speech, Intended to have been Delivered in the House of Commons, in Support of the Petition from the General Congress at Philadelphia.* London, 1775.

[Lee,] *True State of the Proceedings*
[Arthur Lee,] *A True State of the Proceedings in the Parliament of Great Britain, and in the Province of Massachusetts Bay, Relative to the Giving and Granting the Money of the People of that Province, and of all America, in the House of Commons, in which they are not represented.* Philadelphia, 1774.

Leonard, "Massachusettensis"
Daniel Leonard, "Massachusettensis Letters," reprinted in *The American Colonial Crisis: The Daniel Leonard-John Adams Letters to the Press 1774–1775.* Edited by Bernard Mason. New York, 1972.

Letters of Charles Carroll
Unpublished Letters of Charles Carroll of Carrollton, and of his Father, Charles Carroll of Doughoregan. Edited by Thomas Meagher Field. New York, 1902.

Letters of Delegates to Congress
  Letters of Delegates to Congress: 1774–1789. 7 vols. Edited by Paul H. Smith. Washington, D.C., 1976–1981.

"Letters of Dennys De Berdt"
  "Letters of Dennys De Berdt, 1757–1770," *Publications of the Colonial Society of Massachusetts* 13 (1911): 293–461.

Levy, "Freedom, Poverty, and Levellers"
  Michael B. Levy, "Freedom, Property and the Levellers: The Case of John Lilburne," *Western Political Quarterly* 36 (1983): 116–33.

[Lind,] *Englishman's Answer*
  [John Lind,] *An Englishman's Answer, To the Address From the Delegates, To the People of Great-Britain, In a Letter to the Several Colonies which were Represented in the Late Continental Congress.* New York, 1775.

[Lind,] *Thirteenth Parliament*
  [John Lind,] *Remarks on the Principal Acts of the Thirteenth Parliament of Great Britain. Vol. I. Containing Remarks on the Acts relating to the Colonies. With a Plan of Reconciliation.* London, 1775.

[Littleton,] *Groans of Plantations*
  [Edward Littleton,] *The Groans of the Plantations: or a True Account of their Grievous and Extreme Sufferings by the Heavy Impositions upon Sugar, and other Hardships. Relating more particularly to the Island of Barbados.* London, 1689.

[Livingston,] *Other Side*
  [Philip Livingston,] *The Other Side of the Question; or, A Defence of the Liberties of North-America. In Answer to a Late Friendly Address to all Reasonable Americans on the Subject of our Political Confusions* (1774), reprinted in *Extra Number 52 of the Magazine of History with Notes and Queries* (1916): 225–51.

[Lloyd,] *Conduct Examined*
  [Charles Lloyd,] *The Conduct of the Late Ministry Examined; From July, 1765, to March, 1766.* London, 1767.

Locke, *Two Treatises*
  John Locke, *Two Treatises of Government: A Critical Edition with an Introduction and Apparatus Criticus.* 2d ed. Edited by Peter Laslett. Cambridge, England, 1967.

Lockwood, *Connecticut Election Sermon*
  Samuel Lockwood, *Civil Rulers an Ordinance of God, for Good to Mankind. A Sermon Preached Before the General Assembly, of the Colony of Connecticut, at Hartford; On the Day of their Anniversary Election, May 12th, 1774.* New London, Conn., 1774.

Lockwood, *Worth and Excellence*
  James Lockwood, *The Worth and Excellence of Civil Freedom and Lib-*

erty illustrated, and a Public Spirit and the Love of our Country recommended. A Sermon Delivered before the General Assembly of the Colony of Connecticut, at Hartford, on the Day of the Anniversary Election. May 10th 1759. New London, Conn., 1759.

Lofft, *Observations on Wesley's Address*
Capel Lofft, *Observations on Mr. Wesley's Second Calm Address, and Incidently on other Writings upon the American Question. Together with Thoughts on Toleration, and on the Point how Far the Conscience of the Subject is Concerned in a War; Remarks on Constitution in General, and that of England in Particular; on the Nature of Colonial Government, and a Recommendation of a Plan of Peace.* London, 1777.

Logan, *Antidote*
James Logan, *The Antidote, In some Remarks on a Paper of David Lloyd's, called a Vindication of the Legislative Power. Submitted to the Representatives of all the Freemen of Pennsylvania.* Philadelphia, 1725.

London Journal
(Weekly newspaper, London.)

London Magazine
The London Magazine or Gentleman's Monthly Intelligencer. (Monthly magazine, London.)

Lord, *Connecticut Election Sermon*
Benjamin Lord, *Religion and Government subsisting together in Society, Necessary to their Compleat Happiness and Safety. A Sermon Delivered in the Audience of the General Assembly of the Colony of Connecticut, on their Anniversary Election at Hartford, May 9th, 1751.* New London, 1752.

Lord, *Religion and Government*
Benjamin Lord, *Religion and Government subsisting together in Society, Necessary to their Compleat Happiness and Safety.* New London, Conn., 1752.

"Lords Debate on Declaratory Act"
"Debate on the Conway Resolutions. House of Lords, 10 February 1766," in *The Debate on the American Revolution.* 2d ed. Edited by Max Beloff. London, 1960, pp. 106–8.

Lords Manuscripts
The Manuscripts of the House of Lords, 1689–1690. Historical Manuscripts Commission. Twelfth Report. Appendix, Part VI. London, 1889.

Lovejoy, *Glorious Revolution*
David S. Lovejoy, *The Glorious Revolution in America.* New York, 1972.

Lovejoy, *Rhode Island Politics*
David S. Lovejoy, *Rhode Island Politics and the American Revolution 1760–1776.* Providence, R.I., 1958.

Lovejoy, "Virginia's Charter"
> David S. Lovejoy, "Virginia's Charter and Bacon's Rebellion 1675–1676," in *Anglo-American Political Relations, 1675–1775.* Edited by Alison Gilbert Olson and Richard Maxwell Brown. New Brunswick, N.J., 1970, pp. 31–51.

Lovell, *An Oration*
> James Lovell, *An Oration Delivered April 2d, 1771. At the Request of the Inhabitants of the Town of Boston; to Commemorate the bloody Tragedy of the Fifth of March, 1770.* Boston, 1771.

Lowth, *Durham Assize Sermon*
> Robert Lowth, *A Sermon Preached Before the Honourable and Right Reverend Richard, Lord Bishop of Durham, the Honourable Henry Bathurst, One of the Justices of the Court of Common Pleas, and the Honourable Sir Joseph Yates, One of the Justices of the Court of King's Bench; at the Assizes Holden at Durham, August 15, 1764.* 2d ed. Newcastle, England, 1764.

Lucas, *Divelina Libera*
> Charles Lucas, *Divelina Libera: An Apology for the Civil Rights and Liberties of the Commons and Citizens of Dublin.* Dublin, 1744.

Lutz, *Popular Consent and Control*
> Donald S. Lutz, *Popular Consent and Popular Control: Whig Political Theory in the Early State Constitutions.* Baton Rouge, La., 1980.

Macaulay, *Observations on a Pamphlet*
> Catharine Macaulay, *Observations on a Pamphlet, Entitled, Thoughts on the Cause of the Present Discontents.* 4th ed., corrected. London, 1770.

[Madden,] *Reflections*
> [Samuel Madden,] *Reflections and Resolutions Proper for the Gentlemen of Ireland, as to their Conduct for the Service of their Country.* Dublin, 1738, reprinted 1816.

Magna Carta and Liberty
> *Magna Carta and the Idea of Liberty.* Edited by James C. Holt. New York, 1972.

Marcham, *Constitutional History*
> Frederick George Marcham, *A Constitutional History of Modern England, 1485 to the Present.* New York, 1960.

Maryland Votes and Proceedings (September 1765)
> *Votes and Proceedings of the Lower House of Assembly of the Province of Maryland. September Session, 1765. Being the First Session of this Assembly.* Annapolis, Md., n.d.

Maryland Votes and Proceedings (November 1765)
> *Votes and Proceedings of the Lower House of Assembly of the Province*

of Maryland. November Session, 1765. Being the Second Session of this Assembly. Annapolis, Md., n.d.

Maryland Votes and Proceedings (1768)
Votes and Proceedings of the Lower House of Assembly of the Province of Maryland. May Session, 1768. Being the First Session of this Assembly. Annapolis, Md., 1768.

Maryland Votes and Proceedings (1771)
Votes and Proceedings of the Lower House of Assembly of the Province of Maryland. October Session, 1771. Being the First Session of this Assembly. Annapolis, Md., [1772].

[Maseres,] *Canadian Freeholder*
[Francis Maseres,] *The Canadian Freeholder: In Two Dialogues Between an Englishman and a Frenchman, Settled in Canada.* 3 vols. London, 1777, 1779.

[Maseres,] *To Obtain an Assembly*
[Francis Maseres,] *An Account of the Proceedings of the British, And other Protestant Inhabitants, of the Province of Quebeck, In North America, In order to obtain An House of Assembly In that Province.* London, 1775.

Maseres, *Representatives*
[Francis Maseres,] *Considerations on the Expediency of Admitting Representatives from the American Colonies into the British House of Commons.* London, 1770.

Massachusetts Gazette
The Massachusetts Gazette. (Weekly newspaper, Boston.)

Massachusetts Provincial Congresses
The Journals of Each Provincial Congress of Massachusetts in 1774 and 1775, and of the Committee of Safety, with an Appendix, Containing the Proceedings of the County Conventions — Narratives of the Events of the Nineteenth of April, 1775 — Papers Relating to Ticonderoga and Crown Point, and Other Documents, Illustrative of the Early History of the American Revolution. Boston, 1838.

Massacre Orations
Orations Delivered at the Request of the Inhabitants of the Town of Boston, to Commemorate the Evening of the Fifth of March, 1770; When a Number of Citizens were Killed by a Party of British Troops, Quartered Among them, in a Time of Peace. Boston, 1785.

[Mather,] *America's Appeal*
[Moses Mather,] *America's Appeal to the Impartial World. Wherein the Rights of the Americans, as Men, British Subjects, and as Colonists; the Equity of the Demand, and of the Manner in which it is made upon them by Great-Britain are stated and considered. And the Opposition made by*

*the Colonies to Acts of Parliament, their resorting to Arms in their neces-
sary Defence, against the Military Armaments, employed to enforce them,
Vindicated.* Hartford, Conn., 1775.

Mather, *Autobiography*
"The Autobiography of Increase Mather," edited by M. G. Hall, *Proceedings of the American Antiquarian Society* 71 (1961): 271–462.

[Mather,] *A Narrative*
[Increase Mather,] *A Narrative of the Miseries of New-England, By Reason of an Arbitrary Government Erected there Under Sir Edmond Andros*
(1688), reprinted in *The Andros Tracts* 2. Prince Society Publications, vol.
6., 1869, pp. 3–14.

Mather, *Reasons*
Increase Mather, *Reasons For the Confirmation of the Charters of the Cor-
porations in New-England* (1689–1690), reprinted in *The Andros Tracts* 2.
Prince Society Publications, vol. 6, 1869, pp. 225–29.

Mauduit Letters
*Jasper Mauduit: Agent in London for the Province of the Massachusetts
Bay 1762–1765.* Boston, 1918.

Mauduit, *Letters of Hutchinson*
Israel Mauduit, *The Letters of Governor Hutchinson, and Lieut. Governor Oliver, &c. Printed at Boston. And Remarks thereon. With the Assembly's Address, and the Proceedings Of the Lords Committee of Council.
Together with the Substance of Mr. Wedderburn's Speech relating to those
Letters. And the Report of the Lords Committee to his Majesty in Council.* 2d ed. London, 1774.

Mayhew, *Discourse Concerning Unlimited Submission*
Jonathan Mayhew, *A Discourse Concerning Unlimited Submission and Non-
Resistance to the Higher Powers: With some Reflections on the Resistance
made to King Charles I. And on the Anniversary of his Death: In which
the Mysterious Doctrine of that Prince's Saintship and Martyrdom is Un-
riddled* (1750), reprinted in *Pulpit of American Revolution*, pp. 47–104.

Mayhew, *Election Sermon*
Jonathan Mayhew, *A Sermon Preach'd in the Audience of His Excellency
William Shirley, Esq.; Captain General, Governour and Commander in
Chief, the Honourable His Majesty's Council, and the Honourable House
of Representatives, of the Province of the Massachusetts-Bay, in New-
England. May 29th, 1754.* Boston, 1754.

Mayhew, *Snare Broken*
Jonathan Mayhew, *The Snare broken. A Thanksgiving-Discourse Preached
At the Desire of the West Church in Boston, N. E. Friday May 23, 1766
Occasioned by the Repeal of the Stamp-Act.* Boston, 1766.

Memoirs of William Smith
> *Historical Memoirs of William Smith Historian of the Province of New York Member of the Governor's Council and Last Chief Justice of that Province Under the Crown. In Two Volumes.* Edited by William H. W. Sabine. New York, 1969.

[Meredith,] *Letter to Chatham*
> [Sir William Meredith,] *A Letter from Thomas Lord Lyttleton, to William Pitt, Earl of Chatham, on the Quebec Bill.* New York, 1774.

[Meredith,] *Question Stated*
> [Sir William Meredith,] *The Question Stated, Whether the Freeholders of Middlesex lost their Right, by voting for Mr. Wilkes at the last Election?* London, [1769].

[Meredith,] *Remarks on Taxation*
> [Sir William Meredith,] *Historical Remarks on the Taxation of Free States, in a Series of Letters to a Friend.* London, 1778.

Middlekauff, *Glorious Cause*
> Robert Middlekauff, *The Glorious Cause: The American Revolution 1763–1789.* New York, 1982.

Miller, "Glorious Revolution"
> John Miller, "The Glorious Revolution: 'Contract' and 'Abdication' Reconsidered," *Historical Journal* 25 (1982): 541–55.

Missing, *Letter to Mansfield on Instructions*
> John Missing, *A Letter to the Right Honourable William Lord Mansfield, Lord Chief Justice of the Court of King's Bench: Proving that the Subjects of England, lawfully assembled to Petition their King, or to Elect or Instruct their Representatives, are intitled to Freedom of Debate; and that all Suits Prosecutions for Exerting that Right, are Unconstitutional and Illegal.* London, 1770.

Montgomery, *Sermon at Christiana Bridge*
> Joseph Montgomery, *A Sermon Preached at Christiana Bridge and Newcastle, the 10th of July, 1775. Being the Day appointed by the Continental Congress, as a Day of Fasting, Humiliation, and Prayer.* Philadelphia, 1775.

Monthly Review
> *The Monthly Review; or, Liberty Journal: by Several Hands.* (Monthly magazine, London.)

Moore, *Taxing Colonies*
> Maurice Moore, *The Justice and Policy of Taxing the American Colonies, in Great-Britain, considered* (1765), reprinted in *Not a Conquered People: Two Carolinians View Parliamentary Taxation.* Edited by William S. Price, Jr. Raleigh, N.C., 1975, pp. 35–48.

Morgan, *Birth*
Edmund S. Morgan, *The Birth of the Republic, 1763–89.* Chicago, 1956.

Morgan, "Colonial Ideas"
Edmund S. Morgan, "Colonial Ideas of Parliamentary Power 1764–1766," *William and Mary Quarterly* 5 (1948): 311–41.

Morgan, *Gentle Puritan*
Edmund S. Morgan, *The Gentle Puritan: A Life of Ezra Stiles, 1727–1795.* Chapel Hill, N.C., 1962.

Morgan, *Prologue*
Prologue to Revolution: Sources and Documents on the Stamp Act Crisis, 1764–1766. Edited by Edmund S. Morgan. Chapel Hill, N.C., 1959.

Morgan, "Thomas Hutchinson"
Edmund S. Morgan, "Thomas Hutchinson and the Stamp Act," *New England Quarterly* 21 (1948): 459–92.

Morrill, *Revolt of the Provinces*
J. S. Morrill, *The Revolt of the Provinces: Conservatives and Radicals in the English Civil War 1630–1650.* London, 1976.

Mulford, *Speech to New York Assembly*
Samuel Mulford's Speech to the Assembly at New-York, April the Second, 1714. [New York, 1714.]

[Mulgrave] *Letter from a Member*
[Mulgrave, C. J. Phipps, Lord,] *A Letter from a Member of Parliament to One of his Constituents, on the Late Proceedings of the House of Commons in the Middlesex Elections.* London, 1769.

Mullett, *Fundamental Law*
Charles F. Mullett, *Fundamental Law and the American Revolution 1760–1776.* New York, 1933.

Munro, *Bristol*
Wilfred H. Munro, *The History of Bristol, R.I.—The Story of the Mount Hope Lands From the Visit of the Northmen to the Present Time.* Providence, R.I., 1880.

Munro, *Mount Hope*
Wilfred Harold Munro, *The Story of the Mount Hope Lands.* Providence, R.I., 1880.

Murdoch, *Rebellion in America*
Rebellion in America: A Contemporary British Viewpoint, 1765–1783. Edited by David H. Murdoch. Santa Barbara, Calif., 1979.

Namier, *Age of Revolution*
L. B. Namier, *England in the Age of the American Revolution.* London, 1930.

Nelson, *Americanization of the Common Law*
William E. Nelson, *Americanization of the Common Law: The Impact of Legal Change on Massachusetts Society, 1760–1830.* Cambridge, Mass., 1975.

Nenner, *Colour of Law*
Howard Nenner, *By Colour of Law: Legal Culture and Constitutional Politics in England, 1660–1689.* Chicago, 1977.

New Jersey Votes and Proceedings (November 1765)
Votes and Proceedings of the General Assembly of the Province of New-Jersey. At a Session of General Assembly, begun at Burlington, November 26, 1765, and continued till the 30th following. Burlington, N.J., 1765.

New Jersey Votes and Proceedings (1768)
Votes and Proceedings of the General Assembly of the Province of New-Jersey. At a Session of the General Assembly, began at Perth-Amboy, April 12, 1768, and continued till the 10th of May following. Woodbridge, N.J., 1768.

New Jersey Votes and Proceedings (January 1775)
Votes and Proceedings of the General Assembly of the Colony of New-Jersey. At a Session began at Perth-Amboy, Wednesday January 11, 1775, and continued until the 12th Day of February following. Burlington, N.J., 1775.

New York Journal of Votes
Journal of the Votes and Proceedings of the General Assembly of the Colony of New-York. Began the 8th Day of November, 1743; and Ended the 23d of December, 1765. Vol. II. Published by Order of the General Assembly. New York, 1766.

Nicholas, *Present State of Virginia*
Robert Carter Nicholas, *Considerations on the Present State of Virginia Examined* (1774), reprinted in *Revolutionary Virginia* 1:259–85.

[Nicholas,] *Proceedings of 1620–21*
[Edward Nicholas,] *Proceedings and Debates of the House of Commons, in 1620 and 1621.* 2 vols. Oxford, 1766.

Noble, *Some Strictures*
Oliver Noble, *Some Strictures upon the Sacred Story Recorded in the Book of Esther, Shewing the Power and Oppression of State Ministers tending to the Ruin and Destruction of God's People: — And the Remarkable Interpositions of Divine Providence, in Favour of the Oppressed; in a Discourse Delivered at Newbury-Port, North Meeting House, March 8th, 1775. In Commemoration of the Massacre at Boston, March the Fifth, 1770.* Newbury-Port, Mass., 1775.

North Briton
The North Briton. To which is added, By Way of Appendix, The Letters

which passed between the Rt. Hon. Earl Talbot, &c. and John Wilkes, Esq; Previous to their Duel. Together with all the Papers relative to the Confinement and Enlargement of Mr. Wilkes. With many other Curious Particulars. Dublin, 1763.

North Carolina Colonial Records
The Colonial Records of North Carolina, Published Under the Supervision of the Trustees of the Public Libraries, By Order of the General Assembly. Vols. 7, 8, 9, and 10. Edited by William L. Saunders. Raleigh, N.C., 1890.

Northcote, *Observations on Rights*
Thomas Northcote, *Observations on the Natural and Civil Rights of Mankind, the Prerogative of Princes, and the Powers of Government.* London, 1781.

N.S., *Divine Rights*
N.S., *The Divine Rights of the British Nation and Constitution Vindicated.* 2d ed., corrected London, 1710.

[Oldfield,] *History of the Boroughs*
[J. H. B. Oldfield,] *An Entire and Complete History, Political and Personal, of the Boroughs of Great Britain; to which is Prefixed, an Original Sketch of Constitutional Rights, from the Earliest Period Until the Present Time; and the Principles of our Ancient Representation Traced from the Most Authentic Records, Supported by Undeniable Testimonies, and Illustrated by a Variety of Notes and References, Collected from the Most Respectable, Legal, Political, and Historical Authorities.* 3 vols. London, 1792.

Otis, *Rights*
James Otis, *The Rights of the British Colonies Asserted and Proved* (1764), reprinted in Bailyn, *Pamphlets* 1:419–82.

[Otis,] "Substance"
[James Otis,] "Substance of a Memorial Presented [by] the Assembly in Pursuance of the Above Instructions; and by the House Voted to be Transmitted to JASPER MAUDUIT, Esq., Agent for this Province, to be Improved As He May Judge Proper," appendix to Otis, *Rights*, pp. 474–82.

[Otis,] *Vindication*
[James Otis,] *A Vindication of the British Colonies, against the Aspersions of the Halifax Gentleman, in His Letter to a Rhode Island Friend* (1765), reprinted in Bailyn, *Pamphlets* 1:554–79.

Paley, *Essay upon the Constitution*
W. Paley, *An Essay Upon the British Constitution: Being the Seventh Chapter of the Sixth Book of the Principles of Moral and Political Philosophy.* London, 1792.

Paley, *Principles of Philosophy*
>   William Paley, *The Principles of Moral and Political Philosophy*. London, 1785.

Palmer, *Impartial Account*
>   John Palmer, *An Impartial Account of the State of New England: Or, the Late Government there, Vindicated. In Answer to the Declaration Which the Faction Set Forth, when they Over-turned that Government* (1690), reprinted in *The Andros Tracts* 1. Prince Society Publications, vol. 5. Boston, 1868, pp. 23–41.

Papers of Iredell
>   *The Papers of James Iredell: Volume I. 1767–1777.* Edited by Don Higginbotham. Raleigh, N.C., 1976.

Papers of Jefferson
>   *The Papers of Thomas Jefferson.* Edited by Julian P. Boyd. 20 vols. Princeton, N.J., 1950–82.

Papers of William Livingston
>   *The Papers of William Livingston.* 2 vols. Edited by Carl E. Prince. Trenton, N.J., 1979–80.

[Parker,] *Case of Shipmony*
>   [Henry Parker,] *The Case of Shipmony briefly discoursed, according to the Grounds of Law, Policy, and Conscience. And Most Humbly Presented to the Censure and Correction of the High Court of Parliament.* N.i., 1640.

[Parker,] *True Portraiture*
>   [Henry Parker,] *The True Portraiture of the Kings of England; drawn from their Titles, Successions, Raigns, and Ends; or, a short and exact Historical Description of every King, with the Right they have had to the Crown, and the manner of their wearing of it, especially from William the Conqueror* (1650), in *Somers' Tracts* 6, pp. 77–103.

Parliament Register
>   *The Parliamentary Register; or History of the Proceedings and Debates of the House of Commons.* 17 vols. London, 1775–80.

Parliamentary History
>   *The Parliamentary History of England, From the Earliest Period to the Year 1803.* 36 vols. London, 1806–1820.

Parsons, *Election Sermon*
>   Moses Parsons, *A Sermon Preached at Cambridge, Before his Excellency Thomas Hutchinson, Esq; Governor: His Honor Andrew Oliver, Esq; Lieutenant-Governor, The Honorable his Majesty's Council, and the Honorable House of Representatives of the Province of the Massachusetts-Bay in New-England, May 27th, 1772. Being the Anniversary for the Election of His Majesty's Council for said Province.* Boston, 1772.

Patten, *Discourse at Hallifax*
William Patten, *A Discourse Delivered at Hallifax in the County of Plymouth, July 24th 1766. On the Day of Thanks-giving to Almighty God, throughout the Province of the Massachusetts-Bay in New England, for the Repeal of the* STAMP-ACT. Boston, 1766.

Peach, *Richard Price*
Bernard Peach, *Richard Price and the Ethical Foundations of the American Revolution.* Durham, N.C., 1979.

Pease, *Leveller*
Theodore Calvin Pease, *The Leveller Movement: A Study in the History and Political Theory of the English Great Civil War.* Gloucester, Mass., 1965.

Pemberton, *Lord North*
W. Baring Pemberton, *Lord North.* London, 1938.

Pennsylvania Archives (8th series)
Pennsylvania Archives: Eighth Series [Votes and Proceedings of the House of Representatives.] 8 vols. [Harrisburg, Pa.,] 1931–35.

Pennsylvania Council
Minutes of the Provincial Council of Pennsylvania, From the Organization to the Termination of the Proprietary Governor. Vol. IX. Containing the Proceedings of Council From October 15th, 1762, to 17th of October, 1771, Both Days Included. Vol. X. Containing the Proceedings of Council From October 18th, 1771, to 27th of September, 1775, Both Days Included; Together with Minutes of the Council of Safety From June 30th, 1775, to November 12th, 1776, Both Days Included. Harrisburg, Pa., 1852.

Peters, *Massachusetts Constitution*
Ronald M. Peters, *The Massachusetts Constitution of 1780: A Social Compact.* Amherst, Mass., 1978.

Petyt, *Ancient Right*
William Petyt, *The Ancient Right of the Commons of England Asserted; or, a Discourse Proving by Records and the best Historians, that the Commons of England were ever an Essential part of Parliament.* London, 1680.

[Phelps,] *Rights of the Colonies*
[Richard Phelps,] *The Rights of the Colonies, And the Extent of the Legislative Authority of Great-Britain, Briefly Stated and Considered.* London, 1769.

Phillips, *Salem*
James Duncan Phillips, *Salem in the Eighteenth Century.* Boston, 1937.

Plowden, *Rights of Englishmen*
Francis Plowden, *Jura Anglorum: The Rights of Englishmen.* Dublin, 1792.

Plumb, *Growth of Political Stability*
J. H. Plumb, *The Growth of Political Stability in England 1675–1725*. London, 1967.

Pocock, "Commons Debates of 1628"
J. G. A. Pocock, "Book Review: The Commons Debates of 1628," *Journal of the History of Ideas* 39 (1978): 329–34.

Pocock, *Politics*
J. G. A. Pocock, *Politics, Language and Time: Essays on Political Thought and History*. New York, 1971.

Political Register
The Political Register; and Impartial Review of New Books. (Monthly magazine, London.)

Pollock, *Politics*
Sir Frederick Pollock, "The History of English Law as a Branch of Politics," in Sir Frederick Pollock, *Jurisprudence and Legal Essays*. New York, 1961, pp. 185–211.

Popofsky, "Habeas Corpus"
Linda S. Popofsky, "Habeas Corpus and 'Liberty of the Subject': Legal Arguments for the Petition of Right in the Parliament of 1628," *The Historian* 41 (1979): 257–75.

Pownall, *Administration*
Thomas Pownall, *The Administration of the Colonies. Wherein their Rights and Constitution are Discussed and Stated*. 4th ed. London, 1768.

Pownall, *Administration Fifth Edition*
Thomas Pownall, *The Administration of the British Colonies. The Fifth Edition. Wherein their Rights and Constitution are discussed and stated*. London, 1774.

Pownall, *Administration Sixth Edition*
Thomas Pownall, *The Administration of the British Colonies. The Sixth Edition. Wherein their Constitutional Rights and Establishments as also those Disputed Points in the Constitutions and Administration of the Government of the Colonies, from whence the Present American War Sprung, and on which the Final Settlement of a Peace must Turn are discussed and stated*. 2 vols. London, 1777.

[Pownall,] *Considerations*
[Thomas Pownall,] *Considerations on the Points lately brought into Question as to the Parliament's Right of Taxing the Colonies, And of the Measures necessary to be taken at this Crisis. Being an Appendix, Section III, to the Administration of the Colonies*. London, 1766.

Pownall, *Pownall*
> Charles A. W. Pownall, *Thomas Pownall M.P., F.R.S., Governor of Massachusetts Bay*. London, 1908.

[Prescott,] *Calm Consideration*
> [Benjamin Prescott,] *A Free and Calm Consideration of the Unhappy Misunderstandings and Debates, which have of late Years arisen, and yet subsist, Between the Parliament of Great-Britain, and these American Colonies. Contained in Eight Letters, Six whereof, Directed to a Gentleman of Distinction in England, Formerly printed in the Essex Gazette. The other Two, directed to a Friend*. Salem, Mass., 1774.

Price, "Introduction to Two Tracts"
> Richard Price, "Introduction," to Price, *Two Tracts*.

Price, *Nature of Civil Liberty*
> Richard Price, *Observations on the Nature of Civil Liberty, the Principles of Government, and the Justice and Policy of the War with the America*. London, 1776.

Price, *Two Tracts*
> Richard Price, *Two Tracts on Civil Liberty, the War with America, and the Debts and Finances of the Kingdom: with a General Introduction and Supplement* (London, 1778), reprinted New York, 1972.

Price, *Two Tracts: Tract One*
> Richard Price, *Observations on the Nature of Civil Liberty, the Principles of Government, and the Justice and Policy of the War with America*. 8th ed. London, 1778, reprinted in Price, *Two Tracts*, pp. 1–112.

Price, *Two Tracts: Tract Two*
> Richard Price, *Additional Observations on the Nature and Value of Civil Liberty, and the War with America: Also Observations on Schemes for raising Money by Public Loans; An Historical Deduction and Analysis of the National Debt; And a brief Account of the Debts and Resources of France* [3d ed., 1778], reprinted in Price, *Two Tracts*, pp. vii–xiv, 1–216.

Priestley, *First Principles*
> Joseph Priestley, *An Essay on the First Principles of Government; and on the Nature of Political, Civil, and Religious Liberty*. London, 1768.

[Priestley,] *Present State of Liberty*
> [Joseph Priestley,] *The Present State of Liberty in Great Britain and Her Colonies*. London, 1769.

Prince, *Civil Rulers*
> Thomas Prince, *Civil Rulers Raised up by God to Feed His People: A Sermon at the Public Lecture in Boston July 25, 1728*. Boston, 1728.

Prior Documents
> *A Collection of Interesting, Authentic Papers, Relative to the Dispute Between Great Britain and America; Shewing the Causes and Progress of that Misunderstanding From 1764 to 1775.* London, 1777.

Privy Council Copies
> *Copies of papers and letters transmitted to the Council re: the Riots which have lately happened in America in opposition to the Stamp Act . . . [and] copies of all orders etc. issued from the Council Office thereupon.* HM 1947, Huntington Library, San Marino, Calif.

"Proceedings Committee of Correspondence"
> "Proceedings of the Virginia Committee of Correspondence," *Virginia Magazine of History and Biography* 12 (1904–1905): 1–14, 157–69, 225–40, 353–64.

Proceedings and Debates
> *Proceedings and Debates of the British Parliaments respecting North America 1754–1783.* Edited by R. C. Simmons and P. D. G. Thomas. 2 vols. New York, 1983.

Proceedings against Manwaring
> *The Proceedings of the Lords and Commons In the Year 1628. Against Roger Manwaring Doctor in Divinity [The Sacheverell of those Days], For Two Seditious High-flying Sermons, intitled, Religion and Allegiance.* London, 1709.

Protests of Lords
> *A Complete Collection of the Protests of the Lords with Historical Introductions.* Edited by James E. Thorold Rogers. 3 vols. Oxford, 1875.

Protests of the Lords of Ireland
> *A Collection of the Protests of the Lords of Ireland, From 1634 to 1771.* Dublin, 1772.

Providence Gazette
> *The Providence Gazette and Country Journal.* (Weekly newspaper, Providence, R.I.)

Prynne, *Seasonable Vindication*
> William Prynne, *The First and Second Part of a Seasonable, Legal, and Historical Vindication, and Chronological Collection of the Good, Old, Fundamentall Liberties, Franchises, Rights, Laws of all English Freemen.* . . . London, 1655.

Public Records of Connecticut
> Charles J. Hoadly, *The Public Records of the Colony of Connecticut.* Vols. 12–15. Hartford, Conn., 1881–90.

Pulpit of American Revolution
> *The Pulpit of the American Revolution or, The Political Sermons of the Period of 1776.* Edited by John Wingate Thornton, 2d ed. Boston, 1876.

"Putney Debates"
   "The Putney Debates: At the General Council of Officers, 1647," printed
   in *Puritanism and Liberty Being the Army Debates (1647–9) from the Clarke
   Manuscripts with Supplementary Documents.* Edited by A. S. P. Wood-
   house. Chicago, 1974, pp. 1–124.

Pym, *Speech of Summing Up*
   John Pym, *The Speech or Declaration of John Pym, Esquire: After the Re-
   capitulation or summing up of the Charge of High-Treason, Against Thomas
   Earle of Strafford, 12 April 1641.* London, 1641.

Quincy, *Observations with Thoughts*
   Josiah Quincy, Jr., *Observations on the Act of Parliament Commonly Called
   the Boston Port-Bill; with Thoughts on Civil Society and Standing Armies*
   (1774), reprinted in *Memoir of the Life of Josiah Quincy Jun. of Massachusetts: By his Son Josiah Quincy.* Boston, 1825, pp. 355–469.

Quincy, *Reports*
   Josiah Quincy, Jr., *Reports of Cases Argued and Adjudged in the Superior
   Court of Judicature of the Province of Massachusetts Bay.* Boston, 1865.

[Ramsay,] *Historical Essay*
   [Allan Ramsay,] *An Historical Essay on the English Constitution: Or, An
   impartial Inquiry into the Elective Power of the People, from the first Establishment of the Saxons in this Kingdom. Wherein the Right of Parliament, to Tax our distant Provinces, is explained, and justified, upon such
   constitutional Principles as will afford an equal Security to the Colonists,
   as to their Brethren at Home.* London, 1771.

[Ramsay,] *Thoughts on Nature of Government*
   [Allan Ramsay,] *Thoughts on the Origin and Nature of Government. Oc-
   casioned by the late Disputes between Great Britain and her American
   Colonies. Written in the Year 1766.* London, 1769.

[Rawson,] *Revolution in New England*
   [Edward Rawson,] *The Revolution in New England Justified, And the People there Vindicated From the Aspersions cast upon them by Mr. John
   Palmer, In his Pretended Answer to the Declaration, Published by the Inhabitants of Boston, and the Country adjacent, on the Day when they
   secured their late Oppressors, who acted by an Illegal and Arbitrary Commission from the Late King JAMES.* Boston, 1691.

[Reeves,] *Thoughts, Second Letter*
   [John Reeves,] *Thoughts on the English Government. Addressed to the Quiet
   Good Sense of the People of England. In a Series of Letters. Letter the
   Second.* London, 1799.

[Reeves,] *Thoughts, Third Letter*
   [John Reeves,] *Thoughts on the English Government. Addressed to the Quiet*

Good Sense of the People of England. In a Series of Letters. Letter the Third. London, 1799.

Relf, *Petition of Right*
Frances Helen Relf, *The Petition of Right.* The University of Minnesota Studies in the Social Sciences, no. 8. Minneapolis, Minn., 1917.

Remembrancer for 1775
The *Remembrancer, or Impartial Repository of Public Events, for the Year* MDCCLXXV. London, [1776].

Remembrancer for 1776: Part I
The *Remembrancer; or, Impartial Respository of Public Events: Part I For the Year 1776.* London, 1776.

Remembrancer for 1776: Part II
The *Remembrancer; or, Impartial Repository of Public Events: Part II. For the Year 1776.* London, 1776.

Remembrancer for 1776: Part III
The *Remembrancer; or, Impartial Repository of Public Events. Part III. For the Year 1776.* London, 1777.

Remonstrance of the Cities (1659)
The *Remonstrance and Protestation of the Well-affected People of the Cities of London, Westminster, and other the Cities, Counties and Places within the Common-wealth of England, against those Officers of the Army, who put force upon, and interrupted the Parliament; the 13th of Octob. 1659, and against all pretended Powers or Authoritys that they have or shall set up, to Rule or Govern, this Common-Wealth.* London, 1659.

Revolution Documents
Documents of the American Revolution 1770–1783. Edited by K. G. Davies. Vols. 1–16. Dublin, 1972–81.

Revolution Justified
[Edward Rawson and Samuel Sewall,] *The Revolution in New England Justified, And the People there Vindicated From the Aspersions cast upon them By Mr. John Palmer . . .* (1691), reprinted in *The Andros Tracts.* 1: Prince Society Publications, vol. 5., 1868, pp. 65–131.

Revolutionary Virginia
Revolutionary Virginia The Road to Independence — Volume I: Forming Thunderclouds and the First Convention, 1763–1774. A Documentary History. Compiled by William J. Van Schreeven, edited by Robert L. Scribner. *Volume II: The Committees and the Second Convention, 1773–1775. A Documentary Record.* Compiled by William J. Van Schreeven and Robert L. Scribner. *Volume III: The Breaking Storm and the Third Convention, 1775. A Documentary History.* Compiled and edited by Robert L. Scribner. *Volume IV: The Committee of Safety and the Balance of Forces,*

1775. A Documentary History. Compiled and edited by Robert L. Scribner and Brent Tarter. *Volume V: The Clash of Arms and the Fourth Convention, 1775–1776. A Documentary Record.* Compiled and edited by Robert L. Scribner and Brent Tarter. [Charlottesville, Va.,] 1973–79.

Rhode Island Colony Records
  Records of the Colony of Rhode Island & Providence Plantations in New England. Edited by John R. Bartlett. 10 vols. 1856.

Ritcheson, *British Politics*
  Charles R. Ritcheson, *British Politics and the American Revolution.* Norman, Okla., 1954.

[Robertson,] *Liberty, Property, and Religion*
  [William Robertson,] *The Liberty, Property, and Religion of the Whigs.* London, 1713.

Robinson, *Political Catechism*
  Robert Robinson, *A Political Catechism.* 3d ed. London, 1784.

Robson, *American Revolution*
  Eric Robson, *The American Revolution in its Political and Military Aspects 1763–1783.* New York, 1966.

Roeber, *Faithful Magistrates*
  A. G. Roeber, *Faithful Magistrates and Republican Lawyers: Creators of Virginia Legal Culture, 1680–1810.* Chapel Hill, N.C., 1981.

Roebuck, *Enquiry whether the Guilt*
  John Roebuck, *An Enquiry Whether the Guilt of the Present Civil War in America, Ought to be Imputed to Great Britain or America.* New ed. London, 1776.

Rogers, *Empire and Liberty*
  Alan Rogers, *Empire and Liberty: American Resistance to British Authority 1755–1763.* Berkeley, Calif., 1974.

[Rokeby,] *Considerations on the Measures*
  [Matthew Robinson-Morris, Second Baron Rokeby,] *Considerations on the Measures Carrying on with Respect to the British Colonies in North America.* 2d ed. London, [1774].

[Rokeby,] *Further Examination*
  [Matthew Robinson-Morris, Second Baron Rokeby,] *A Further Examination of our Present American Measures and of the Reasons and the Principles on which they are founded.* Bath, England, 1776.

Rossiter, *Political Thought*
  Clinton Rossiter, *The Political Thought of the American Revolution.* New York, 1963.

Rossiter, *Six Characters*
> Clinton Rossiter, *Six Characters in Search of a Republic: Studies in the Political thought of the American Colonies.* New York, 1964.

[Rous,] *Letter to Jurors*
> [George Rous,] *A Letter to the Jurors of Great-Britain. Occasioned by an Opinion of the Court of King's Bench, read by Lord Chief Justice Mansfield in the Case of the King and Woodfall; and said to have been left by his Lordship with the Clerk of Parliament.* London, 1771.

Rous, *Thoughts on Government*
> George Rous, *Thoughts on Government; Occasioned by Mr. Burke's Reflections, &c. in a Letter to a Friend. To which is added a Postscript, in Reply to a Vindication of Mr. Burke's Reflections.* London, 1791.

Rushworth, *Historical Collections: Third Part*
> John Rushworth, *Historical Collections: The Third Part; in Two Volumes.* Vol. 1. London, 1692.

Russell, *Parliaments and Politics*
> Conrad Russell, *Parliaments and English Politics 1621–1629.* Oxford, 1979.

"Rusticus," *Remarks*
> "Rusticus," *Remarks on A Late Pamphlet Entitled Plain Truth.* Philadelphia, 1776.

Rutherforth, *Natural Law*
> T. Rutherforth, *Institutes of Natural Law Being the substance of a Course of Lectures on Grotius de Jure Belli et Pacis Read in S. Johns College Cambridge.* 2 vols. Cambridge, England, 1754–56.

Ryder, "Parliamentary Diaries"
> "Parliamentary Diaries of Nathaniel Ryder, 1764–7," edited by P. D. G. Thomas. *Camden Miscellany Vol. XXIII.* Camden Society, 4th ser, vol. 7. London, [1969].

Saint-John, *Speech or Declaration*
> [Oliver St. John,] *The Speech or Declaration of Mr. St. John, His Majesties Solicitor-Generall. Delivered at a Conference of both Houses of Parliament, held 16. Caroli, 1640. Concerning Ship-Money. As it is revised, and allowed.* London, 1641.

Samson, *Sermon at Roxbury-Camp*
> Ezra Samson, *A Sermon Preached at Roxbury-Camp, Before Col. Cotton's Regiment; On the 20th of July, P.M. 1775. Being a Day set apart for Fasting and Prayer, throughout all the United Colonies in America.* Watertown, Mass., 1775.

Scots Magazine
> *The Scots Magazine.* (Monthly magazine, Edinburgh.)

[Scott,] *Remarks on the Patriot*
[John Scott,] *Remarks on the Patriot. Including some Hints Respecting the Americans: with an Address to the Electors of Great Britain.* London, 1775.

[Seabury,] *Congress Canvassed*
[Samuel Seabury,] *The Congress Canvassed: or, an Examination into the Conduct of the Delegates, at their Grand Convention, Held in Philadelphia, Sept. 1, 1774. Addressed to the Merchants of New-York.* New York, 1774.

Selden, *Table Talk*
Table Talk of John Selden. Edited by Frederick Pollock. London, 1927.

Select Collection of Letters
A Select Collection of the Most Interesting Letters on the Government, Liberty, and Constitution of England; Which have appeared in the different News-papers from the elevation of Lord Bute, to the death of the Earl of Egremont. 3 vols. 2d ed. London, 1763–64.

[Serle,] *Americans against Liberty*
[Ambrose Serle,] *Americans against Liberty: or, an Essay on the Nature and Principles of True Freedom, Shewing that the Design and Conduct of the Americans tend only to Tyranny and Slavery.* 3d ed. London, 1776.

[Sewall,] *Americans Roused*
[Jonathan Sewall,] *The Americans Roused, in a Cure for the Spleen.* New York, [1775].

[Shaftesbury,] *Person of Quality*
[Anthony Ashley Cooper, earl of Shaftesbury,] *A Letter from a Person of Quality, to his Friend in the Country.* London, 1675.

Sharp, *Legal Means*
Granville Sharp, *The Legal Means of Political Reformation, Proposed in Two Small Tracts.* 8th ed. London, 1797.

[Shebbeare,] *Fifth Letter*
[John Shebbeare,] *A Fifth Letter to the People of England, on the Subversion of the Constitution: And, The Necessity of it's being restored.* 2d ed. London, 1757.

Shepard, "Sovereignty"
Max Adams Shepard, "Sovereignty at the Crossroads: A Study of Bodin," *Political Science Quarterly* 45 (1930): 580–603.

[Sheridan,] *Observations on the Doctrine*
[Charles Francis Sheridan,] *Observations on the Doctrine laid down by Sir William Blackstone, Respecting the extent of the Power of the British Parliament, Particularly with relation to Ireland. In a letter to Sir William Blackstone, with a Postscript Addressed to Lord North Upon the Affairs of that Country.* 2d ed. London, 1779.

[Sheridan,] *Review*
> [Charles Francis Sheridan,] *A Review of the Three Great National Questions Relative to the Declaration of Right, Poynings' Law, and the Mutiny Bill.* Dublin, 1781.

[Shipley,] *Intended Speech*
> [Jonathan Shipley,] *A Speech Intended to have been Spoken on the Bill for Altering the Charter of the Colony of Massachusetts-Bay.* Boston, 1774.

[Shippen,] *Four Speeches*
> [William Shippen,] *Four Speeches Against Continuing the Army, &c. As they were spoken on Several Occasions in the House of Commons.* London, 1732.

Shirley, *Richard Hooker*
> F. J. Shirley, *Richard Hooker and Contemporary Political Ideas.* London, 1949.

Shute, *Election Sermon*
> Daniel Shute, *A Sermon Preached before his Excellency Francis Bernard, Esq.; Governor, his Honor Thomas Hutchinson, Esq; Lieutenant-Governor, the Honourable His Majesty's Council, and the Honourable House of Representatives, of the Province of the Massachusetts-Bay in New-England, May 25th, 1768.* Boston, 1768.

[Sinclair,] *Lucubrations*
> [Sir John Sinclair,] *Lucubrations During a Short Recess.* London, 1782.

Smith, *Appeals*
> Joseph H. Smith, *Appeals to the Privy Council from the American Plantations.* New York. 1950.

Smith, *English Legal System*
> Joseph H. Smith, *The English Criminal Law in Early America,* in *The English Legal System: Carryover to the Colonies: Papers Read at the Clark Library Seminar November 3, 1973* (1975).

Smith, "1758 Pennsylvania Brief"
> William Smith, "Brief in Matter of Smith," "Law and Liberty: In the Matter of Provost William Smith of Philadelphia, 1758," *William and Mary Quarterly* 38 (1981): 681–701.

Smith, *Writs of Assistance*
> M. H. Smith, *The Writs of Assistance Case.* Berkeley, Calif., 1978.

Society for Constitutional Information
> Two publications distributed by the Society for Constitutional Information without title, imprint, or binding. The copies at the Huntington Library, San Marino, Calif., are numbered, for 1782, rare book 310802 and, for 1783, rare book 305204.

Somers, *Security of Englishmen's Lives*
John Lord Somers, *The Security of Englishmen's Lives: Or, the Trust, Power and Duty of Grand Juries of England Explained according to the Fundamentals of the English Government, and the Declaration of the same made in Parliament by many Statutes. First printed in the Year 1681.* London, 1766.

Somers' Tracts
A Collection of Scarce and Valuable Tracts, on the Most Interesting and Entertaining Subjects: But Chiefly such as Relate to the History and Constitution of these Kingdoms. Selected from an Infinite Number in Print and Manuscript, in the Royal, Cotton, Sion, and other Public, as well as Private, Libraries; Particularly that of the Late Lord Somers. Edited by Walter Scott. Vols. 4–6. London, 1809–15.

South-Carolina Gazette
(Weekly newspaper, Charles Town, S.C.)

Speeches
Speeches of the Governors of Massachusetts From 1765 to 1775; And the Answers of the House of Representatives to the Same; with their Resolutions and Addresses for that Period. Boston, 1818.

Stanlis, *Burke and Natural Law*
Peter J. Stanlis, *Edmund Burke and the Natural Law*. Ann Arbor, Mich., 1965.

State Trials
A Complete Collection of State Trials and Proceedings for High Treason and Other Crimes and Misdemeanors From the Earliest Period to the Year 1783, With Notes and Other Illustrations. Compiled by T. B. Howell. 34 vols. London, 1816–28.

Stearns, *View of the Controversy*
William Stearns, *A View of the Controversy subsisting between Great-Britain and the American Colonies. A Sermon, Preached at a Fast, in Marlborough in Massachusetts-Bay. On Thursday May 11, 1775. Agreeable to a Recommendation of the Provincial Congress.* Watertown, Mass., 1775.

Steinberg, *Idea of Consent*
Jules Steinberg, *Locke, Rousseau, and the Idea of Consent: An Inquiry into the Liberal-Democratic Theory of Political Obligations.* Westport, Conn., 1978.

[Stephens,] *Modest Reply*
[William Stephens,] *A Modest Reply to the Unanswerable Answer to Mr. Hoadly. With Some Considerations on Dr. Sacheverell's Sermon before the Lord Mayor, Novemb. 5, 1709.* London, 1709.

Stevens, *Election Sermon*
> Benjamin Stevens, *A Sermon Preached at Boston, Before the Great and General Court or Assembly of the Province of the Massachusetts Bay in New England, May 27. 1761. Being the Day appointed by Royal Charter for the Election of his Majesty's Council for said Province.* Boston, 1761.

Stone, "Results of Revolutions"
> Lawrence Stone, "The Results of the English Revolutions of the Seventeenth Century," in *Three British Revolutions: 1641, 1688, 1776.* Edited by J. G. A. Pocock. Princeton, N.J., 1980, pp. 23–108.

[Strafford,] *Briefe and Perfect Relation*
> [Thomas Wentworth, earl of Strafford,] *A Briefe and Perfect Relation, of the Answeres and Replies of Thomas Earle of Strafford; To the Articles exhibited against him, by the House of Commons on the thirteenth of April, An. Dom. 1641.* London, 1647.

[Stuart,] *Historical Dissertation*
> [Gilbert Stuart,] *An Historical Dissertation Concerning the Antiquity of the English Constitution.* Edinburgh, 1768.

Sullivan, *Lectures on the Constitution*
> Francis Stoughton Sullivan, *Lectures on the Constitution and Laws of England: With a Commentary on Magna Charta, and Illustrations of Many of the English Statutes. To which Authorities are added, and a Discourse is prefixed, concerning the Laws and Government of England by Gilbert Stuart, LL.D.* 2d ed. London, 1776.

Sydney, *Discourses Concerning Government*
> Algernon Sydney, *Discourses Concerning Government*, reprinted in *The Works of Algernon Sydney: New ed.* London, 1772, pp. 1–542.

[Talbot,] *Speech in Lords*
> [William Talbot,] *The Bishop of Oxford His Speech in the House of Lords on the First Article of the Impeachment of Dr. Henry Sacheverell.* London, 1710.

Tanner, *Constitutional Conflicts*
> J. R. Tanner, *English Constitutional Conflicts of the Seventeenth Century, 1603–1689.* Cambridge, England, 1971.

Taylor, "Mauduit-Pamphleteer"
> Robert J. Taylor, "Israel Mauduit: Antirevolutionary Pamphleteer," in *The Colonial Legacy: Volume I, Loyalist Historians.* Edited by Lawrence H. Leder. New York, 1971, pp. 118–34.

Thacher, *Sentiments*
> Oxenbridge Thacher, *The Sentiments of a British American* (1764), reprinted in Bailyn, *Pamphlets* 1:490–98.

They Preached Liberty
    They Preached Liberty: With an Introductory Essay and Biographical Sketches by Franklin P. Cole. Indianapolis, [1977].

Thomas, "British Imperial Policy"
    Robert Paul Thomas, "A Quantitative Approach to the Study of the Effects of British Imperial Policy Upon Colonial Welfare: Some Preliminary Findings," *Journal of Economic History* 25 (1965): 615–38.

Thompson, *Whigs and Hunters*
    E. P. Thompson, *Whigs and Hunters: The Origin of the Black Act.* New York, 1975.

Thomson, *Constitutional History*
    Mark A. Thomson, *A Constitutional History of England 1642 to 1801.* London, 1938.

Thornton, "Introduction and Notes"
    John Wingate Thornton, "Introduction and Notes" to *Pulpit of American Revolution.*

Throop, *Thanksgiving Sermon*
    Benjamin Throop, *A Thanksgiving Sermon, Upon the Occasion, of the glorious News of the repeal of the Stamp Act; Preached in New-Concord, in Norwich, June 26, 1766.* New London, Conn., 1766.

Tierney, *Religion, Law, and Growth*
    Brian Tierney, *Religion, Law, and the Growth of Constitutional Thought 1150–1650.* Cambridge, England, 1982.

Toohey, *Liberty and Empire*
    Robert E. Toohey, *Liberty and Empire: British Radical Solutions to the American Problem 1774–1776.* Lexington, Ky., 1978.

Tooke, *Letter on Reform*
    John Horne Tooke, *A Letter on Parliamentary Reform; Containing the Sketch of a Plan.* 2d ed. London, [178?].

[Towers,] *Juries as Judges*
    [Joseph Towers,] *An Enquiry into the Question, Whether Juries are, or are not, Judges of Law, as well as of Fact; With a particular Reference to the Case of Libels.* London, 1764.

[Towers,] *Letter to Wesley*
    [Joseph Towers,] *A Letter to the Rev. Mr. John Wesley; In Answer to his late Pamphlet, Entitled, "Free Thoughts on the Present State of Public Affairs."* London, 1771.

[Towers,] *Observations on Liberty*
    [Joseph Towers,] *Observations on Public Liberty, Patriotism, Ministerial*

Despotism, and National Grievances. With Some Remarks on Riots, Petitions, Loyal Addresses, and Military Execution. London, 1769.

Town and Country Magazine
> *The Town and Country Magazine; or Universal Repository of Knowledge, Instruction, and Entertainment.* (Monthly magazine, London.)

Trial of Daniel Disney
> *The Trial of Daniel Disney, Esq.* Quebec, 1767.

Trial of Sacheverell
> *The Tryal of Dr. Henry Sacheverell, before the House of Peers, For High Crimes and Misdemeanors; Upon an Impeachment by the Knights, Citizens and Burgesses in Parliament Assembled, in the Name of themselves, and of all the Commons of Great Britain: Begun in Westminster Hall the 27th Day of February, 1709/10; and from thence continu'd by several Adjournments until the 23d Day of March following.* London, 1710.

Trumbull, *Discourse at New Haven*
> Benjamin Trumbull, *Discourse, Delivered at the Anniversary Meeting of the Freemen of the Town of New-Haven, April 12, 1773.* New Haven, Conn., 1773.

Tuck, *Natural Rights Theories*
> Richard Tuck, *Natural Rights Theories: Their Origin and Development.* Cambridge, England, 1979.

Tucker, *Election Sermon*
> John Tucker, *A Sermon Preached at Cambridge, Before his Excellency Thomas Hutchinson, Esq; Governor; His Honor Andrew Oliver, Esq; Lieutenant-Governor, the Honorable His Majesty's Council, and the Honorable House of Representatives, of the Province of the Massachusetts-Bay in New England, May 29th, 1771. Being the Anniversary for the Election of His Majesty's Council for the Province.* Boston, 1771.

Tucker, *Four Letters to Shelburne*
> [Josiah Tucker'] *Four Letters on Important National Subjects, Addressed to the Right Honourable the Earl of Shelburne, His Majesty's First Lord Commissioner of the Treasury.* 2d ed. London, 1773.

Tucker, *Tract Five*
> Josiah Tucker, *Tract V. The Respective Pleas and Arguments of the Mother Country, and of the Colonies, Distinctly Set Forth; and the Imposibility of a Compromise of Differences, or a Mutual Concession of Rights, Plainly Demonstrated. With a Prefatory Epistle to the Plenipotentiaries of the late Congress at Philadelphia.* London, 1775.

Tucker, *Treatise*
> Josiah Tucker, *A Treatise Concerning Civil Government, In Three Parts.* London, 1781.

Tully, *Discourse on Property*
James Tully, *A Discourse on Property: John Locke and His Adversaries.* Cambridge, England, 1980.

Turner, *Election Sermon*
Charles Turner, *A Sermon Preached Before His Excellency Thomas Hutchinson, Esq; Governor: The Honourable His Majesty's Council, and the Honourable House of Representatives, of the Province of the Massachusetts-Bay in New-England, May 26th, 1773. Being the Anniversary of the Election of His Majesty's Council for said Province.* Boston, 1773.

Twysden, *Certaine Considerations*
Sir Roger Twysden, *Certaine Considerations Upon the Government of England.* Camden Society, vol. 45. London, 1849.

[Twysden,] *Commoners Liberty*
[Sir Roger Twysden,] *The Commoners Liberty: or, The English-Mans Birth-Right.* N.i., 1648.

Tyrrell, *Politica*
James Tyrrell, *Bibliotheca Politica: Or, An Enquiry into the Antient Constitution of the English Government, With Respect to the Just Extent of the Regal Power, and the Rights and Liberties of the Subject.* London, 1718.

Ubbelohde, *Vice-Admiralty*
Carl Ubbelohde, *The Vice-Admiralty Courts and the American Revolution.* Chapel Hill, N.C., 1960.

Valentine, *Lord North*
Alan Valentine, *Lord North.* 2 vols. Norman, Okla., 1967.

Vattel, *Law of Nations*
Emmerich de Vattel, *The Law of Nations; or, Principles of the Law of Nature: Applied to the Conduct and Affairs of Nations and Sovereigns.* Dublin, 1792.

Viner, "Possessive Individualism"
Jacob Viner, "'Possessive Individualism' as Original Sin," *Canadian Journal of Economics and Political Science* 29 (1963): 548–66.

Walsh, *Appeal from the Judgments*
Robert Walsh, Jr., *An Appeal from the Judgments of Great Britain Respecting the United States of America. Part First, Containing an Historical Outline of their Merits and Wrongs as Colonies; and Strictures upon the Calumnies of the British Writers.* 2d ed. Philadelphia, 1819.

Warrington, *Works*
Henry Booth, earl of Warrington, *The Works of the Right Honourable Henry late L[ord] Delamer, and Earl Warrington.* London, 1694.

[Watson,] *Answer to Disquisition*
[Richard Watson,] *An Answer to the Disquisition on Government and Civil Liberty; in a Letter to the author of Disquisitions on Several Subjects.* London, 1782.

West, *Election Sermon*
Samuel West, *A Sermon Preached Before the Honorable Council, and the Honorable House of Representatives, of the Colony of the Massachusetts-Bay, in New-England. May 29th, 1776. Being the Anniversary for the Election of the Honorable Council for the Colony.* Boston, 1776.

[Whately,] *Considerations on Trade*
[Thomas Whately,] *Considerations on the Trade and Finances of this Kingdom, and on the Measures of Administration, with Respect to those great National Objects since the Conclusion of the Peace.* 3d ed. London, 1769.

[Whately,] *Regulations Lately Made*
[Thomas Whately,] *The Regulations Lately Made Concerning the Colonies and the Taxes imposed Upon Them, Considered.* London, 1765.

[Whitby,] *Historical Account*
[Daniel Whitby,] *An Historical Account of Some Things Relating to the Nature of the English Government, and the Conceptions which our Forefathers had of it.* London, 1690.

White, *Coke and the Grievances*
Stephen D. White, *Sir Edward Coke and "The Grievances of the Commonwealth," 1621–1628.* Chapel Hill, N.C., 1979.

White, *Connecticut Election Sermon*
Stephen White, *Civil Rulers Gods by Office, and the Duties of such Considered and Enforced. A Sermon Preached before the General Assembly of the Colony of Connecticut, at Hartford, on the Day of their Anniversary Election, May the 12th, 1763.* New London, Conn., 1763.

Wickwire, *Subministers*
Franklin B. Wickwire, *British Subministers and Colonial America 1763–1783.* Princeton, N.J., 1966.

Wilkes, *English Liberty*
John Wilkes, *English Liberty: Being a Collection of Interesting Tracts, From the Year 1762 to 1769. Containing the Private Correspondence, Public Letters, Speeches, and Addresses, of John Wilkes, Esq. Humbly Dedicated to the King.* London, [1770].

[Wilkes,] *Letter to Johnson*
[John Wilkes,] *A Letter to Samuel Johnson, L.L.D.* [London,] 1770.

Willcox, *Age of Aristocracy*
William B. Willcox, *The Age of Aristocracy 1688–1830.* Lexington, Mass., 1966.

[Willes,] *Present Constitution*
[Sir John Willes,] *The Present Constitution, and the Protestant Succession Vindicated: In Answer to a late Book Entituled, The Hereditary Right of the Crown of England Asserted, &c.* London, 1714.

William Peere Williams
Reports of Cases Argued and Determined in the High Court of Chancery. 3 vols. 5th ed. London, 1793.

Williams, *Election Sermon*
Abraham Williams, *A Sermon Preach'd at Boston, Before the Great and General Court or Assembly of the Province of the Massachusetts-Bay in New-England, May 26, 1762. Being the Day appointed by Royal Charter, for the Election of His Majesty's Council for said Province.* Boston, 1762.

[Williams,] *Essential Rights*
[Elisha Williams,] *The Essential Rights and Liberties of Protestants. A Seasonable Plea for the Liberty of Conscience, and the Right of private Judgment, In Matters of Religion, Without any Controul from human Authority. Being a Letter, from a Gentleman in the Massachusetts-Bay to his Friend in Connecticut.* Boston, 1744.

[Williams,] *Letters on Liberty*
[David Williams,] *Letters on Political Liberty. Addressed to a Member of the English House of Commons, on his being Chosen into the Committee of an Associating County.* London, 1782.

[Williams,] *Letters on Liberty (3d ed.)*
[David Williams,] *Letters on Political Liberty, and the Principles of the English and Irish Projects of Reform.* 3d ed. London, 1789.

[Williamson,] *Plea of the Colonies*
[Hugh Williamson,] *The Plea of the Colonies On the Charges brought against them by Lord Mansfield, and Others in a letter to His Lordship.* Philadelphia, 1777.

Willman, "Blackstone and Caroline Law"
Robert Willman, "Blackstone and the 'Theoretical Perfection' of English Law in the Reign of Charles II." *Historical Journal* 26 (1983):39–70.

Wills, *Inventing America*
Garry Wills, *Inventing America: Jefferson's Declaration of Independence.* Garden City, N.Y., 1978.

Wilson, *Considerations*
James Wilson, *Considerations on the Nature and Extent of the Legislative Authority of the British Parliament (1774),* reprinted in *The Works of James Wilson* 2. Edited by Robert Green McCloskey. Cambridge, Mass., 1967, pp. 721–46.

Wilson, "Speech in the Pennsylvania Convention"
James Wilson, "Speech in the Pennsylvania Convention, January 1775," in Beloff, *Debate*, pp. 178–79.

Wilson, "Speech of 1775"
James Wilson, "Speech Delivered in the Convention for the Province of Pennsylvania," in *The Works of James Wilson* 2. Edited by Robert Green McCloskey. Cambridge, Mass., 1967, pp. 747–58.

Wood, *Creation*
Gordon S. Wood, *The Creation of the American Revolution 1776–1787*. Chapel Hill, N.C., 1969.

[Wood,] *Institute of the Laws*
[Thomas Wood,] *A New Institute of the Imperial or Civil Law*. London, 1704.

Wooddeson, *Jurisprudence*
Richard Wooddeson, *Elements of Jurisprudence Treated of in the Preliminary Part of a Course of Lectures on the Law of England*. Dublin, 1792.

Wright, *Grand Jury Speech*
John Wright, *The Speech of John Wright, Esq; One of the Magistrates of Lancaster County, to the Court and Grand-Jury, on his Removal from the Commission of the Peace at the Quarter-Sessions held at Lancaster for the said County in May 1741*. [Philadelphia, 1741.]

Wynne, *Eunomus*
Edward Wynne, *Eunomus: or, Dialogues Concerning the Law and Constitution of England with an Essay on Dialogue*. 2d ed. 2 vols. London, 1785.

Wyvill, *Defence of Price*
Christopher Wyvill, *A Defence of Dr. Price, and the Reformers of England*. London, 1792.

Wyvill, *State of Representation*
Christopher Wyvill, *A State of the Representation of the People of England, on the Principles of Mr. Pitt in 1785; with an Annexed State of Additional Propositions*. York, 1793.

Yale, "Hobbes and Hale"
D. E. C. Yale, "Hobbes and Hale on Law, Legislation and the Sovereign," *Cambridge Law Journal* 31 (1972):121–56.

York Address of January 1781
An Address From the Committee of Association of the County of York, to the Electors of Great-Britain. To which are prefixed the Resolutions of that Committee, at their Meetings, Held on the 3rd and 4th of January, 1781, and the Instrument of Instructions to their Deputies. N.i., n.d.

[Yorke,] *Forfeitures for High Treason*
[Charles Yorke,] *Considerations on the Law of Forfeitures, for High Treason. With an Appendix concerning Estates-Tail in Scotland.* 4th ed. London, 1775.

Young, *Constitution Safe*
Arthur Young, *The Constitution Safe without Reform: Containing Some Remarks on a Book Entitled the Commonwealth in Danger, by John Cartwright, Esq.* Bury St. Edmund's, England, 1795.

Young, *Political Arithmetic*
Arthur Young, *Political Arithmetic. Containing Observations on the Present State of Great Britain; and the Principles of her Policy in the Encouragement of Agriculture.* London, 1774.

[Young,] *Political Essays*
[Arthur Young,] *Political Essays Concerning the Present State of the British Empire.* London, 1772.

[Zubly,] *Humble Enquiry*
[John J. Zubly,] *An Humble Enquiry into the Nature of the Dependency of the American Colonies upon the Parliament of Great-Britain, and the Right of Parliament to lay Taxes on the said Colonies.* [Charles Town, S.C.,] 1769.

Zubly, *Law of Liberty*
John J. Zubly, *The Law of Liberty. A Sermon on American Affairs, Preached at the Opening of the Provincial Congress of Georgia. Addressed to the Right Honourable the Earl of Dartmouth.* Philadelphia, 1775.

[Zubly,] *Right to Tax*
[John Joachim Zubly,] *Great Britain's Right to Tax her Colonies. Placed in the Clearest Light, by a Swiss.* London, 1774.

NOTES

Introduction

1 Speech of John Wilkes, Commons Debates, 26 October 1775, *Scots Magazine* 37 (1775): 613; *Freeman Letters*, p. 20; Grand Jury charge, March term 1769, Quincy, *Reports*, p. 306.

2 Failed to define: Leder, *Liberty*, p. 126; Excise: *Gentleman's Magazine* 34 (1764): 115; Press: Anon., *Considerations on Information*, p. 2; Benefit: Anon., *To the Princess of Wales*, p. 52; Abrogate: Anon., *Fact without Fallacy*, p. 26. Also, freedom of religion did not mean separation of church from government, but that government would not impose doctrine. West, *Election Sermon*, pp. 44–45.

3 Leder, *Liberty*, p. 146; "Irrelevance of the Declaration," pp. 47–69.

4 *Freeman Letters*, p. 58; [Meredith,] *Remarks on Taxation*, p. 6; "Junius," *Junius*, 1:iii; Cartwright, *Appeal on Constitution*, p. 29; Cartwright, *Constitution Produced*, p. 31 (quoting Letter to Almon [1764]).

5 Concord Returns, 22 October 1776, Handlin, *Popular Sources*, p. 153; Bridge: *They Preached Liberty*, p. 71; *Political Register* 7 (1770): 152; [Hartley,] *Appeal to Juries*, p. 4; Petition of Middlesex, 30 March 1770, *Political Register* 6 (1770): 301; Dickinson quoted in Aldridge, "Paine and Dickinson," p. 135. See also Burke quoted in Stanlis, *Burke and Natural Law*, pp. 54–55.

6 Letter from William Jones to Thomas Yates, 7 June 1782, *Society for Constitutional Information,*" p. 35 (also in Cartwright, *Constitution Produced*, p. 34); Robinson, *Political Catechism*, p. 38; Abingdon, *Thoughts on Burke's Letter*, p. 24.

7 Anon., *Conduct of a Gentleman*, p. 51; Letter 95, 22 September 1722, "Cato's Letters, at 225; Speech of 28 January 1729, [Shippen,] *Four Speeches*, pp. 37–38.

CHAPTER ONE: THE ENGLISHNESS OF RIGHTS

1 Boston Resolves, 8 May 1770, *Boston Evening-Post*, 14 May 1770, p. 3, col. 2; Stamp Act Petition and Stamp Act Declarations, October 1765, Morgan, *Prologue*, pp. 64, 62; Letter of Lebanon Town Meeting, 11 April 1768, *South-Carolina Gazette*, 13 June 1768, p. 2, col. 2; Letter from Virginia Committee to Agent, 28 July 1764, 12 "Proceedings Committee of Correspondence" 12:9; Letter from New Hampshire Representatives to Virginia Burgesses, 1768, *Documents of New Hampshire*, p. 190.

2 [Lee,] *Speech Intended*, p. 2.

3 *Scots Magazine* 35 (1763): 393.

4 New York Resolves, 18 December 1765, *New York Journal of Votes*, p. 807. See also Resolutions of North Carolina Convention, 27 August 1774, *American Archives* (4th Ser.) 1:734; Southwick Instructions, February 1769, *Cambridge Magazine*, p. 115; Speech of George Johnstone, Commons Debates, 16 December 1774, *Gentleman's Magazine* 44 (1774): 597–98.

5 Anon., *British Liberties*, p. 161–62; Blackstone, *Commentaries* 1:6, 126–27, 129.

6 [Galloway,] *Political Reflections*, p. 13; Tucker, *Election Sermon*, p. 43; Anon., *Rights Asserted*, p. 12; Anon., *North-Country Poll*, p. 2. See also Fortescue-Aland, "Preface," pp. xxxiv–xxxv; Shute, *Election Sermon*, pp. 51–52; [Bolingbroke,] *Dissertation*, p. 206.

7 White, *Connecticut Election Sermon*, p. 25. See also *London Journal* 769 (23 March 1733/34): 1, col. 1; Anon., *Letter to Freemen of New York*, p. 4.

8 [Young,] *Political Essays*, p. 50; [Johnson,] *Important Observations*, p. 28; Johnson, *Integrity and Piety*, p. 13. See also Lockwood, *Worth and Excellence*, p. 18.

9 Anon., *Critical Review of Liberties*, p. 11; [Keld,] *Polity of England*, p. 426; Fletcher, *Vindication of Wesley*, p. 66. Astonishingly, most writers boasting of British rights asserted that their blessings rained equally on the Irish. [Brooke,] *Liberty and Common Sense*, p. 10.

10 Gordon, *Evil Speaking*, p. 14; Dodgson, *Assize Sermon*, p. 11.

11 Speech of Humphry Sydenham, Commons Debates, 23 January 1745, *Parliamentary History* 13: 1064; Anon., *Compleat View*, p. 31. For a remarkable example of cherishing rights, see *Collection of Letters*, p. 222–30.

12 Petition of New York Assembly to House of Lords, 31 December 1768, *Boston Post-Boy*, 1 May 1769, p. 1, col. 2; Anon., *Plea for Poor*, p. 5. See also Cumings, *Thanksgiving Sermon*, p. 19.

13 Anon., *Remarks upon a Discourse*, p. 9. Similarly, see *Gazette & News-Letter*, 9 March 1775, p. 1, col. 1.

14 Address to Inhabitants of Quebec, 26 October 1774, *Commemorative Ceremony*, p. 122.

CHAPTER TWO: RIGHTS IN GENERAL

1 *Gentleman's Magazine* 34 (1764): 105.

2 Resolves of Maryland Convention, 14 December 1774, *London Magazine* 44 (1775): 130; "Parliamentary History," *London Magazine* 45 (1776): 402. For standing army and police role, see *In Defiance of the Law*, pp. 172–228.

3 Address of the Provincial Congress of Georgia to President Archibald Bullock, 7 June 1776, *Remembrancer of 1776: Part II*, p. 311; Declaration of Rights, 14 October 1774, *Journal of the First Congress*, p. 62; Georgia Commons House Resolves, January 1775, *American Archives* (4th ser.) 1:1157.

4 Resolves of the Georgia Commons House of Assembly, January 1775, *American Archives* (4th ser.) 1:1157; Morgan, "Colonial Ideas," p. 314; Address to Quebec, 26 October 1774, *Journal of the First Congress*, p. 122; Virginia Resolves, Morgan, *Prologue*, pp. 47–48.

5 Declaration of Rights, 14 October 1774, *Journal of the First Congress*, pp. 60–63; Resolves of the Delaware Convention, 2 August 1774, *American Archives* (4th ser.) 1:667–68; Resolves of Connecticut Representatives, May 1774, *Public Records of Connecticut* 14:348.

6 Letters to British and to Quebec, 5 September and 26 October 1774, *Extracts of Votes and Proceedings* (Rivington), pp. 12, 16, 26. For importance of "arbitrary," see "In Legitimate Stirps," at 459–99; "Irrelevance of Declaration," pp. 85–87.

7 Memorial to the Inhabitants of the Colonies, 21 October 1774, *Extracts from the Votes and Proceedings* (Gaine), p. 41; Boast: Anon., *Rights of People to Petition*, p. 19; Charles I: *Answer to a Book*, p. 28; Strafford impeachment and Charles II: Anon., *Rights of People to Petition*, pp. 23, 24; James II: Declaration of the Nobility, Gentry, and Commonalty assembled at Nottingham, 22 November 1688, [Bohun,] *Desertion*, p. 78; Memorial: *Parliamentary History* 5:1255; Resolve: [Musgrave,] *Letter from a Member*, p. 83n.

8 Rokeby quoted in *Gentleman's Magazine* 45 (1775): 34; *York Address of January 1781*, p. 9; *Collection of Letters* 1:64. Similarly, see *Select Collection of Letters* 1:92, 113; Missing, *Letter to Mansfield on Instructions*, pp. 9–13.

9 Valentine, *Lord North* 1:201; Letter from the Lord Chamberlain to Lord Mayor, 12 April 1775, and Letter from Lord Mayor to Lord Chamberlain, 2 May 1775, *London Magazine* 44 (1775): 210, 263; First resolution: *Gentleman's Magazine* 45 (1775): 348. Similar resolves: *Petition in Favour of Americans*, also printed in *Remembrancer for 1775*, p. 108.

10 "[I]t is the Right of the *British* Subjects in these Colonies, to Petition the King, or either House of Parliament." Declarations of the Stamp Act Congress,

Morgan, *Prologue*, p. 63. Similarly, South Carolina Resolves, 29 November 1765, ibid., p. 59.

11 "Extract of a Letter from London, dated February 16, 1765," *South-Carolina Gazette*, 20 July 1765, p. 2, col. 1; Cooper, *Crisis*, p. 17. A second American whig complaint was that their assemblies were frequently unable to draft petitions because they were not permitted to meet and the reason that they were not allowed to meet was to prevent their petitioning. "Virginius," June 1775, *American Archives* (4th ser.) 2:1130; Resolves of Second Provincial Convention, 7 April 1775, *North Carolina Colonial Records* 9:1185.

12 Thomson, *Constitutional Law*, p. 205; Speeches of Yonge, Winnington, and Sandys, Commons Debates, 8 March 1733, *Parliamentary History* 8:1261–66; Speech of Sir John Barnard, Commons Debates, 8 March 1733, *Gentleman's Magazine* 3 (1733): 510; Walsh, *Appeal from the Judgments*, pp. 9–10.

13 [Ramsay,] *Thoughts on the Nature of Government*, p. 35n.; Letter from Charles Carroll to Henry Graves, 15 September 1765, *Letters of Charles Carroll*, p. 90; Letter from London, *Massachusetts Gazette* (Supplement), 23 January 1766, p. 1, col. 3; Letter from Jasper Mauduit to the Speaker, 8 April 1763, *Mauduit Letters*, p. 100; Speech of Robert Viner, Commons Debates, 9 December 1754, *Parliamentary History* 15:376.

14 Speech of Lord North, Commons Debates, 15 May 1775, *American Archives* (4th ser.) 1:1819; Fox, *Speeches* 1:42; [Hutchinson,] *Strictures Upon the Declaration*, p. 29; *Gazette & News-Letter*, 9 May 1765, p. 3, col. 1, and 4 April 1765, p. 3, col. 2; Kammen, *Rope*, p. 172–73; Langford, *Rockingham Administration*, p. 153.

15 "Journal of the Continental Congress," entry for 25 July 1775, *Monthly Review* 54 (1776): 155.

16 Georgia Resolves, January 1775, *American Archives* (4th ser.) 1:1157; Letter from Sir William Jones to Thomas Yates, 7 June 1782, *Society for Constitutional Information*, p. 36; Cartwright, *Constitution Produced*, pp. 34–35; [Fowle,] *Appendix to Eclipse*, p. 17; Maryland Resolves, 2 November 1765, *Maryland Votes and Proceedings* (November 1765), p. 15. See also Pole, *Pursuit of Equality*, pp. 15–16.

17 Anon., *Foundation of British Liberty*, p. 7; [Serle,] *Americans against Liberty*, p. 11. See also Thompson, *Whigs and Hunters*, p. 266; Dickinson, *Liberty and Property*, pp. 89–90 (quoting Locke).

18 Price, "Introduction to Two Tracts," p. vii; *Political Register* 2 (1768): 285; Anon., *State Necessity*, p. 6; Mayhew, *Election Sermon*, p. 20; William Markham, "Sermon Preached," reprinted in Peach, *Richard Price*, p. 263. See also [Meredith,] *Question Stated*, pp. 53–54. For other eighteenth-century aspects of the "rule of law," see London Instructions quoted in Brewer, "Wilkites and the law," p. 163 (similarly see South Carolina Resolves, 8 July 1774, *American Archives* (4th ser.) 1:525); [Auckland,] *Principles of Penal Law*, p. 84; *Scots Magazine* 30 (1768), p. 344; [Wilkes,] *Letter to Johnson*, pp. 42–43.

19 Middlesex Resolves, quoted in Rossiter, *Political Thought*, pp. 124–25; Declaration of Rights, 14 October 1774, *Journal of the First Congress*, pp. 62–63.

20 Letter to British People, 5 September 1774, *Extracts from Votes and Proceedings* (Rivington), p. 14; [Forster,] *Answer to the Question Stated*, p. 4; Prynne, *Seasonable Vindication*, pp. 60–64; "Declaration of 1689," p. 14; Logan, *Antidote*, p. 8; Anon., *Letter to Freemen of New York*, p. 4; Lovejoy, *Glorious Revolution*, pp. 116–17; Howard, *Road to Runnymede*, pp. 64, 182.

CHAPTER THREE: THE RIGHT TO PROPERTY

1 Anon., *Rights of East-India*, p. 23; Tucker, *Treatise*, p. 98 (quoting Molyneux); De Lolme, *Constitution: New Edition*, p. 100. It has been overlooked how closely the arguments of British defenders of the East India Company paralleled American whig arguments against taxation. The reason they did was the unity of constitutional principles. See, e. g., Petition of East-India General Court to Commons, 3 April 1773, *Gentleman's Magazine* 43 (1773): 247–48; "The British American, No. VI," 7 July 1774, *American Archives* (4th ser.) 1:521.

2 Speech of Sir Dudley Digges to the Lords, 7 April 1628, Popofsky, "Habeas Corpus," p. 266, n. 40 (for a similar speech in which Digges used the term "common law," see Speech of Sir Dudley Digges, 3 April 1628, *Conference of Both Houses*, p. 3); Nenner, *Colour of Law*, p. 37 (quoting duke of Buckingham); [Robertson,] *Liberty, Property, and Religion*, p. 4.

3 Lord Keeper Sir John Finch was just one of several judges impeached for rulings "against . . . the Subjects Right of Property." Articles of Impeachment, 14 January 1640/41, Rushworth, *Historical Collections: Third Part* 1:138. Similarly, see Articles of the Irish Commons Charging High Treason against Sir Richard Bolton, Lord Chancellor et al., 1641, ibid., p. 219. Even Roger Mainwaring was accused of attacking "the property rights of the subject." Cragg, *Freedom and Authority*, p. 96.

4 Anon., *Letter to Freeholders* (1742), p. 6; Rogers, *Empire and Liberty*, p. 42 (quoting Governor Robert Morris). In 1728, Maryland's Daniel Dulany wrote: "I have no Notion of a Certainty, in any Thing, that I hold by so slender a Tenure, as the Will of another; but think it vain, and arrogant, to call it Mine." Dulany, *English Laws*, p. 13.

5 Brown, *Estimate of Manners*, p. 15; "Book Review," *Monthly Review* 46 (1772): 584–90; Blackstone, *Commentaries* 2:2; see also "Book Review," *Critical Review* 27 (1769): 47; Hay, "Property," p. 19; Kramnick, *Bolingbroke's Circle*, pp. 248–49.

6 Marcham, *Constitutional History*, p. 199. For applications of the principle, see Plumb, *Growth of Political Stability*, p. 26; *In Defiance of the Law*, p. 142. For the contrary, see Rous, *Thoughts on Government*, p. 27.

7 Letter from *Junius* to John Wilkes, 7 September 1771, *Gentleman's Magazine* 41 (1771): 586; Boorstin, *Mysterious Science of Law*, p. 175. For other contemporary assumptions that the owner of rotten boroughs "owned" a vested property right that could not be taken without compensation, see Tooke, *Letter on Reform*, pp. 14–15; [Sinclair,] *Lucubrations*, p. 21; Letter from

C. Wyvill to the Belfast Committee, 1783, *Collection of Irish Letters*, pp. 35–36; [Almon,] *Free Parliaments*, p. 30. For the contrary, see Carysfort, *Letter to Huntingdonshire*, p. 4; [Carysfort,] *Serious Address*, pp. 22–23.

8 Davis, *Reports*, preface, p. 20; Hill, *Intellectual Origins*, p. 230; Speech of Commissary-General Henry Ireton, 29 October 1647, "Putney Debates," p. 69. For similar arguments that property is the product of positive law, see Harrington, *Prerogative of Popular Government*, p. 458; Halifax, *Charles II*, p. 73; Hoadly, *Works* 2:113; Priestly, *First Principles*, pp. 41, 42. See also Hart, "Bentham and America," p. 550. For the contrary, see Locke, *Two Treatises*, book 1, sec. 92.

9 It is sometimes said that colonial whigs thought property was derived from nature, not from positive law. This interpretation would be true only if we took our law from the clergy or letter writers and not from lawyers or public officials. E.g., [Williams,] *Essential Rights*, p. 3; Hobart, *Connecticut Election Sermon*, p. 15; Lord, *Religion and Government*, p. 26; Williams, *Election Sermon*, p. 7. See also Baldwin, *New England Clergy*, p. 48.

10 Viner, "Possessive Individualism," p. 558. For a clear statement of the principle by an American whig, see [Joseph Hawley,] "To the Inhabitants of Massachusetts," 30 March 1775, *American Archives* (4th ser.) 2:248. See also [Lind,] *Thirteenth Parliament*, pp. 55–56.

11 Although it was occasionally said that ownership of property was an exclusive right (Burnet, *Essay upon Government*, p. 22), it was generally understood by lawyers that the right was subject to other claims. Rutherforth, *Natural Law* 1:81–83. For discussion, see Larkin, *Property in Eighteenth Century*, pp. 104, 130; Thompson, *Whigs and Hunters*, p. 241.

12 [Lind,] *Thirteenth Parliament*, p. 56; Burnet, *Sermon . . . 31st of January 1688*, quoted in Breen, *Good Ruler*, p. 155; [Parker,] *Case of Shipmony*, p. 4.

13 Historians: Pocock, "Commons Debates of 1628," p. 332; Leveller: Speech of Colonel Thomas Rainborough, 29 October 1647, "Putney Debates," p. 71; Hill, *Upside Down*, p. 389; Ireton: Speech of 29 October 1647, "Putney Debates," pp. 72, 73; Rule: Twysden, *Certaine Considerations*, p. 82; Prerogative tax: Speech of William Pierrepont to the two Houses on the Impeachment of a Shipmoney Judge, 6 July 1641, in *Somers' Tracts* 4:305. A general seventeenth-century theory of liberty was to balance the subject's property against the Crown's prerogative. Speech of the Speaker to the King, 22 June 1641, Rushworth, *Historical Collections: Third Part* 1:296; Warrington, *Works*, pp. 36–37, 651.

14 Hudson, "Penn's *English Liberties*," p. 581; Breen, *Good Ruler*, p. 183. See also Breen's discussion of a 1678 Boston pamphlet, pp. 119–20.

15 Resolves of the Delaware House of Assembly, 3 June 1766, *Delaware House Minutes* (1765–1770), p. 54; *Independent Reflector*, 3 May 1753, p. 220; Rossiter, *Six Characters*, p. 197 (quoting Bland).

16 Lee, *Appeal to Justice*, p. 14; Speech of John Dickinson, 25 April 1769, *American Gazette*, p. 43; *Boston Gazette*, 22 February 1768, p. 1, col. 2.

17 Association of Members of the Late House of Burgesses, [27 May 1774,] *Papers of Jefferson* 1:107–8; Hill, *Century of Revolution*, p. 107 (quoting Davies).

CHAPTER FOUR: THE RIGHT TO SECURITY

1 Locke, *Two Treatises*, book 2, sec. 124 (also sec. 94); Anon., *British Liberties*, p. lvi (quoting Locke); Anon., *Vindication of the Livery*, p. 5 (citing Locke); [Joseph Hawley,] "To the Inhabitants of Massachusetts," 30 March 1775, *American Archives* (4th ser.) 2:248 (elaborating on Locke); Stone, "Results of Revolutions," pp. 32–33; Morgan, *Birth*, p. 16.

2 Lord, *Connecticut Election Sermon*, p. 27; Anon., *Middle Line*, p. 17; Pym, *Speech of Summing Up*, pp. 18–19; Marcham, *Constitutional History*, p. 243 (quoting Lord Camden). See also Resolves of 24 May 1775, *American Archives* (4th ser.) 1:347; "Grand Jury Charge," Warrington, *Works*, p. 467; Smith "1758 Pennsylvania Brief," p. 694; Bailyn, *Pamphlets* 1:257, 262–63 (quoting Joseph Galloway).

3 "The Cyder-Act," *Gentleman's Magazine* 33 (1763): 446; [Stephens,] *Modest Reply*, p. 13; Mulford, *Speech to New York Assembly*, p. 6; Hobart, *Connecticut Election Sermon*, pp. 6–7, 9. See also Williams, *Election Sermon*, pp. 7–8.

4 Burnet, *Essay upon Government*, p. 20; *London Journal* 694 (14 October 1732): 1, col. 1; "Putney Debates," p. 71; Anon., *Letter to Freeholders* (1742), p. 6. See also Anon., *Representative of London*, p. 5; Anon., *Letter to Member*, p. 6; *Hiberian Magazine* 3 (1773): 66, reprinted in *Gazette & Post-Boy*, 26 July 1773, p. 2, col. 1; Trenchard, Letter 84, 7 July 1722, "Cato's Letters," p. 212; St. John, *Speech or Declaration*, p. 7; Lord Strange's Commons Speech (1742), quoted in Burgh, *Political Disquisitions* 2:64; Hurstfield, *Freedom, Corruption and Government*, p. 73; Pocock, "Commons Debates of 1628," p. 332.

5 [Otis,] "Substance," p. 474; Johannesen, "Dickinson," p. 43.

6 Namier, *Age of Revolution*, p. 36, n. 4; Petition of New York, 18 October 1764, *New York Journal of Votes*, p. 771, Gordon, Letter 68, 3 March 1721, "Cato's Letters," pp. 177–78; [Cluny,] *American Traveller*, pp. 62–64; Quincy, *Observations with Thoughts*, pp. 399–400.

7 Letter from Massachusetts House to Shelburne, 15 January 1768, *Speeches*, p. 139; Letter from Massachusetts House to Agent De Berdt, 12 January 1768, *Speeches*, p. 126; Nowell, *Abraham in Arms* (1678), discussed in Breen, *Good Ruler*, pp. 120, 136; Letter from Abel Stiles to Ezra Stiles, 18 April 1766, Morgan, *Gentle Puritan*, p. 233; Letter from Abel Stiles to Ezra Stiles, 18 April 1766, Namier, *Age of Revolution*, p. 36, n. 4.

CHAPTER FIVE: THE RIGHT TO GOVERNMENT

1 Lutz, *Popular Consent and Control*, p. 39; Genovese, "Book Review," *Harvard Law Review* 91 (1978): 726, 732; Hay, "Property," p. 18; "doctrine:"

Stone, "Results of Revolutions," pp. 36–37; Thompson, *Whigs and Hunters*, pp. 21, 197, 207.

2 Locke, *Two Treatises*, book 2, sec. 27; [Williams,] *Essential Rights*, p. 3; Thompson, *Whigs and Hunters*, p. 244; Dickinson, *Liberty and Property*, p. 318.

3 Kern, *Kingship and Law*, p. 186. But see Duncan Kennedy, "The Structure of Blackstone's Commentaries," *Buffalo Law Review* 28 (1979): 205–382.

4 Burnet, *Essay upon Government*," p. 20; Anon., *Representative of London*, p. 5; Anon., *Vindication of the Livery*, p. 6.

5 *American Archives* (4th ser.) 1:242 (quoting *London Gazetteer*, 7 April 1774); [Ramsay,] *Historical Essay*, p. 197. See also Foster, *Short Essay*, p. 27. For an important American explanation of the constitutional theory as based on contract, see Anon., *Essay upon Government*, pp. 67–68.

6 Trenchard, Letter 100, 27 October 1722, "Cato's Letters," p. 232; Rossiter, *Six Characters*, p. 197 (quoting Bland); Speech of Dickinson, 24 April 1768, *American Gazette*, p. 43.

7 Congress Resolves of 31 July 1775, *Papers of Jefferson* 1:233; Leder, *Liberty*, p. 122; Breen, *Good Ruler*, p. 155.

8 *Boston Gazette*, 4 March 1771, p. 1, col. 1; Middlesex Resolutions, July 1774, *Revolutionary Virginia* 1:144; Burgh, *Political Disquisitions* 2:328; Anon., *To Tax Themselves*, p. 109.

9 See, e.g., Address of Lower House to Governor Eden, 22 November 1771, *Maryland Votes and Proceedings* (1771), p. 65.

10 Langford, *Excise Crisis*, p. 162 (quoting untitled pamphlet).

11 [Knox,] *Extra Official Papers*, appendix, p. 2; [Carysfort,] *Serious Address*, p. 18. The theory that property, not people, was represented was not seriously questioned until near the close of the American Revolution. E.g., [Williams,] *Letters on Liberty*.

12 Gordon, Letter of 20 October 1722, *Cato's Letters* 3:288; Letter from John Adams to James Sullivan, 26 May 1776, *Letters of Delegates to Congress* 4:74; Pocock, *Politics*, p. 91. Some of these theories can be traced back at least to Ireton at Putney. Ireton Speech, 29 October 1647, "Putney Debates," p. 57; Hill, "Norman Yoke," p. 80; Tully, *Discourse on Property*, p. 174; J. R. Pole, *The Seventeenth Century: The Sources of Legislative Power*. Charlottesville, Va., 1969, pp. 18–19.

13 Anon., *Civil Liberty Asserted*, p. 19. A related theory was that "*Power* is founded in *Property*; and, that the *Liberty* of the People grew with their *Possessions*." *Daily Gazetteer* 30 (2 August 1735): 1, col. 2.

14 Resolutions of 26 May 1628, *Commons Debates 1628* 2:138, 125, 132, 142, 135, 141; Propriety: Laslett, "Introduction to Locke," p. 116, n. 14; Larkin, *Property in the Eighteenth Century*, pp. 52–53. In the eighteenth century, law dictionaries defined property not in physical terms but in terms of abstract right. See Jacob, *New Law Dictionary* (1762); Cowell & Manly, *Interpreter* (1701). See also "Book Review," *Monthly Review* 53 (1775): 522; *Demophoon* in *Political Register* 7 (1770): 152; [Rokeby,] *Considerations on the Measures*, p. 12; Anon., *Vindication of the Livery*, p. 6; Anon., *British Liberties*, pp. xxxi–xxxii; Locke, *Two Treatises*, book 2, sec. 138.

15 Hopkins, *Rights*, p. 507; Providence Resolves, 19 January 1774, *Records of Rhode Island* 7:272-73. See also Stearns, *View of the Controversy*, pp. 16-17.

16 New York Petition to the King, 18 October 1764, *New York Journal of Votes*, p. 771; "Junius Americanus" to "Junius," *Political Register* 9 (1771): 325; Speech of John Wilkes, *Hibernian Magazine* 5 (1775): 163. A member of the Middle Temple contended that "the levying taxes in America by the sole authority of a British legislature, whereof America constitutes not one single member, would be the grossest violation of American Property." Canning, *Letter to Hillsborough*, p. 18. See also Philadelphia Resolves, 18 October 1773, *Hibernian Magazine* 4 (1774): 100; Philadelphia Instructions, 30 July 1768, *American Gazette*, p. 90; *Scots Magazine* 30 (1768): 689; *New-London Gazette*, 20 September 1765, quoted in *Boston Evening-Post*, 14 October 1765, p. 1, col. 2.

17 Resolves of Georgia Congress, 10 July 1775, *Remembrancer for 1776: Part I*, p. 12; New York Petition to Commons, 18 October 1764, Morgan, *Prologue*, p. 9. Similarly, see Message from Virginia Burgesses to Massachusetts Representatives, 9 May 1768, *American Gazette*, p. 20; Address of Delaware House to the King, 27 October 1768, *Delaware House Minutes* (1765-1770), p. 168; Instructions of Boston, 24 May 1764, *Boston News-Letter*, 31 May 1764, p. 2, col. 2; Letter from *Boston Gazette*, 24 August 1767, reprinted in *Political Register* 2 (1768): 97.

18 Boston newspaper of 27 June 1774, *American Archives* (4th ser.) 1:488. It must be stressed that the right to property and security were asserted as rights in many situations other than attempts by Parliament to tax. The Boston Port Act and the Massachusetts Government Act of 1774 are only two examples, for which see Connecticut Resolutions, May 1774, ibid., p. 356; North Carolina Resolutions, 27 August 1774, ibid., p. 735; Philadelphia newspaper, 1 June 1774, reprinted in ibid., p. 378; Petition from Natives of America to the King, 19 May 1774, ibid., p. 96; Memorial from New York Assembly to House of Lords, 25 March 1775, ibid., p. 1317; Letter from New York General Committee to the Mayor et al., of London, 5 May 1775, *Addresses and Petitions of Common Council*, p. 86.

CHAPTER SIX: THE JURY RIGHT

1 Care, *English Liberties Boston Edition*, p. 203; Anon., *British Liberties*, p. 373; [Fowle,] *Appendix to Eclipse*, p. 17; [Brooke,] *Liberty and Common-Sense*, p. 1-2; *Monthly Review* 50 (1774): 454 (quoting Wynne, *Eunomus*); William Henry Drayton's Address to Camden District Grand Jury, November Session, 1774, *London Magazine* 44 (1775): 127 (quoting Blackstone); Sullivan, *Lectures on the Constitution*, p. 352; Petition of Mayor et al., to King, 23 June 1774, *London Magazine* 43 (1774): 302; Instructions of Middlesex to John Wilkes, et al., 25 September 1775, Remembrancer of 1775, p. 296; Johnstone, *Speech on American Affairs*, p. 6; Throop, *Thanksgiving Sermon*, p. 11; Anonymous, *The Constitution. With Some Account*

of a Bill lately rejected by the H[ouse] of L[ords]. Number III (London, 1757), p. 32; Anon., *Considerations on Information*, pp. 30, 7; *Collection of Letters* 1:243.

2 *Collection of Letters* 1:256; Blackstone, *Commentaries* 1:138–39; Cartwright, *Constitution Produced*, pp. 263, 262 (also p. 138).

3 Address to Quebec, 26 October 1774, *Journal of the First Congress*, pp. 121–22. For contrasting British and American definitions, see *Guide to Rights*, p. 151; Resolutions of South Carolina Inhabitants, 8 July 1774, *Revolutionary Virginia* 2:139; *Scots Magazine* 36 (1774): 412.

4 Maryland Resolves, 28 September 1765, Morgan, *Prologue*, p. 53; Speech of Lord Chatham, Lords Debates, 17 June 1774, *Scots Magazine* 36 (1774): 304; New York Resolves, 14 December 1765, *Boston Post-Boy*, 6 January 1766, p. 2, col. 1; Resolution of 21 June 1770, *Journal of Burgesses* 12:85.

5 Hale, *History*, pp. 249–61; Quebec Petition to House of Commons, 12 November 1774, [Maseres,] *To Obtain an Assembly*, p. 257; Wright, *Grand Jury Speech*, p. 2; Patten, *Discourse at Hallifax*, p. 14; Adams, *Legal Papers* 1:210–16, 219–30 (quoting John Adams); [Fowle,] *Appendix to Eclipse*, p. 12.

6 [Care,] *English Liberties Second Edition*, pp. 220–27; Care, *English Liberties Boston Edition*, pp. 212–23; Care, *English Liberties Providence Edition*, pp. 226–39; *Guide to Rights*, pp. 200–14; Hudson, "Penn's English Liberties," p. 579.

7 Remonstrance to the King, 15 November 1770, *Addresses and Petitions of the Common Council*, p. 25; Address of Grand Jury to the Justices, 10 February 1775, *American Archives* (4th ser.) 1:1227; Maryland Resolves, 28 September 1765, *Maryland Votes and Proceedings* (September 1765), p. 10; Answer to Governor Francis Bernard, 3 November 1764, *Speeches*, p. 18. See also Trumbull, *Discourse at New Haven*, pp. 19–20; *Collection of Letters*, 1:250, 257; *Critical Review* 20 (1765): 424.

8 Salem Instructions, 21 October 1765, Phillips, *Salem*, p. 287; *Political Register* 9 (1771): 189.

9 *Jury-Man's Judgement*, p. 13; Pease, *Leveller Movement*, pp. 344–45.

10 Carroll, *First Citizen*, p. 202; Anon., *Constitutional Answer to Wesley*, p. 8; [Rokeby,] *Further Examination*, p. 106. See also [Ramsay,] *Historical Essay*, p. 165; [Rous,] *Letter to Jurors*, p. 3; Brewer, "Wilkites and the Law," pp. 153–55.

11 Petition from the Stamp Act Congress to King, and New York Resolves, 18 December 1765, Morgan, *Prologue*, pp. 64, 61; Middlesex Resolves, 31 August 1774, *American Archives* (4th ser.) 1:751; Blackstone, *Commentaries* 4:350; [Fowle,] *Appendix to Eclipse*, pp. 17–18; [Towers,] *Juries as Judges*, p. 9. For "arbitrary," see "In Legitimate Stirps."

12 Hamilton, *Duty of Obedience to Laws*, p. 16; Day, *Two Speeches*, p. 4; Gallaway, *Sermon at St. Mary's*, p. 18; Lowth, *Durham Assize Sermon*, p. 13.

13 Entry for 12 February 1771, *Diary of John Adams* 2:3; Adams, *Legal Papers* 1:229; Peters, *Massachusetts Constitution*, pp. 169–70 (quoting Adams, "Clarendon" letter).

14 Untitled paper, June 1776, *Papers of Iredell* 1:393; Trumbull, *Discourse at*

New Haven, p. 20. Interestingly, the South Carolina Regulators were said to have rebelled against trial by jury at faraway Charles Town because "they are not tried there by their peers . . . by which means the honest man is not secure in his property." Letter from Peedee to Charles Town, *Scots Magazine* 30 (1768): 547.

15 Instructions of Boston, 18 September 1765, *Boston News-Letter*, 19 September 1765, p. 2, col. 1. See also To Americans, Philadelphia newspaper, 1 June 1774, *American Archives* (4th ser.) 1:375; Dummer, *Defence of the Charters*, p. 27; Pease, *Leveller Movement*, p. 344.

16 Some matters pertaining to the jury that caused controversy between Britain and the colonies are not discussed in this book. An example is New York's celebrated Cunningham case involving the authority of the executive to set aside jury verdicts. It was concerned less with the right to jury trial than with London's authority to invest a colonial governor with power by mere instructions and more properly belongs in a study of the authority of London to govern. See Minutes of 14 December 1765, *Journal of New York Assembly* 2:803–6. By the same measure, some of the legal issues relating to the "dockyards" resolution discussed in this section more properly belong in a volume dealing with the authority of Parliament to legislate than here in a volume on colonial rights.

17 New York Petition to Commons, 18 October 1764, Morgan, *Prologue*, p. 13; Letter from the General Court [1764] and Resolves of House of Representatives, 29 June 1769, *Speeches*, pp. 24–25, 179; *Freeman Letters*, p. 5. Imperial equality was another, less convincing, explanation why vice-admiralty was constitutional. *Monthly Review* 54 (1776): 146–47.

18 Throop, *Thanksgiving Sermon*, p. 11. See also Philadelphia letters, *Scots Magazine* 27 (1765): 550, 610.

19 Declaration of Stamp Act Congress and the Stamp Act resolves of Pennsylvania, Connecticut, Massachusetts, South Carolina, and New Jersey, Morgan, *Prologue*, pp. 63, 52, 55, 57, 58, 60; Maryland Instructions, 26 September 1765, *Maryland Votes and Proceedings* (September 1765), p. 7; Instrument of 21 September 1765, *Delaware House Minutes* (1765–1770), p. 35–36; Adams, *Braintree Instructions*, pp. 2–3; Instructions of Newburyport and of Beverly, 21 October 1765, *Boston Post-Boy*, 4 November 1765, p. 1, col. 2, and p. 2, col. 1.

20 For a detailed discussion, see *In a Defiant Stance*, pp. 27–73. For the best account by an imperial law officer of jury nullification and whig law, see remarks of New Hampshire's attorney general, who asked: "[C]an juries be found that will convict their neighbours of treason or felony for doing those things which they thought were for their necessary self-preservation?" Letter from Samuel Livermore to Governor John Wentworth, 11 January 1775, *Resolution Documents* 9:28–29.

21 New York Resolves, 8 March 1775, *American Archives* (4th ser.) 1:1302; [Erskine,] *Reflections on the Rise*, p. 38. See also Continental Congress Resolves, 14 October 1774, *Extracts from the Votes and Proceedings* (Rivington), p. 4.

22 Anon., *Letter to People of Great Britain*, pp. 34–35; Speeches of Sir John Hynde Cotton and Sir William Yonge, Commons Debates, 13 March 1734, *Parliamentary History* 9:441–42, 453; Thompson, *Whigs and Hunters*, pp. 22, 155.

23 [Auckland,] *Principles of Penal Law*, p. 154. See also Anon., *History of George III*, pp. 352–53. But see Ritcheson, *British Politics*, p. 124.

24 35 Henry VIII, cap. 2; 12 George III, cap. 24; Declaration of the Continental Congress, 14 October 1774, and Petition to the King, 26 October 1774, *Commemoration Ceremony*, pp. 98, 127; New York Remonstrance, 25 March 1775, *Scots Magazine* 37 (1775): 236.

25 Knollenberg, *Growth of Revolution*, p. 324, n. 23; Letter from Attorney and Solicitor Generals to Earl of Dartmouth, 11 February 1774, *Revolution Documents* 8:47–48. For evidence that the official might be indicted, see generally *In a Defiant Stance* and *In a Rebellious Spirit*.

26 South Carolina Resolutions, 8 July 1774, *Revolutionary Virginia* 2:140; Message of the Georgia Committee, 10 August 1774, ibid., 2:158; Resolves of Connecticut, May 1774, and of New York, 3 and 25 March 1775, *American Archives* (4th ser.) 1:356, 1299, 1314; New Jersey Petition to King, 13 February 1775, *Revolution Documents* 9:50.

27 Address to the King, 17 May 1769, *Journal of Burgesses* 11:215; Minutes of 21 October 1774, *Journal of the First Congress*, p. 113. See also Letter from Governor Sir James Wright to Earl of Dartmouth, 1 February 1775, *Revolution Documents* 9:42; Trumbull, *Discourse at New Haven*, p. 24.

28 Necessity: [Hutchinson,] *Strictures upon the Declaration*, pp. 23–24; Lord Coke: Instructions of 8 May 1769, *Boston Town Records* 16:288. For an especially strong denunciation of the jury deprivation and a threat to resist "by all lawful means," see New Jersey Petition to King, 13 February 1775, *Revolution Documents* 9:50.

29 Petition of Mayor et al., to King, 10 April 1775, *American Archives* (4th ser.) 1:1853; Burke, *Letter to Sheriffs*, pp. 7–8. For other British comment, see [Rokeby,] *Further Examination*, p. 118; Hope, *Letters*, pp. 16–17 (describing statute of Henry as "sending out a Star Chamber order"); Anon., *History of George III*, pp. 352–53.

30 *Public Ledger*, 13 July 1769, reprinted in *Gazette & Post-Boy*, 6 November 1769, p. 4, col. 1; *North Briton No. 43*, p. 249; Address of Devon, 23 May 1763, *Gentleman's Magazine* 33 (1763): 300. See also *Gentleman's Magazine* 33 (1763): 447. For a condemnation of statutes depriving the British of jury trial in language echoing American whigs, see [Scott,] *Remarks on the Patriot*, p. 15.

31 Petition of the Corporation of London to King, *Gentleman's Magazine* 44 (1774): 248. See also [Erskine,] *Reflections on the Rise*, p. 40; [Maseres,] *To Obtain an Assembly*, p. 211. Use of the vice-admiralty in Britain to enforce the act prohibiting commerical intercourse with the North American colonies was protested on precisely the grounds Americans had objected to the jurisdiction. Protest of 15 December 1775, *Complete Protests*, pp. 55–56. Similarly, see Clark, *British Opinion*, p. 179.

32 Instructions of Westminster, 25 January 1769, *Cambridge Magazine*, p. 74. The East India Bill, of no concern in the colonies, was protested in Great Britain on the grounds of property right and right to jury. Anon., *Letter to North on East-India Bill*, p. 36.

33 Anon., *Magna Charta Opposed to Privilege*, p. 67; Instructions of Middlesex, 12 January 1769, *Cambridge Magazine*, p. 38; Address of the Lord Mayor et al., 21 November 1770, *Town and Country Magazine* 2 (1770): 615. See also Petition of London Livery to King, 5 July 1769, Wilkes, *English Liberty*, p. 336.

34 *Political Register* 5 (1769): 44. For other contemporary arguments of liberty depending on jurors as triers of law and fact, see [Towers,] *Juries as Judges*; [Rous,] *Letter to Jurors*, p. 10; Anon., *Considerations on the Imposition*, p. 3; [Ramsay,] *Historical Essay*, p. 169; *Gentleman's Magazine* 33 (1763): 345; [Jacob,] *Laws of Liberty*, pp. 58–59.

35 Anon., *British Liberties*, p. xxxvi; *Gentleman's Magazine* 39 (1769): 547. For the ideal in New England, see Nelson, *Americanization*, pp. 3–4, 20–32; Adams, *Legal Papers* 1:215, 229–30.

36 Anon., *"Taxation no Tyranny" Considered*, p. 121. See also [Rous,] *Letter to Jurors*, pp. 18–19; Anon., *British Liberties*, pp. 384–88; De Lolme, *Constitution: New Edition*, p. 177n.; Speech of Serjeant Glynn, Commons Debates, 6 December 1770, *Parliamentary History* 16:1213; *Political Register* 9 (1771): 189; *Monthly Review* 50 (1774): 454; Foss, *Judges of England* 8:358. But for the opposite view, see Anon., *Letter to Robert Morris*, pp. 101–3; Hawles, *Englishman's Right*, pp. 13–21.

CHAPTER SEVEN: EQUALITY OF RIGHTS

1 Speech of Richard Hussey, Commons Debates, 3 February 1766, Ryder, "Parliamentary Diaries," p. 271; Instructions of New York Freemen, 26 November 1765, *Boston Post-Boy*, 9 December 1765, p. 2, col. 3. See also Petition of Massachusetts Council and House to House of Commons, *Providence Gazette*, 16 March 1765, p. 2, col. 1; Letter from Philadelphia, 7 September 1765, *Scots Magazine* 27 (1765): 550; Trumbull, *Discourse at New Haven*, p. 24.

2 Instructions of 8 May 1769, *Boston Town Records* 16:287. Similarly, Instructions of 20 May 1772, ibid., 18:85; "Letter to the Colonists," 21 October 1774, *Journal of the First Congress*, p. 95.

3 Petition of Governor and Company of Rhode Island to King, 29 November 1764, *Rhode Island Colony Records* 6:415. See also Letter from Governor Samuel Ward to Secretary of State Henry Seymour Conway, 6 November 1765, ibid., 6:473; "To the Planters etc.," *South Carolina Gazette*, 22 June 1769, reprinted in Gadsden, *Writings*, p. 78.

4 Instructions of Cambridge, 14 October 1765, *Boston Post-Boy*, 21 October 1765. p. 2, col. 1. See also Stamp Act Congress Petitions to the Lords and the Commons, Morgan, *Prologue*, pp. 66, 67; Continental Congress Letter to the British People, 5 September 1774, *London Magazine* 43 (1774):

628; New York Assembly Memorial to House of Lords, 25 March 1775, *American Archives* (4th ser.) 1:1317; *South Carolina Gazette*, 24 December 1764, p. 2, col. 1; Instructions of Salem, 27 May 1769, *Boston Post-Boy*, 5 June 1769, p. 1, col. 1.

5 Lords Second Protest, 17 March 1766, *Boston Evening-Post* (Supplement), 16 June 1766, p. 1, col. 1; [Whately,] *Considerations on Trade*, p. 227; [Hutchinson,] *Strictures upon the Declaration*, pp. 23–24; [Dalrymple,] *Address to the People*, p. 39; Johnson, *Political Tracts*, p. 230; [Lloyd,] *Conduct Examined*, p. 36; Anon., *Constitutional Right*, pp. 56–57; *Gentleman's Magazine* 54 (1766): 108. For the contrary view, see *Monthly Review* 54 (1776): 146–47.

6 Address from the Committee to Governor, 17 November 1765, *Boston Post-Boy*, 20 January 1766, p. 2, col. 2; Letter from Continental Congress to British People, 5 September 1774, *London Magazine* 43 (1774): 628; Delaware Resolves, 3 June 1766, *Delaware House Minutes* (1765–1770), p. 54; Resolves of Caroline County, 14 July 1774, *Revolutionary Virginia* 1:115; New York Resolves, 17 December 1765, *Boston Post-Boy*, 30 December 1765, p. 3, col. 2; Instructions of Boston, 18 September 1765, *Boston Evening-Post*, 23 September 1765, p. 1, col. 2; Instructions of Boston, May 1764, Adams, *Writings* 1:5.

7 For example, the right of petition: New York Resolves, 30 December 1768, *Journal of New York Assembly* (1766–1776), p. 70; tenure of judges: Price, *Two Tracts: Tract One*, p. 22; Letter from Massachusetts House to Earl of Dartmouth, 5 March 1773, *Revolution Documents* 6:98; [Allen,] *American Alarm*, p. 28 (for the constitutional theory for the right, see American Petition, in Burgh, *Political Disquisitions* 2:336–37; Dickinson, *Letters*, at 367, 370–71; for denial Americans shared the right, see [Hutchinson,] *Strictures upon the Declaration*, p. 18); the right to an independent judiciary: Minutes of 3 March 1775, *Journal of New York Assembly* (1766–1776), p. 54; Massachusetts Resolves, 3 May 1773, Mauduit, *Letters of Hutchinson*, pp. 53–54; Petition of Boston to Governor Hutchinson, 29 October 1772, *Gazette & Post-Boy*, 2 November 1772, p. 3, col. 1; *Extract of a Letter to De Berdt*, p. 9. Similar constitutional questions were raised in Great Britain when Parliament appointed judges for the territories of the East India Company and paid them "out of the Company's revenue . . . an outrage on all the rights of property." Lords Protest, *Gentleman's Magazine* 43 (1773): 263; right to representation: Instructions of Portsmouth, N.H., 23 December 1765, *Boston Evening-Post*, 6 January 1766, p. 2, col. 3.

8 Pownall, *Administration*, p. 140; Virginia Resolutions, 3 June 1765, Morgan, *Prologue*, p. 48; [Knox,] *Controversy*, appendix, p. xxxii.

9 [Knox,] *Considerations on the Present State*, p. 50; "Book Review," *Critical Review* 27 (1769): 50; [Knox,] *Controversy*, p. 10.

10 Anon., *Remarks on the New Essay*, pp. 10–11; Wilson, *Considerations*, p. 731; "Analysis of the British Constitution," *Political Register* 5 (1769): 75. See also [Chandler,] *What think Ye of Congress*, pp. 6–7; [Keith,] *Two Papers on Taxing*, p. 17.

CHAPTER EIGHT: AUTHORITY OF RIGHTS

1 Lee, "Preface," p. 290; Howard, *Road from Runnymede*, p. 178.

2 Resolution of 21 June 1770, and Petition of 27 June 1770, *Journal of Burgesses* 12:85, 102.

3 [Fitch et al.,] *Reasons Why*, p. 26; "Non-Conformist," *Gazette & News-Letter*, 30 March 1775, p. 2, col. 1. For an excellent "official" claim in this language, see New York Petition, 18 October 1764, Morgan, *Prologue*, p. 10. For "blood," see Anon., *Fair Trial*, p. 75; Johnson, *Notes on Pastoral*, p. 61; Anon., *Observations upon the Authority*, p. 33; Anon., *Conduct of Mansfield*, pp. 4–5. For an excellent sample of British language defending British rights, see Anon., *North-Country Poll*, p. 2.

4 Petition of 24 June 1769, *Addresses and Petitions of Common Council*, p. 6; East India Petition to House of Commons, 14 December 1772, *Scots Magazine* 35 (1773): 122; Speech of the Earl of Chatham, Lords Debates, 26 May 1774, *American Archives* (4th ser.) 1:167; Petition of Lord Mayor et al., to House of Commons, 28 May 1773, *London Magazine* 43 (1774): 417. See also Address of Ward of Bridge Inhabitants to Lord Mayor Bass Crosby, [April 1771], Anon., *Magna Charta Opposed to Privilege*, p. 196.

5 Hopkins, *Rights*, p. 511; Willman, "Blackstone and Caroline Law," p. 45; [Erskine,] *Reflections on the Rise*, p. 40; [Towers,] *Observations on Liberty*, p. 16; Anon., *Rights Asserted*, p. 52.

6 Chauncy, *Civil Magistrates*, p. 32; Turner, *Election Sermon*, p. 18.

7 Howard, *Halifax Letter*, p. 535; Lockwood, *Worth and Excellence*, pp. 10, 13; Isaac Norris, *The Speech Delivered from the Bench in the Court of Common Pleas held for the City and County of Philadelphia, the 11 Day of September, 1727* [Philadelphia, 1727], p. 2; *Monthly Review* 52 (1775): 85; *Collection of Letters* 2:135. Some statements, as from the constitutionally eccentric Samuel Johnson, may have been made to shock contemporaries. See, e.g., Hawkins, *Life of Johnson*, pp. 505–6.

8 Ashton, "Tradition and Innovation," p. 211 (quoting James); Speech of the Lord Keeper to Both Houses, 28 April 1628, *State Trials* 3:172 (speaking for Charles).

9 Twysden, *Certaine Considerations*, p. 82; Sydney, *Discourses Concerning Government*, pp. 263–70; Earl, "Procrustean Feudalism," p. 38; *New York Evening Post*, 7 December 1747, reprinted in *Boston Evening-Post*, 28 December 1747, p. 1, col. 2; Birdsall, "Non Obstante," p. 40, n. 10.

10 *Boston Gazette*, 10 May 1756, p. 1, col. 1; Meeting of 22 March 1782, *Society for Constitutional Information*, p. 9 (quoting Somers). See also [Joseph Hawley,] "To the Inhabitants of Massachusetts," 30 March 1775, *American Archives* (4th ser.) 2:248–49; Anon., *British Liberties*, p. 21; [Williams,] *Essential Rights*, p. 65; Anon., *Defence of English History*, p. 13; Anon., *Old Constitution*, p. 23. The same theory was applied to the Bill of Rights and the Petition of Right, Cartwright, *Appeal on Constitution*, p. 31; Robinson, *Political Catechism*, pp. 34–35; Relf, *Petition of Right*, p. 56.

11 Brady, *Complete History*, "Preface" (no pagination); Speech of the Earl of

Chatham, Lords Debates, 2 February 1770, *Parliamentary History* 16:818; *Daily Gazetteer* 6 (5 July 1735): 1, col. 1; Pollock, "Politics," p. 207; Brand, *Defence of Reeves*, pp. 66, 62–63; Price, *Two Tracts: Tract Two*, p. 86.

12 Lovejoy, *Glorious Revolution*, p. 332. But note that one colonial assembly spoke of "privileges" secured by "grants." Resolves of 30 November 1765, *New Jersey Votes and Proceedings* (November 1765), p. 7.

13 Middlekauff, *Glorious Cause*, p. 118 (quoting Selden); Johnson, *Notes on Pastoral*, p. 102; [Fowle,] *Appendix to Eclipse*, pp. 22–23. For British theorists locating government authority in "grants from the people," see [Keld,] *Polity of England*, p. 83; Cartwright, *Appeal on Constitution*, p. 15; Price, *Two Tracts: Tract Two*, p. 4; Sydney, *Discourses Concerning Government*, p. 267. See also Thomas Hutchinson, Charge to the Grand Jury, March 1769, in Quincy, *Reports*, pp. 306–7. For the principle summed up in terms more acceptable to British constitutional thought, see Anon., *Considerations on the Addresses*, pp. 6–7.

14 Tucker, *Four Letters to Shelburne*, p. 53; Anon., *Second Answer to Wesley*, p. 13. For an important "advance" by Americans to the doctrine of reserved rights, see *Essex Result*, pp. 13–14, 15. For a British warning that rights should not depend on "parliamentary edicts," see Speech of Temple Luttrell, Commons Debates, 27 February 1775, *London Magazine* 44 (1775): 559.

15 Massachusetts Resolves, 29 October 1765, Morgan, *Prologue*, p. 56. See also Petition of Westmoreland County Freeholders, Minutes of 2 April 1768, *Journal of Burgesses* 11:146.

16 Letter from A.B.C., *Boston Evening-Post*, 25 January 1773, p. 1, col. 2. For a claim to the benefits of a presettlement statute (Westminster I), see Message from Pennsylvania Assembly to Governor John Penn, 21 February 1767, *Pennsylvania Council* 9:373. For an assertion that colonial rights might come from parliamentary grants, see Pownall, *Administration Fifth Edition* 2:46–47.

17 South Carolina Resolves, 29 November 1765, Morgan, *Prologue*, p. 58; Massachusetts Resolves, 29 October 1765, ibid., p. 57; Hopkins, *Rights*, p. 511 (quoting the statute); [Knox,] *Controversy*, p. 177. See also Instructions to Jasper Mauduit, 1762, *Mauduit Letters*, pp. 41–42; Letter from Samuel Adams to John Smith, 19 December 1765, Adams, *Writings* 1:45–46; Letter from Aquus, 16 January 1766, *London Magazine* 35 (1766): 33.

18 Connecticut Resolutions, June 1774, *Revolutionary Virginia* 2:116. For the irrelevance of charter due to possession, see "Monitor V" [Arthur Lee], *Virginia Gazette* [Rind], 24 March 1768, p. 1, col. 1.

19 Instructions of Providence, 13 August 1765, *Boston Evening-Post*, 19 August 1765, p. 2, col. 2; New York Petition to King, 18 October 1764, *New York Journal of Votes*, p. 770; Resolves of Virginia's Richmond County (29 June 1774) and Caroline County (14 July 1774), *American Archives* (4th ser.) 1:492, 540.

20 [Joseph Hawley,] "To Inhabitants," 13 April 1775, *American Archives* (4th ser.) 2:332; *Craftsman* 466 (7 June 1735): 2; Wooddeson, *Jurisprudence*, pp.

35–36. For a leading English appeal to custom for the authority of rights, see Petition of Grievances (1610), *State Trials* 2:519–20. See also Chauncy, *Discourse on "the good News,"* p. 15; Jenkins, *Lex Terrae*, p. 99.

21 Resolves of Connecticut House, May 1774, *American Archives* (4th ser.) 1:356. For examples from colonial past, see Speech of the Speaker to Lieutenant Governor, 11 November 1736, *South-Carolina Gazette*, 20 November 1736, p. 2, col. 1; Howard, *Road to Runnymede*, pp. 29, 51. See also Canning, *Letter to Hillsborough*, p. 17; Chauncy, *Discourse on "the good News,"* p. 14.

CHAPTER NINE: CONSTITUTIONAL AUTHORITY

1 Anon., *To Tax Themselves*, pp. 5–6.

2 Dicey, *Introduction*, pp. 193, 199; Greene, *Quest*, p. 411 (quoting Lee); Pownall, *Administration Fifth Edition* 1:86; Mayhew, *Snare Broken*, p. 24; Brand, *Defence of Reeves*, p. 77. See also Campbell, *Duty of Allegiance*. For one claim that rights were "derived from" the constitution, see Address of President John Rutledge to General Assembly, 11 April 1776, Gibbes, *Documentary History*, p. 274.

3 Resolves of First Provincial Congress, 27 August 1774, *North Carolina Colonial Records* 9:1045; Resolves of Lower House of Assembly, 22 June 1768, *Maryland Votes and Proceedings* (1768), p. 204; Instructions to Jasper Mauduit, 1762, *Mauduit Letters*, p. 41. See also Otis, *Rights*, p. 466; Cumings, *Thanksgiving Sermon*, p. 18.

4 [Knox,] *Controversy*, pp. 11–12.

5 Voting: [Forster,] *Answer to the Question Stated*, p. 8. For an instance of "common law" being used in today's sense of constitutional law, see Howard, *Halifax Letter*, p. 537.

6 "Constitution": Estwick, *Letter to Tucker*, p. 83; Protective: [Galloway,] *Political Reflections*, pp. 12, 19–20; Thomson, *Constitutional History*, p. 119; Yale, "Hobbes and Hale," pp. 143–44; Legislature: Rutherforth, *Natural Law* 2:297, 301–6; [Bolingbrooke,] *Freeholder's Catechism*, p. 9. An ambiguous term, "fundamental law" was sometimes used ambiguously. See [Hawley,] "To Inhabitants," 30 March 1775, *American Archives* (4th ser.) 2:248. One distinction is clear. Fundamental rights should not be equated with natural rights as is sometimes done. See, e.g., Conkin, *Truths*.

7 Unalienable: Abingdon, *Thoughts on Burke's Letter*, p. vii; Boundaries: Fiske, *Importance of Righteousness*, p. 31. For an argument, probably by Joseph Galloway, why unalterable fundamental law was necessary, see Anon., *Letter*, p. 257.

8 Letter from *Junius* to John Wilkes, 7 September 1771, *Gentleman's Magazine* 41 (1771): 586; [Ramsay,] *Historical Essay*, p. 143; Gray, *Doctor Price's Notions*, p. 43. See also Anon., *British Liberties*, p. xxiv; Paley, *Principles of Philosophy*, pp. 426–27, 464; Thomson, *Constitutional Law*, pp. 265–66; Barker, "Natural Law," p. 321.

9 Anon., *Abuse of Standing Parliaments*, pp. 10–11; *Crisis*, 1 April 1775, p. 63; "Book Review," *Monthly Review* 52 (1775): 256; Demophoon, "Disserta-

tion," *Political Register* 7 (1770): 155; Lawyers: Rutherforth, *Natural Law* 2:632–33; Sheridan, *Observations on the Doctrine*, pp. 6–7; Anon., *Legality of Putting Soldiers to Death*, p. 19; *Junius*: Letter from *Junius* to John Wilkes, 7 September 1771, *Gentleman's Magazine* 41 (1771): 587. Lord Chancellor Camden supported the principle of immutable fundamental law.

10 [Joseph Hawley,] "To Inhabitants," 9 March 1775, *American Archives* (4th ser.) 2:96–97; Tucker, *Election Sermon*, pp. 29–30; [Johnson,] *Important Observations*, p. 31.

11 Speech of George Johnstone, Commons Debates, 25 March 1774, *American Archives* (4th ser.) 1:56; Anon., *Necessity of Repealing the Stamp Act*, p. 18.

12 Shute, *Election Sermon*, p. 24; Jensen, *Revolution Within*, p. 32; [Williams,] *Essential Rights*, p. 5.

13 Burlamaqui, *Politic Law*, p. 142. In seventeenth-century England, the people's safety was frequently said to be government's end. E.g., Tuck, *Natural Rights Theories*, p. 151 (quoting Ireton at Putney); Jordan, *Men of Substance*, p. 163 (quoting Henry Parker); *Monarchy Asserted to Be the Best* (1660), reprinted in *Somers' Tracts* 6:364.

14 "Peace and Order": Warrington, *Works*, p. 433; objectives: N.S., *Divine Rights*, p. 46. The "great end of Government," a 1764 writer said, was "to detect criminals, and bring them to justice." Anon., *Examination of the Legality*, p. 6. See also Jones, *Fear of God*, pp. 29–30.

15 But see [Parker,] *True Portraiture*, p. 80; [Reeves,] *Thoughts, Second Letter*, p. 171. Similarly, Wyvill, *State of Representation*, p. 35.

16 Message from Representatives to Governor Hutchinson, 14 June 1771, *Gazette & Post-Boy*, 24 June 1771, p. 1, cols. 1–2.

17 Anon., *Fatal Consequences*, p. 2; Lofft, *Observations on Wesley's Address*, p. 32; Stevens, *Election Sermon*, p. 7; West, *Election Sermon*, p. 14. See also [Downer,] *Discourse in Providence*, p. 5; Robert Yates, "Plan of Union," *William & Mary Quarterly* 34 (1977): 302; Price, *Nature of Civil Liberty*, p. 11.

18 Anon., *Vindication of the Livery*, p. 5 (quoting John Locke); Tucker, *Election Sermon*, p. 22; Message from the Congress to Governor Thomas Gage, 13 October 1774, *Gazette & Post-Boy*, 17 October 1774, p. 3, col. 1. See also [Seabury,] *Congress Canvassed*, p. 20; Williams, *Election Sermon*, pp. 7–8, 14; [Williams,] *Essential Rights*, p. 4; Macaulay, *Observations on a Pamphlet*, p. 10.

19 Tucker, *Election Sermon*, p. 20; [Blount,] *William and Mary Conquerors*, pp. 41–42; Anon., *Dialogue between High and Low*, p. 5.

20 Dickinson, *Connecticut Election Sermon*, p. 5; Mayhew, *Discourse Concerning Unlimited Submission*, p. 60; Anon., *Legality of Impressing Seamen*, pp. 10–11.

21 [Talbot,] *Speech in Lords*, p. 3. James Otis said the "end" was "the good of the whole." Otis, *Rights*, p. 424.

22 Subject: Allen, *Magistracy an Institution*, p. 28; People: *The Freeman's Journal or New-Hampshire Gazette*, 29 June 1776, p. 1, col. 2; Green, *Observations on Reconciliation*, p. 10; Welfare: Hunn, *Welfare of a Government*,

p. 9; Safety: Mayhew, *Discourse Concerning Unlimited Submission*, p. 86. See also [Mather,] *America's Appeal*, p. 65; Lathrop, *Innocent Blood*, p. 15; Anon., *Philosophical Survey of Nature*, p. 86.

23 Protest of 26 March 1760, *Protests of the Lords of Ireland*, p. 82. See also "Some Thoughts on the Constitution," *American Archives* (4th ser.) 2:965; Williams, *Election Sermon*, pp. 20–21; Peters, *Massachusetts Constitution*, p. 104 (quoting Phillips Payson); Rossiter, *Political Thought*, p. 164; Hoadly, *Sermon before Lord Mayor*, p. 7; Browning, *Court Whigs*, p. 244 (quoting Archbishop Herring).

24 Address from New Jersey Assembly to Governor William Livingston, 24 September 1776, *Remembrancer for 1776: Part III*, p. 227; Instructions to Pennsylvania Representatives, 15 July 1774, *American Archives* (4th ser.) 1:565; Massachusetts Proclamation, 23 January 1776, *Remembrancer for 1776: Part II*, p. 53; Anon., *With Respect to America*, p. 139; Young, *Constitution Safe*, p. 61; Anon., *Civil Liberty Asserted*, p. 13; Anon., *Thoughts on Quebec Act*, p. 9; Anon., *Liberty in Two Parts*, p. 78; [Willes,] *Present Constitution*, p. 1.

25 "To Author," *American Gazette*, p. 49; Priestley, *First Principles*, p. 36; [Braxton,] *Address to the Convention*, p. 5; Paley, *Essay upon the Constitution*, p. 11; [Meredith,] *Letter to Chatham*, p. 20; Tyrrell, *Politica*, p. 48; Hoadly, *Works* 2:33.

26 Wilson, *Considerations*, p. 723; West, *Election Sermon*, pp. 41–2; Anon., *Essay upon Government*, p. 44; Burnet, *Essay upon Government*, p. 45; Burnet, *Divine Authority of Government*, p. 15.

27 [Drinker,] *Observations*, p. 18. See also Instructions of 20 May 1772, 18 *Boston Town Records*, p. 83; "Vindex," *Boston Gazette*, 19 December 1768, reprinted in Adams, *Writings*, 1:269.

28 Hobart, *Connecticut Election Sermon*, p. 3.

29 Thomas Hutchinson, Charge to the Grand Jury, March Term 1767, Quincy, *Reports*, p. 234; Anon., *Letter to Cooper*, p. 11; Gordon, *Evil Speaking*, p. 9. Also, "the end of government is the greatest happiness of the greatest number." Adams, *Works* 4:318; Quincy, *Observations with Thoughts*, p. 394; "Book Review," *Critical Review* 23 (1767): 252.

30 Hamilton, *Duty of Obedience to Laws*, p. 11; Mayhew, *Election Sermon*, p. 9. Also, "public Peace and Happiness," Hoadly, *Works* 2:21; "safety and happiness," Hamowy, "Jefferson and Scottish Enlightenment," p. 506 (quoting Francis Hutcheson).

31 [Fowle,] *Appendix to Eclipse*, p. 16; [Barwis,] *Three Dialogues*, p. 66.

32 Anon., *Civil Liberty Asserted*, p. 9; Foster, *Short Essay*, p. 40.

33 Somers, *Security of Englishmen's Lives*, p. 7; Rutherforth, *Natural Law* 2: 133.

34 Declaration of Congress, 6 July 1775, *Papers of Jefferson* 1:213; Letter from R. H. Lee to Samuel Adams, 4 February 1773, Lee, *Richard Henry Lee* 1:87; Petition from Natives of America, 19 May 1774, *American Archives* (4th ser.) 1:96. The standard could also be used as a political test. Thus, as the end of government was happiness, it was manifest that Hutchinson

was not a fit governor for Massachusetts. Instructions of 20 May 1772, *Boston Town Records* 18:83–84.

35 Instructions of Pennsylvania, 21 July 1774, *American Archives* (4th ser.) 1:565–66; Trumbull, *Discourse at New Haven*, p. 31. See also [Joseph Hawley,] "To Inhabitants," 30 March 1775, *American Archives* (4th ser.) 2:248.

CHAPTER TEN: THE RIGHT TO ISONOMY

1 Dickinson, "Address to Friends and Countrymen," reprinted in Dickinson, *Writings*, p. 202; [Dickinson,] *New Essay*, p. 4.

2 *Boston Evening-Post* (Supplement), 23 July 1770, p. 2, col. 1.

3 For unqualified colonial insistence on equality with the British, see [Mather,] *A Narrative*, p. 10; Lovejoy, *Glorious Revolution*, p. 229; New York Resolves, 31 December 1768, *Gentleman's Magazine* 39 (1769): 82; [Fitch et al.,] *Reasons Why*, p. 6; Letter from Committee to Charles Garth, 4 September 1764, Gibbes, *Documentary History*, p. 3; Lovejoy, "Virginia's Charter," p. 38.

4 Pennsylvania Resolutions, 15 July 1774, *Gentleman's Magazine* 44 (1774): 438. Similarly, Resolves of Georgia Congress, 10 July 1775, *Remembrancer for 1776: Part I*, p. 12; New York Assembly to House of Lords, 25 March 1775, *American Archives* (4th ser.) 1:1317; Delaware Convention Resolves, 2 August 1774, *American Archives* (4th ser.) 1:667; South Carolina Resolves, 6, 7, 8 July 1774, *Scots Magazine* 36 (1774): 412; Connecticut Resolves, May 1774, *Public Records of Connecticut* 14:347; Stamp Act Congress Resolves, *Account of Stamp Act Congress*, p. 5; South Carolina Resolves of 29 November 1765, Massachusetts Resolves of 29 October 1765, and Pennsylvania Resolves of 21 September 1765, Morgan, *Prologue*, pp. 58, 56–57, 51; New Jersey Resolves, 30 November 1765, *New Jersey Votes and Proceedings* (November 1765), p. 7.

5 Letter from Massachusetts House to Earl of Shelburne, 15 January 1768, printed in [Hollis,] *True Sentiments*, p. 13. See similar explanation in 1728. Dulany, *English Laws*, p. 10.

6 Cooke, *Election Sermon*, p. 15; Letter from Massachusetts House to Henry Seymour Conway, 13 February 1768, *Boston Post-Boy*, 28 March 1768, p. 2 col. 1; Hopkins, *Rights*, p. 507; Kronenberger, *Kings*, p. 41 (quoting Burke). See also Williams, *Election Sermon*, p. 5; [Williams,] *Essential Rights*, pp. 2–4; Carysfort, *Letter to Huntingdonshire*, p. 6. For the claim to an equality of rights made from the American perspective, see South Carolina Resolves, 8 July 1774, *Boston Evening-Post*, 25 July 1774, p. 2, col. 1; Petition from Virginia Burgesses to the King, 27 June 1770, *Revolution Documents* 2:129; Letter from New York Congress to Merchants of Canada, 12 June 1775, *American Archives* (4th ser.) 2:1294. From a British or Irish perspective, see Speech of Alderman Frederick Bull, Commons Debates, 18 November 1777, *Parliamentary History* 19:427; Anon., *Examination of Rights of the Colonies*, pp. 26–27; Stanlis, *Burke and Natural Law*, p. 42;

Anon., *Critical Review of Liberties*, p. 29. See also Lee, *Appeal to Justice*, pp. 11–12; Anon., *Application of Political Rules*, p. 55.

7 Providence Resolves, 19 January 1774, *Gazette & Post-Boy*, 31 January 1774, p. 3, col. 1. See also Instructions to Congressional Delegates, June 1776, *Colonial Records of Connecticut* 15:414–15; Anon., *To Tax Themselves*, pp. 140–41; Anon., *Constitutional Right*, p. 57.

8 Hopkins, *Rights*, p. 510; Baptists: [Backus,] *Letter to a Gentleman*, pp. 19–20; [Allen,] "To Council and House," p. 9; Bishop: *Boston Chronicle*, 1 February 1768, p. 1, col. 3. See also Otis, *Rights*, p. 470; Worcester County Declaration, 9 August 1774, *Boston Evening-Post*, 5 September 1774, p. 1, col. 3.

9 Griffith, *Passive Obedience*, p. 21. See also Lee, *Appeal to Justice*, pp. 11–12; Wilson, *Considerations*, p. 724.

10 Letter from Thomas Hutchinson to Thomas Whately, 20 January 1769, Hutchinson, *Letters*, p. 16; Pemberton, *Lord North*, p. 215 (quoting George III). American whigs rejected the argument that distance determined civil rights. Address to British People, 5 September 1774, *Journal of the First Congress*, p. 81; Letter from Massachusetts House to Lords of Treasury, 17 February 1768, *Boston Post-Boy*, 4 April 1768, p. 2, col. 2; Cambridge Resolutions, *Gentleman's Magazine* 35 (1765): 586–87; *Boston News-Letter*, 17 October 1765, p. 3, col. 1; *South-Carolina Gazette*, 4 April 1768, p. 1, col. 4; Anon., *Plan to Reconcile*, p. 2.

11 It was argued "That the British colonists are entitled to the same privileges, in all parts of the British dominions, as the subjects born in England would enjoy in those parts." Anon., *Remarks on the New Essay*, p. 56. For a writer who mentioned that Americans as a people were not equal but as individuals were entitled to every British right, see [Lind,] *Englishman's Answer.*

12 Anon., *Constitutional Considerations*, p. 8; Anon., *Inquiry into the Nature*, pp. 20–21. See also Leonard, "Massachusettensis," p. 36; "J. H." in London *Daily Advertiser*, 21 February 1767, reprinted in *Boston Evening-Post*, 4 May 1767, p. 2, col. 1.

13 *Boston Evening-Post*, 7 February 1774, p. 2, col. 3, and 14 February 1774, p. 2, col. 3; Anon., *Considerations upon Rights of Colonists*, p. 17.

CHAPTER ELEVEN: THE AUTHORITY OF NATURE

1 [Bollan,] *Continued Corruption*, p. 79; Instructions of 14 June 1762, *Mauduit Letters*, p. 39; Resolves of Sheffield, 12 January 1773, *Boston Evening-Post*, 15 February 1773, p. 2, col. 1; Sheridan, *Observations on the Doctrine*, p. 33. Dudley Digges in 1644 said the concept should be called right of nature, not law of nature. Tuck, *Natural Rights Theories*, pp. 102–3.

2 Otis, *Vindication*, p. 563; Wilson "Speech of 1775," p. 753; Dickinson, *To Barbados*, p. 262. See also Bailyn, *Pamphlets* 1:107–9.

3 Taxation: Letter from Maryland House to Massachusetts House, 24 June 1768, *Massachusetts Gazette*, 11 July 1768, p. 2, col. 2; Letters from Massachusetts House to Lord Chatham, 2 February 1768, and to Lord Camden, 29

February 1768, *Boston Post-Boy*, 4 April 1768, p. 2, col. 2, and p. 1, col. 1; Liberty: Hamilton, *Farmer Refuted*, p. 104. See also Otis, *Rights*, p. 426; Joseph Warren (1775), *Massacre Orations*, p. 58.

4 Granville County Resolutions, 15 August 1774, *North Carolina Colonial Records* 9:1034; Instructions of 14 June 1762, *Mauduit Letters*, p. 39.

5 Selden, *Table Talk*, p. 69; [Sheridan,] *Observations on the Doctrine*, p. 32. See also Rutherforth, *Natural Law* 2:405; Fish, *Discourse at Worcester*, p. 9; [Cartwright,] *American Independence*, p. 54.

6 [Drayton,] *Letter from Freeman*, p. 40; Resolves of 13 September 1768, *Boston Town Records* 18:261. See also Rossiter, *Political Thought*, pp. 105–6.

7 Wynne, *Eunomus* 1:66; Massachusetts Instructions to Agent, 1768, *Scots Magazine* 30 (1768): 463–64; [Rokeby,] *Considerations on the Measures*, pp. 7–8; Blackstone, *Commentaries* 1:54; Tucker, *Treatise*, pp. 235–36; *Hibernian Magazine* 5 (1775): 790; *Gentleman's Magazine* 46 (1776): 450.

8 Hall, *Apology for Freedom*, p. 49; Paley, *Principles of Philosophy*, p. 75.

9 [Bacon,] *Short Address*, p. 5; [Lind,] *Thirteenth Parliament*, p. 191n. For the best statement of the law by the imperial side, see [Knox,] *Controversy* (Dublin edition), pp. 17–18, 11–12; [Knox,] *Letter to a Member*, p. 12.

10 Lyme Resolves, January 1766, *Massachusetts Gazette* (Supplement), 23 January 1766, p. 2, col. 2; Massachusetts Resolves, 29 October 1765, Morgan, *Prologue*, p. 56. See also Letter from Governor Samuel Ward to Secretary of State Henry Seymour Conway, 6 November 1765, *Rhode Island Colony Records* 6:472–73; Petition of Native Americans, 25 March 1774, *American Archives* (4th ser.) 1:47.

11 *Briefs of American Revolution*, pp. 46–48; "Irrelevance of the Declaration," p. 48; Debate: *Letters of Delegates to Congress* 1:46–49 (also quoting Adams, *Diary*); *Monthly Review* 46 (1772): 579 (quoting Young, *Political Essays*). See also Tucker, *Tract Five*, p. 34; Becker, *Declaration*, p. 122; Wills, *Inventing America*, pp. 60–61.

12 In addition to Congress's declaration, see the unusually long list of New Jersey grievances, not one remotely connected with natural law. Petition of House of Representatives to King, 13 February 1775, *New Jersey Votes and Proceedings* (January 1775), pp. 59–60.

13 [Drayton,] *Letter from Freeman*, pp. 13–14. Otis claimed authority for the emigration purchase on the basis of "the laws of nature and of nations" which may or may not be an alternative authority. [Otis,] "Substance," p. 474.

14 See, e.g., Beloff, *Debate*, p. 35. For a discussion of the irrelevance of natural law in general, not just natural rights, see "Irrelevance of the Declaration," pp. 47–69.

15 Cohen, "Revolution and Natural Law," p. 494. For whether Otis applied or rejected natural law, compare Beloff, *Debate*, p. 25, to J. R. Pole, *The Pursuit of Equality in American History* (Berkeley, Calif., 1978), p. 15.

16 Rossiter, *Political Thought*, p. 58; Conkin, *Truths*, p. 34; Aldridge, "Paine and Dickinson," p. 127.

17 Ferguson, "Reason in Madness," p. 199.

18 *Craftsman* 14 (7 June 1735): 1–2; *Daily Gazetteer* 6 (5 July 1735): 1, col. 1. See also Grey, "Unwritten Constitution," p. 861.

19 Speech of Earl Camden, Lords Debates, 20 January 1775, *American Archives* (4th ser.) 1:1501. Thomas Jefferson seems to have claimed the right to free trade on the strength of natural law alone. Christie and Labaree, *Empire*, p. 206.

20 Cambridge Resolves, 14 October 1765, *Privy Council Copies*, p. 202; Letters from Massachusetts House to Earl of Shelburne and Dennys de Berdt, 15 January 1768 and 12 January 1768, Adams, *Writings* 1:156–57, 135; Georgia Resolves, 24 December 1768, *Georgia Commons House Journal* 14:655.

21 E.g., Virginia Petition (1770), *Boston Evening-Post*, 15 April 1771, p. 4, col. 1.

22 R. R. Palmer, *The Age of Democratic Revolution; A Political History of Europe and America, 1760–1800: The Challenge* (Princeton, N.J., 1959), p. 181; Pennsylvania Resolves, 21 September 1765, Morgan, *Prologue*, p. 51; Dugdale, *Origines Juridicales*, p. 3, col. 2; Goodhart, *Law of the Land*, p. 54; Otis, *Vindication*, p. 558; Anon., *Defence of Resolutions*, p. 40.

CHAPTER TWELVE: RIGHTS AS PROPERTY

1 F. W. Maitland, *Equity also the Forms of Action at Common Law: Two Courses of Lectures* (Cambridge, England, 1913), p. 1.

2 E.g., Letter from Massachusetts House to Agent Dennys de Berdt, 12 January 1768, Adams, *Writings* 1:137–38; Foster, *Short Essay*, p. 8.

3 Thomson, *Constitutional History*, p. 169; Nenner, *Colour of Law*, p. 36; *New London Gazette*, 20 September 1765, reprinted in *Boston Evening-Post*, 14 October 1765, p. 1, col. 2.

4 Burnett, *Continental Congress*, p. 13, For the proposition that "property" meant material goods, see Kenyon, "Republicanism in Revolution," p. 10; Russell, *Parliaments and Politics*, p. 351.

5 Locke, *Two Treaties*, book 2, sec. 27, 87, 123; Nenner, *Colour of Law*, pp. 38–39; Larkin, *Property in Eighteenth Century*, pp. 58–59; Laslett, "Introduction to Locke" p. 101; Viner, "Possessive Individualism," pp. 554, 563–64; Hexter, "Hobbes and the Law," p. 489; Tully, *Discourse on Property*, p. 115; Levy, "Freedom, Property, and Levellers"; Goebel, "Matrix of Empire," p. xxii; Roeber, *Faithful Magistrates*, p. 90, n. 35.

6 Jenkins, *Works of Judge Jenkins*, p. 128; *Gentleman's Magazine* 35 (1765): 586 [sic], 570; Anon., *Licentiousness Unmask'd*, p. 27; *Remembrancer of 1776: Part III*, p. 339; Speech of Sir George Moore, Commons Debates, 15 December 1621, [Nicholas,] *Proceedings of 1620–21*, 2:330; Hawles, *Englishman's Right*, pp. 28, 39.

7 Blackstone, *Commentaries* 1:122–23; ibid., 3:119; *Trial of Sacheverell*, p. 48. See also Argument of the Attorney General, In re Sir Thomas Darnell, et al., *State Trials* 3:1, 36 (1627); St. John, *Speech or Declaration*, p. 2; Barker, *Essays*, pp. 138–39; Boorstin, *Mysterious Science of Law*, p. 162.

8 Sharp, *Legal Means*, p. 75; James Howell, *The Preheminence of Parlement*

(1644), *Somers' Tracts*, 5:48; Prynne, *Seasonable Vindication*, p. 7; Anon., *Court of Star Chamber*, p. 13.

9 Popofsky, "Habeas Corpus," p. 270; Address of Sir Edward Coke, Conference with the Lords, 3 April 1628, *Parliamentary History* 2:270, *State Trials* 3: 131; Speech of Sir Thomas Hammer, Commons Debates, 6 December 1717, *Parliamentary History* 7:522; Anon., *Privileges of Jamaica*, pp. 44–45; Dickinson, "Letter to Inhabitants," p. 470.

10 Speech of Lord Mayor, 12 April 1770, *Political Register* 6 (1770): 303; Address of John Wilkes, 18 June 1768, Wilkes, *English Liberty*, p. 192, and *Scots Magazine* 30 (1768): 375; Anon., *Late Occurences*, p. 36. See also Sharp, *Legal Means*, p. 77; Declaration of Lords and Commons, 12 July 1642, Rushworth, *Historical Collections: Third Part* 1:611; *Guide to Rights*, p. iv; Duchal, *Sermons*, p. 170.

11 Lucas, *Divelina Libera*, p. 5; Speech of Sir Edward Coke, 3 April 1628, *Conference of Both Houses*, p. 69; Howard, *Road from Runnymede*, p. 89 (quoting Penn); Speech of Edward Hyde, *Conference of Both Houses*, 22 April 1641, Rushworth, *Historical Collections: Third Part* 1:232.

12 *Crisis*, 20 January 1775, p. 6; Protestation of 5 June 1628, *Commons Debates 1628* 4:133; Schuyler, *Empire*, p. 41 (quoting Irish Commons 1641); Petition to Lord Protector, 25 May 1657, *Somers' Tracts* 6:404; Howard, *Road to Runnymede*, p. 62 (quoting Dulany); Virginia Address to the King, 18 December 1764, *Revolutionary Virginia* 1:11; Anson County Address to Governor Josiah Martin, [1775,] *North Carolina Colonial Records* 9:1162.

13 [Johnson,] *Important Observations*, p. 27; Gregor, "Preface," p. xl.

14 Anon., *Licentiousness Unmask'd*, p. 27; Lofft, *Observations on Wesley's Address*, pp. 34–35. Another theory was expounded by the seventeenth-century common lawyer Henry Parker. It blended government and society into one unit and made society's ownership higher than the individual's. "[T]here is a Liberty of the whole State, as well as of any particular subject, and that Liberty of the whole State must supersede the Liberty of every particular subject, whensoever both accord not." Tuck, *Natural Rights Theories*, p. 151.

CHAPTER THIRTEEN: PROPERTY IN RIGHTS

1 Cartwright, *People's Barrier*, p. 2; Anon., *Judgment of Whole Kingdoms*, p. 65. For discussion, see Nenner, *Colour of Law*, p. 33; Hexter, "Hobbes and the Law," p. 489; Russell, *Parliaments and Politics*, p. 139.

2 Chapman, *Burke*, p. 158; De Lolme, *Constitution*, p. 63. De Lolme's "new" edition in 1807 retained the exact language. De Lolme, *Constitution: New Edition*, p. 100. See also *Boston Gazette*, 10 May 1756, p. 1, col. 1; [Meredith,] *Remarks on Taxation*, pp. 6–7.

3 [Yorke,] *Forfeitures for High Treason*, pp. 17–23; Collier, *Essay on Charters*, p. 1; Burke, *Revolution in France*, pp. 34–35.

4 For the concept's uses in times of controversy, see Marcham, *Constitutional History*, pp. 144–47; Hill, *Century of Revolution*, p. 61; Hume, *History*

5:80–81; White, *Coke and the Grievances*, pp. 175–76; Speeches of Thomas Crewe and Sir Edward Coke, Commons Debates, 15 December 1621, [Nicholas,] *Proceedings of 1620–21* 2:336, 337; Letter from James to Secretary Calvert, 16 December 1621, ibid., pp. 339–40; Tanner, *Constitutional Conflicts*, p. 49.

5 Birdsall, "Non Obstante," p. 37; Kern, *Kingship*, p. 185; Laslett, "Introduction to Locke," p. 305, n. 27 (reprinting Richard Baxter [1680]); Hexter, "Hobbes and the Law," p. 489; Address to Lord Mayor Brass Crosby from Ward of Lime-Street, 25 April 1771, Anon., *Magna Charta Opposed to Privilege*, p. 163; *New York Evening Post*, 7 December 1747, reprinted in *Boston Evening-Post*, 28 December 1747, p. 1, col. 2; [Ferguson,] *Brief Justification*, p. 12; Anon., *Judgment of Whole Kingdoms*, p. 18; Meeting of 22 March 1782, *Society for Constitutional Information*, p. 9.

6 [Burnet,] *Sermon at Salisbury*, p. 6. See also Declaration of Lords and Commons, 26 May 1642, Rushworth, *Historical Collections: Third Part* 1:578–79; Prynne, *Seasonable Vindication*, p. 8; [Oldfield,] *History of the Boroughs*, 1:175; Judson, *Crisis*, pp. 34–40. For the contrary view, see [Robertson,] *Liberty, Property, and Religion*, p. 7.

7 "They are much mistaken, who imagine the Prerogative of the Crown is a peculiar estate of the King, in which the People have no interest: for in this also, they have an inheritance as one of the guards and securities of their Liberties." Anon., *Fair Trial*, p. 230.

8 Rous, *Thoughts on Government*, p. 36. See also Priestly, *First Principles*, p. 41; Anon., *Protest of a Private Person*, p. 29. For the contrary view, see Anon., *Spirit and Principles*, pp. 30–31.

9 The vocabulary of ownership was used by lawyers arguing the most important constitutional litigation involving colonial rights. Arguments of Alleyne for plaintiff and Hargrave for defendant, *Campbell v. Hall*, 20 *State Trials* 239, 273, 296 (Kings Bench, 1774). See also Speech of Temple Luttrell, Commons Debates, 27 February 1775, *London Magazine* 44 (1775): 560; Pownall, *Administration*, pp. 71–72; [Sheridan,] *Observations on the Doctrine*, p. 5; Candidus, *Two Letters*, p. 14; Anon., *To Tax Themselves*, p. 92.

10 Resolution of 6 December 1775, *Letters of Delegates to Congress* 2:449.

11 Patten, *Discourse at Hallifax*, p. 11; Lockwood, *Worth and Excellence*, p. 26; "Notes of Proceedings," 7 June to 1 August 1776, *Papers of Jefferson* 1:326. See also Newburyport Instructions, 21 October 1765, *Boston Post-Boy*, 4 November 1765, p. 1, col. 1; Adams, *Religious Liberty*, p. 54; Nicholas, *Considerations on the Present State of Virginia Examined* (1774), reprinted in *Revolutionary Virginia* 1:260.

12 Breen, *Good Ruler*, p. 160 (quoting Mather); Anon., *Consideration upon Rights of Colonists*, p. 16 (see also pp. 12, 17); Petition of New Jersey Representatives to King, 7 May 1768, *Scots Magazine* 30 (1768): 522; [Hopkins,] *Grievances of the Colonies*, p. 17; Instructions of Boston, 28 May 1764, *Gazette & News-Letter*, p. 2, col. 2; Delaware Resolves, 3 June 1766, *Delaware House Minutes* (1765–1770), p. 54. Of course, they also claimed by descent. Petition to the King, 14 April 1768, *Journal of Burgesses* 11:165.

See also the argument of *Allison* v. *Long* (1770), in Smith, *Appeals*, p. 477 (Jamaica, 1770).

13 "A Native," *South-Carolina Gazette*, 5 October 1765, p. 3, col. 1; Connecticut Resolves, May 1774, *Public Records of Connecticut*, 14:347–48. See also Delaware Resolves, 2 August 1774, *American Archives* (4th ser.) 1:667; Connecticut Resolves, June 1774, *Revolutionary Virginia* 2:116; Letter to Lord North, *Gentleman's Magazine* 44 (1774): 68.

14 Protestation of 18 December 1621, Cragg, *Freedom and Authority*, p. 88; Petition of Lords and Commons, 14 December 1641, Rushworth, *Historical Collections: Third Part* 1:458; [Downley,] *Sentiments*, p. 51; *Collection of Letters* 1:64.

15 Young, *Political Arithmetic*, p. 5; [Cartwright,] *Take Your Choice*, p. 19; Cartwright, *Legislative Rights*, p. 29. "Liberty is the darling Property of *Englishmen*," and "by the Constitution of this Kingdom, committed to us, and secured in our own Possession." *Craftsmen* 14.488 (8 November 1735): 173.

16 *Guide to Rights*, p. 2; Carysfort, *Thoughts on Constitution*, p. 4.

17 Keir, *Constitutional History*, p. 341; Thomson, *Constitutional History*, p. 190; Marcham, *Constitutional History*, p. 226; [Almon,] *Free Parliaments*, p. 30. "If a vote for a Member of Parliament be property, why may not the voter sell it, or why is a corrupt exercise of any one branch of Executive Government an High Crime and Misdeameanor?" Rous, *Thoughts on Government*, p. 27. See also Sharp, *Legal Means*, pp. 87–88; Northcote, *Observations on Rights*, p. 10; [Shaftesbury,] *Person of Quality*, p. 10.

18 New York Assembly Petition to the King, 11 December 1765, *New York Journal of Votes*, p. 795; Maryland Resolves, 28 September 1765, *Maryland Votes and Proceedings* (September 1765), p. 10; Message from the House to Governor John Penn, 21 February 1767, *Pennsylvania Archives* (8th ser.) 7:6001–5; Gadsden, *Writings*, p. 20 (quoting South Carolina Commons House).

19 Answer of the Council, 25 January 1773, *Briefs of American Revolution*, p. 37; Resolves of Worcester County, Maryland, Committee, 7 June 1775, *American Archives* (4th ser.) 2:924; Bland, *Colonel Dismounted*, pp. 22–23; "To the Electors," 5 February 1763, Gadsden, *Writings*, p. 47; Bailyn, *Pamphlets*, p. 109 (quoting James Otis).

20 Commons' Declaration, *Proceedings against Manwaring*, p. 6; Petition to Lord Protector, 25 May 1657, *Somers' Tracts* 6:406; Letter from the *North Briton*, no. CXXXV, *London Magazine* 34 (1765): 101.

21 "A British American," *Gentleman's Magazine* 36 (1766): 612 (reprinted from colonial newspapers). A less frequently mentioned authority for the right was a grant of equal rights and equal property interests. Connecticut Resolves, 25 October 1765, Morgan, *Prologue*, p. 55. For other variations, see Petition from Pennsylvania Assembly to King, 22 September 1768, *Pennsylvania Archives*, 7:6272; *New-London Gazette*, 20 September 1765, reprinted in *Boston Evening-Post*, 14 October 1765, p. 1, col. 2; Westmoreland Articles, 27 February 1766, Lee, *Richard Henry Lee* 1:34; Virginia

Petition to the King, 18 December 1764, *Journal of Burgesses* 10:302. In Barbados, where the right's authority was doubted, it was termed "that *seeming birthright* of every BRITON." Dickinson, *To Barbados*, p. 255.

22 New York Representatives Votes, 31 December 1768, *London Magazine* 38 (1769): 97. For the right claimed on the authority of equality, see Resolves of Accomack County, 27 July 1774, *Revolutionary Virginia* 1:111.

23 Remonstrance of the Council and Burgesses to the House of Commons, December 1764, *Revolutionary Virginia* 1:13; Letter from Philadelphia, 9 November 1765, *Gentleman's Magazine* 36 (1766): 96.

24 Petition to King from the Continental Congress, 26 October 1774, *Commemoration Ceremony*, p. 128; *New-London Gazette*, 20 September 1765, reprinted in *Boston Evening-Post*, 4 November 1765, p. 2, col. 1; Speech of Lord Chatham, Lords Debates, 20 January 1775, *Hibernian Magazine* 5 (1775): 89–90; [Knox,] *Claim of the Colonies*, pp. 5–6; Address to the People, 9 February 1775, *American Archives* (4th ser.) 1:1332; "To the Inhabitants of New-York," 28 April 1775, *American Archives* (4th ser.) 2:429.

CHAPTER FOURTEEN: THE AUTHORITY OF MIGRATION

1 Virginia Resolves, June 1765, Morgan, *Prologue*, p. 47. The exact words were incorporated into other resolutions: Rhode Island Resolves, September 1765, and Maryland Resolves, 28 September 1765, ibid., pp. 50, 52; Maryland Resolves, 22 June 1768, *Maryland Votes and Proceedings* (1768), p. 204; Resolves of Richmond Town Meeting, 28 February 1774, *Records of Rhode Island* 7:276. See also Petition from Council and Burgesses to House of Lords, 14 April 1766, and Petition from same to Commons, 14 April 1768, *Journal of Burgesses* 11:166, 169.

2 Resolves of Congress, 14 October 1774, *Commemoration Ceremony*, p. 97; Georgia Resolves, January 1775, *American Archives* (4th ser.) 1:1156–57; *Trial of Daniel Disney*, p. 15.

3 New York Memorial to House of Lords, 25 March 1775, *American Archives* (4th ser.) 1:1316; Pennsylvania Petition to King, 22 September 1768, *Pennsylvania Archives* 7:6272; Dickinson, "Non-Importation," p. 411.

4 "A brief Examination of *American* Grievances; being the heads of a Speech . . . at Leweston, on Delaware, July 28, 1774," *American Archives* (4th ser.) 1:658; Howard, *Road from Runnymede*, p. 60; [Hopkins,] *Grievances of the Colonies*, p. 10.

5 "Answer to Wesley," *Hiberian Magazine* 5 (1775): 790. See also [Johnson,] *Political Tracts*, p. 208.

6 Kliger, *Goths*, p. 131 (quoting Hunton); [Stuart,] *Historical Dissertation*, p. 59 (see also p. 282). "The Saxons . . . brought into England the customs of that country, customs very similar to, and, in many instances, exactly the same with those used abroad on the continent." Sullivan, *Lectures on the Constitution*, p. 243.

7 Jefferson, *Summary View*, p. 122; *Gentleman's Magazine* 43 (1773): 513–14.

8 Anon., *Policy of the Laws*, pp. 24–25; [Madden,] *Reflections*, p. 82.

9 [Barron,] *History of Colonization*, p. 144; *Boston Evening-Post*, 17 April 1769, p. 4, col. 1.

10 Speech of Lord Mansfield, Lords Debates, 10 February 1766, "Lords Debate on Declaratory Act," p. 188; Letter from Arthur Lee to Samuel Adams, 25 January 1773, Lee, *Arthur Lee* 1:227. For a seventeenth-century lawyer who agreed with Mansfield, see Palmer, *Impartial Account*, p. 39. See also Anon., *Inquiry into the Nature*, p. 50; Anon., *Some Fugitive Thoughts*, pp. 4–5.

11 Leder, *Liberty*, p. 102; Resolutions of 26 May 1768, *Maryland Votes and Proceedings* (1768), p. 158; [Littleton,] *Groans of Plantations*, p. 16.

12 *Campbell* v. *Hall*, State Trials 20:239, 265, 269 (King's Bench, 1774); *Lloyd* v. *Mansell*, *William Peere Williams* 2:73, 74–75 (1722); Blackstone, *Commentaries* 1:106–7.

13 Smith, *English Legal System*, pp. 12–22; [Phelps,] *Rights of the Colonies*, p. 9.

14 New York Petition, 18 October 1764, and New York Resolves, 18 December 1765, *New York Journal of Votes*, pp. 769, 807–8; Jefferson. *Summary View*, p. 121; Rossiter, *Political Thought*, p. 110; Burlamaqui, *Politic Law*, p. 119. See also Mullett, *Fundamental Law*, p. 131.

15 [Strafford,] *Brief and Perfect Relation*, p. 32; Wynne, *Eunomus* 4:198. The writ means "Do not let him leave the realm."

16 Wynne, *Eunomus* 4:198–99; Pownall, *Administration Sixth Edition* 2:22–23; Plowden, *Rights of Englishmen*, p. 68.

17 Memorial of Council and Burgesses to House of Lords, 18 December 1764, *Revolutionary Virginia* 1:11; Declaration of Rights, 14 October 1774, *Journal of the First Congress*, p. 61; Letter from Virginia House of Burgesses to Pennsylvania House of Representatives, 9 May 1768, *Pennsylvania Archives* 7:6190; Address of Judge Drayton to Camden District Grand Jury, November Session, 1774, *London Magazine* 44 (1775): 126; Chatham, "Speech on Quartering Act of 1774," p. 152; [Downer,] *Discourse in Providence*, p. 4.

18 Declaration of Rights, 14 October 1774, *Journal of the First Congress*, p. 60; Petition from Jamaica to King, *Gentleman's Magazine* 45 (1775): 617n.

19 Instructions of Massachusetts to Jasper Mauduit, 1762, *Mauduit Letters*, pp. 40–41; Petition of General Assembly to the House of Lords, 16 April 1768, *Revolutionary Virginia* 1:57; [Madden,] *Reflections*, p. 83.

20 Smith, *English Legal System*, p. 12. See also *Massachusetts Gazette*, 6 March 1766, p. 2, col. 2; Pownall, *Pownall*, pp. 224–25; Barker, *Essays*, pp. 149–50.

21 Chalmers, *Opinions*, p. 206. See also ibid., pp. 206–32; Pownall, *Administration Sixth Edition* 2:37.

22 [Rawson,] *Revolution in New England*, p. 43; "To the Gentlemen Electors," 5 February 1763, Gadsden, *Writings*, p. 31; Dickinson, "Address," 25 April 1768, *Scots Magazine* 30 (1768): 524. See also [Fitch et al.,] *Reasons Why*, pp. 7–8.

23 Petition of 7 May 1768, *New Jersey Votes and Proceedings* (1768), p. 37. See also Anon., *To Tax Themselves*, at title, p. 126; Bland, *Colonel Dismounted*, pp. 20–21.

24 Letter to Lord Halifax, n.d., "Letters of Dennys De Berdt," p. 428. See also Anon., *Considerations upon Rights of Colonists*, p. 4.

25 Resolves of Bristol, Rhode Island, 28 February 1774, Munro, *Bristol*, p. 193. See also Resolves of Westerly, Rhode Island, 2 February 1774, Denison, *Westerly*, p. 110.

26 Petition from the House of Representatives to the House of Commons, 22 September 1768, *Pennsylvania Archives* 7:6275. See also Petition from the General Assembly to the King, 22 September 1768, ibid., at 6271; Address of Fincastle County, Virginia, to Congress Delegate, 20 January 1775, *American Archives* (4th ser.) 1:1166; Lovell, *An Oration*, p. 7; "Book Review," *Political Register* 4 (1769): 373.

27 "Book Review," *Monthly Review* 52 (1775): 259 (quoting Hutchinson, *History*). It was a current historical theme in Great Britain that the Germans migrating to Britannia brought freedom with them. Stuart, *Historical Dissertation*, pp. 282–83.

28 "To the Author," *American Gazette*, p. 50. See also [Dulany,] *Considerations on the Propriety*, p. 29.

29 Anon., *Rights of Parliament*, p. 15; Letter X, *Boston Evening-Post*, 5 June 1769, p. 4, col. 3.

30 [Erskine,] *Reflections on the Rise*, p. 15; "Book Review," *Gentleman's Magazine* 36 (1766): 628. See also Augusta County Instructions, 22 February 1775, *Revolutionary Virginia*, 2:299; Speech of Lord Chatham, Lords Debates, 20 January 1775, *Scots Magazine* 37 (1775): 81; Speech of Lord Chatham, Lords Debates, 26 May 1774, *American Archives* (4th ser.) 1:167. For an example of the forensic dispute over "historical" facts, see Anon., *Tyranny Unmasked*, pp. 34–35.

31 New Jersey Petition, 7 May 1768, *Scots Magazine* 30 (1768): 522; North Carolina Petition, 10 November 1768, *Boston Chronicle*, 20 March 1769, p. 91, col. 3. See also Remonstrance from Assembly to the King, 5 December 1768, *North Carolina Colonial Records*, 7:981; Remonstrance from Rhode Island to the King, *Boston Post-Boy*, 15 May 1769, p. 2, col. 1; Resolves of 30 May 1765, *Journal of Burgesses* 10:360; "An Act for regulating . . . ," May 1775, *Public Records of Connecticut*, 15:18–19; Instructions to Jasper Mauduit, 1762, *Mauduit Letters*, p. 41–42.

32 Jamaica Petition to the King, 28 December 1774, *Revolutionary Virginia* 2:363–64. For a striking version of the argument from Barbados in 1689, see [Littleton,] *Groans of Plantations*, pp. 24–25.

33 Anon., *Application of Political Rules*, p. 55; [Madden,] *Reflections*, p. 83; Anon., *Evidence of Common and Statute Laws*, p. iii.

34 Letter of 3 June 1774, *Scots Magazine* 36 (1774): 283; Petition of 29 October 1768, *Documents of New Hampshire*, pp. 248–49. For British discussion of the migration principle, see Anon., *Present Crisis*, pp. 11–12; "Answer

to Wesley," *Hibernian Magazine* 5 (1775): 785–86; Anon., *Constitutional Right*, p. 9; Pownall, *Administration*, p. 51. See also "A British American," *Gentleman's Magazine* 36 (1766): 613; Anon., *Letter* pp. 270–71.

CHAPTER FIFTEEN: THE MIGRATION PURCHASE

1 Declaration of 6 July 1775, Commager, *Documents*, pp. 92–93; Gloucester Resolves, 27 March 1770, *Boston Evening-Post*, 16 April 1770, p. 4, col. 1. See also Bristol, Rhode Island Resolves, 28 February 1774, Munro, *Bristol*, p. 194; *Public Advertiser*, 15 January 1770, reprinted in *Franklin's Letters to the Press*, p. 177; Haven; *Election Sermon*, p. 45.

2 Allen, *American Crisis*, p. 16; [Galloway,] *Americanus*, pp. 6–7; American answer: *London Chronicle*, 11 April 1767, reprinted in *Franklin's Letters to the Press*, p. 88 (this item was widely reprinted in the colonies: *South-Carolina Gazette*, 27 July 1767, p. 1, col. 1; *Boston Post-Boy*, 22 June 1767, p. 1, col. 1); Bland, *An Inquiry*, pp. 13–14; Anon., *Necessity of Repealing the Stamp Act*, pp. 7–9.

3 [Mather,] *America's Appeal*, p. 53. See also Jefferson, "Summary View," reprinted in *Commemoration Ceremony*, p. 65; Instructions of 21 October 1765; Thomas Franklin Waters, *Ipswich in the Massachusetts Bay Colony* (Ipswich, Mass., 1917) 2:294; Anon., *History of George III*, p. 242.

4 See, e.g., Andrews, *Settlements*, pp. 1–3; Robson, *American Revolution*, p. 4.

5 *Massacre Orations*, p. 60. See also Adams, *Historical View*, p. 66. For the most important debate on the facts and law of migration purchase, see Hutchinson, Address of January 1773, *Briefs of American Revolution*, pp. 15–16; Answer of the Council, 25 January 1773, and Answer of the House, 26 January 1773, ibid., pp. 34–36, 54–58; [Prescott,] *Calm Consideration*, p. 35; Vattel, *Law of Nations* 1:166 (book 1, chapter 18, sec. 210). It would seem that when speaking officially, Hutchinson intentionally argued forensic history. His private interpretation of the facts was close to that of the whigs. See his letter quoted in Becker, *Declaration*, pp. 83–84.

6 [Downer,] *Discourse in Providence*, p. 9; Wallingford Resolves, 13 January 1766, *Gazette & News-Letter*, 6 February 1766, p. 3, col. 1; Suffolk Resolves, 9 September 1744, *Massachusetts Provincial Congresses*, p. 601.

7 Dorset Declaration, 15 June 1648, Morrill, *Revolt of the Provinces*, p. 207; Anon., *Conduct of Mansfield*, pp. 4–5. See also Address of Cripplegate Within to the Lord Mayor, 30 April 1771, Anon., *Magna Charta Opposed to Privilege*, p. 194. Edmund Burke probably meant purchased with money when he spoke of the "bought" rights of the East India Company. Speech of Edmund Burke, Commons Debates, 18 December 1772, *Scots Magazine* 35 (1773): 127. Similarly, Dissent of the Lords, 25 December 1772, ibid., p. 129. Also, Americans thought of the English civil war as a time when rights had been purchased. Montgomery, *Sermon at Christiana Bridge*, pp. 23–69, 24.

8 *Select Collection of Letters* 3:123.

9 Resolves of Westerly, Rhode Island, 2 February 1774, Denison, *Westerly*, p. 110. See also Cooke, *Election Sermon*, p. 33, 174: Resolves of Lower House, 2 November 1765, *Maryland Votes and Proceedings* (November 1765), p. 15; [Devotion,] *The Examiner*, p. 13.

10 Cohen, "Revolution and Natural Law," pp. 498–99 (quoting John Adams); "To Inhabitants of Salem," 11 July 1768, *Scots Magazine* 30 (1768): 523; Dickinson, *Speech*, p. 44. See also Instructions of Fincastle to Continental Congress Delegates, 20 January 1775, *Revolutionary Virginia* 2:256; Petition from Assembly to King, 5 December 1768, *North Carolina Colonial Records* 7:981; New York Petition to the House of Commons, 18 October 1764, Morgan, *Prologue*, p. 9; Cambridge Petition, 1688, [Mather,] *A Narrative*, pp. 8–9; Patten, *Discourse at Hallifax*, pp. 12, 15–16.

11 Brown, *Revolutionary Politics*, p. 116; Mayhew, *Snare Broken*, p. 16; Chauncy, *Civil Magistrates*, p. 33; Baldwin, *New England Clergy*, p. 108 (quoting Amos Adams); [Johnson,] *Important Observations*, p. 35; Gorham Resolves, 7 January 1773, *Boston Evening-Post*, 15 February 1773, p. 1, col. 2; "Statement," 17 December 1764, *Boston Evening-Post*, 29 August 1774, p. 1, col. 2.

12 *Gentleman's Magazine* 44 (1774): 63; Concord Resolves, 24 January 1774, *Boston Evening-Post*, 7 February 1774, p. 1, col. 3.

13 *Boston-Gazette*, reprinted in *South Carolina Gazette* (Supplement), 26 August 1765, p. 1, col. 2; Anon., *Case of Great Britain*, p. 3; Instructions to Pennsylvania's Agent Richard Jackson, 22 September 1764, *Franklin-Jackson Letters*, pp. 183–84. Yet another word was "debt": "a debt due to these brave adventurers, and their immediate descendants." Anon., *Right of British Legislature*, pp. 12–13.

14 Mather, *Reasons*, p. 225. For a somewhat similar 1675 argument on behalf of Virginia's rights, see Lovejoy, "Virginia's Charter," p. 39.

15 New York Resolves, 18 December 1765, Morgan, *Prologue*, p. 61. See also Petition from the Pennsylvania Assembly to the House of Commons, 22 September 1768, *Boston Post-Boy*, 20 February 1769, p. 2, col. 1. For details of how the colonies increased Britain's wealth, see Rusticus, *Remarks*, pp. 13–14; *Boston Evening-Post*, 4 November 1765, p. 1, cols. 2–3.

16 "Hutchinson's Essay on Colonial Rights," in Morgan, "Thomas Hutchinson," p. 488; New Jersey Petition to the King, 7 May 1781, *Scots Magazine* 30 (1768): 523. It was also claimed that the first colonists enriched Britain because "their astonishing efforts greatly facilitated the settlement of other British colonies in America." Address from Salem Whigs to General Thomas Gage, 21 June 1774, Phillips, *Salem*, p. 325.

17 [Bernard,] *Appeal to the Public*, p. 53; Johnson, *Political Tracts*, p. 160; Anon., *Application of Political Rules*, p. 75. See also Taylor, "Mauduit-Pamphleteer," p. 124.

18 [Gray,] *Right of the Legislature*, pp. 47–48. For an important lawyer and judge who rejected Gray's law, see Camden, "Speech on American Taxation," pp. 123–24.

CHAPTER SIXTEEN: THE ORIGINAL CONTRACT

1 Anon., *Letter on Corruption*, p. 56; Hamilton, *Farmer Refuted*, p. 88. See also Principles and Resolutions of the Constitutional Society at Cambridge, 1783, Wyvill, *Defence of Price*, pp. 98–99.

2 Willcox, *Age of Aristocracy*, p. 7; Kenyon, *Revolution Principles*, p. 2; "In Our Contracted Sphere," pp. 22–24.

3 Wood, *Creation*, p. 283. For writers who treat the two contracts as one, see Dickinson, "Debate on Glorious Revolution," p. 42; Dickinson, *Liberty and Property*, p. 72; Einaudi, "Burke's Political Philosophy," p. 582; J. C. Holt, "Rights and Liberties in Magna Carta," reprinted in *Magna Carta and Liberty*, pp. 45–46.

4 E.g., Acherley, *Britannic Constitution*, p. 102; [Barwis,] *Three Dialogues*, p. 65; *Monthly Review* 55 (1776): 263; Rutherforth, *Natural Law* 2:78–82. But see a critic of the contract theory who compounds the two, Tucker, *Treatise*, p. 42.

5 See Barker, "Natural Law," at p. 274, n. 1; Miller, "Glorious Revolution," p. 544; *Political Register* 10 (1772): 329; Locke, *Two Treatises*, book 2, sec. 97. But see Laslett, "Introduction to Locke," p. 113.

6 Shirley, *Richard Hooker*, p. 210; Tierney, *Religion, Law and Growth*, pp. 36– 37; Burlamaqui, *Politic Law*, p. 28.

7 Burlamaqui, *Politic Law*, p. 28; Gough, *Social Contract*, pp. 2–3. For the contrary view, see Paley, *Principles of Philosophy*, p. 415.

8 Anon., *Rights Asserted*, p. 52; Letter of 26 November 1768, Anon., *National Mirror*, p. 26. See also Anon., *In Behalf of the Constitution*, pp. 88–89.

9 Baldwin, *New England Clergy*, p. 67 (quoting Williams); Instructions to the Representatives, July 1774, [Dickinson,] *New Essay*, p. 11–12; Blackstone, *Commentaries* 1:237. See also Francis Stoughton Sullivan, "A Discussion," *Political Register* 11 (1772): 156; Turner, *Election Sermon*, p. 16.

10 Patten, *Discourse at Hallifax*, p. 10; Letter of 20 December 1768, Anon., *National Mirror*, p. 61; "To the King," February 1777, *Papers of Iredell* 1:436. See also [Allen,] *Watchman's Alarm*, p. 6; Dulany, *Considerations*, p. 634; Hoadley, *Works* 2:256; Kenyon, *Revolution Principles*, p. 17.

11 *Delaware Declaration of Rights* (1776), p. 2; Dickinson's Notes for a Speech, [24? January 1776,] *Letters of Delegates to Congress*, 3:134; Eliot, *Give Cesar His Due*, p. 31; *Maryland Gazette*, 10 February 1748, p. 1, col. 2; Baldwin, *New England Clergy*, p. 39 (quoting Joseph Moss) and p. 180 (quoting Jonas Clark). See also Anon., *Confutation of Sherlock*, p. 5.

12 [Barwis,] *Three Dialogues*, p. 73; *Monthly Review* 55 (1776): 262; Abington Resolves, 19 March 1770, *Boston Gazette*, 2 April 1770, p. 3, col. 1.

13 E.g., Brady, *Complete History*, "Preface" (no pagination); Blackall, *Exeter's Answer*, pp. 20–21; Anon., *Defence of English History*; Bentham, *Fragment on Government*, p. 428; [Reeves,] *Thoughts, Third Letter*, p. 83.

14 E.g., [Whitby,] *Historical Account*, p. 48; Anon., *Divine Rights*, p. 68; [Watson,] *Answer to Disquisition*, p. 29. See also Gough, *Locke's Political Philosophy*, p. 33.

15 Paley, *Principles of Philosophy*, pp. 417–18. See also Wooddeson, *Jurisprudence*, p. 36; Answer to Sir Robert Atkyns, Lords Debates, 30 January 1689, *Lords Manuscripts*, p. 15.

16 *Craftsman* 13 (16 November 1734): 70–71; Anon., *Essay upon Government*, pp. 67–68; Johnson, *Remarks on Sherlock*, p. x–xi. For ridicule, saying the contract would base rights "in Dreams and Forgery," see Anon., *Defence of English History*, p. 13. See also Instructions from the Committee, [July 1774,] [Dickinson,] *New Essay*, p. 10n. But see Wooddeson, *Jurisprudence*, p. 69.

17 The extensive history of the original contract in England, going back to Saxon times, belongs with a study of Parliament's authority to legislate more than it belongs here and is therefore deferred. See "In Our Contracted Sphere," pp. 22–25; Judson, *Crisis*, p. 74.

18 *London Magazine* 34 (1765): 274; [Shebbeare,] *Fifth Letter*, p. 12; Tucker, *Election Sermon*, p. 17. See also Anon., *Defence of Resolutions*, p. 85; [Reeves,] *Thoughts, Second Letter*, p. 170; [Galloway,] *Candid Examination*, p. 17. For an excellent English statement of the contract and specific references to the authorities, documents, and writings that contain the terms of the contract, see [Whitby,] *Historical Account*, pp. 44–45.

19 Tucker, *Treatise*, p. 142; Wooddeson, *Jurisprudence*, pp. 13–15, 32, 35. See also Barker, *Essays*, p. 147; Shepard, "Sovereignty," p. 593.

CHAPTER SEVENTEEN: THE ORIGINAL COLONIAL CONTRACT

1 Richmond Resolves, 29 June 1774, *Revolutionary Virginia* 1:155; Address to British People, 5 September 1774, *Journal of the First Congress*, p. 79; Westerly Resolves, 2 February 1774, Denison, *Westerly*, p. 111.

2 Cooke, *Election Sermon*, pp. 45–46; Bland, *An Inquiry*, reprinted in *Revolutionary Virginia* 1:35.

3 Anon., *Policy of the Laws*, pp. 24–31; [Rawson,] *Revolution in New England*, p. 43.

4 Wilson, "Speech in the Pennsylvania Convention," p. 178; [Dulany,] *Considerations on the Propriety*, p. 30.

5 "To British Inhabitants," September 1774, *Papers of Iredell* 1:252.

6 Petition to King, 22 October 1765, *Account of Stamp Act Congress*, p. 11; Resolves of 2 November 1765, *Maryland Votes and Proceedings* (November 1765), p. 15. See also Quincy, *Observations with Thoughts*, pp. 453–54.

7 Massachusetts House Petition to the King, 20 January 1768, *Boston Post-Boy*, 21 March 1768, p. 1, col. 1; *Boston Evening-Post*, 1 July 1765, p. 1, col. 2. See also Cooke, *Election Sermon*, pp. 33–34.

8 Roxbury Declaration, 14 December 1772, *Boston Evening-Post*, 21 December 1772, p. 1, col. 2; Anon., *Letter*, p. 265; *Revolution Justified*, p. 125; Lovejoy, *Glorious Revolution*, p. 333 (quoting Mather); *The Freeman's Journal or New-Hampshire Gazette*, 6 July 1776, p. 1, col. 2. See also Anon., *Justice and Necessity*, pp. 18–19; Hall, *Edward Randolph*, p. 223 (quoting William Penn).

9 Petition from the New York Assembly to the King, n.d., *Boston Evening-Post*,

17 April 1769, p. 2, col. 1; Richard Henry Lee's Draft Address, October 1774, *Letters of Delegates to Congress* 1:175; Moore, *Taxing Colonies*, p. 45. The same "encouragement" was said to have induced English settlers to Ireland. Anon., *Narrative of Lords of Ireland*, p. 33; Anon., *Critical Review of Liberties*, p. 97.

10 [Livingston,] *Other Side*, p. 16. See also *Boston Evening-Post*, 1 July 1765, p. 1, col. 2.

11 *Boston Post-Boy*, 11 August 1766, p. 1, col. 3.

12 Instructions to Richard Jackson, 22 September 1764, *Pennsylvania Archives* 7:5643–44; Connecticut Resolves, 25 October 1765, Morgan, *Prologue*, p. 55. This "purchase" consideration seems to have been the one most favored by colonial assemblies. *Extract of Letter to De Berdt*, pp. 4–5; Petition to the King, 7 May 1768, *New Jersey Votes and Proceedings* (1768), p. 37; Petition from New Hampshire House of Representatives to King, 29 October 1768, *Documents of New Hampshire*, p. 249. See also *Massachusetts Gazette & News-Letter*, 30 March 1775, p. 2, col. 1; Anon., *To Tax Themselves*, p. 63 (quoting Hutchinson's *History*); Patten, *Discourse at Hallifax*, pp. 13, 15–16; Adams, *Religious Liberty*, p. 53.

13 *Boston Evening-Post* 1 July 1765, p. 1, col. 2.

14 Letter from Boston, 5 August 1765, *Prior Documents*, p. 9; Letter from Massachusetts House to Dennys De Berdt, 12 January 1768, Adams, *Writings* 1:140; Dover Resolves, 10 January 1774, *Boston Evening-Post*, 31 January 1774, p. 1, col. 3.

CHAPTER EIGHTEEN: THE REALITY OF CONTRACT

1 Steinberg, *Idea of Consent*, pp. 26–27.

2 See e.g., [Goodricke,] *Observations on Price's Theory*, p. 22.

3 Tucker, *Treatise*, p. 163; Instructions of Pennsylvania Congress to Continental Congress Deputies, 15 July 1774, *London Magazine* 43 (1774): 584 (the judge referred to was Bracton, quoted in Blackstone, *Commentaries* 1:227); *Maryland Gazette*, 16 March 1748, p. 2, col. 1.

4 Speech of Lord Lyttleton, "Lords Debates on Declaratory Act," p. 109; "Some Thoughts on the Constitution," *American Archives* (4th ser.) 2:963 (Philadelphia, 12 June 1775).

5 [Draper,] *Thoughts of a Traveller*, pp. 22–23; Proceedings of Bellingham, 19 May 1773, *Boston Evening-Post*, 18 October 1773, p. 1, col. 1.

6 [Maseres,] *Canadian Freeholder* 1:152; *Town and Country Magazine* 9 (1777): 453. See also Second Letter from a London Merchant to a Noble Lord, *Gazette & News-Letter*, 2 January 1766, p. 1, col. 3; Preamble, *Constitution of New-Jersey* (1776), p. 3.

7 "Hutchinson Essay on Colonial Rights," in Morgan, "Thomas Hutchinson," p. 482; [Hopkins,] *Grievances of the Colonies*, p. 8. See also [Dulany,] *Considerations on the Propriety*, p. 30.

8 Roxbury Declaration, 14 December 1772, *Boston Evening-Post*, 21 December 1772, p. 1, col. 2; Rhode Island Petition to King, 29 November 1764,

Rhode Island Colony Records 6:415. See also Patten, *Discourse at Hallifax*, p. 13; Anon., *To Freemen of Pennsylvania*, p. 1.

9 Mather, "Autobiography," p. 327; [Mather,] *America's Appeal*, p. 25; Resolutions of the General Assembly, October 1765, *Public Records of Connecticut* 12:422; Petition of William Bollan to House of Commons, February 1769, *Massachusetts Gazette*, 24 April 1769, p. 2, col. 1.

10 [Bancroft,] *Remarks*, p. 7. See also Anon., *Privileges of Jamaica*, pp. 30–31; Hamilton, *Farmer Refuted*, pp. 90–91.

11 Letter from Samuel Adams to John Smith, 19 December 1765, Adams, *Writings* 1:45; Anon., *To Tax Themselves*, p. 95. Equally wonderful was the certitude of writers commenting on the terms of the original colonial contract. They knew what it said, sometimes referring to the "words" and saying they had "read" them. Anon., *Remarks on the New Essay*, p. 42. For the most detailed discussion of the terms of the contract by a British lawyer disagreeing with the whig interpretation, see Abercromby, *De Jure*, pp. 65–66.

12 For a splendid instance of the custom of contract, applied against the colonies by a whig lawyer who became a loyalist, see Letter from William Smith to Committee of the Provincial Congress, 4 July 1776, *Memoirs of William Smith* 1:280. For Smith's explanation of how prior promise and later usage combined in the original-contract theory to legitimize civil rights, see diary entry for 9 June 1776, ibid., pp. 271–72. In Great Britain the custom of the original contract was often argued as proof of parliamentary supremacy. See, e.g., Lord Rockingham quoted in Guttridge, *English Whiggism*, p. 74.

13 [Whately,] *Regulations Lately Made*, pp. 19, 22–23; Proclamation of 7 October 1763, Special Verdict, *Campbell* v. *Hall, State Trials* 20:239 (King's Bench, 1774), p. 244. See also *Scots Magazine* 25 (1763): 576–77; *Gentleman's Magazine* 33 (1763): 477; *American Archives* (4th ser.) 1:172–80.

14 Anon., *Considerations Upon the Act*, p. 4: Maryland Resolves, 28 September 1765, Morgan, *Prologue*, pp. 52–53. For promises that the settlers, including dissenters, could retain civil and religious rights, attributed to Charles II and said to have been relied upon, see Anon., *Case of Presbyterians*, pp. 3–4; Anon., *Privileges of Jamaica*, pp. 30–31. For a leading loyalist saying the promise was needed for settlement of western lands, see Galloway, *Speech in Answer*, pp. 5–6.

15 For examples of the implied encouragement contract, see "Aequus," *London Chronicle*, 12 December 1765, quoted in *Boston Post-Boy*, 10 March 1766, p. 1, cols. 2–3; Greene, *Quest*, p. 1 (quoting William Bull); Anon., *Late Occurences*, p. 36; Anon., *To Tax Themselves*, pp. 126–27.

16 "Humble Representation of the Lords Spiritual and Temporal," 17 October 1719, *Protests of the Lords of Ireland*, p. 41.

17 *South-Carolina Gazette* (Supplement), 1 October 1764, p. 2, col. 2. See also [Bollan,] *Continued Corruption*, p. 61.

18 Speech of Lord Chatham, Lords Debates, 17 June 1774, *Scots Magazine* 36 (1774): 305; Speech of Lord Camden, Lords Debates, 17 May 1775, *Scots*

Magazine 37 (1775): 242. A writer who favored the act and attacked Chatham admitted that settlers would not have gone to Quebec but for the proclamation. [Meredith,] *Letter to Chatham*, pp. 6–7.

19 London Petition, June 1774, *Gentleman's Magazine* 44 (1774): 248; *Scots Magazine* 36 (1774): 307; *Hibernian Magazine* 4 (1774): 404; *Addresses and Petitions of the Common Council*, p. 49; *American Archives* (4th ser.) 1:215. See also Anon., *History of Lord North*, p. 159.

20 Quebec Petitions of November 1774, [Maseres,] *To Obtain an Assembly*, pp. 202–22, 239, 254; [Knox,] *Justice and Policy*, p. 74; *American Archives* (4th ser.) 1:1849. See also Memorial of Freeholders to Lord Dartmouth, 15 January 1774, *American Archives* (4th ser.) 1:1844–45.

21 Speeches of Attorney General Edward Thurlow and Sergeant John Glynn, Commons Debates, 26 May 1774, *American Archives* (4th ser.) 1:183–84.

22 Speech of Lord Mansfield, Lords Debates, 3 February 1766, Holliday, *Life of Mansfield*, pp. 245–46.

23 "To the Printer," *Political Register* 11 (1772): 107.

24 [Whately,] *Regulations Lately Made*, p. 23; *Political Register* 6 (1770): 166, 59.

25 Arguments for the plaintiff by Alleyne and Glynn, and for the defendant by Thurlow, *Campbell* v. *Hall*, 20 *State Trials* 239 (King's Bench, 1774) pp. 262, 312, 313, 316.

26 Opinion of Lord Mansfield, *Campbell* v. *Hall*, ibid., pp. 328–29.

27 Speech of Lord Camden, Lords Debates, 17 May 1775, *Parliamentary History* 18:659; *Scots Magazine* 37 (1775): 241.

CHAPTER NINETEEN: THE EVIDENCE OF CHARTER

1 Weymouth Instructions, n.d., *Boston Evening-Post*, 21 October 1765, p. 2, col. 2; *Boston Evening-Post*, 1 July 1765, p. 1, col. 2.

2 For contrary arguments that charters were authority for rights, see Cooke, *Election Sermon*, p. 33; Noble, *Some Strictures*, p. 21n.; [Shipley,] *Intended Speech*, pp. 25–26; Ipswich Instructions, 21 October 1765, *Boston Post-Boy*, 4 November 1765, p. 2, col. 1; Allen, *Magistracy an Institution*, p. 8; Dulany, *English Laws*, p. 24; Mather, *Reasons*, p. 226 (Massachusetts); [Fitch et al.,] *Reasons Why*, pp. 7–9 (Connecticut).

3 Chauncy, *Civil Magistrates*, p. 54; Rowley Instructions, 10 October 1765, *Boston Evening-Post*, 21 October 1765, p. 1, col. 3.

4 Prince, *Civil Rulers*, p. 22; Mather, "Autobiography," p. 327.

5 [Goodricke,] *Observations on Price's Theory*, p. 22; *Papers of Jefferson* 1:340; [Galloway,] *True and Impartial State*, p. 33; [Hawley,] "To Inhabitants," 9 March 1775, *American Archives* (4th ser.) 2:95; "Essay," *Papers of Iredell* 1:164. See also [Devotion,] *The Examiner*, p. 14.

6 Bristol Resolves, 28 February 1774, *Rhode Island Colony Records* 7:274; Instructions to Jasper Mauduit, 1762, *Mauduit Letters*, p. 46. See also Cooke, *Election Sermon*, pp. 33–34; Anon., *Second Answer to Wesley*, p. 12.

7 "To his Majesty," February 1777, *Papers of Iredell* 1:432; Dummer, *Defence*,

p. 13. See also Letter from a London Merchant, *Boston News-Letter* (Supplement), 2 May 1765, p. 1, col. 1; Crane, "Franklin and Stamp Act," p. 63.

8 Speech of Richard Hussey, Commons Debates, 3 February 1766, *Proceedings and Debates* 2:141; Price, *Nature of Civil Liberty*, p. 40. See also Patten, *Discourse at Hallifax*, p. 15; *New York Journal*, reprinted in *Boston Evening-Post* (Supplement), 8 March 1773, p. 1, col. 1.

9 Worcester County Resolves, 9 August 1774, *Boston Evening-Post*, 5 September 1774, p. 1, col. 3.

10 Dulany, *Considerations*, p. 634.

11 Petition to the King, May 1768, *Public Records of Connecticut* 13:87; [Fitch, et al.,] *Reasons Why*, pp. 25–26.

12 Message from the Massachusetts Council to Governor Hutchinson, 5 April 1771, *Boston Evening-Post*, 8 April 1771, p. 2, col. 1; Pomfret Resolves, 25 December 1765, *Gazette & News-Letter*, 9 January 1766, p. 1, col. 2; Hampshire County Resolves, 23 September 1774, *Gazette & Post-Boy*, 10 October 1774, p. 1, col. 1. See also Georgia Committee to Virginia Committee, 10 August 1774, *Revolutionary Virginia* 2:158; Parsons, *Election Sermon*, p. 16; [Allen,] *Watchman's Alarm*, pp. 10–11; Dummer, *Defence*, p. 7.

13 Haven, *Election Sermon*, p. 45; Otis, *Vindication*, pp. 558–59; Dulany, *Considerations on the Propriety*, pp. 15–16.

14 Resolves of Albermarle County, 26 July 1774, *Revolutionary Virginia* 1:112; Suffolk Resolves, 9 September 1774, *Massachusetts Provincial Congresses*, p. 602; Instructions to Richard Jackson, 22 September 1764, Franklin-Jackson, *Letters*, p. 183. See also Resolves of Georgia Commons House, January 1775, *American Archives* (4th ser.) 1:1157.

15 Instructions of Boston, 17 May 1764, *Boston Evening-Post*, 28 May 1764, p. 2, col. 1; *London Magazine* 43 (1774): 243. See also Galloway, *Speech in Answer*, p. 23; Price, *Nature of Civil Liberty*, p. 40; Palmer, *Impartial Account*, p. 40; "Answer to Wesley," *Hibernian Magazine* 5 (1775): 785. The same doctrine was true for British charters. [Ramsay,] *Historical Essay*, pp. 53–54.

16 [Drayton,] *Letter from Freeman*, p. 30; Gadsden, *Writings*, p. xx.

17 [Ramsay,] *Thoughts on Nature of Government*, p. 53.

18 [Howard,] *Halifax Letter*, p. 535; [Lind,] *Thirteenth Parliament*, p. 86. See also Anon., *Civil Liberty Asserted*, p. 68; [Gray,] *Right of the Legislature*, pp. 47–48; Abercromby, "De Jure," pp. 62, 65–66; Hinkhouse, *Preliminaries*, p. 94.

19 "In the First Line of Defense," pp. 194–204; Petersham Instructions, 4 January 1773, *Boston Evening-Post*, 18 January 1773, p. 2, col. 2.

20 Hopkins, *Rights*, p. 508; [Hawley,] "To the Inhabitants," 6 April 1775, *American Archives* (4th ser.), 2:290, 291; Lee's Draft Address, October 1774, *Letters of Delegates to Congress* 1:175; Maryland Resolves, 28 September 1765, Morgan, *Prologue*, p. 53. See also Hazeltine, "Influence," p. 8.

21 [Dulany,] *Considerations on the Propriety*, p. 30; vagueness: "In the First Line of Defense," pp. 183–89; Rhode Island Resolves, September 1765, Morgan,

Prologue, p. 50; Hopkins, *Rights*, p. 508. See also Letter of 16 January 1766, *London Magazine* 35 (1766): 33; Dulany, *English Laws*, pp. 27–30; Creasy, *Imperial Constitutions*, p. 92.

22 *Massachusetts Gazette* (Supplement), 27 February 1766, p. 1, col. 1.

23 Hinkhouse, *Preliminaries*, p. 95.

24 Increase Mather, *A Brief Account Concerning Several of the Agents of New-England, their Negotiation at the Court of England* (London, 1691), pp. 17, 22.

25 Connecticut Resolves, 25 October 1765, Morgan, *Prologue*, p. 54.

26 *Boston Evening-Post*, 21 October 1765, p. 1, col. 1.

27 *Boston Gazette*, 4 May 1767, p. 3, col. 1.

28 *Examination of Franklin*, p. 15.

29 Bailyn, *Pamphlets*, p. 111 (quoting Dickinson).

30 Connecticut Resolves, *Boston Evening-Post*, 20 June 1774, p. 4, col. 1. See also Resolves of Town of Groton, 25 January 1773, *Boston Evening-Post*, 22 March 1773, p. 2, col. 1; Letter from Town of North Yarmouth to Boston Selectmen, 18 January 1773, *Boston Evening-Post*, 19 July 1773, p. 4, col. 1.

31 *Boston Evening-Post*, 28 October 1765, p. 1, col. 1 (quoting *New London Gazette*); Massachusetts Resolves, 29 October 1765, *Boston Evening-Post*, 4 November 1765, p. 1, col. 1.

32 Connecticut Resolves, 25 October 1765, Morgan, *Prologue*, p. 54. For British support of this constitutional theory, see *Boston Evening-Post*, 2 December 1765, p. 1, col. 1; *Massachusetts Gazette*, 6 February 1766, p. 1, col. 3 (quoting London *Public Advertiser*). For another authority, see "In the First Line of Defense," pp. 208–15.

CHAPTER TWENTY: THE COLONIAL GRIEVANCES

1 *Remonstrance of the Cities* (1659), p. 1; Declaration of the Nobility et al. at Nottingham, 22 November 1688, in [Bohun,] *Desertion*, pp. 77–79; [Jacob,] *Laws of Liberty*, p. 114; Irish: Schedule of Grievances by Irish House of Lords, 18 February 1640/41, Rushworth, *Historical Collections: Third Part* 1:222; Coke: White, *Coke and the Grievances*.

2 Answer of John Wilkes to the Grand Jury of Carmarthen County, 4 May 1771, Anon., *Magna Charta Opposed to Privilege*, p. 202. See also Petition to King, 24 June 1769, and Remonstrance to King, 15 November 1770, *Addresses and Petitions of the Common Council*, pp. 6, 26; Petition of Bristol to King, 25 July 1769, *Political Register* 6 (1770): 115–16; [Baillie,] *Appendix to a Letter*, p. 79; [Priestly,] *Present State of Liberty*, pp. 20–22; [Towers,] *Observations on Liberty*, p. 30.

3 Speech of Edmund Burke, Commons Debates, 22 March 1775, *Burke on American Revolution*, p. 86.

4 Resolution of Richard Oliver, House of Commons, 27 November 1775, *Hibernian Magazine* 6 (1776): 57; Petition to King, 24 June 1769, *Addresses and Petitions of Common Council*, p. 8; Petition of Lord Mayor, Alder-

men, and Livery of London to the King, 11 April 1775, *London Magazine* 44 (1775): 209.

5 Suffolk Resolves, 9 September 1774, *Massachusetts Provincial Congresses*, p. 602; Petition of Continental Congress to the King, 26 October 1774, *London Magazine* 44 (1775): 68.

6 Constitutional grievances: Resolutions of New York General Assembly, 8 March 1775, *American Archives* (4th ser.) 1:1302–03, 1302; *Examination of Franklin*, p. 4; Pomfret Resolves, 25 December 1765, *Gazette & News-Letter*, 9 January 1766, p. 1, col. 2; Anon., *To Committee of London Merchants*, p. 13; Continental Congress Petition to the King, 26 October 1744, *London Magazine* 44 (1775): 67. A related but different category of grievances was that arising from imperial governance practice rather than from parliamentary legislation. A New England newspaper illustrated one of these grievances when objecting that "our legislature has been dissolved without allowing them time to go through the most important business." That was a governance grievance. It may have involved rights of the colonial assemblies, but not individual rights of the people. *Boston Evening-Post* (Supplement), 18 July 1768, p. 2, col. 1.

7 Letter from F. B., 27 August, *Scots Magazine* 36 (1774): 418 (reprinting *London Chronicle*, 5–7 January 1768).

8 "Virginia Resolutions on Lord North's Conciliatory Proposal," 10 June 1775, *Papers of Jefferson* 1:171–72; Address of New York General Committee of Association to Cadwallader Colden, 11 May 1775, *Remembrancer for 1775*, p. 215.

9 Petition to the King, 13 February 1775, *New Jersey Votes and Proceedings* (January 1775), pp. 59–60; Resolutions of New York Assembly, 3 March and 8 March 1775, *American Archives* (4th ser.) 1:1297–1303; "An Act for regulating and ordering the Troops that are or may be raised for the Defence of this Colony," May 1775, *Public Records of Connecticut* 15:18–21.

10 Continental Association of 20 October 1774 and Declarations setting forth the Causes and Necessity of taking up Arms, 6 July 1775, *Papers of Jefferson* 1:150, 214–15; "To the Inhabitants of the Colonies," 21 October 1774, *Journal of the First Congress*, pp. 104–7.

11 Petition to the King, 26 October 1774, *Revolution Documents* 8:216–17; Declaration of Rights, 14 October 1774, *Journal of the First Congress*, pp. 63–64.

Chapter Twenty-One: The Admiralty Grievance

1 [Allen,] *Beauties of Liberty*, pp. 20–21; Instructions of 8 May 1769, *Boston Town Records* 16:287; *South-Carolina Gazette*, 12 October 1765, p. 1, col. 1 (quoting *Connecticut Gazette*, 30 August 1765); Instructions of Providence, 13 August 1765, *Boston Evening-Post*, 19 August 1765, p. 2, col. 3; *Gazette & News-Letter*, 28 November 1765, p. 3, col. 1 (quoting *Public Ledger*, 23 September 1765).

2 Connecticut Resolves, May 1774, *American Archives* (4th ser.) 1:356. See also

Continental Congress's Declaration and Resolves, 14 October 1774, and
Memorial to Inhabitants, 21 October 1774; Petition from the Stamp Act
Congress to the King (1765), Morgan, *Prologue*, pp. 64–65.

3 Letter II from Philadelphia, *Boston Evening-Post*, 27 June 1774, p. 1, col. 2.

4 Petition from the General Court to the House of Commons, 3 November 1764,
Speeches, p. 22; Cambridge: *Boston Post-Boy*, 21 October 1765, p. 2, col.
1. See also Answer from the Council and House to Governor Francis Bernard, 3 November 1764, *Speeches*, p. 19; Instructions of 8 May 1769, *Boston Town Records* 16:288; Instructions of New York Freeholders, 26 November 1765, *Boston Evening-Post*, 9 December 1765, p. 3, col. 1.

5 One removal: Knollenberg, *Growth of Revolution*, p. 222; Ubbelohde, *Vice-
Admiralty*, p. 48–105; new courts: Barrow, *Trade*, p. 224; church courts:
John Bastwick, *The Letany of John Bastwick* (1637), in *Somers' Tracts* 5:413;
[Dulany,] *Considerations on the Propriety*, p. 23n. See also Hopkins, *Rights*,
pp. 515–16; [Whately,] *Considerations on Trade*, p. 229.

6 Dickerson, *Acts*, p. 169; Answer from the Council and House to Governor
Francis Bernard, 3 November 1764, *Speeches*, p. 19. The Sugar Act is reprinted in Morgan, *Prologue*, pp. 4–8.

7 Thacher, *Sentiments*, p. 495. See also Petition from New York Assembly to
the House of Commons, 25 March 1775, *American Archives* (4th ser.) 1:
1319; "Junius Americanus," *Boston Evening-Post*, 28 January 1771, p. 1,
col. 1.

8 "Junius Americanus," *Boston Evening-Post*, 17 December 1770, p. 1, col. 2.

9 Address from the Continental Congress to the King, 26 October 1774, and
Petition from the New Jersey Assembly to the King, 13 February 1775, *American Archives* (4th ser.) 1:935, 1132; Answer from the Council and House
to Governor Francis Bernard, 3 November 1764, *Speeches*, p. 18; Thacher,
Sentiments, p. 493; "Brutus," Address to County, July 1775, *Revolutionary
Virginia* 3:128; [Lee,] *True State of the Proceedings*, p. 37; Speech of Edmund Burke, Commons Debates, 22 March 1775, *Burke on American Revolution*, p. 111. See also Goodhart, *Law of the Land*, p. 59 (quoting John
Adams); Wickwire, *Subministers*, p. 122.

10 "L.," *Letter to G[renville]*, p. 46; Instructions of Newburyport, 21 October
1765, *Boston Post-Boy*, 4 November 1765, p. 1, col. 2; Instructions of 8 May
1769, *Boston Evening-Post*, 15 May 1769, p. 1, col. 2.

11 Letter from the Continental Congress to British People, 5 September 1774,
London Magazine 43 (1774): 630; [Bollan,] *Free Britons Memorial*, p. 21.
See also [Hurd,] *Moral and Political Dialogues*, p. 304; Bourguignon, *First
Federal Court*, p. 35; Kellogg, *Colonial Charter*, p. 227.

12 *Boston Evening-Post*, 2 January 1769, p. 2, col. 1. Another admiralty grievance was that the "single judge" did not have to sit, but could depute another to hold court in his place "and pass Judgment upon the Property of
English Subjects." *Boston Gazette*, 2 October 1769, p. 3, col. 2.

13 Letter from the Massachusetts House to the Earl of Dartmouth, 5 March 1773,
Revolution Documents 6:98; Instructions of 20 May 1772, *Boston Town
Records* 18:85. See also [John Adams,] Braintree Instructions, *Gazette &*

News-Letter, 10 October 1765, pp. 2–3; Hopkins, *Rights*, pp. 515–16; Lovejoy, *Rhode Island Politics*, pp. 97–98; Wickwire, *Subministers*, pp. 190–91.

14 Resolution of 21 June 1770, *Journal of Burgesses* 12:85; [Hopkins,] "Vindication of a Pamphlet," 9 March 1765, p. 1, col. 3. For defense of single judges on grounds of imperial necessity, see [Hutchinson,] *Strictures upon the Declaration*, p. 24; Howard, *Halifax Letter*, p. 541–42; [Pownall,] *Considerations*, p. 43.

15 Instructions of 27 May 1769, Phillips, *Salem*, p. 304. For the best expressions of the inequality grievance, see Instructions of 20 May 1772, *Boston Town Records* 18:85; Instructions of Boston, 8 May 1769, *Boston Post-Boy*, 15 May 1769, p. 1, col. 2. See also Thacher, *Sentiments*, pp. 493–94; Letter from Samuel Adams to John Smith, 19 December 1765, Adams, *Writings* 1:46.

16 [Hutchinson,] *Strictures upon the Declaration*, p. 24; *Journal of the Times*, 14 May 1769, p. 99, col. 1, and 7 January 1769, p. 46, col. 2; Thacher, *Sentiments*, p. 494; [Baillie,] *Appendix to a Letter*, p. 24.

17 Instructions of the Pennsylvania Congress to Deputies, 15 July 1774, *London Magazine* 43 (1774): 586. For the last and perhaps best statements of the grievance by a colonial assembly, see Petition of the New York Assembly to King, 25 March 1775, *American Archives* (4th ser.) 1:1314; Representation of the New York Assembly to House of Commons, 25 March 1775, *Scots Magazine* 37 (1775): 236 (also in *Gentleman's Magazine* 45 (1775): 247–48; *Hibernian Magazine* 5 (1775): 359); Resolution of New York Assembly, 8 March 1775, *American Archives* (4th ser.) 1:1302. See also Minutes of 3 March 1775, *Journal of New York Assembly* (1766–1776), pp. 52–54.

Chapter Twenty-Two: The Duty of Rights

1 Letter "from another Gentleman, London, Feb. 11, 1766," *South Carolina Gazette*, 16 June 1766, p. 2, col. 2; Speech of Lord Chatham, Lords Debates, 26 May 1774, and Resolutions of the North Carolina Convention, 27 August 1774, *American Archives* (4th ser.) 1:168, 735.

2 Anon., *British Liberties*, pp. 161–62; Anon., *Fair Trial*, p. 1.

3 Anon., *Considerations on Information*, p. 20; Anon., *Fair Trial*, p. 228. See also Hind, *Sermon at St. Margaret's*, p. 16.

4 Adams, *Religious Liberty*, pp. 50–51; Resolutions of the North Carolina Convention, 27 August 1774, *American Archives* (4th ser.) 1:736; Chauncy, *Civil Magistrates*, pp. 32–33. See also Statement of Suffolk County Grand Jurors, *Gazette & Post-Boy*, 5 September 1774, p. 2, col. 2.

5 Anon., *Conduct of Mansfield*, pp. 4–5. Similarly, see *Remonstrance of the Cities* (1659), pp. 2–3; Anon., *British Liberties*, pp. 52–53.

6 Suffolk Resolves, 9 September 1774, *Massachusetts Provincial Congresses*, p. 602; Johnson, *Notes on Pastoral*, p. 61; Essex County Resolutions, 11 June 1774, *Papers of William Livingston* 1:17; "To the Good People of Virginia" (1766), Lee, *Richard Henry Lee* 1:39; [Shebbeare,] *Fifth Letter*, pp. 52–53; *Guide to Rights*, p. iii. See also Concord Resolves, 31 August 1774,

Gazette & Post-Boy, 12 September 1774, p. 1, col. 3; Resolves of Middlesex County, Massachusetts, 31 August 1774, *American Archives* (4th ser.) 1:752; Resolves of Worcester County, Maryland, 7 June 1775, *American Archives* (4th ser.) 2:924; Botetourt Instructions, 11 March 1775, *Revolutionary Virginia* 2:324–25.

7 [Dickinson,] Pennsylvania Instructions, 21 July 1774, *London Magazine* 43 (1774): 585. See also Resolves of the Delaware Convention, 2 August 1774, and Fairfax County (Virginia) Association, 17 January 1775, *American Archives* (4th ser.) 1:668, 1145; Letter from Town of Duxborough to Boston Committee, 29 March 1773, *Boston Evening-Post*, 12 July 1773, p. 2, col. 1.

8 [Keld,] *Polity of England*, p. 434 (quoting Blackstone). See also Towers, *Letter to Wesley*, pp. 47–48; Message from John Wilkes to Electors of Middlesex, 25 March 1769, *Cambridge Magazine*, p. 145.

9 [Johnson,] *Some Important Observations*, p. 23.

10 "Americanus," *Letter to Freeholders*, p. 2. See also [Allen,] *Beauties of Liberty*, p. 19; Patten, *Discourse at Hallifax*, pp. 15–16.

11 Resolves of the First Provincial Congress, 27 August 1774, *North Carolina Colonial Records* 9:1044; Message from the Council to Governor Thomas Gage, 9 June 1774, *Boston Evening-Post*, 20 June 1774, p. 1, col. 2.

12 Resolutions of New Kent County Committee, 11 May 1775, *Revolutionary Virginia* 3:118. See also Resolves of New Windsor, New York, 14 March 1775, *American Archives* (4th ser.) 2:132; Resolves of Charles Town, S.C., July 1774, Resolves of Prince William County, Virginia, 6 June 1774, Resolves of Prince George's County, Virginia, June 1774, and New Jersey Assembly Petition to the King, 13 February 1775, *American Archives* (4th ser.) 1:316, 388, 494, 1133; Instructions of Cambridge, 14 October 1765, *Boston Evening-Post*, 21 October 1765, p. 2, col. 1; [Johnson,] *Important Observations*, p. 29.

13 *Gentleman's Magazine* 35 (1765): 351; [Ramsay,] *Historical Essay*, p. 143; Answer of Brass Crosby to the Inhabitants of Farrington Without, 26 April 1771, Anon., *Magna Charta Opposed to Privilege*, p. 172. See also Plowden, *Rights of Englishmen*, p. 493; Speech of Thomas Crewe, Commons Debates, 15 December 1621, [Nicholas,] *Proceedings of 1620–21* 2:335.

14 New York Association, 29 April 1775, *Revolutionary Virginia*, 3:96; Charge to Grand Juries of Camden and Cheraws Districts, 5 and 15 November 1774, *American Archives* (4th ser.) 1:959–60.

15 Resolutions of Chester, 15 May 1775, *American Archives* (4th ser.) 2:588; Petition of the Lord Mayor, Aldermen, and Livery of London, 24 June 1775, ibid., p. 1073; Johnson, *Notes on Pastoral*, p. 101; Speech of Marquis of Granby, Commons Debates, 5 April 1775, *Gentleman's Magazine* 45 (1775): 627. See also Connecticut Resolves, May 1774, *Gazette & Post-Boy*, 20 June 1774, p. 4, col. 2; Resolves of Hunterdon County, New Jersey, 8 July 1774, *American Archives* (4th ser.) 1:524; Suffolk Resolves, 9 September 1774, *Massachusetts Provincial Congresses*, p. 602; Speech of Lord Chatham, Lords Debates, 20 January 1775, *Hibernian Magazine* 5 (1775): 90.

CHAPTER TWENTY-THREE: THE EXIGENCY OF RIGHTS

1 Petition from the New York Assembly to the King, 25 March 1775, *American Archives* (4th ser.) 1:1314.

2 12 George III, cap. 24; Letter from the Massachusetts House to the Earl of Dartmouth, 5 March 1773, *Revolution Documents* 6:98.

3 [Lee,] *True State of the Proceedings*, p. 37; Petition of Mayor et al. to the King, 10 April 1775, *American Archives* (4th ser.) 1:1853; Suffolk Resolves, 9 September 1774, *Massachusetts Provincial Congresses*, p. 602.

4 5 George III, cap. 33; 14 George III, cap. 54; *In a Defiant Stance*, pp. 100–17.

5 Camden, C. J., *Entick v. Carrington*, 19 *State Trials* 1030, 1063–64 (C. P. 1765); Campbell, *Chancellors* 5:251 (quoting *Leach v. Money*). See also Resolution of 21 February 1764, *Addresses of the Common Council*, p. 55; *Gentleman's Magazine* 34 (1764): 117; *London Magazine* 34 (1765): 283; *Monthly Review* 28 (1763): 490; *Annual Register 1764*, pp. [19–20].

6 Protest of 30 March 1763, *Protests of Lords* 2:67; Petition of Lord Mayor et al., *London Magazine* 32 (1763): 256; Address from Freeholders of Cullompton to Lord Mayor William Beckford, 21 May 1763, *London Magazine* 32 (1763): 289; Presentation of 23 March 1763, *London Magazine* 32 (1763): 166. See also [Dowdeswell,] *Address to Electors*.

7 Minutes of 20 July 1764, *Acts of the Privy Council* 4:677–78.

8 "Lucius," *Political Register* 9 (1771): 126; *Journal of the Times*, 28 April 1769, p. 93, col. 1. For a comparison of British and American writs, see Wickwire, *Subministers*, pp. 132–33.

9 Address to the King from the Continental Congress, 26 October 1774, and New Jersey Assembly Petition to the King, 13 February 1775, *American Archives* (4th ser.) 1:935, 1132; Petition of Lord Mayor et al., 10 April 1775, ibid., p. 1853. See also Letter from Virginia Committee of Correspondence to Connecticut Committee, 6 January 1774, *Journal of Burgesses* 13:136; Hutchinson, *History* (1828), pp. 94–95; Rogers, *Empire and Liberty*, p. 103 (quoting *Boston Gazette*, 4 January 1762); Smith, *Writs of Assistance*, p. 157 (quoting *Boston Gazette*, 7 December 1761); Gough, *Fundamental Law*, p. 192; Wood, *Creation*, pp. 262–63.

10 Dickerson, "Writs," pp. 40–75.

11 *In a Rebellious Spirit*, pp. 11–19.

CHAPTER TWENTY-FOUR: THE ISSUE OF RIGHTS

1 North Carolina Address, 8 September 1775, *Remembrancer for 1776: Part I*, p. 172; Anon., *Remarks on the New Essay*, p. 4; Toohey, *Liberty and Empire*, p. 84 (quoting Macaulay); Letter from John Wesley to Lord Dartmouth, 14 June 1775, *Dartmouth Manuscripts* 1:378–79.

2 Letter from Benjamin Franklin to Joseph Galloway, 18 February 1774, Franklin, *Writings* 6:196; Letter from the Massachusetts Subcommittee to the Virginia Committee, 21 October 1773, *Revolutionary Virginia* 2:45–46.

3 Rowley Instructions, 10 October 1765, *Boston Evening-Post*, 21 October 1765, p. 1, col. 3.

4 Pennsylvania Instructions, 22 July 1774, and North Carolina Instructions, 14 September 1774, *Commemoration Ceremony*, pp. 83, 86; Instructions of Massachusetts, 17 June 1774, and New Hampshire Instructions, 21 July 1774, *American Archives* (4th ser.) 1:894, 893–94; New Hampshire Instructions, August 1774, *Revolution Documents* 8:171.

5 Instructions of Salem, 27 May 1769, Phillips, *Salem*, p. 304; Fairfax Resolutions, 18 July 1774, *American Archives* (4th ser.) 1:599; "Proceedings of the Freeholders in Rowan County," 8 August 1774, *North Carolina Colonial Records* 9:1025.

6 Duane's Speech, 8 September 1774, *Letters of Delegates to Congress* 1:51; Declaration and Resolves, First Continental Congress, 14 October 1774, Commager, *Documents*, p. 83.

7 South Carolina Provincial Congress, 11 January 1775, *American Archives* (4th ser.) 1:1116; Maryland Instructions, 29 April 1775, *American Archives* (4th ser.) 2:380; Declaration of the Continental Congress, 6 July 1775, *Gentleman's Magazine* 45 (1775): 360.

8 New York Petition to the King, 25 March 1775, *American Archives* (4th ser.) 1:1314.

9 London Merchants Petition to the House of Commons, 23 February 1775, *American Archives* (4th ser.) 1:1633–34; Hartley Motion of 1 April 1776, "Parliamentary History," *London Magazine* 45 (1776): 520; Preamble of 18 George III, cap. 13. For a revealing plan that specified which American demands and guarantees of rights should be granted, a plan offered by a former colonial secretary, see General Conway's Bill for Conciliation, 5 May 1780, Conway, *Peace Speech*, pp. 43–51.

10 Leder, *Liberty*, pp. 10–13.

11 Boston Instructions, 20 May 1772, *Gazette & News-Letter*, 28 May 1772, p. 1, col. 1; Letter from Samuel Cooper to Thomas Pownall, 14 November 1771, Cooper, "Letters," pp. 325–26; Proclamation of Governor Pownall, 4 November 1758, *Boston News-Letter*, 16 November 1758, p. 1, col. 1; Letter from Joseph Warren to Josiah Quincy, November 1774, Thornton, "Introduction and Notes," p. 194.

CHAPTER TWENTY-FIVE: THE CAUSATION OF RIGHTS

1 Resolves of Continental Congress, 2 January 1776, *Revolutionary Virginia* 5:312; Resolves of Georgia Congress, 10 July 1775, *Remembrancer for 1776: Part I*, pp. 12–13; New York County General Committee to Mayor and Corporation of London, 5 May 1775, *American Archives* (4th ser.) 2:511.

2 Letter from Governor Trumbull to Earl of Dartmouth, 10 March 1775, *Revolution Documents* 9:75; Anon., *Remarks on the New Essay*, p. 28; Bristol Resolves, 28 February 1774, Munro, *Bristol*, p. 194. See also Fairfax County (Virginia) Association, 17 January 1775, *American Archives* (4th ser.) 1:

1145; "An American," Salem, Massachusetts, 1 June 1775, *American Archives* (4th ser.) 2:875; Letter from Richard Price to Charles Chauncy, 25 February 1775, Peach, *Richard Price*, p. 294.

3 Samson, *Sermon at Roxbury-Camp*, p. 17. Similarly, see Resolves of Westmoreland, Pennsylvania, 16 May 1775, *American Archives* (4th ser.) 2:615.

4 Marblehead Town Meeting, 14 January 1775, *Gazette & Post-Boy*, 16 January 1775, p. 3, col. 2; Montgomery, *Sermon at Christiana Bridge*, p. 10.

5 Speeches of the Duke of Grafton and Lord Chatham, Lords Debates, 30 May 1777, *Parliamentary History* 19:324, 318; Speech of David Hartley, Commons Debates, 29 February 1776, *Hibernian Magazine* 6 (1776): 487. See also Speech of David Hartley, Commons Debates, 5 December 1777, and speech of John Wilkes, Commons Debates, 10 December 1777, *Parliamentary History* 19:555, 568; Speech of James Luttrel, Commons Debates, 12 March 1778, *Parliament Register* 9:44.

6 Speech of Edmund Burke, Commons Debates, 22 March 1775, *Hibernian Magazine* 5 (1775): 404–5.

7 E.g., [Anderson,] *Free Thoughts*, pp. 2–3. For a rare writer on the imperial side who makes an economic argument, see "To Merchants," *Scots Magazine* 37 (1775): 22–23.

8 Ernst, "Ideology," p. 165. See also Hacker, "First American Revolution," pp. 138, 141; Boyer, "Borrowed Rhetoric," pp. 348–49.

9 Christie, "Quest for the Revolution," p. 186. See also Bailyn, "Central Themes," pp. 12–13; Bailyn, *Pamphlets*, p. viii; Jones, *O Strange*, p. 340 (quoting Colyer Meriwether).

10 [Williamson,] *Plea of the Colonies*, p. 9.

11 [Downer,] *Discourse in Providence*, pp. 4–5; [Boucher,] *Letter from a Virginian*, pp. 17–18; De Pinto, *Letters on Troubles*, p. 7. For a loyalist writer who believed that the controversy *was* constitutional but implied that the economic risks outweighed the constitutional considerations, see "To Inhabitants of New-York," 20 October 1774, *American Archives* (4th ser.) 1:886–88.

12 Address from Continental Congress to Jamaica, 25 July 1775, *Scots Magazine* 38 (1776): 203; Christie, "Quest for the Revolution," p. 190; Letter from John Dickinson to Arthur Lee, 29 April 1775, *American Archives* (4th ser.) 2:445. For cost to colonies of British imperial policy, see generally Thomas, "British Imperial Policy."

13 Letter from Thomas Hutchinson to Israel Williams, 6 May 1769, Bailyn, *Ordeal*, p. 191, n. 66; [Galloway,] *A Candid Examination*. For a loyalist lawyer answering whig arguments about rights, see [Sewall,] *Americans Roused*, p. 9.

14 Lee, *Second Appeal*, pp. 75–77 (quoting imperial officials in the colonies); Letter from Thomas Gage to Lord Barrington, 4 May 1772, Gage, *Correspondence* 2:604; Letter from Lord Dartmouth to Colonial Governors, 3 March 1775, *American Archives* (4th ser.) 2:27. For a whig writer who was ignorant of the constitution yet argued that all aspects of the controversy were constitutional, see Zubly, *Right to Tax*; Zubly, *Humble Enquiry*.

15 18 George III, cap. 13; Speech of Duke of Richmond, Lords Debates, 18 November 1777, *Parliamentary History* 19:399.

16 Address of Governor James Wright to Commons House, 18 January 1775, and Message from Upper House to Governor Wright, 20 January 1775, *American Archives* (4th ser.) 1:1153, 1154–55; Zubly, *Law of Liberty*, p. 24.

17 Petition of New Jersey Assembly to the King, 13 February 1775, *American Archives* (4th ser.) 1:1132; New York Representation to House of Commons, 25 March 1775, *Gentleman's Magazine* 45 (1775): 249.

18 [Serle,] *Americans against Liberty*, p. 47.

CHAPTER TWENTY-SIX: THE REDRESS OF RIGHTS

1 Instructions of the Delaware Assembly to Congressional Deputies, 29 March 1775, *American Archives* (4th ser.) 2:129; Speech of Bishop of Peterborough, Lords Debates, 30 May 1777, *Parliamentary History* 19:329.

2 *Journal of the Times*, 7 January 1769, p. 46, col. 2; Instructions of 8 May 1769, *Boston Town Records* 16:288; Instructions of Leicester, Spencer, and Paxton, *Boston Gazette*, 5 June 1769, p. 3, col. 3; Instructions of Salem, 27 May 1769, Phillips, *Salem*, p. 304; Conway, *Peace Speech*, p. 46. The chief exception was the plan of Edmund Burke. He sought to solve the vice-admiralty grievance by redressing the "fees" grievance, not the jurisdiction grievance. Speech of Edmund Burke, Commons Debates, 22 March 1775, *Parliamentary History* 18:525.

3 New York Remonstrance to the House of Commons, 25 March 1775, *Scots Magazine* 37 (1775): 237. See also Petition from Continental Congress to the King, 26 October 1774, *Commemoration Ceremony*, p. 129. Thus the second "conciliatory act" of 1778, although intended primarily to redress the legislative controversy, had a secondary purpose of redressing some of the rights grievances when it authorized peace commissions to suspend "the Operation and Effect of any Act or Acts of Parliament which have passed since the Tenth Day of February One thousand Seven hundred and Sixty-three." 18 George III, cap. 13.

4 "Extract of a Letter from a Gentleman of Philadelphia, to a Member of the British Parliament, Dated December 26, 1774," *American Archives* (4th ser.) 1:1067; Howard, *Road from Runnymede*, p. 179. (quoting Rutledge); New York Petition to the King, 25 March 1775, and Debates of New York General Assembly, 24 March 1775, *American Archives* (4th ser.) 1:1314, 1309.

5 Perhaps the most famous plans were offered by Edmund Burke. See plan of 22 March 1775 and plan of 16 November 1775, *Parliamentary History* 18: 517, 519–20, 525, 978–82. These plans, however, did not deal with rights except for the vice-admiralty "fees" grievance, as noted in the first part of this chapter, n. 2.

6 Speech of David Hartley, Commons Debates, 9 April 1778, *Parliamentary History* 19:1078. For other proposals by Hartley, see Speeches, *Parliamen-*

tary History 18:570–71, 1051–52; *Gentleman's Magazine* 46 (1776): 246–47; Hartley, *Speech and Motions*; Hartley, *Letters on the War.*

7 Conway's Bill, 5 May 1780, Conway, *Peace Speech*, pp. 47, 44–45. Conway would have repealed nine statutes (listed in ibid., p. 48).

8 "A Provisional Act for settling the Troubles in America, and for asserting the Supreme Legislative authority and superintending power of Great Britain over the Colonies," *Parliamentary History* 18:199–200, 202, 202–3; Speech of Earl Gower, Lords Debates, 1 February 1775, ibid., p. 208; Message from the Burgesses to Governor Lord Dunmore, 12 June 1775, *American Archives* (4th ser.) 2:1205–6.

9 Speeches of Lord Chatham and Earl Gower, Lords Debates, 30 May 1777, *Parliamentary History* 19:318, 343–44, 343, 320.

10 Speech of Lord Chatham, Lords Debates, 18 November 1777, ibid., p. 365.

CHAPTER TWENTY-SEVEN: CONCLUSION

1 Instructions to Congress Deputies from North Carolina, 27 August 1774, *American Archives* (4th ser.) 1:737.

2 Speech of John Aubrey, Commons Debates, 19 February 1778, *Parliamentary History* 19:774.

3 John Adams's Notes and James Duane's Speech, 8 September 1774, *Letters of Delegates to Congress* 1:52, 47, 53.

4 Anon., *Inquiry into the Nature*, p. 10; Speech of Earl Gower, Lords Debates, 30 May 1777, *Parliamentary History* 19:320–21.

5 Speech of James Luttrell, Commons Debates, 3 December 1777, *Parliamentary History* 19:536.

6 For what may be the only contemporary British (i.e., Irish) discussion of creating a declaration of rights, see [Sheridan,] *Review*, p. 45.

7 Speech of Lord Chatham, Lords Debates, 18 [*sic*, 20] November 1777, *Parliamentary History* 19:373–74, 375, 374.

8 In fact, the contemporary pamphlet of this speech, which the title page explains was "Taken Verbatim as his Lordship spoke it," does not report these words or the plan. Chatham, *Speech of 20 November.* They are also not reported in *Gentleman's Magazine, London Magazine,* or other publications.

9 Speech of the Earl of Abingdon, Lords Debates, 18 [*sic*, 20] November 1777, *Parliamentary History* 19:380. It may be indicative of how little the plan was understood that the early edition of Chatham's speeches reports him as saying that he sought "the establishment of recoverable law," the exact opposite of what he sought, "the establishment of irrevocable laws." Compare *Anecdotes of the Life of the Right Hon. William Pitt, Earl of Chatham* (7th ed., London, 1810) 2:313, to Chatham, *Speech of 20 November,* p. 19.

10 Letter from Jonathan Trumbull to Lord Dartmouth, March 1775, *American Archives* (4th ser.) 2:109.

INDEX

DESIGNED BY IRVING PERKINS ASSOCIATES
COMPOSED BY METRICOMP, GRUNDY CENTER, IOWA
MANUFACTURED BY BRAUN-BRUMFIELD, INC., ANN ARBOR, MICHIGAN
TEXT AND DISPLAY LINES ARE SET IN CALEDONIA

Library of Congress Cataloging-in-Publication Data
Reid, John Phillip.
Constitutional history of the American Revolution.
Includes bibliographical references and index.
1. Civil rights — United States — History.   2. United States — Constitutional history.   3. United States — History — Revolution, 1775–1783.   I. Title.
KF4749.R45   342.73'085   86-40058
ISBN 0-299-10870-8   347.30285